D0078666

MENTAL HEALTH
A Challenge to the Black Community

Edited by
Lawrence E. Gary

DORRANCE & COMPANY • *Philadelphia and Ardmore, Pa.*

Copyright © 1978 by Institute for Urban Affairs and Research
All Rights Reserved
ISBN 0-8059-2493-0
Printed in the United States of America

CONTENTS

PREFACE

In my experience in training social workers, psychologists, guidance counselors, special educators, teachers and other helping professionals, I became aware of a profound need for a book devoted to a realistic analysis of factors and issues affecting the mental health of Black people. This collection of articles was stimulated by a federal grant for the development of a position paper on the mental health status of Black people. In the process of developing and organizing materials for that task, I found it clear that based on the current literature, I would be forced to concentrate on the pathological aspect of Black mental health.

Therefore, with the encouragement of several colleagues, I decided to ask several practitioners and scholars for their input to make a comprehensive analysis of the mental health of Black people. I contacted numerous friends and colleagues who, I felt—based upon my personal knowledge of their professional reputation and commitment to the Black community—were indeed competent and experienced in working with mental health and related problems. Moreover, I was interested in writers who would focus not only on the negatives but also on the strengths of Black people and the positive aspects of their mental health. In general, I believe the contributors to this book have tended to follow this emphasis. The chapters cover the developmental process of the Black person's mental health from childhood through old age. They examine his environment and the conditions within it which may lead to stress and conflict. Below is a brief summary of each chapter.

Chapter 1 gives a conceptual overview of mental health. It discusses some of the problems encountered in defining mental health and the different theoretical approaches in these definitions, and provides a tentative definition of mental health. Various models of human behavior or mental health are described since the conceptual model used influences the treatment strategy. The authors suggest a model for viewing the mental health of Black people which is designed to aid researchers and practitioners in solving the problems in the Black community.

Chapter 2 examines the social problems aspect of mental health; statistical data on mental health problems among Blacks; research as a social problem; the politics of social policy and treatment modalities; and racism and its effects on the Black professional and on interpersonal functioning in the Black community.

Chapter 3 explores the etiology of mental disabilities in the Black community. It emphasizes the importance of understanding the relationship among behavioral disability, the nervous systems, and environmental stresses. In this connection, the ecological, biological, socio-cultural, and political-economic bases of mental disabilities are discussed within the framework of racism or white supremacy.

Chapter 4 reviews the concept of the family and focuses on the support function of the Black family. Historical reflections are made and some structural concerns are discussed. Adaptation styles within the Black family are examined and predictions are made about the future of the Black family.

Statistics on infant morbidity and mortality rates are provided in Chapter 5. There is a discussion on growth and development which links cohesiveness and strength in the family with optimum growth and development. Supports and strengths, hostile forces, and limitations of the environment and the culture are explored. The school as a part of the social system is analyzed. Finally, adoption, transracial adoption, and day care are shown as three alternative modes for mental health consideration.

In the discussion on the concept of adolescence in Chapter 6, the author compares and contrasts the Euro-American view with the African view and the Black American view. He looks at the social and training needs of the adolescent, such as peer affiliation, heterosexual ties, contact with the adult support systems, preparation for provider role, and cooperative ties versus competition. Events and circumstances leading to deviance, delinquency, and disorder are also discussed briefly.

Chapter 7 is an exploration into the world of work of the adult. It examines those work factors which have been found to contribute to positive and negative attitudes and outcomes for workers in general, and Black workers in particular. Several variables in the world of work are discussed, such as stress, job fulfillment, employment patterns, health, and working conditions.

Chapter 8 gives a profile of the elderly in the Black community and describes their role and function. Adjustment or failure to adjust to the aging process are discussed in relation to economic stress factors such as income, quality of housing, and health care. Other social and psychological stress factors and support systems available to the elderly are also covered in this chapter.

The focus in Chapter 9 is on community health and survival. In this context, the various mutual support systems of the Black community are identified. These survival settings include clubs, fraternal orders, the church, and recreational areas, all of which, the author notes, provide gratification and tension release. The strengths and pitfalls of various social movements in the Black community are examined, and finally the author shares some thoughts on the future of the networks in the Black community.

Chapter 10 looks at the concept of ecology and provides a classification of ecological factors—physical, social, and economic. Air, land, water, food supply, density of people, architecture, noise, and odor are ecological factors which are relevant to the discussion of mental health of urban communities. Housing density and crowding have had an impact on urban Blacks and have contributed to mental pathology.

Chapter 11 discusses models of mental health service delivery at the organizational level. Selected service models are health maintenance organizations, public and private mental hospitals, community mental health centers, and neighborhood centers. The author discusses the scope, target, strengths, limitations, and plans under the various models described. She traces the early developments of service and concerns for service delivery, and analyzes organizational theories relative to mental health. Finally, the author offers suggestions for a new organizational model for Black people.

Chapter 12 provides reflections on selected aspects of public policy in the mental health field. The author defines traditional concepts and approaches to the study of public policy, explores mental health policy issues, discusses some legal aspects of mental health, and identifies some issues that Black professionals and leaders should raise concerning new health legislation.

Chapter 13 cites the manpower developments in mental health. It shows the lack of Black mental health manpower and illustrates the criticical need for training Black mental health personnel. Training needs are in four major areas, namely, research, treatment, administration, and policy. Since training is directly related to educational institutions, the authors discuss the emerging role that Black colleges must play in developing programs in the mental health disciplines at the highest degree level.

Chapter 14 looks at mental health research that has been conducted on Black people. The author emphasizes the importance of following the basic methodological rules and procedures of research when conducting research on mental health problems in the Black community. He discusses the role of the Center for Minority Group Mental Health Programs in the development of research centers under the control and direction of minority scholars.

This book does not claim to cover all the past, present, and future aspects of mental health in the Black community. Moreover, it does not claim final answers to the increasingly perplexing mental health problems facing Black people in the United States. An important value of this book is that it presents a Black perspective on social interaction within the Black community and between Black and white people. In this volume, one can observe that there is diversity of opinion within the Black community as reflected by the authors and their approaches and analyses of current mental health concerns. This is not surprising since the Black community is not monolithic. Indeed, there is heterogeneity within the Black community. Hence, the notion of the Black community is a general term including the diverse aspects of Black life. Understanding and appreciating this diversity is important for practitioners who are engaged in helping to solve the problems confronting the Black community. It is my hope that this book would serve as a resource for parents, teachers, social workers, psychologists, psychiatrists, political leaders, students and others concerned with, and responsible for, programs dealing with the growth and development of Black people.

ACKNOWLEDGMENTS

I am gratefully indebted to the people whose contributions are included in this volume. Since all of the articles were written specifically for this effort, the contributors' cooperation and commitment made it possible to complete this book.

As in the production of any work, there are many detailed tasks which have to be performed. Loretta Burgess, Arlene B. Enabulele, Roneé Harris, Katrinka O. Stringfield, Evelyn M. Gunn, and Eva M. Bell, played important roles in assisting me in the development of this manuscript. I here record my thanks to all of the above.

Special thanks is due to Dionne J. Jones. She was involved in this undertaking from beginning to end. She provided not only technical aid—criticisms, wisdom, and meticulous attention to details—but also warm support and encouragement.

The book itself was made possible in part through the financial generosity of the Center for Minority Group Mental Health Programs, National Institute of Mental Health. I especially appreciate the guidance, support, and understanding which I received from Drs. James R. Ralph and Mary S. Harper, who are affiliated with the Minority Center.

Finally, I should like to thank my wife, Robenia, and my children, Lisa Ché, Lawrence Charles André, and Jason Edward, for their patience and forbearance during my total involvement with this document. They were extremely considerate and took pride in my effort.

CONTRIBUTORS

Lewis P. Clopton, Ph.D.
Assistant Professor,
School of Architecture and Planning,
Columbia University,
New York, New York

William Denham, Ph.D.
Director,
Division of Manpower and Training Programs,
National Institute of Mental Health,
Rockville, Maryland

David L. Ford, Jr., Ph.D.
Associate Professor,
School of Management and Administration,
University of Texas at Dallas,
Dallas, Texas

Lawrence E. Gary, Ph.D.
Director,
Mental Health Research and Development Center, and
Institute for Urban Affairs and Research,
Howard University,
Washington, D.C.

Thomas A. Gordon, Ph.D.
Director,
Early Childhood Services Linkage Program,
Thomas Jefferson University Hospital,
Philadelphia, Pennsylvania

Brin Hawkins, Ph.D.
Associate Professor,
School of Social Work,
Howard University,
Washington, D.C.

Audreye E. Johnson, D.S.W.
Associate Professor,
Graduate School of Social Work,
University of North Carolina,
Chapel Hill, North Carolina

Dionne J. Jones, M.S.W.
Research Associate,
Mental Health Research and Development Center,
Howard University,
Washington, D.C.

Norman L. Jones, M.A.
Psychologist,
Early Childhood Services Linkage Program,
Thomas Jefferson University Hospital,
Philadelphia, Pennsylvania

James R. Ralph, M.D.
Chief,
Minority Center,
National Institute of Mental Health,
Rockville, Maryland

Pearl L. Rosser, M.D.
Professor,
School of Medicine, and
Director, Institute for Child Development and
   Urban Family Life,
Howard University,
Washington, D.C.

Stanley H. Smith, Ph.D.
Dean,
College of Human Resources,
Southern Illinois University,
Carbondale, Illinois.

Robert E. Staples, Ph.D.
Associate Professor of Sociology,
University of California,
San Francisco, California

Theodis Thompson, Ph.D.
Chairman,
Department of Health Services Administration,
School of Business and Public Administration,
Howard University,
Washington, D.C.

Frances Cress Welsing, M.D.
Private Psychiatrist,
Washington, D.C.

Willie S. Williams, Ph.D.
Associate Dean,
Medical College,
Case Western Reserve University,
Cleveland, Ohio

1 MENTAL HEALTH: A CONCEPTUAL OVERVIEW

Lawrence E. Gary, Ph.D., and Dionne J. Jones, M.S.W.

Introduction

This chapter describes some of the problems involved in defining mental health and conceptual approaches to classifying and assessing human behavior with appropriate attention given to strengths and limitations. There is substantial disagreement in the social and behavioral sciences literature as to the definitions of mental health and illness. According to Minear (1974, p. 294):

> One problem in dealing with mental illness has been that there [are] so many ways of classifying and defining it. Aside from the general public, different professions view it from different perspectives and even within the medical profession, there are a variety of definitions.

Mental illness has been classified according to (1) cause—demon theory, imbalance of body fluids, physiological interactions, unresolved conflicts of early development, and so forth; (2) degree of disability—deviant behavior requiring hospitalization versus home care; (3) law—insanity defense, involuntary hospitalization, the concept of danger, legal certification for business contracts, estate management, and education; and (4) behavior—the degree of deviation from what is considered normal behavior, and the frequency and intensity with which deviation occurs (Minear, 1974, pp. 294–299).

The line of demarcation between mental illness and mental health is not very clear because both of these concepts are usually defined by symptomatic or behavioral traits. Miller (1974, p. 31) defines mental illness as "occurrence of psychological or neurological conditions giving rise to gross deviation from a designated range of desirable behavioral variability." On the other hand, Theodorson and Theodorson (1969, p. 253) state: "Mental illness is a nonorganic, social-psychological disorder in which the individual is unable to protect his ego or social self sufficiently to participate in ordinary social life and obtain at least a minimal degree of social and psychological rewards." These definitions, like most definitions of mental illness, are based on symptoms which are related in a direct way to the concept of normality (Offer and Sabshin, 1974; Miller, 1974). Given these definitions, the crucial ethical question becomes: Who determines the norms?

The Concept of Mental Health

In recent years greater emphasis has been placed on the concept of mental health primarily because it connotes positiveness. In their discussion of mental health, Schwartz and Schwartz (1968) observe that this emphasis is an outgrowth of the mental hygiene movement in the United States and the development of psychotherapy and personality research. Rather than focusing exclusively on the cause and treatment of the emotional disturbance, this movement gave special attention to the prevention of mental disorder and social and psychological maladjustment.

The concept of mental health is just as difficult to define as is mental illness. Not surprisingly, the experts do not agree on what it is (Insel and Roth, 1976; Minear, 1974; Offer and Sabshin, 1974; Jahoda, 1958; Kaplan, 1976). In attempting to define mental health, some writers use a traditional medical approach based on the absence of illness or the dominant influence of biological processes upon mental functioning (Fine, 1973; Kubie, 1975; Margolis and Favazza, 1971; Ausubel, 1961). Other theorists formulate their definitions from an adaptive behavior approach which utilizes principles of learning theory (Ullman and Krasner, 1969; Fester, 1965). The social conformity definition of mental health views the individual's ability to function within the context of a social situation (Bandura, 1969; Kaplan, 1976; Caplan, 1975). Several scholars (White, 1959; White, 1960; Phillips, 1967) have used the concept of competence as an operational definition of mental health. In this connection, the mental health of an individual is described in terms of his "fitness or ability to carry on transactions with the environment" (White, 1971, p. 301).

In arriving at a definition of mental health, Insel and Roth (1976, pp. 56–57) have taken a different approach by analyzing what mental health *is not*. They argue that normality, a statistical concept, is not the same as mental health. What is normal is related to "whatever state most of the people in the population are in at a given time." Moreover, they suggest that the absence of symptoms or of problems does not necessarily mean that a person is mentally healthy. In other words, some healthy people may have problems, and some unhealthy people may not have any significant symptoms. "Everlasting happiness is not a criterion for a mentally healthy person simply because no one is happy all the time; healthy people have ups and downs." The ability to function in areas of life should not be taken as the standard for mental health. According to Insel and Roth (1976, p. 56), "Never having had help or adjustment to society or reality is not a sure sign of a healthy person."

Although there are different theoretical approaches to the definition of mental health, there is some agreement as to the basic aspects of the concept. For example, Miller (1974, p. 31) states:

> Positive mental health suggests that an individual has a realistic or non-distorted orientation toward his social and physical environment, that he has (and is able to exercise) social skills in interpersonal relations, that his emotional life is personally satisfying, and that he meets reasonable role expectations of others who know him as, for example, fellow workers or members of a family.

Fromm's (1955) definition of mental health is as follows:

> Mental health is characterized by the ability to love and to create, by the emergence from incestuous ties to clay and soil, by a sense of identity based on one's experience of self as the subject and agent of one's power, by the grasp of reality inside and outside of ourselves; that is, by the development of objectivity and reason.

In an article, "Toward A Working Definition of Mental Health," Kaplan (1976, p. 8) reviewed various definitions of mental health and arrived at the following conclusions:

> Mental health is a sequence of states of mind that unfolds when the emergence, functioning, and integration of mental processes become differentiated from and integrated with the emergence, function, and

integration of physical maturational processes as both sets of phenomena fit with each other and, taken together, are in keeping with the individual's adaptation to the environment.

Keezer (1971, pp. 18–19) states that mental health is more than "simple freedom from mental disease." Further, it is the ability "to understand and accept one's own feelings, to make mature and appropriate emotional responses to situations, [to] endure frustration and to gain satisfaction from constructive achievement." Keezer concludes that mental and emotional health exists when individuals go about their daily lives with reasonable satisfaction, and are "unhampered by feelings of constant conflict, either in themselves or with the world around." It is apparent that such a non-conflictive perspective of mental health does not take into consideration the social and environmental factors which impinge upon Black people and other minorities. For if these factors had been considered, Keezer would surely know that many Black persons exist in total frustration and despair precisely because they are prevented by systemic forces from constructive achievements. Hence, according to Keezer's criteria, few Black persons possess positive mental health.

In a longitudinal, community-based mental health study of Black children, Kellan, Branch, and co-workers (1975) developed a two-dimensional view of mental health: (1) social adaptational status—a societal dimension involving the adequacy of social performance as judged by others (an aspect of the concept which is external to the individual), and (2) psychological well-being—an individual dimension in that it deals with how the individual is feeling inside. In a comprehensive review of the literature on what constitutes positive mental health, made to the Joint Commission on Mental Illness and Health, Jahoda (1958) identified six major categories or parameters of this concept:

1. An attitude toward one's self in which self inspection leads toward acceptance of weaknesses and pride in strengths; a clear image of what one really is and identity with it so that one is motivated toward inner stability
2. Growth and development toward self-realization of one's potentialities; a blending of one's total personality toward achieving the best of what one might become
3. Integration of personality involving a balance of psychic forces, a unified outlook on life, and some capacity for withstanding anxiety and stress

4. Autonomy of action in which the individual determines behavior from within instead of drifting with the impact of present stimuli— independence in the face of difficulties
5. A perception of reality which is relatively free from what one wishes things might be and which involves his being attentive to and concerned with the welfare of others
6. Mastery of the environment through (a) the ability to love, (b) being adequate in love, work and play, (c) competence in human relations, (d) capacity to adapt oneself to current circumstances, (e) ability to draw satisfaction from one's environment, and (f) willingness to use problem-solving approaches in life processes

Although Jahoda's review is comprehensive, these categories are value-laden, and they do not adequately deal with the issue of racism, especially in white individuals (Pettigrew, 1973). Since definitions of mental health influence the modes of intervention used in practice, Black social and behavioral scientists, and a number of their white colleagues, are recognizing the need to develop definitions of mental health for Black people (McGhee and Clark, 1974; Wilcox, 1973; Jones, 1972). These scientists agree that white behavior as a normative standard for all Black people should be rejected. They argue that promotion of mental health in the Black community rests on the ability of Black people to utilize their resources to fight the debilitating effects of the system (Myers, 1973). Jones (1972) urges theorists to de-emphasize the deficiency-based hypothesis of Black behavior and emphasize instead its positive aspects.

In developing alternative parameters for studying the mental health of Black people, Black scholars are especially cognizant of the functional significance of physical, social, political, economic, and other environmental forces which influence the mental health of an individual and, thus, his community in general. In developing a working definition of mental health, Thomas and Comer (1973, pp. 165–166) state:

> . . . mental health includes people's feelings of worth in the context of the total cultural and societal system as well as within the identifiable groups to which they belong. . . . Mental health encompasses the issue of the availability of the good life within a given social, political and economic context.

They also view a positive state of mental health as the ability "to cope or function within society in an adaptive way." They define positive adaptation as "the results of everyday endeavors to cope which produce in turn a heightened capacity to cope and increased willingness to engage society'' (p. 166). Wilcox (1973, pp. 467–468) identified the following factors which are crucial for understanding positive mental health in the Black community.

1. Conscious awareness that this society is hostile to one's existence—that it is organized to destroy Black people as Blacks: that they live in a society where it is illegal to be Black and to be human. Black men earn ''acceptance'' when they deny their Blackness or feign whiteness.

2. A constant state of dynamic tension. Perpetual conflict becomes a static condition. Most mainstream crises do not have to be crushed—they will peter out if not escalated by oppressive or resistive tactics. ''Conscious living'' and resisting are the normal status of tension for Black people.

3. Ability to deal with superordinated. The most consummate skill of Black people is to exercise power from a presumed position of powerlessness.

4. Lack of a desire to oppress or to be oppressed and a will to sustain one's existence on his own terms; refusing to be abused or to abuse.

5. A need to be involved in shaping and/or controlling one's own destiny; being suspicious of bewilderers and gatekeepers, that is, those who have a need to believe that they can save you or have a need to adjust your expectations.

6. Steady involvement in self-confrontation—engaging one's ''I'' institution *first* before confronting other institutions, that is, killing one's old inner self first.

7. Being steeped in an identity of one's own culture—history and values—at a gut level.

8. A basic knowledge of the society's destructive characteristics; racism, capitalism, classism, sexism, materialism, and the like.

9. An ability to perceive the humanity of oppressed people and to enable them to utilize it in their own liberation; ability to perceive the relationship between the exploiters and those they exploit.

Drawing inferences from the foregoing discussion, we may define mental health as the ability of an individual to control or modify his or her environment so that he or she is able:

1. to exercise sound and realistic judgment and strategies for dealing with problems

2. to satisfy basic biological and derived human needs

3. to establish meaningful physical and emotional relationships with others

4. to take responsibility for personal feelings and action

5. to have a functional and integrated self-image with an awareness of how freedom, autonomy and morality relate to one's self-image

6. to support efforts to promote the growth and development of one's own cultural or social group

This tentative definition has limitations, but it is a rather comprehensive statement which has some potential for measurement from a research perspective. This definition has some relevance for the various models of human behavior and different treatment approaches to dealing with problems of living.

Models of Human Behavior

Students of human behavior have proposed a variety of models for explaining behavior; at least six of these major models will be discussed. These models are not mutually exclusive, and they have been used to interpret and misinterpret the behavior and action of Black people. It is generally known that these conceptual schemes influence how an individual deals with reality and life events and how problems are defined. Moreover, practitioners, in developing a treatment strategy, use one or several of these models (Burgess and Lazare, 1976), often without realizing it. A brief discussion appears below of several models of human behavior or mental health.

The Biological Model. The biological model—sometimes referred to as the biomedical or medical model—assumes that biological components, such as genes, hormones, enzymes, neurons, audition, and vision, have a tremendous impact on human behavior (Insel and Roth, 1976; Page, 1975; Siegler and Osmond, 1976). According to Page (1975, p. 141):

> The [biological factors] influence particularly the range and level of the organism's learning aptitudes, physiological drives, basic temperament, stress tolerance, adaptive resources, and response capabilities. Individual differences in these and other functions are partly due to individual variations in neurophysiological and biochemical traits.

This model suggests that behavioral disturbances or abnormalities are due to underlying brain or biochemical defects or imbalances (Page,

1975, p. 141; Burgess and Lazare, 1976, p. 304). Other sources of biological individuality that have special mental health significance include nutritional deficiencies, especially during infancy and early childhood, genetic endowment, debilitating physical illnesses, and too much toxic substance intake. Clearly, this model assumes that psychiatric diseases, like other illnesses, can be subdivided into categories, each of which has a specific organic course, distinguishable symptoms, and a predictable outcome.

Recent discoveries in genetics, biochemistry, and psychology suggest that the biological model has increased our understanding of human behavior (Minear, 1974, p. 294), but there are also some serious criticisms of this approach. Insel and Roth (1976, p. 63) observe:

> . . . in the case of major psychotic illnesses, this approach has had major successes. New drugs have been developed that alleviate human suffering associated with some kinds of mental illness. Yet, the biological approach is an incomplete one. It tends to explain complex human problems on the basis of a few chemical compounds. Even though this approach is likely to turn out to be valid for understanding illnesses such as schizophrenia, it will probably be of less value in the understanding of neurosis or of ordinary problems of living.

Moreover, in establishing a causal relationship between biological variables and behavioral abnormalities, one will need more than supportive statistical evidence. Page (1975, p. 141) suggests that one will need "specific information on the ways in which genetic and other biological factors contribute to the development of abnormal behavior and the reasons the effects of these variables differ so much from individual to individual."

A recent controversial book, *Sociobiology: The New Synthesis* (Wilson, 1975), discusses the biological basis of social behavior and suggests that much of human behavior is genetically determined. Drawing on facts and theories from several disciplines and with a modified Darwinian theoretical frame of reference, Wilson has attempted to develop a set of principles for understanding social instincts in living communities and for identifying inheritable traits that mold individual societies and the biological commonalities that underlie all societies. However, Wilson has not worked out all the details of how social traits or behavior, such as altruism, coyness, spite, jealousy, and selfishness, relate specifically to genes. In addition to having methodological and conceptual deficiencies, the biosociological perspective in human behavior is a conservative world view which can be used to justify the current political and economic system and to support the notion that racial difference in intelligence is related to genetics. Black scholars and researchers must be suspicious of any discussion concerning the genetic basis of behavior, for it is possible to see policy directives and programs based on this approach in the very near future.

The Intrapsychic Model. The intrapsychic model—often referred to as the psychodynamic or psychoanalytic model—has been developed primarily by Freud, although there have been significant modifications by scholars such as Erik Erikson, Harry Stack Sullivan, Erich Fromm, and Karen Horney (Page, 1974, p. 107). This model assumes that the deviant behavior is due to inner conflict or personal disunity which may be related to early childhood experiences. According to Freud's theory of psychosexual development, the basis for disorder is one or more conflicts between the components of personality—id, ego, and superego—and external reality. Psychoanalytic theory assumes that there is a biologically predetermined sequence in human psychosexual development. Freud referred to this sequence as the oral stage, the anal stage, the phallic stage, the latency stage, and the genital stage. If libidinal energy is fixated at any stage of psychosexual development, the individual may be unable to cope with succeeding stages and conflicts. The concept assumes that the stage at which fixation or difficulty occurs influences the type of psychopathology that is manifested.

If there is a behavioral problem as viewed from an intrapsychic perspective, therapy is usually in the form of psychoanalysis on an individual or group basis (Page, 1974, p. 107; Whittaker, 1976, pp. 227-229). The principal objective of psychoanalytic therapy is to uncover hidden conflicts and defenses which, it is believed, prevent effective functioning so that the patient can be freed from childhood fixations. This is achieved in part by reconstructing a developmental picture of the patient's personality and identifying the stage at which the disturbed state arose. The second objective of the therapy is to help the patient to understand and cope with the unconscious material so that he no longer has to use repression. Finally, the analyst must reconstruct a sounder personality which can cope effectively with problems of living. The main analytic techniques used are free association, dream analysis, interpretation, and transference (Daves, 1975, p. 534; Eysenck, 1973, p. 7).

The intrapsychic model has been criticized because its treatment methods are intensive, long-term and expensive. Some opponents of the model argue that "as many patients are likely to recover spontaneously as do through long-term individual psychotherapy or psychoanalysis" (Gottesfeld, 1972, p. 69). Others are apprehensive about the model because of Freud's preoccupation with sex, the unconscious defenses, and his belief that childhood experiences determine behavior. Furthermore, cross-cultural studies have failed to document or confirm the universality of several concepts, such as the Oedipus complex, and it is difficult empirically to test others, such as id, ego, superego, and preconscious (Page, 1975, p. 116; Yates, 1970, pp. 7–10). Finally, the treatment method relies heavily on the patient's motivation to continue therapy, his ability to express his thoughts and feelings, and the subjective interpretation of behavioral dynamics by the therapist.

The Behavioral Model. The behavioral model (or learning theory) does not distinguish between abnormal and normal behavior. Any distinction is assumed to be the result of value judgment and the cultural environment (Ullman and Krasner, 1969, p. 1). According to Insel and Roth (1976, pp. 63, 65):

> The behaviorists see humans as machines. They differ from the biologist, though, in emphasizing function instead of structure. They focus on how something reacts rather than how it is put together. The "atoms" the behaviorists work with are stimulus-response bits, bits of behavior that can be measured. . . . Mental health from the behaviorist viewpoint is a matter of learning or conditioning. A person can be only what he or she has been programmed or conditioned to be. If the organism is not functioning efficiently, it must first be deconditioned, then reconditioned.

It is clear that this model holds that all behavior is a learned way of coping with the demands of the environment. Hence, behavioral theorists are most concerned with the observable symptoms which, it is assumed, constitute the disorder, and often do not need to know the origin of the behavior in order to influence it, since they are not concerned with speculation about internal states and psychodynamics. The behaviorist treatment methodology implies unlearning the maladaptive or undesirable behavior and learning substitute behavior which would be more effective in coping with the environment. Behavioral theoretical methods include role playing, desensitization, emotional flood, assertiveness training, aversive conditioning, token economics, and model imitation (Whittaker, 1974, p. 207; Thomas, 1973, pp. 1235–1236; Stuart, 1974, pp. 400–417).

Although there is a great deal of enthusiasm concerning the behavioral aproach and its potential for helping people, there are some serious shortcomings (Yates, 1970; Breger and McGaugh, 1965; Page, 1974). The behavioral model does not adequately explain why maladaptive behavior, such as fear or guilt, is not exhibited by all people, even though everyone may experience difficult or traumatic situations. According to Page (1974, p. 127):

> At some time or another, everyone is exposed to dramatic situations and makes undesirable responses that are reinforced. Why, then, doesn't everyone acquire fears, guilt feelings, and faulty habit patterns? Secondly, learning theory holds that "wrong" responses that lead to negative reinforcement are supposed to extinguish or die out. Why do the maladaptive and distressing symptoms of the neurotic persist?

What is implied is that the concept of neurosis in behavioral therapy is based on faulty assumptions. Other faulty assertions are advanced by behavioral therapists; among these are (1) that the overt discrete response is the most significant unit of human behavior, (2) that complex human behavior can be accounted for in terms of simple conditioning, and (3) that rewards play an essential role in all learning phenomena (Yates, 1970, p. 397). Although some behaviorists claim that their approach is more scientifically based than other psychotherapeutic approaches and that it has a higher cure rate than other forms of therapy, these conclusions have not been supported with adequate documentation (Yates, 1970, p. 395; Breger and McGaugh, 1965). In spite of its shortcomings, however, the behavioral approach appears to be making significant advances in the areas of social learning, cognition, and attitude change, as is noted in the work of Bandura and Walters (1965). Also, it should be noted that behavioral therapy was initiated with studies of regressed psychotic adults, autistic children, and the severely mentally retarded, for whom traditional methods had not been effective; but there is a need to extend this approach to new clients with less severe difficulties and to those in open, rather than closed, settings (Whittaker, 1974, pp. 207–208). As behavioral therapy is expanded, more consideration must be given to the ethics of this approach (Yates, 1970, pp. 402–423).

The Humanistic Model. The humanistic model is based upon the assumption that behavior is caused and meaningful and is the result of a complex series of physical, psychological, and sociocultural factors. Humanistic theorists have been influenced by existentialism and phenomenology (Frankl, 1962). Their theories stress man's potential for constructive, healthy living, given a wholesome and accepting environment. Theoreticians and practitioners associated with this approach include Abraham Maslow (1962); Viktor Frankl (1967); Donald Krill (1969); Carl Rogers (1974); Frederick Perls (1969); William Glasser (1965); and Eric Berne (1967). According to Whittaker (1974, pp. 103–107), the major assumptions and tenets of the humanistic approach are as follows:

1. Man has potential freedom to make choices.
2. Man can be helped to find meaning in life through the liberation of inner strengths.
3. Dignity is inherent in the human condition.
4. Man is in the process of becoming. As stated by Camus, "Man's greatness lies in his decision to be stronger than his condition."
5. Man is viewed in his wholeness, in the totality of his humanness.
6. Humanness is not a fixed state of being, but a constant process of becoming, unfolding and venturing forth.
7. Man is a free agent who achieves his meaning through responsible choice and through the stance he adopts toward life's pain and suffering.
8. Man, faced with an absurd and unpredictable world and burdened with doubt and anxiety, nonetheless chooses to act in a way that is responsible to his innermost being and in doing so authenticates his existence, is safe from total despair, and gains his freedom.

Based on these assertions, the humanistic model assumes that when an individual feels safe and accepted, his development is enhanced. However, personality disorder results when a person is unable to achieve actualizing experiences and realize his potential. The form of disorder is dependent upon factors such as the level of anxiety created and the degree to which the self image is denied. The major treatment approaches or techniques based on this model are client center therapy, gestalt therapy, and existential psychotherapy (Page, 1974; Whittaker, 1974; Insel and Roth, 1975).

The limitation of the humanistic model lies in its simplistic approach to life problems. It tends to assume that most disorders and conflicts result from inferiority feelings. Furthermore, the approach seems to be more of a philosophy of life rather than a theory of human behavior. Thus a basic problem in treatment is whether "the client needs to accept the philosophy in order to get help" (Whittaker, 1974, p. 107). By combining philosophy with a technology of helping, this approach can create many problems for the client. Finally, more systematic documentation is needed of the relative importance and significance of this model in solving problems for clients.

The Sociocultural Model. The sociocultural model is perhaps a misnomer in that several theories and constructs are involved. In general, this model assumes that cultural and social conditions have a tremendous influence on human behavior and that these factors determine, to a large extent, the way in which an individual copes with life stresses (Page, 1975, p. 180; Offer and Sabshin, 1974, pp. 67–82; Siegler and Osmond, 1976, pp. 42–88; Margolis and Favazza, 1971, p. 776).

This general approach has several theoretical themes or submodels, such as anomie (Merton, 1957), labeling or conspiratory theory (Lemert, 1967; Becker, 1963; Szasz, 1961; Scheff, 1966), societal reaction theory (Siegler and Osmond, 1976; Cohen, 1966; Kaplan, 1976), and cultural support theory (Page, 1975, p. 161–171; Offer and Sabshin, 1974, pp. 68–74; Horton and Leslie, 1974, pp. 39–40; Perrucci and Wallach, 1975). What these partial theories have in common is their view that deviant behavior and psychiatric illness stem from social rather than personal causes (Burgess and Lazare, 1976, p. 8; Horton and Leslie, 1975, p. 37). In this connection, it is conceivable that a society or a "social context" may be sick rather than an individual whose behavior is defined as being deviant or abnormal.

Szasz (1961) posits that there was a conspiracy among mental health professionals which promoted and perpetuated the use of the term mental illness. He suggests redefining mental disorders as "problems in living" which may involve deviations from socially accepted norms. Szasz (1971) maintains that psychiatry is endangering personal liberties and human rights because the patient is defined and labeled as mentally ill by others. Further exemplifying the conspiracy, Szasz points to the legal power of the American mental health movement as demonstrated by its ability to have an incarcerated individual subjected to treatment against his will.

The social component of this model tends to focus on pathology, even though society is viewed as primarily responsible for deviant behavior. According to Page (1975, p. 161), "Most sociocultural theories either are of a global nature or deal with some specific factor such as the relation of psychopathology to economic status, social disorganization, and change." Variables such as age, sex, marital status, and income are correlated with the incidence of mental disorder, and data tend to show "a definite relationship between social class and source of referral for treatment [and the] duration of treatment" (Hollingshead and Redlich, 1958; Reissman, et al., 1964; Dunham, 1971).

From a developmental perspective, the sociocultural model tends to emphasize strengths rather than weaknesses (Albee, 1972). The cultural emphasis of this model generally takes a developmental frame of reference. Cultural relativity becomes an important concept in understanding human behavior from the perspective of this mode. Offer and Sabshin (1974, p. 68) state:

> In its purest form, a cultural relativity position views all behavior as relative to its particular cultural context and states positively that no form of behavior is abnormal in all cultures.

There have been many studies which show the behavioral relationship between culture and mental disorder (Linton, 1956; Leighton and Hughes, 1961; Wallace, 1967; Dunham, 1971; Giordano and Giordano, 1976). However, most of these studies have focused on cross-cultural comparisons between foreign countries rather than looking at the diverse ethnic groups within the United States (Carpenter and Strauss, 1974; Kiev, 1972). In addition, much of what is known about ethnicity is based on research conducted over thirty years ago (Giordano and Giordano, 1976, p. 4). Some scholars and practitioners argue that there is a gap between current mental health practice and our knowledge of the impact of culture on human behavior (Abel and Metraux, 1974; Brandt, 1974; Leighton, 1972; Waggoner, 1970).

Black mental health professionals have, in recent years, begun seriously to question the applicability of traditional models of mental health to the Black community. These professionals believe that individual functioning must be viewed within the context of the social, political, economic and other institutional forces with which the individual must cope. Thomas and Comer (1973) have posited that the mental health of Black individuals cannot be properly assessed in a vacuum. Rather, the mental health of Blacks must be viewed within the context of the total cultural and societal systems as well as within the perspective of the Black group.

Wilcox (1973) and Billingsley (1968) have provided assumptions and hypotheses about positive Black functioning. Wilcox postulated that the mental health states of Blacks are largely reactions and adaptations to the conditions of white institutional racism. Billingsley stated that when Black people do not conform to the norms of the dominant culture, they are considered social and mental deviants. It must be noted that much of this "deviant" behavior is tolerated and absorbed by the Black community. Poor communities have had to adjust to a certain level of chaotic and socially disruptive behavior because of the multiple problems that exist within and are perpetuated against them.

Some Black scholars are currently developing a Pan-Africanist cultural model for viewing the mental health of Black people. They propose the development of Black psychology as a discipline (Williams, 1974; Clark, 1972; Nobles, 1974; Mosby, 1972; White, 1972). William Hayes (1972) is opposed to the notion of Black psychology as a discipline, but urges acceptance of his proposed new discipline "Radical Black Behaviorism," a science of Black behavior which he contends can be observed, measured, and reproduced, and which is individualistic in its approach, and can meet the needs of Black people. Wade Nobles (1972, p. 26), notes that "African [Black] psychology is rooted in the nature of Black culture which is based on particular indigenous [African] philosophical assumptions." Nobles notes further that the African concept of man is fundamentally different from the European concept. While the two assume a duality in man's nature (mind and body functions), the African concept does not divide them; instead, there is concern with notions of unity, being "one with nature," and "survival of the people." Hence, Nobles concludes that from a Pan-Africanist perspective, it would be useless to develop theories or make analyses based on a mind-body dichotomy.

A Black cultural approach is affective and group-focused, and it recognizes the Africanness in Black family structure, sex role definitions, behavior, and attitudes toward money (Jackson, 1976). For example, there is a qualitatively different value placed on money in the African culture than that assigned in the European culture. In the African culture, money is a means of obtaining needed goods and services (Nobles, 1974), whereas in the European tradition, money is saved and invested as though it were an end in itself. If this distinction could be understood by mental health professionals, they would cease their accusations that Blacks in general, and low-income Blacks in particular, have misplaced priorities and are present-oriented.

It has been suggested that the Black culture and the Black experience be included as treatment variables in the development of a new paradigm (Jackson, 1976). Recognizing that many Black clients are hesitant in seeking professional assistance, Jackson advocates broadening the concept of client selection so that the client is sought out in his natural environment. It was also suggested that the appointment system be abandoned and professional involvement be initiated in the Black community so as to desensitize Black clients to the role of the professional.

The Systems Model. The use of "systems theory" to describe and analyze human behavior is relatively new, but it is becoming an important theoretical approach in the social and behavioral sciences (Buckley, 1977; Parson, 1964; Olsen, 1968; Churchman, 1968; Anderson and Carter, 1974). The systems model combines the theoretical boundaries of biochemistry, biophysics, genetics, biology, physiological and ecological sciences, psychiatry, psychology, sociology, anthropology, business administration, social organization, communication engineering, and group management (Margolis and Favazza, 1971, p. 780). Thus the approach cuts across many disciplinary areas of concern. Ruesch (1966, p. 577) states:

> The modern task orientation of science requires new theories that are neither bound to unique situations nor associated with particular professions.

To a large extent, the goal of the systems model is the development of general theories of (1) molecular biology, which lays stress on man's constituent processes; (2) the biological sciences, which focus specifically on man's transactions with his environment; (3) the behavioral sciences, which treat man's behavior alone and in groups; and (4) social operations, which attempt to understand how social behavior is organized, managed, and changed (Margolis and Favazza, 1971, p. 780).

In summarizing the major assumptions and tests of the systems model, Whittaker (1974, pp. 103–105) stated:

1. Systems theory assumes an interaction and interdependency between systems and a high degree of organization within each system.
2. Change in one part of a system will have implications for all other parts of the system and may have effects in contiguous systems as well, e.g., ripple effect.

3. Man is viewed not as an isolated entity, but as a participant in a number of interacting and interdependent dynamic social systems.

This approach to understanding human behavior is particularly well suited to the mental health field, especially the practice modality of community psychiatry, public health and community mental health centers (Freedman and Kaplan, 1967; Margolis and Favazza, 1971; Hearns, 1969; Lieberman, 1975). For one thing, the model provides a mode for conceptualizing a mental health problem with adequate consideration to time span, interrelationship of various elements or variables, the identification and selection of targets of intervention, and a more functional view of symptoms. In addition, with a systems approach, less emphasis is placed on a linear causal perspective on behavior or mental health problems while more emphasis is given to functional relationships (Janchill, 1969; Lippitt, Watson, and Westley, 1958).

The professional operating from a systems frame of reference has to develop strategies for intervening in one or several functional areas or subsystems, such as individual, group, community organization, or society (Lippitt, Watson, and Westley, 1958). Although the systems approach has many advantages, there are some limitations which Whittaker (1974, p. 107) has identified: (1) the problem of the closeness with which the social systems model fits the real world; (2) the problem of changing systems; the need for further clarification of the role of change agents; and (4) the use of specific strategies and techniques for action.

Concluding Remarks

With this somewhat limited review of some definitional and conceptual issues related tto mental health and human behavior, it becomes increasingly clear that it will be difficult to develop a functional model for analyzing the mental health of Black people. Nonetheless, a model for viewing the mental health of Black people is suggested. Given our definition of mental health, this model is based on the view that mental health is one means toward maximum human growth and development. In this connection, mental health can be viewed as an evolutionary process from infancy through succeeding stages of growth and development, resulting from the expressions of generative processes, action systems, and environmental factors. In other words, the "systems model" approach seeks an answer to the question of how the mental health of Black people can be explained with consideration given to biological, psychological, sociological, economic, political, ecological, religious, and cultural factors.

From this theoretical perspective, the individual and his mental health are viewed as a system of actions continuously interacting with self and environment. The core of these views of mental health is *interaction*. It can be argued that mental health and its variations are the result of interaction between and within internal and external action systems and their impact on the individual. The nature of the interaction and intra-action between these action systems and the self-generated processes (thinking, learning, believing, judging, etc.) constitutes the core of positive mental health.

Figure 1 illustrates the various components of this model. Black people are born into society with certain potentials for the development of positive mental health. These potentials are developed or undeveloped as a function of two interrelated subsystems: (1) biopsychological or internal and (2) sociocultural or external.

The specific components of this model include the following:

1. *Individual* (I): The individual is in constant interaction with both subsystems. Among the characteristics of this variable are behavior, attitudes, perception, motivation, learning, sensation, and reaction.

2. The elements of the sociocultural subsystem are as follows:

   a. *Family life* (II): family structure, size of family, family mobility, family values, decision-making processes in the family, family interaction, and family roles.

   b. *Social environment* (III): from the informal social network to formal or complex organization—peer groups, church, night clubs and bars, barber and beauty shops, recreation groups, social clubs, schools, hospitals, government, and business organizations.

   c. *Physical environment* (IV): the interior of the house; space; physical design; industrial pollutants such as smoke, soot, dust, gases, and fumes; biological pollutants such as rats and cockroaches; and street design and lighting.

A PRACTICE AND
RESEARCH MODEL
FOR THE
BLACK COMMUNITY

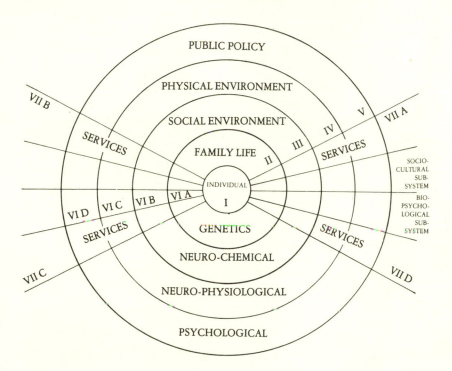

d. *Public policy* (V): administrative rules and regulations, legislation, and judicial decisions.

3. The elements of the biopsychological subsystem are as follows:

a. *Genetic* (VI-A): dominant genes, recessive genes, sex-linked genes, chromosomal abnormalities, and multi-factorial inheritance.

b. *Neurochemical* (VI-B): ATP (adenosine triphosphate), enzyme, hormone, neuron, and organelle.

c. *Neurophysiological* (VI-C): gastrointestine, respiratory, kidneys, cardiovascular, endocrine, and reproduction.

d. *Psychological* (VI-D): cognitive development, social and emotional development, motivation reaction, sensation and perception, vision, and audition.

Of course, there are other elements of these two subsystems that also influence mental health—for example, the mental health services (VII) linkage that interfaces with the individual and each element of the two subsystems. In other words, an intervention strategy for modifying the mental state of an individual must be given to all of the elements identified in the model. However, differential emphases are expected to form the basis for implementing a services modality.

This model should aid the researcher and the practitioner in solving problems confronting the Black community. To a larger extent, this model of mental health not only unifies various definitions of mental health, but also suggests experimentation, research and development, and practice areas which are worthy of performing. The suggested model, however tentative it may be, calls for new concepts, definitions, hypotheses, theories, interpretations, techniques, and methods for dealing with the mental health of Black people.

References

Abel, T., and Metraux, R. *Culture and Psychotherapy*. New Haven: College and University Press, 1974.

Albee, G. W. "The Sickness Model of Mental Disorder Means a Double Standard of Care." In Harry Gottesfeld (ed.), *The Critical Issues in Community Mental Health*, pp. 217–233. New York: Behavioral Publications, 1972.

Anderson, R. E., and Carter, I. E. *Human Behavior in the Social Environment: A Social Systems Approach*. Chicago: Aldine, 1974.

Ausubel, D. P. "Personality Disorder is Disease." *American Psychologist* 61 (1961): 69–74.

Bandura, A. *Principles of Behavior Modification*. New York: Holt, Rinehart and Winston, 1969.

Bandura, A., and Walters, D. H. *Social Learning and Personality Development*. New York: Harper & Row, 1963.

Becker, H. S. *Outsider: Studies In the Sociology of Deviance*. New York: Free Press, 1963.

Berne, Eric. *Games People Play*. New York: Grove Press, 1967.

Billingsley, A. *Black Families in White America*. Englewood Cliffs, New Jersey: Prentice-Hall, 1968.

Branch, J. D. et al. *Mental Health and Going to School*. Chicago: University of Chicago Press, 1975.

Brandt, A. *Reality & Police: The Experience of Insanity in America*. New York: W. Morrow, 1974.

Breger, L., and McGaugh, J. L. "Critique and Reformulation of 'Learning Theory' Approaches to Psychotherapy and Neurosis," *Psychological Bulletin*, 63 (1965): 338–358.

Buckley, W. *Sociology and Modern Systems Theory*. Englewood Cliffs, New Jersey: Prentice-Hall, 1977.

Burgess, A. W., and Lazare, A. *Community Mental Health: Target Populations*. Englewood Cliffs, New Jersey: Prentice-Hall, 1976.

Caplan, N., and Nelson, S. D., "On Being Useful: The Nature and Consequences of Psychological Research on Social Problems." In Irving Horowitz (ed.), *The Use and Abuse of Social Science*, pp. 136–161. New Brunswick, New Jersey: Transaction Books, 1975.

Carpenter W., and Strauss, J. "Cross-Cultural Evaluation of Schneider's First Rank Symptoms of Schizophrenia: a Report from the International Pilot Study of Schizophrenia." *American Journal of Psychiatry* 131, (1974): 682–687.

Churchman, C. W. *The Systems Approach*. New York: Dell, 1968.

Clark, C. "Black Studies or the Study of Black People?" In Reginald L. Jones (ed.), *Black Psychology*, pp. 3–17. New York: Harper & Row, 1972.

Cohen, A. K. *Deviance and Control*. Englewood Cliffs, New Jersey: Prentice-Hall, 1966.

Daves, W. F. *A Textbook of General Psychology*. New York: Thomas Y. Crowell, 1975.

Dunham, H. W. "Socio-Cultural Studies of Schizophrenia." *Archives of General Psychiatry* 24 (1971): 206–214.

Eysenck, H. J. (ed.). *Handbook of Abnormal Psychology*. London: Sir Isaac Pitman and Sons, 1973.

Fester, C. B. "Classification of Behavioral Pathology." In L. Krasner and L. Ullman (eds.), *Research in Behavioral Modification*, pp. 6–26. New York: Holt, Rinehart & Winston, 1965.

Fine, R. *The Development of Freud's Thought*. New York: Jason Aronson, 1973.

Frankl, V. E. *Man's Search for Meaning*. Boston: Beacon Press, 1962.

_____. *Psychotherapy and Existentialism*. New York: Washington Square Press, 1967.

Freedman, A., and Kaplan, H. *Comprehensive Textbook of Psychiatry.* Baltimore: Williams & Watkins, 1967.

Fromm, E. *The Sane Society.* New York: Holt, Rinehart & Winston, 1955.

Giordano, J. and Giordano, G. P. "Ethnicity and Community Mental Health." *Community Mental Health* 1 (1976): 1, 4, 14, 26.

Glasser, W. *Reality Therapy.* New York: Harper & Row, 1965.

Gottesfeld, H. *The Critical Issues of Community Mental Health.* New York: Behavioral Publications, 1972.

Hayes, W. A. "Radical Black Behaviorism." In Reginald L. Jones (ed.), *Black Psychology,* pp. 51–59. New York: Harper & Row, 1972.

Hearns, G. (ed.). *The General Systems Approach: Contributions toward an Holistic Conception of Social Work.* New York: Council on Social Work Education, 1969.

Hollingshead, A., and Redlich, J. *Social Class and Mental Illness: A Community Study.* New York: Wiley, 1958.

Horton, P. B. and Leslie, G. R. *The Sociology of Social Problems.* 5th ed. Englewood Cliffs, New Jersey: Prentice-Hall, 1974.

Insel, P. M. and Roth, W. T. *Health In a Changing Society.* Palo Alto, California: Mayfield, 1976.

Jackson, G. G. "Cultural Seedbeds of the Black Backlash in Mental Health." *Journal of Afro-American Issues* 4 (1976): 70–91.

Jahoda, M. *Current Concepts of Positive Mental Health.* New York: Basic Books, 1958.

Janchill, M. P. "Systems Concepts in Casework Theory & Practice." *Social Casework* 50 (1969): 74–82.

Jones, R. L. (ed.). *Black Psychology.* New York: Harper & Row, 1972.

Kaplan, B. L. "Towards a Working Definition of Mental Health." *Community Mental Health Review* 1 (1976): 1, 4–9.

Keezer, W. S. *Mental and Human Behavior.* Dubuque, Iowa: W. C. Brown, 1971.

Kellam, S. G.; Branch, J. D.; Agrawal, K. C.; and Ensminger, M. E. *Mental Health and Going to School.* Chicago: University of Chicago Press, 1975.

Kiev, A. *Transcultural Psychiatry.* New York: Free Press, 1972.

Krasner, L., and Ullman, L.P. *Research in Behavior Modification.* New York: Holt, Rinehart & Winston, 1965.

Krill, D. F. "Existential Psychotherapy and the Problem of Anomie." *Social Work* 14 (1969): 33–49.

Kubie, L. "The Language Tools of Psychoanalysis: A Search for Better Tools Drawn from Better Models." *The International Review of Psychoanalysis* 2 (1975): 11–24.

Leighton, A. H., and Hughes, J. M. "Culture as a Causative of Mental Disorder." *Milbank Memorial Fund Quarterly* 39 (1961): 446–470.

Leighton, D. "Culture Determinants of Behavior: A Neglected Area." *American Journal of Psychiatry* 128 (1972): 117–118.

Lemert, E. M. *Human Deviance: Social Problems & Social Control.* Englewood Cliffs, New Jersey: Prentice-Hall, 1967.

Lieberman, E. J. (ed.). *Mental Health, the Public Health Challenge.* Washington, D.C.: American Public Health Association, 1975.

Linton, R. *Culture and Mental Disorder.* Springfield, Illinois: Charles C. Thomas, 1956.

Lippitt, R.; Watson, J.; and Westley, B. *The Dynamics of Planned Change.* New York: Harcourt Brace, 1958.

Margolis, P., and Favazza A. R. "Mental Health and Illness." *Encyclopedia of Social Work,* Vol. 1, No. 16. New York: National Association of Social Workers, 1971, 773–783.

Maslow, Abraham. *Toward a Psychology of Being.* Princeton, New Jersey: Van Nostrand, 1962.

McGee, D. P., and Clark, C. X. "Critical Elements of Black Mental Health." *Journal of Black Health Perspectives* 1 (1974): 52–58.

Merton, R. K. *Social Theory and Social Structure.* New York: Free Press, 1957.

Miller, D. *Community Mental Health.* Lexington, Mass.: Lexington Books, 1974.

Minear, R. "Mental Illness." In Jean Mayer (ed.), *Health,* p. 294. New York: Van Nostrand, 1974.

Mosby, D. P. "Toward a New Specialty of Black Psychology." In Reginald L. Jones (ed.), *Black Psychology,* pp. 33–42. New York: Harper & Row, 1972.

Myers, E. R. "Implications of the Emerging Discipline of Community Psychology for Black Social Workers." In *Nation Building Time: Proceedings of the 5th Annual Conference of NABSW,* April 1973.

Noble, P. *The Negro in Films.* New York: Arno Press, 1970.

Nobles, W. W. "Africanity: Its Role in Black Families." *The Black Scholar* 5 (1974): 10–17, 18–32.

Offer, D., and Sabshin, M. *Normality: Theoretical and Clinical Concepts of Mental Health.* Rev. ed. New York: Basic Books, 1974.

Olsen, M. *The Process of Social Organization.* New York: Holt, Rinehart & Winston, 1968.

Page, J. D. *Psychopathology: The Science of Understanding Deviance.* 2nd ed. Chicago: Aldine, 1975.

Page, R. *How to Be Prepared for Any Crisis.* New York: Hawks Publishers, 1974.

Parsons, T. *The Social System.* New York: Free Press, 1964.

Perls, F. S. *Gestalt Therapy: Excitement and Growth and the Human Personality.* New York: Julian Press, 1969.

Perrucci, R., and Wallace S. D. "Models of Mental Illness and Duration of Hospitalization." *Community Mental Health Journal.* 11 (1975): 271–279.

Pettigrew, T. F. "Racism and the Health of White Americans: A Social Psychological View." In C. Willie; B. Kramer; and B. Brown (eds.), *Racism and Mental Health,* pp. 269–298. Pittsburgh: University of Pittsburgh Press, 1973.

Phillips, D. L. "Identification of Mental Illness: Its Consequences for Rejection." *Community Mental Health Journal* 3 (1967) 262–266.

Reissman, F.; Cohn, J.; and Pearl, A. (eds.). *Mental Health of the Poor.* New York: Free Press, 1964.

Reusch, T. "Social Progress." *Archives of General Psychiatry* 15 (1966): 577.

Rogers C. R. "In Retrospect: Forty-Six Years." *American Psychologist* 29 (1974): 115–123.

Schwartz, M. S., and Schwartz, C. G. "Mental Health: The Concept." In David L. Sills (ed.), *International Encyclopedia of the Social Sciences,* Vol. 10, pp. 216–221. New York: Macmillan and Free Press, 1968.

Scheff, T. J. "A Sociological Theory of Mental Disorders." In J. D. Page (ed.), *Approaches to Psychopathology.* Wolfe City, Texas: University Press, 1966.

Siegler, M., and Osmand, H. *Models of Madness, Models of Medicine.* New York: Harper Colophon Books, 1976.

Stuart, R. B. "Behavior Modification: A Technology of Social Change." In Frances J. Turner (ed.), *Social Work Treatment,* pp. 400–417. New York: Free Press, 1974.

Sullivan, H. S. *The Interpersonal Theory of Psychiatry.* New York: Norton, 1953.

Szasz, T. S. *The Myth of Mental Illness: Foundations of a Theory of Personal Conduct.* New York: Hoeber-Harper, 1961.

——————. "The Mental Health Ethic." In Harry Gottesfeld (ed.), *The Critical Issues of Community Mental Health.* New York: Behavioral Publications, 1972.

Theodorson, G. A., and Theodorson, A. *Modern Dictionary of Sociology.* New York: Thomas Y. Crowell, 1969.

Thomas C. S., and Comer, J. P. "Racism and Mental Health Services." In C. Willie; B. Kramer; and B. Brown (eds.), *Racism and Mental Health,* pp. 165–181. Pittsburgh: University of Pittsburgh Press, 1973.

Ullman, L. P., and Krasner, L. (eds.) *A Psychological Approach to Abnormal Behavior.* Englewood Cliffs, New Jersey: Prentice-Hall, 1969.

Waggoner, R. "The Presidential Address: Cultural Dissonance and Psychiatry." *American Journal of Psychiatry* 127 (1970): 1–8.

Wallace, A. F. C. "Anthropology and Psychiatry." In A. M. Freedman; H. I. Kaplan; and H. S. Kaplan (eds.), *A Comprehensive Textbook of Psychiatry,* pp. 195–201. Baltimore, Maryland: Williams and Wilkins, 1975.

White J. "Toward a Black Psychology." In R. L. Jones (ed.), *Black Psychology,* pp. 43–50. New York: Harper & Row, 1972.

White, R. "Motivation Reconsidered: The Concept of Competence." *Psychological Review* 66 (1959): 297–333.

_____. "Competence and the Psychological States of Development." In J. Rosenblith, and W. Allensmith (eds.), *The Causes of Behavior,* pp. 300–308. Boston: Allyn and Bacon, 1966.

_____. *Right to Health: The Evolution of an Idea.* Iowa City: University of Iowa Graduate Program in Hospital and Health Administration, 1971.

Whittaker, J. K. *Social Treatment: An Approach to Interpersonal Helping.* Chicago: Aldine, 1974.

Wilson, E. A. *Sociobiology: The New Synthesis.* Cambridge: Harvard University Press, 1975.

Wilcox, P. "Positive Mental Health in the Black Community: The Black Liberation Movement." In C. Willie; B. Kramer; and B. Brown (eds.), *Racism and Mental Health,* pp. 463–524. Pittsburgh: University of Pittsburgh Press, 1973.

Williams, L. N. *Black Psychology.* Washington, D.C.: Nuclassics and Science Publishing Company, 1974.

Yates, A. *Behavior Therapy.* New York: Wiley, 1970.

2 MENTAL HEALTH: THE PROBLEM AND THE PRODUCT

Lawrence E. Gary, Ph.D.

Introduction

Although the experts do not agree on the definition of mental health or illness, it is clear that a major service industry has developed around this concept. In this chapter the following broad areas will be discussed: (1) the social problems aspects of mental health, (2) statistical and other data on the extent of mental health problems in the Black community, (3) research as a social problem, (4) the politics of social policy and treatment modalities, (5) racism and the Black professional, and (6) interpersonal functioning in the Black community. There is no attempt to cover all problem areas related to mental health in the Black community. Issues related to psychobiological aspects of mental health or illness are not within the scope of this discussion.

In many respects, the mental illness–mental health continuum can be discussed or viewed as a social problem. Horton and Leslie (1974, p. 4) define a social problem as:

> . . . a condition affecting a significant number of people in ways considered undesirable, about which it is felt something can be done through collective social action. This definition has four distinct ideas (1) a condition affecting a significant number of people, (2) in ways considered undesirable, (3) about which it is felt something can be done, (4) through collective social action.

With these criteria, one can assume that mental health/illness has been a social problem for a long time in the Black community. The concept of social deviance has also been used to cover mental health problems. According to Wheller (1973, p. 650), deviant behavior is defined as "conduct that people of a society generally regard as aberrant, disturbing, improper or immoral, and for which specific social control efforts are likely to be found."

The terms "social problem" and "social deviance" are interrelated, are used to cover issues related to mental health problems, and have relevance to the concept of cultural relativity. Horton and Leslie (1974, pp. 31–32) stated:

> The concept of cultural relativity implies that a trait has no meaning by itself; it has meaning only in its cultural setting. . . . Every idea or practice must be understood in terms of its relation to other parts of the culture within which it occurs. This concept helps us understand some of the stresses within our own society and some of the difficulties in finding agreeable relief from them.

What is implied is that since Black people have a culture (Butcher, 1956; Ellison, 1966; Herskovits, 1958; Keil, 1966; Szwed, 1970; Whitten and Szwed, 1970), it is necessary for us to examine mental health problems from the perspective of Black people. In other words, mental health problems are those conditions affecting a significant number of Black people in ways which they consider undesirable, and there is a strong commitment through social action to changing the situation or condition so that a significant number of individuals can become, or remain, functioning members of their communities. With this broader notion, many issues and problems are part of the mental health service industry. Among these problems are crime and delinquency, family and generational conflict, alcoholism, drug abuse, conflict and anxiety, sexual attitudes and behavior, self-concept and personality, inadequate economic participation, discrimination, racism and prejudice, urban deterioration, physical decay and pollution, involvement and alienation, and inadequate health and medical care (Horton and Leslie, 1974; Freeman and Jones, 1970; Keezer, 1971; Insel and Roth, 1976).

Stressful Life Events

Stress, defined as "something that disturbs a person's psychological or biological equilibrium" (Insel and Roth, 1976, p. 555), is an important concept to consider in determining the extent of mental health problems in a given community. Data have shown that stress-provoking situations, especially if continued over an extended period of time, will damage body tissues and thus lead to physical illness and psychiatric disorder (Levi, 1971; Insel and Roth, 1976; Dohrenwend and Dohrenwend, 1974). A body of knowledge has developed which documents the relationship between magnitude of changes in life events and susceptibility to somatic and psychiatric disorders. Holmes and Rahe (1967) argue that events leading to significant change (pleasant or unpleasant) will increase the probability of one's susceptibility to illness. Some of these life events, suggested by the authors, are (1) death of spouse, (2) divorce, (3) marital separation, (4) jail term, (5) personal injury or illness, (6) marriage, (7) loss of job, (8) pregnancy, (9) change in financial state, (10) death of close family member or close friend, (11) trouble with boss, (12) change in work, (13) change in residence, (14) change in school, (15) change in number of family get-togethers, and (16) minor violations of the law. A supportive environment is a strong positive factor in preventing illness and death (Insel and Roth, 1976, pp. 18–19; Mayer, 1974, pp. 489–515).

Social ecology, which analyzes the impact of physical and social environments on human beings, provides a useful perspective in discussing mental health problems in the Black community because it is assumed that the environment of an individual has a tremendous impact on his health, especially his mental health. According to Insel and Roth (1976, pp. 18–19):

> How people interact with each other—and how they deal with their feelings about these interactions—has a great influence on individual health. . . . Illness is one of the ways an individual can adapt to his or her environment and patterns of illness in a family or other unit are sometimes indicators of stress imposed by the social climate of the environment.

The above assertion emphasizes the importance of the social environment (family, peer relationships, organizations, neighborhoods, personality variables, etc.); similar conclusions can be made about the physical environment. Mayer (1974, p. 469) states:

> Man alone has the ability to regulate his external environment in accordance with his own ideas and hence to extend his habitat into physical environments that otherwise would be inhospitable. Nevertheless, it has become possible for modern man to alter adversely his natural environment so greatly that his internal environment becomes unable to maintain its accustomed uniformity and disease results. When this occurs, the environment is called polluted.

In an article, "Black Ecology," Hare (1970) was very critical of the ecology movement because it has not given proper recognition to the fact that Black and white environments not only differ in degree but in nature as well; and this conclusion has a direct bearing on the causes of, and solutions to, ecological and mental health problems. One general distinction is that there are greater problems with pollutants such as smoke, soot, dust, flying ash, fumes, gases, stench, carbon monoxide, rats, lead, cockroaches, overcrowding and excessive noise in the physical environment of most Black people.

Given the comprehensive nature of problem areas related to mental health, it is difficult to assess the impact of these problems on the Black community. Getting appropriate and meaningful statistical data on stressful life events in the Black community would appear impossible. Kramer, Rosen, and Willis (1973, pp. 353–354) tried to generate data on the definition and distribution of mental disorders in the Black community, but they reached the following conclusions:

> . . . it is impossible to provide a precise description of the frequency of occurrence of the mental disorder by age, sex, race, marital status, occupation, place of residence, and a variety of other social and economic variables as of a given point in time or over time for the United States as a whole, its various geographic regions, divisions or separate states. The major impediments to the development . . . are the continued absence of standardized case-finding techniques capable of uniform application from place to place and from time to time for detecting persons in the general populations with these disorders, lack of reliable differential diagnostic techniques for assigning each case to a specific category and the dearth of methods for determining dates of onset and termination.

Moreover, since experts differ on the definition of mental health, it is also impossible to determine the size and cost of the problem in the general population as well.

Although the data base is very weak and somewhat inadequate, research studies have reached some conclusions concerning selected mental health problems in the Black community:

Crime. Although the statistics on crime are inadequate, it is safe to say that crime has a significant differential impact on the Black community (Pinkney, 1969; Staples, 1976; Gary and Brown, 1976). According to Staples (1976, p. 218):

> Although the burden of poverty rests equally on all members of the underclass, it is colonized Blacks who bear most heavily the oppressive aspects of the American criminal justice system. Due to the inequity of colonial rule, Blacks are more likely to be arrested, brutalized by the police, disenfranchised in the courtroom, and punished severely.

In 1975, Blacks, made up 54 percent of the nationwide arrests for murder and 47 percent of the victims of homicide (Kelley, 1976, p. 20). Fifty-nine percent of the persons arrested for robbery were Blacks in 1976 (Kelley, 1976, p. 192). These data, although inadequate, show that for the most serious crimes, Blacks are disproportionately represented as both the victim and the perpetrator. According to the U.S. Census Bureau, in 1970, there were 140,821 nonwhite inmates in correctional institutions, representing 43 percent of the total inmate population.

Mortality. Life expectancy and mortality rates are basic indices of health and the extent of stress in a given community. Blacks of both sexes can expect a shorter life span than that indicated for whites (Levitan, et al., 1975, p. 129). Both maternal and infant mortality rates are higher for Blacks than for whites. Data seem to suggest that, in general, Blacks have a higher incidence of fatal illness and accidents than whites. Levitan and his co-workers (1975, pp. 131–132) state:

> Adjusting for age, Blacks are more likely to suffer almost all kinds of fatal illness and accidents. Though the overall incidence of heart disease and cancer are lower among Blacks, standardization by age reveals that Blacks are 25 to 35 percent more likely than whites to die from these two most serious diseases. . . . Sharp differentials are evident for other diseases. Pneumonia, diabetes, and cirrhosis of the liver are twice as common among Blacks as whites.

Mental Illness. Although the data are contradictory, most reports show that there is a differential incidence of mental illness between Blacks and whites (Pinkney, 1969, p. 131).

Blacks are 4.3 percent more likely to be in mental institutions than whites and twice as likely to suffer fatal consequences from psychoses and neuroses (Levitan, et al., 1975, p. 133). Data tend to show that problems such as lack of transportation, lack of citizen participation and control of mental health services, cumbersome intake procedures, and impersonal treatment settings affect the accessibility of mental health services to the Black community (Garfield, 1963; Warren, 1973; Gilbert, 1972).

With respect to type of treatment, it has been reported that the treatment Blacks receive in mental health agencies is different from that of whites. The following differences have been observed:

1. Diagnoses are less accurate for Blacks (Gross, et al., 1969; Cooper, 1973).

2. Dispositions of Black cases are more nonspecific (Lowenger and Dobie, 1966).

3. Blacks are more likely to be seen for diagnosis only (Jackson, et al., 1974).

4. Blacks are less likely to be selected for insight-oriented therapy than whites (Rosenthal and Frank, 1958).

5. Blacks are less likely to be selected for long-term psychotherapy than whites (Wildner and Coleman, 1963).

6. Some data suggest that the attitudes of the therapists toward Blacks have not been too positive in terms of their assessment of the potential benefits that Black clients can receive from certain types of treatment (Hendre and Hanson, 1972).

Alcoholism and Drug Abuse. Blacks are more than eight times as likely to become institutionalized for drug addiction as whites; death from alcoholism is three times more common among Blacks; and problem drinking is considerably more common among Blacks than whites (Levitan, et al., 1975, p. 133). Furthermore, in 1975, 96,660 Blacks were arrested for violation of narcotic drug laws, and 224,417 were detained for public drunkenness (Kelly, 1975, p. 192). Commenting on these problems, Staples (1976, pp. 232–233) stated:

> Because of the oppressive conditions under which they live, Blacks consume more alcoholic beverages to cope with the stress in their lives and escape from reality. No law ever stopped a man from drinking, and alcoholism is not going to be solved by putting people in jail because it is a medical problem, not a crime. . . . The use of heroin by poor Blacks can only be seen as an effort to cope with the stress related to survival.

Racism. Both personal and institutional racism must be seen as key variables related to stressful events in the life of Black people. Several authors (Staples, 1976; Knowles and Prewitt, 1969; Willie, et al., 1973) have shown that racism is also a significant factor which influences the delivery of social and health services to the Black community. Moreover, other stressful events, such as family instability, child abuse and neglect, inadequate nutrition, poor physical environment, and inequitable economic participation in the Black community, are clearly linked to race and discrimination in the American society. However, further discussion of these problems can be found in other sections of this book.

Research as a Problem

Increasingly, Black people are beginning to see research, especially in the social and behavioral sciences, as a major problem confronting their community. The problem is related to the structure of the research industry, ethnic issues related to human experimentation, manpower and training, and deficiencies in the research. In response to the need to solve a range of problems, including mental health or illness in the United States, research has become a major business enterprise (Gary, 1975). Millions of dollars are spent each year for research. For example, in 1974, it was estimated that $32.1 billion was spent on research and development (R&D) activities (National Science Foundation, 1974, p. 1).

With respect to the sources of funding for R&D projects, in 1974, 53 percent of funds for these activities came from the federal government. Unfortunately, most of the federal support (about 70 percent) was in the areas of defense and space (National Science Foundation, 1974, pp. 1, 4–5). Although the federal share of R&D efforts has been declining, this trend should be reversed during the latter part of this decade, given the increased emphasis on health and energy.

In a comprehensive study by the Committee on Social Sciences of the National Science Foundation (1976, p. 11), it was estimated that in 1975, $475 million was appropriated for the social and behavioral sciences by the federal government. The category of behavioral and social sciences includes the disciplines of psychology, anthropology, economics, history, linguistics, political science, sociology, law, and socioeconomic geography. Of this $475 million, $129.5 million was spent on basic research, while $345.5 million was allocated to applied research. The four largest federal agencies supporting social and behavioral sciences research in 1975 were (1) the Department of Health, Education and Welfare ($186.1 million); (2) the Department of Agriculture ($52.6 million); (3) the Department of Defense ($51.6 million); and (4) the National Science Foundation ($51.6 million).

From a historical perspective, federal government support for social science research has doubled from 1966 to 1976 (*Federal Support of Social Science Research,* 1975, p. 38). Mental health research has been supported primarily by the federal government through the National Institute of Mental Health (NIMH). A recent NIMH study of its research programs revealed that its research budget grew from less than $1 million in 1968 to $112 million in 1972 (*Research in the Service of Mental Health,* 1975, p. 27). In 1972, however, only $82.5 million was devoted to extramural research programs. Moreover, in a ten-year period, the social science share of all federal support has risen from 3.1 percent to 4.3 percent. During the period from 1966 to 1976, the average annual growth rate for federally funded social science research was 7.9 percent (*Federal Support of Social Science Research,* 1975, p. 38). While federal support for social science research has increased, it is rising at a slower rate.

Federal support for social science research varies according to the discipline and the agency sponsoring the research. For example, HEW is the chief agency supporting research in the social sciences, and the focus has been primarily on multidisciplinary areas related to education in sociology (poverty) and in the economics of medical and social services. Almost all of the Department of Agriculture research funds go to research in economics (*Federal Support of Social Science Research,* 1975, p. 38). In the study of NIMH research grants and funds in 1972, the data showed that psychologists received 45 percent of research funds; psychiatrists received 18 percent; other medical sciences, 13 percent; and social science, 11 percent (*Research in the Service of Mental Health,* 1975, p. 42).

Since it has been shown that research is a major business enterprise in the United States, an important question is: What role has the Black community played in this important business-educational activity? As indicated above, the major disciplines receiving federal support for social science and mental health research are economics, psychology, psychiatry, and sociology. The next question is: How many Blacks with terminal or professional degrees are there in these fields? Blacks constitute less than 3 percent of the professionals in these fields. These data would suggest that one major research problem facing the Black community is how to get more Black students interested in research careers in those disciplines mentioned above.

In 1976, it was estimated that universities and colleges performed 27 percent of the social science research sponsored by the federal agencies (*Federal Support for Social Science Research,* 1975, p. 38). In 1972, the greatest proportion of NIMH research grant awards and funds went to colleges and universities (*Research in the Services of Mental Health,* 1975, p. 37). Robinson (1971) conducted a study of 552 minority research projects funded by the federal government. He found that 48 percent of these projects used Black subjects. Out of the 552 projects, 388 (70.3 percent) were carried out at colleges and universities, but only 18 projects (3 percent) involved traditionally Black colleges and universities (Robinson, 1971, p. 3). In a recent article, Gary (1975) concluded that the federal government, including NIMH, has not supported research at Black colleges and universities even though the institutions have the capabilities for developing quality research programs. It is interesting to note that although NIMH had $82.5 million available for extramural research, the Center for Minority Group Mental Health Programs, which was developed to assist minority researchers, had only $1.10 million to support research projects (*Research in the Service of Mental Health,* 1975, p. 31). What these data suggest is that Blacks and other minorities continue to be targets for research conducted largely by white investigators.

Most of the research conducted in the Black community is under the control of white scholars, but they have not done a good job. A special research task force of a conference convened by the Minority Center at NIMH made these observations concerning research on Black people by white scientists:

1. White middle-class behavior constitutes the norms against which Black behavior is evaluated.

2. There has been a failure to take account of the interrelated forces that create and maintain racism and hence influence the mental health of Black people.

3. There has been a tendency to engage in interminable victim analysis, comparisons of Blacks and whites, and deficiency-deprivation explanations of Black behavior.

Several Black scholars (Billingsley, 1968; Gary, 1976; Jackson, 1976; Smith, 1972; Gordon, 1973) have identified additional deficiencies in much of the research of white scientists on problems confronting the Black community. Some of the deficiencies are given below:

1. Oversimplified reasoning from group (statistical aggregates) to individuals.

2. A tendency to assume the uniformity of the Black experience.

3. A propensity to focus primarily on lowest-income groups of Black subjects.

4. A tendency to concentrate on captive subjects (prisoners, mental patients, school children).

5. Inadequate conceptual schemes for problem definition.

6. Poor sampling and research design.

7. Inappropriate and unreliable instruments.

8. A tendency to underemphasize cultural factors or deny the importance of culture in influencing behavioral patterns in the Black community.

9. A reluctance to treat racism as an important variable.

10. A biased perspective, given the socialization of the researcher.

Of course, this list of deficiencies in the social and behavioral sciences research conducted in the Black community is incomplete, but such tendencies are viewed as a major problem by many Black people.

The Politics of Social Policy

In 1969, the National Science Foundation appointed a committee to study ways "for increasing the useful application of the social sciences in the solution of contemporary social problems" (*Report of the Special Commission*, 1969, p. xi). The report, entitled *Knowledge into Action: Improving the Nation's Use of the Social Sciences*, covered a range of issues including problems such as the social sciences and the professions; the social sciences and the federal government; the social sciences, business and labor; the social sciences and community organizations; and the social sciences, the public, and social problems research institutes. This report clearly documents the linkages between social and behavioral sciences research and social policy.

In an article, "Social Science for Social Policy," Gans (1975, p. 4) defines social policy as "any proposal for deliberate activity to affect the working of society or any of its parts." He elaborates further: "The distinct quality of social policy is its aim for what might be called programmatic rationality; it seeks to achieve substantive goals through instrumental action that can be proven logically or empirically, to achieve these goals'' (Gans, 1975, p. 4). While one can see the positive role for the social and behavioral sciences in solving social problems, Chaplan and Nelson (1975, p. 192) suggested that it is necessary for us to be aware of some serious consequences when they concluded:

> Whether or not the problems we study are true social problems or whether they deserve the attention they receive vis-à-vis other social ills, is open to debate. However, a more serious and less obvious danger is the use of social science and social scientists to displace the blame for prior political and technological failures. Such failures are often the end result of a series of short-run political and technological accommodations for which there may no longer be either short- or long-term political, technological or social solutions. But because breakdowns in the political-economic system produce serious social consequences, social scientists are called on to deal with it. The implication is that socially undesirable behavior is the problem rather than the inevitable by-product of political trade-off and technological fixes, thereby distracting attention from the real cause.

In relating this problem to the Black community, one can see the relationship between social research and social programs and policies (Yette, 1971). There are instances where concepts such as cultural deprivation, inadequate mother thesis, genetic determinism, learning disabilities, helper therapy principle, etc., have served as theoretical foundations for a variety of social programs in the Black community, such as infant stimulation, special education, career education, and paraprofessional programs (Gary, 1975, pp. 45–46).

Politics has tremendous impact on the research industry as well as on the research process. Over the past several years, there has been a significant shift in the political climate in this country relative to the support of social programs designed to broaden opportunities for disadvantaged groups in our society. Leading white intellectuals, such as Jensen (1969), Herrnstein (1971), Jencks (1972), and Banfield (1968) have advanced arguments which question the utility of compensatory programs for helping poor—especially Black—people to improve or change their social and personal conditions. The governments at both the federal and state levels are supporting research on Black people, but the research conclusions are being used to justify the government's objective of ''benign neglect.'' It is no accident that James Coleman, long an advocate of busing for integrating public schools, has changed his mind. Supposedly, his current research suggests that he was wrong.

Since he changed his mind, he will be able to get significant research dollars for his projects.

Politics of Treatment Modalities

One important mental health problem of importance to the Black community is the relationship between politics and treatment modalities. Stress has a significant impact on the mental functioning of Black people, and often public policy decisions contribute to the stress level in the Black community. Brenner (1967, 1968) has documented the relationship between economic instability and the incidence of health disabilities. Fieve (1975) has shown the dramatic growth in drug therapy since the 1950s. Before the 1960s, the major treatment modality for mental illness (about 60 percent of the cases) was based on a psychological frame of reference (group therapy, casework, individual therapy) rather than on a chemotherapeutic model (drugs). Today the mode of treatment is the reverse. In other words, the major treatment modality for mental illness is now based on psychopharmacological procedures. When a person gets upset or depressed, he usually gets some type of antidepressant pill. The Black community is no exception to this trend. Too many people are on psychotropic medication in our society.

It is interesting to note that prescriptions for mental health–related problems are written mainly by internists and general practitioners rather than by psychiatrists. Moreover, one must ask these questions: Who goes to the psychiatrist for mental health problems? Who goes to the general practitioner or the emergency ward or the city hospital for their mental health problems?

Class and racial variables are important factors in understanding the mental health delivery system. Lower-income people—especially Blacks—tend to go to the internists or the emergency room rather than to a psychiatrist or private physician when there is a mental health problem. On the other hand, upper-class people tend to utilize the services of a psychiatrist somewhat more than do the poor. The upper class is experimenting with encounter groups, religious meditation, and alternative life styles as well as going to psychiatrists who are not necessarily prescribing drugs.

In accepting the notion that drug therapy is useful or effective in treating mental problems, we are indirectly supporting the concept that the cause of the problem is related to biological rather than to socioeconomic factors. With this frame of reference, one can see how genetics is becoming an important discipline in relationship to studying behavior and feelings. In fact, in the future, more money will be allocated to research into the genetic basis of behavior. The important question, then, is how many Blacks are there who are trained in genetics?

The political implications of the above discussion are becoming clear. In the educational field, some white scientists are saying that poor academic performance by Blacks is related to their genetics; moreover, these scientists are claiming that maladaptive behavior in Blacks is also related to genetics. In addition, there is an apparent tendency among professionals to support a political and ideological strategy in which the victim is blamed for his decline (Ryan, 1971). Data seem to be suggesting that the economy is to blame for the rise in mental illness, but professionals are giving medication to the victim rather than trying to change the economic system. Given the high incidence of drug abuse in the Black community, it is necessary for us to raise issues with professionals who are advocating a chemotherapeutic approach to the mental health problems of Black people. This is a major challenge for Black mental health professionals.

Interpersonal Relations

Interpersonal functioning in the Black community is a problem area for the community, but Black scholars and practitioners have not dealt in any significant way with this problem. Theodorson and Theodorson (1969) define interpersonal relations as "the patterns of personal relationships that develop out of sustained social interaction." Volkart (1964) states that this concept refers to everything that goes on between one person and another by way of perception, evaluation, understanding, and mode of reaction. Given the level of social and interpersonal conflict within the Black community, as expressed in the crime statistics, particularly "Black-on-Black crime," Black social practitioners and researchers must develop meaningful instruments for assessing interpersonal development in areas such as (1) friendship—the ability to establish, maintain, and experience satisfaction from close relationships with others; (2) work relationship—the ability to function with satisfaction vis-à-vis other people according to the demands of the job; and (3) sexual relationship—the ability to establish, sustain, and gain satisfaction from broadly defined sexual relationships.

Developing mechanisms for improving the quality of interpersonal functioning in the community must be seen as an immediate goal for Black people. Research and practice skills in this area have important social and political implications, such as (1) reducing crime in the community, (2) organizing citizens to solve community or social problems at the local level, (3) improving the quality of education, (4) fund raising in the Black community for social purposes, (5) developing a community approach to mental health problems, (6) designing a meaningful health education program, (7) improving the support base of Black institutions, and (8) understanding economic behavior in the Black community.

Within the confines and constraints of the urban environment, Blacks have developed their own strategies, survival or coping mechanisms for dealing with personal crises and external pressures which have a direct bearing on their mental health (Billingsley, 1969; Comer, 1972; Keil, 1966). Many Black people with personal problems customarily turn to informal organizations in their environment rather than to professionals. These informal groups and voluntary associations, such as bars, barbershops, peer groups, gangs, and storefront churches, make up the social network of the Black community. Authors such as Malcolm X (1965) and Claude Brown (1965) cite, in their autobiographies, examples of how these informal organizations and similar ones have enabled many Blacks to develop the necessary talent for functioning in a hostile, racist environment.

Within the past ten years, there has been considerable social change in the Black community which has relevance for studying the mental health of Black people (White, 1970). Former social network groups are beginning to disintegrate. A communication lag exists in the Black churches. For many Black people, the bars, barbershops, and Saturday night "joints" are no longer seen as meeting spots to come, "rap," and "hash out" problems. On the other hand, these organizations continue to exist and provide services to the Black community. Little research has been conducted to determine the significance of social networks in the

Black community, and most mental health workers do not integrate the social support systems with treatment plans when working with Black clients.

By using a social networks framework, one can get a different view of economic behavior in the Black community, Fusfeld (1973) has developed the term "irregular economy" to describe this aspect of economic behavior in the Black community. Black people have always had to rely on innovative means for surviving in a hostile economic environment. When one cannot afford goods in the regular economy, he purchases them through the irregular economy, and it is not all illegal—some purchases are legal. The following occupational types operate in the irregular economy in our inner-city communities:

1. *The artist:* entertainers, painters, craftsmen, etc.
2. *The hustler:* supersalesmen, drug dealers, bookies, pimps, and prostitutes.
3. *The fixer:* repairmen who work on (or "fix") cars, appliances, etc., and do plumbing and electrical work.
4. *The information broker:* individuals who receive cash in exchange for information, i.e., job opportunities, specific information concerning the welfare system, help to locate friends and enemies and to find stolen goods.
5. *The product developer:* individuals who develop products and sell them to residents of the inner city or citizens in general.

It is important for us to understand how these individuals operate in the community for they are important sources of community strength and viability, but they can also create interpersonal conflict and problems which will have a direct bearing on the mental health of the community.

The Black Professional and Racism

In recent years, an increased interest has developed in looking at the impact of racism, both individual and institutional, on Black professionals (Back and Simpson, 1964; Beisser and Harris, 1966; Blackwell and Haug, 1973; Daniel, 1973; Sanders, 1972; Williams, 1974; Wilson, 1975; Better, 1972; Calnek, 1970; Funnye, 1970). As

Black people begin to move into professions or professional fields in increasing numbers, it seems that a variety of mechanisms have been used by white-dominated institutions to restrict or limit their opportunities. Considerable pressures have been placed on Black professionals who have tried to "make it" in these institutions. Yet few studies have been conducted on what is happening to the best Black minds as a result of institutional racism. According to Jackson (1976, p. 70):

> . . . One apparent reality is that there has been little scholarly effort either to ferret out the ramifications of the subtle pressure exerted on Black professionals or to synthesize how Black professionals have reacted to it. Of particular interest to me is the articulation of the cultural and theoretical links among professionals because of a failure to examine this dimension of the problem, it is espoused is contributing to conflicts among them.

White-dominated institutions use a variety of strategies or mechanisms to create stress for Black professionals. The following are examples of such tactics:

1. Strategies of promoting the less talented Black at the expense of the talented Black. Result: intragroup conflict and intrapsychic stress.

2. Strategies of isolating a Black professional into a unit where there are few other Blacks. Result: intrapsychic stress and conflict.

3. Strategies of putting a Black professional over a program or activity which is being phased out. Result: intragroup conflict and intrapsychic stress.

4. Strategies of systematically questioning the competencies of the Black professional even though he might have excellent credentials and experience. Result: intrapsychic stress.

5. Strategies of using biased assessment instruments for selection, placement, and promotion in such a manner as to limit the mobility of the Black professional. Result: intrapsychic conflict.

These tactics—and there are others—create much stress for Black professionals, and this factor is viewed as a serious mental health problem. As suggested earlier, the notion of stress implies inordinate exposure to forces that can harm a person's well-being. The conditions under which many Black professionals work make them particularly susceptible to the impact of stressors. The prevalence of overt and covert discrimination from whites makes these professionals consistently open to assaults on their tranquility as well as their material status.

In simple terms, it is necessary to be concerned about the training needs and requirements of the Black professional for the different environments in which he works and the responses he makes to the multitude of stressors he encounters in his daily life (Gary, 1976). One can also argue that there is a need for research or training information to answer the following questions:

1. What are the common stressors found in the environment of Black professionals? What are their frequencies of incidence?

2. What responses to these stressors are included in the repertoires of Black professionals? What are their frequencies of use?

3. What are the rules and conditions governing the choice of particular responses to various stressors?

4. Given situational constraints, how "adequate" are the typical responses made to stressors?

5. In instances in which stressors are inadequate, what are the origins of the inadequacies?

6. Can measures be taken to increase the use of adequate stressor responses by given Black professionals in a given environment?

With answers to these questions, the Black professional, as well as Black people in general, should be able to deal more effectively with complex organizations and their racist ideology and behavior.

Conclusion

Although there are many mental health problems in the Black community, adequate information is not available which could be used to assess how these problems impact on the community. A needs assessment which takes into consideration factors such as geography, class, sex, age, migration, and neighborhoods is very important in determining the mental health status of the Black community. Several stressful life events have been discussed; however, to understand fully the causal factors related to stress in the Black community, racism must be viewed as the key variable. Given this factor, one can see why social and behavioral sciences research, social policies, and treatment modalities are seen by many Blacks as major problems confronting the Black community. Some stressful areas such as interpersonal relations are ignored in professionals. Yet the quality of interpersonal functioning in the Black community is crucial for its own survival. As Black professionals try to change the direction of white-dominated social organizations, so they will deal with issues important to the Black community; they will experience, and are experiencing, considerable stress. Racism, then, has a tremendous impact on mental health problems in the Black community.

References

Back, K., and Simpson, I. "The Dilemma of the Negro Professional." *Journal of Social Issues* 10 (1964): 60–70.

Banfield, E. E. *The Unheavenly City.* Boston: Little, Brown, 1968.

Beisser, A., and Harris, H. "Psychological Aspects of the Civil Rights Movement and the Negro Professional Man." *American Journal of Psychiatry* 12 (1966): 733–738.

Beisser, R. et al. *Mental Health Consultation and Education.* Palo Alto, California: National Press Books, 1972.

Better, S. "The Black Social Workers' Role in the Black Community Altering the System." *Black World* 22 (1972): 4–14.

Billingsley, A. *Black Families in White America.* Englewood Cliffs: Prentice-Hall, 1968.

_____. "Black Families and White Social Sciences." *Journal of Social Issues* 26 (1970): 127–142.

Blackwell, J., and Haug, M. "Relations Between Black Bosses and Black Workers." *Black Scholar* 4 (1973): 36–43.

Brenner, M. H. "Economic Change and Mental Hospitalization: New York State 1910–1960." *Social Psychology* 2 (1967): 180–188.

_____. "Patterns of Psychiatric Hospitalization Among Different Socioeconomic Groups in Response to Economic Stress." *Journal of Nervous and Mental Diseases* 148 (1968): 31–8.

Brown, C. *Manchild in a Promised Land.* New York: American Library, 1965.

Butcher, M. *The Negro in American Culture.* New York: Knopf and Mentor Books, 1956.

Calneck, M. "Racial Factors in the Counter-Transference: The Black Therapist and Black Client." *American Journal of Orthopsychiatry* 40 (1970): 39–46.

Chaplan, N., and Nelson, S. D. "On Being Useful: The Nature and Consequences of Psychological Research of Social Problems." In Irving Horowitz (ed.), *The Use and Abuse of Social Science.* New Brunswick, New Jersey: Transaction Books, 1975.

Comer, J. C. *Beyond Black and White.* New York: Quadrangle Books, 1972.

Cooper, S. "Look at the Effect of Racism on Clinical Work." *Social Casework* 54 (1973): 76–83.

Daniel, J. "Black Academic Activism." *Black Scholar* 4 (1973): 44–52.

Dohrenwend, B. S., and Dohrenwend, B. P. *Stressful Life Events: Their Nature and Effects.* New York: Wiley, 1974.

Ellison, R. *Shadow and Act.* New York: Signet, 1966.

Fieve, R. R. *Moodswing: The Third Revolution in Psychiatry.* New York: William Morrow, 1975.

Freeman, H. E., and Jones, W. C. *Social Problems: Causes and Controls.* Chicago: Rand McNally, 1970.

Funnye, C. "The Militant Black Social Worker and the Urban Hustle." *Social Work* 15 (1970): 5–13.

Fusfeld, R. *The Basic Economics of the Urban Racial Crisis.* New York: Holt, Rinehart & Winston, 1973.

Gans, H. J. "Federal Support of Social Science Research Rising at Slower Pace." *Mosiac* 6 (1975): 38.

——————. "Social Science for Social Policy." In Irving L. Horowitz (ed.), *The Use and Abuse of Social Science,* 2nd ed., p. 4. New Brunswick, New Jersey: Transaction Books, 1975.

Garfield, S. L. "A Note on Patients' Reasons for Terminating Therapy." *Psychological Report* 13 (1963): 38.

Gary, L. E. "The Significance of Research for the Survival of Black Colleges." *Journal of Black Studies* 6 (1975): 45–46.

——————. "Understanding Institutional Racism in Mental Health." Unpublished paper, 1976.

Gary, L. E., and Brown, L. P. *Crime and Its Impact on the Black Community.* Washington, D.C.: Howard University Press, 1976.

Gilbert, J. "A Study of Equity in Providing Community Mental Health Services." Interim Report prepared for NIMH by Public Sector, Inc., New York, September, 1972.

Gordan, T. "Notes on White and Black Psychology." *Journal of Social Issues* 29 (1973): 87–89.

Gross, H. S. et al. "The Effect of Race and Sex on the Variation of Diagnosis and Disposition in a Psychiatric Emergency Room." *Journal of Nervous and Mental Diseases* 148 (1969): 638–642.

Hare, N. "Black Ecology." *Black Scholar* 1(1970): 2–8.

Hendrie, H. C., and Hanson, D. "A Comparative Study of Psychiatric Care of Indians and Metis." *American Journal of Orthopsychiatry* 42 (1972): 480–489.

Herrnstein, P. "I.Q." *Atlantic Quarterly* 12 (1971): 13–64.

Herskovits, M. *The Myth of the Negro Past.* Boston: Beacon Press, 1958.

Holms, T. H., and Rahe, R. H. "The Social Readjustment Rating Scale." *Journal of Psychosomatic Research* 10 (1967): 255–262, 355–366.

Horton, P. B., and Leslie, G. R. *The Sociology of Social Problems.* 5th ed. Englewood Cliffs, New Jersey: Prentice-Hall, 1974, pp. 4, 31–32.

Insel, P. M., and Roth, W. T. *Health in a Changing Society.* Palo Alto California: Mayfield, 1976, pp. 1, 18, 19, 55.

Jackson, A. M.; Berkowitz, H.; and Farley, G. "Race as a Variable Affecting the Treatment Involvement of Children." *Journal of American Academy of Child Psychiatry* 13 (1974): 20–31.

Jackson, G. G. "Cultural Seedbeds of the Black Backlash in Mental Health." *Journal of Afro-American Issues* 4 (1976): 70.

Jencks, C. et al. *Inequality: a Reassessment of Effects of Family and Schooling in America.* New York: Basic Books, 1972.

Jensen, R. "How Much Can We Boost IQ and Scholastic Achievement?" *Harvard Educational Review* 39 (1969): 1–123.

Keezer, W. S. *Mental Health and Human Behavior.* Dubuque, Iowa: W. C. Brown, 1971.

Keil, C. *Urban Blues.* Chicago: University of Chicago Press, 1966.

Kelly, C. M. *Crime in the United States, 1975.* Washington, D.C.: U.S. Government Printing Office, 1976, pp. 20, 192, 194.

Knowles, L. L., and Prewitt, K. (eds.), *Institutional Racism in America.* Englewood Cliffs, New Jersey: Prentice-Hall, 1969.

Levi, L. (ed.). *Society, Stress and Disease.* London: Oxford University Press, 1971.

Levitan, S. R. et al. *Minorities in the United States: Problems, Progress, and Prospects.* Washington, D.C.: Public Affairs Press, 1975.

Lowenger, P., and Dobie, S. "Attitudes and Emotions of the Psychiatrist in the Initial Interview." *American Journal of Psychotherapy* 20 (1966): 17–32.

Malcolm X. *The Autobiography of Malcolm X.* New York: Grove Press, 1965.

Mayer, J. *Health.* New York: D. Van Nostrand, 1974, pp. 469, 489–515.

National Science Foundation. *National Patterns of Resources, Funds and Manpower in the United States: 1953-1974.* (National Science Foundation 74-304). Washington, D.C.: U.S. Government Printing Office, 1974, pp. 1, 4–5.

Pinkney, A. *Black Americans.* Englewood Cliffs, New Jersey: Prentice-Hall, 1969.

Research in the Service of Mental Health: Report of the Research Task Force of the National Institute of Mental Health. D.E.W. Publication No. (ADM) 75–236. Washington, D.C.: U.S. Government Printing Office, 1975, pp. 27, 37, 42.

Robinson, T. N. "Minority Research Studies." Unpublished paper, 1971.

Rosenthal, D., and Frank, J. "Fate of Psychiatric Clinic Outpatients Assigned to Psychotherapy." *Journal of Nervous and Mental Diseases* 14 (1958): 330–343.

Ryan, W. *Blaming the Victim.* New York: Random House, 1971.

Sanders, C. L. *Black Professionals' Perceptions of Institutional Racism in Health and Welfare Organizations.* Fairlawn, New Jersey: R. E. Burdick, 1972.

Smith, C. H. "Organizational Model for Parental Involvement in Inner City Schools." *Journal of Afro-American Issues* 1 (1972): 247–256.

Special Commission on the Social Sciences of National Science Board. *Knowledge Into Action: Improving the Nation's Use of the Social Sciences.* Washington, D.C.: National Science Foundation, 1969.

Staples, R. *Introduction to Black Sociology.* New York: McGraw-Hill, 1976.

Szwed, J. F. (ed.). *Black America.* New York: Basic Books, 1970.

Theodorson, G. A., and Theodorson, A. *Modern Dictionary of Sociology.* New York: Thomas Y. Crowell, 1969.

U.S. Bureau of the Census. *Current Population Reports,* 1, 1970 series p. 20, No. 271.

Volkart, P. "Interpersonal Relations." In J. Gould, and W. L. Kolb (eds.), *Dictionary of Social Sciences.* New York: Free Press, 1964.

Warren, D. "Neighborhood Helping Networks in Urban Community." Proposal submitted to the Center for Studies of Metropolitan Problems. NIMH, 1973.

Wilder, J., and Coleman, M. "The 'Walk-In' Psychiatric Clinic: Some Observations and Follow-up." *International Journal of Social Psychiatry* 11 (1963): 192–199.

Williams, A. "Black-Related Diseases: An Overview." *Journal of Black Health Perspectives* 1 (1974): 35–40.

Willie, C. V.; Kramer, B. M.; and Brown, B. S. (eds.). *Racism and Mental Health.* Pittsburgh: University of Pittsburgh Press, 1973.

Wilson, E. A. *Sociobiology: The New Synthesis.* Cambridge, Massachusetts: Harvard University Press, 1975.

Wheller, S. "Deviant Behavior." In N. J. Smelser (ed.), *Sociology: An Introduction,* 2nd ed., p. 650. New York: Wiley, 1973.

White, J. "Guidelines for Black Psychologists." *Black Scholar* 3 (1970): 6–10.

Whitten, E., Jr., and Zwed, F. *Afro-American Anthropology: Contemporary Perspective.* New York: Free Press, 1970.

Yette, S. F. *The Choice: The Issues of Black Survival in America.* New York: Putnam, 1971.

3   MENTAL HEALTH: ETIOLOGY AND PROCESS

Counterracist Psychiatry

Frances C. Welsing, M.D.

The National Institute of Mental Health (NIMH) recently labeled mental illness as "America's primary health problem." It stated that at least 20 million Americans suffer some form of mental illness, and about one-seventh of them receive some psychiatric care.

One year after the Kerner Commission (the Presidential Commission on Violence) labeled American society as a "racist society," Black psychiatrists at the 1969 annual meeting of the American Psychiatric Association declared racism to be the number-one mental health problem in the area of the world known as the United States of America. They further labeled racism as the major cause of all other mental health problems. Thus, using current NIMH statistics, Black psychiatrists have labeled racism as the cause of America's primary health problem and as the major mental health problem.

For close to 2000 years, Western medicine has been characterized by the attempt to understand in depth the cause(s) or etiology of disease states, reasoning that once the cause is understood, the disease can be efficiently and effectively attacked. This means that proper treatment can be instituted, with the possibility of disease cure and even, perhaps, the prevention of disease.

Thus, if racism is the cause of mental disability, as so stated in 1969 by many Black psychiatrists, the fundamental question for psychiatrists, for psychiatry, and for mental health advocates from all disciplines is: Can racism, as itself a disease state and as the cause of other disease states, be sufficiently understood so that it can be adequately attacked, eradicated (cured), and prevented? Similarly, can the disease states which arise secondary to the primary dynamic of racism also be treated, cured, and prevented?

It is of major significance that some Black psychiatrists and other Black behavioral scientists are now setting forth their views as to the etiology of mental illness and disability at a period in history when the established edifice of psychiatry in America is experiencing an inner crisis of theory and practice. Past theory and practice no longer seem adequate, and from within, there is a rising criticism of the profession, e.g., *The Death of Psychiatry,* by E. Fuller Torrey. Another commentator has said that "At the present time, the field of psychiatry is undergoing an identity crisis from within and a crisis of public confidence from without" (Ludwig, 1967).

The present disillusionment with past theoretical models and their therapy correlates and the current proliferation of schools of therapy have led many to fear that the only alternatives to control or to alter behavior are those of the behaviorist psychology of B. F. Skinner, J. M. R. Delgado, and Perry London, which claim to modify behavior through drugs, brain surgery, and genetic alteration (Lasch, 1976).

It is this writer's view, however, that the current crisis in psychiatry is directly related to the cowardice of the psychiatrists and the psychiatry and behavioral science establishment in confronting the reality of the major social-environmental dynamic of racism. Failure to do so has necessitated a head-in-the-sand attitude toward confronting those societal determinants of behavior-pattern organization and thus a refusal to probe and dissect all of the aspects of the social dynamic which produce socially dysfunctional patterns of conduct.

Instead of probing how certain patterns of dysfunctional and socially destructive behavior are programmed into the brain computer by specific societal dynamics and a specific social experience, the focus has shifted to probing and cutting out portions of the brain, or destroying certain groups of cells in the brain, so that those unwanted behaviors cannot be expressed. Instead of focusing on the dynamic interaction between the totality of the social dynamic and the genetic and constitutional make-up, the focus shifts toward genetic alteration and manipulation while steadfastly ignoring major aspects of the societal dynamic. Similarly, the use of drugs proliferates as a means of controlling and modifying behaviors in adults and children alike, rather than focusing on the dynamic societal determinants of disturbed behavior-pattern formation.

One cannot help but conclude that in the present social dynamic the basic societal dynamic must remain unexamined as a whole and thereby untouched, while that which the societal dynamic acts upon can be subjected to alteration: genes, brain tissue, and individual neurochemistry.

However, from the perspective of this writer, any discussion of mental disability must begin with the basic understanding that firstly, mental disability is discerned through the observation (in the context of an established behavior system) of patterns of logic, thought, speech, action, emotional response, and perception, as carried out in one or more of the various areas of people activity: economics, education, entertainment, labor, law, politics, religion, sex, and war.

Secondly, behavior must be understood as the by-product of the activity of the nervous system—namely, the brain, the peripheral nervous system (sensory and motor aspects), and the autonomic nervous system—as the total nervous system encounters a specific surrounding environment. Of course, the fundamental basis for nervous system functioning is the genetic and constitutional make-up of the organism.

In order to understand behavior and therefore behavior disability or mental disability, one must be able to understand basically how the brain and the other major aspects of the nervous system function in relationship to the totality of the surrounding environment. Most simply stated, the brain is the organ responsible for logic, thought, speech, action, emotional response, and perception. It functions as a central computer decoding, analyzing, and correlating all of the various forms of environmental data brought to it by the sensory receptors (sight, taste, touch, smell, hearing) of the peripheral nervous system. The data are derived from the totality of the physical and social environment which surrounds the human organism. Sensory data input to the brain is information about the environment, its quality, its structure, and its process.

Data are also brought to the brain computer from the internal environment of the human organism. By and large, the body's internal environment is also influenced by the surrounding external environment. For example, the functioning of the total body is influenced by the food and quality of air and oxygen that is brought from the external environment to the body to sustain the internal life processes. This information is also taken to the central brain computer. All of the data that are brought to the computer brain are for the purpose of solving the problems posed to the human organism by the surrounding environment so that the organism may relate successfully to that environment, i.e., thrive, develop, and propagate itself.

The brain and the peripheral nervous system in the human organism, as well as in the lower animals, have been designed by nature during the long process of evolution, for the sole purpose of solving problems posed to the organism by the surrounding environment. The bases for successful problem solution are the accuracy and completeness of data brought to the brain by the sensory nervous system; the efficiency with which that data is processed, decoded, and analyzed by the brain computer; and finally, the development by the computer brain of an appropriate behavior response to the environment which will permit survival and development for the organism, as expressed through the motor apparatus of the nervous system.

The brain computer, upon receiving information about the environment, acts as a highly complex computer analyzer of the environmental data, combining new and past stored data, and thereby producing the potentiality for environmental problem solution, as the informed organism acts back upon the environment through learned and/or newly designed or created patterns of behavior in all areas of people activity.

From this description of the dynamic interaction between the brain and nervous system and the environment, the following definition of intelligence is possible. *Intelligence* is the ability of the brain and the nervous system to decode (analyze) the environmental totality and then to organize an appropriate, efficient, and effective behavioral response (which is environmental problem-solving), thus permitting survival and the development of the organism in harmony with the surrounding environmental totality.

Figure 1 illustrates this writer's conception of the dynamic origin of all behavior-pattern formations in human beings in the context of an established social system or system of specific power relationships. These behavior patterns cannot be fully understood or, if need be, adequately treated, without an accurate analysis of the existing power relationships of the social system and, more fundamentally, without full knowledge of the major objective which these power relationships have been designed to achieve.

The individual patterns of behavior response or reaction to the environmental system of power relationships or the total social dynamic can be referred to as personality or character formations. In general, these personality and character configurations serve in turn to give further support to the established power relationships within the social-

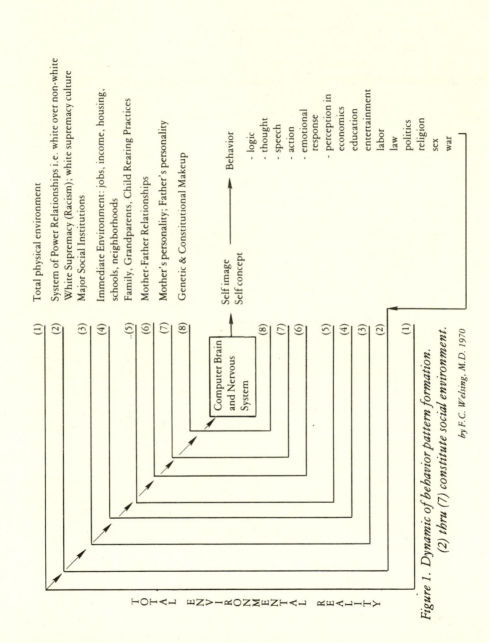

(1)　Total physical environment

(2)　System of Power Relationships i.e. white over non-white
White Supremacy (Racism); white supremacy culture
Major Social Institutions

(3)

(4)　Immediate Environment: jobs, income, housing,
schools, neighborhoods

..(5)　Family, Grandparents, Child Rearing Practices

(6)　Mother-Father Relationships

(7)　Mother's personality; Father's personality

(8)　Genetic & Constitutional Makeup

Self image　　　　　　Behavior
Self concept

- logic
- thought
- speech
- action
- emotional
  response
- perception in
  economics
  education
  entertainment
  labor
  law
  politics
  religion
  sex
  war

Computer Brain
and Nervous
System

Figure 1. Dynamic of behavior pattern formation.
(2) thru (7) constitute social environment.

by F. C. Welsing, M.D. 1970

system context. This is the nature of a behavior system and the dynamic which permits the system to survive and exist over a given expanse of time.

All social systems have specific goals and objectives which are either explicitly or implictly stated. When these goals and objectives are not overtly stated, it is necessary for the behavioral scientist to decode them from observation of the patterns and direction, over time, of the total internal behavior process, so that individual and group behavior within the power system can be fully understood and/or treated.

All individual and collective patterns of behavior within the framework of a total behavior power system relate directly or indirectly to the ultimate goals of the power system in which the behavior occurs. The established power relationships can be viewed most fundamentally as the perception of their survival necessity by a specific people who control the balance of power within the power system. It is also their view of themselves in relationship to the total environment. The behaviors are also an expression of the genetic base of the individuals and the collective, since the behavior end-product results from the dynamic interaction of the total environment and the genetic and constitutional make-up of individuals.

From birth (possibly at the point of conception), as the environment acts upon the genetic and constitutional make-up and the nervous system, each individual develops patterns of behavior in all areas of activity which, when carried out in the environment, are either functional or dysfunctional toward the solution to the environmentally determined problems confronted by the individual.

Functional patterns of behavior are those which solve or help to produce solutions to the problems posed by the total environment. When these are used by the individual, he or she experiences a sense of harmony with the environment or power over the environment and thus a sense of self-respect in relationship to the total environment.

Dysfunctional patterns of behavior fail to solve environmentally posed problems, giving a sense of disharmony with the environment, a sense of frustration, anxiety, and despair; thus the individual experiences a sense of powerlessness and a low level of self-esteem and self-respect in relationship to the environment.

Functional patterns of behavior can only develop in the presence of accurate and sufficient data about the total environment and an ac-

curate decoding and analysis of the environmental data by the individual computer brain.

Dysfunctional patterns of behavior, on the other hand, result from
insufficient, confusing, inaccurate, contradictory, and/or false data for
brain computer analysis or faulty data input. Dysfunctional patterns of
conduct can also result from a damaged brain computer and nervous
system, whether or not that damage is genetically determined.

Functional patterns of behavior—meaning efficient and effective
problem-solving behavior in relationship to environmental issues and
problems—can be viewed as synonymous with mental health, while
dysfunctional patterns of behavior—those which fail to produce
solutions to environment-posed problems—are synonymous with
mental disability or mental illness in varying degrees. Sometimes these
dysfunctional patterns of conduct result from a steadfast refusal to face
and confront the environmental reality. Sometimes there is fear of facing that reality.

In the course of lived experience in the total environment, each
individual develops a concept and image of the self. This is, in turn,
reflected in the expressed behaviors of logic, thought, speech, action,
emotional response, and perception in all areas of people activity:
economics, education, entertainment, labor, law, politics, religion, sex,
and war (see figure 2).

In relationship to the total environment, the self functions either
effectively or ineffectively in the various areas of people activity.

The self-image and self-concept formed during the lived experience
is, on balance, either positive or negative, seldom neutral. The
distinction is made by this writer between self-image and self-concept
only in the sense that the *self-image* is the composite of conscious as
well as unconsciously held perceptions of the self, while the *self-concept*
is only the conscious description and picture of the self. Behavior is
controlled by the composite self-image.

Returning to figure 1, generally speaking, a sum total of *stress* at the
various levels of the environmental dynamic results in the development
of a negative image of the self, low levels of self-respect, and dysfunctional patterns of behavior in relationship to problem-solving in the
environment. The composite self-image becomes negative in
relationship to the environment as a whole because the environment
relates to the individual as though he or she lacks value and/or because,
lacking the specific and appropriate behaviors to solve problems in the

ENVIRONMENT

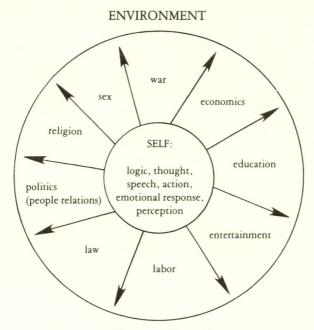

Figure 2. The self.

environment, the individual has actually become overwhelmed by the problems affecting his or her survival and development in the environment and by the total environmental dynamic.

Being so overwhelmed implies that the individual lacks the necessary functional, problem-solving patterns of conduct required to neutralize the environmental stress. The individual self is then engulfed by a sense of social environment-imposed powerlessness. The individual perceives an actual inability to remove the experienced environmental stress. Under such extreme stress, behavior becomes disorganized and chaotic; it becomes self- and group-negating.

Stress is here defined as an unresolved problem in the environment or an accumulation of unresolved problems confronting the individual organism. These unresolved problems are posed in one or more of the areas of people activity or at various levels of the total environmental dynamic and are perceived by the individual as affecting his or her survival and development (see figure 3).

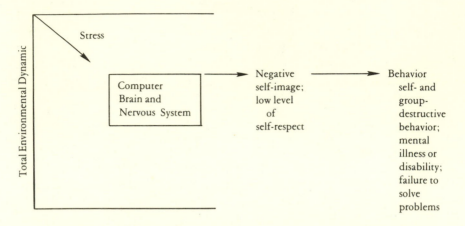

Figure 3. Environmental stress and dysfunctional patterns of behavior.

Contrary to the effect of environmental stress, a sum total of *supports* at the various levels of the environmental dynamic in the various areas of people activity result in the development of a positive image of the self, self-confidence, high levels of self-respect, and thereby functional patterns of problem-solving behavior in relationship to the environment. The individual therefore does not sense being overwhelmed by the environmental dynamic. Self- and group-supporting and enhancing behaviors thus evolve (see figure 4).

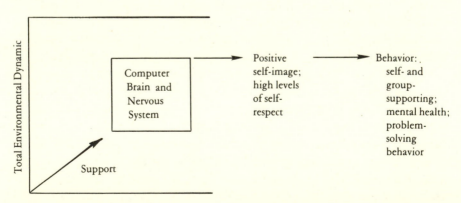

Figure 4. Environmental support and functional patterns of behavior.

The actual power relationships between people, which are established and maintained in a given social power system, determine the amount of stress or support that each individual receives relative to his or her classification or power status in the power system. Power status or classification is, by and large, determined at birth by the classification or power status of one's parents, who are themselves either classified as those with a relative degree of power or those who lack power.

Those with relative power receive more supports from the total social dynamic, while those who are powerless receive more stress. Those who suffer more stress will, of course, develop more dysfunctional patterns of behavior when compared with those who receive more social supports.

The established power relationships confer either a sense of relative power or powerlessness in each individual born into the power system framework. Indeed, the very real life condition in which the powerless live and function daily not only reinforce a sense of powerlessness but convince the powerless of their inability to produce their own solutions to life problems, thereby influencing their level of expressed intelligence, which is not to say their intelligence potential.

Thus power status or classification is the most powerful determinant of self- and group-image formation and conceptualization. These power relationships, once established, condition, limit, and determine the specific behavior patterns in all areas of people activity.

Racism is viewed by this writer (after Neely Fuller), as a global behavior power system with a constant and specific set of power relationships. Racism evolved with the singular goal of white supremacy or white power domination by the global white minority over the vast non-white global majority. This ''colored global collective'' has been forced into the position of relative powerlessness compared to the ''global white collective,'' establishing the power equation of white over non-white ($_{N=W}^{W}$). As such, racism is the dominant power dynamic in the world today, establishing and maintaining the specific power relationship between the earth's peoples of white supremist domination and control.

It is this writer's view, as stated in 1970 in The Cress Theory of Color-Confrontation and Racism (White Supremacy), that whether consciously or unconsciously determined, racism evolved as a survival necessity for the tiny, global white minority, due to their awareness of their minority status and the fact of their genetic-recessive status as albino variants (mutants) in a world of skin-color genetically dominant black, brown, red, and yellow peoples.

Indeed, had the global white minority not evolved this specific system of power relationships (whites over non-whites) wherein whites control all of the behavior activity of non-whites in all areas of people activity (economics, education, entertainment, labor, law, politics, religion, sex, and war) as a survival mechanism, in the presence of the genetically dominant colored world majority, the mutant albino genetic-recessive minority would find itself genetically annihilated. That is, there would be no "white" people except for the new mutations to albinism produced by skin-melaninated or colored peoples. Thus, to prevent the genetic annihilation of skin whiteness, a behavior power system was evolved—the power system of racism or white supremacy domination.

Racism can thus be viewed as a behavior system evolved to compensate for the problems posed to a genetic-recessive mutant minority population that feared for its genetic survival, a population that also sought to compensate for a sense of white genetic inferiority by establishing a global system and culture of white superiority or supremacy.

In the context of the now-established power system of racism, all dominant behavior patterns of logic, thought, speech, action, emotional response, and perception as expressed in all areas of people activity (economics, education, entertainment, labor, law, politics, religion, sex, and war) are consciously and/or unconsciously structured to establish, maintain, expand, and refine the system of white supremist domination, producing the white supremist system, its institutions, and its culture.

Occurring simultaneously as a necessary corollary dynamic to the establishment and maintenance of white supremacy (racism) is the process of constant and continuous non-white victimization and inferiorization. This writer defines the term "inferiorization" as the systematic stress-attack (through the entire social environmental dynamic) on the genetic and constitutional make-up of individuals classified as non-white, within the system of white supremist domination, so as to achieve dysfunctional and chaotic patterns of logic, thought, speech, action, emotional response, and perception in all areas of people activity. These dysfunctional patterns of behavior in the non-white collective prevent environmental problem analysis and problem solution. Thus, through the inferiorization process, Blacks and other non-whites are programmed so that they may be dominated and controlled by people who classify themselves as "white."

Persons thus classified as "non-whites" in the context of the white supremist system are molded into functional inferiors. That is, they become socially conditioned so as to be incapable of solving their own problems, while persons classified as white, through a dynamic of systematic support from the social system dynamic, are molded into functional superiors—not genetic superiors—but persons always capable (within the white supremist system context) of solving their own environmental problems by any means necessary.

Mental illness or mental disability (failure to solve one's own problems) is thus established, in the context of the white supremist system, as a way of life for the powerless non-white collective, in contrast to a pattern of mental health or self-generated problem solution, which is established for the white collective.

Dominant language patterns within the white supremist system, once learned by peoples of color, inform all non-whites that the very color of their physical appearance is negatively valued. "Black," for example, is used to convey all that is bad, unfortunate, evil, dysfunctional (e.g., "black sheep"), and sinful, etc., while "white" is used to denote good and purity. "Yellow" is used to denote cowardice; "red" is used to denote a major political enemy. Currently, the word "kinky," which describes the typical quality of Black hair, is used as a pejorative adjective.

Black children in the white supremist system and culture also learn very early how they are valued and thus how to evaluate their own worth based upon the exact shade of color of their skin, which reflects the level of melanin pigment in their skin melanocytes. Black children are still being taught, "If you're black, stay back; if you're brown, stick around; if you're yellow, you're mellow; if you're white, you're all right!"

These thought patterns, imposed by the white supremist dynamic, aid in the development of negative Black self-imagery and thereby dysfunctional, self- and group-negating patterns of conduct. Further, the white supremist system actually distributes support to non-whites directly in proportion to the relative absence of melanin pigment in the skin melanocytes. The darker the hue, the fewer the privileges and supports; the lighter the hue, the more privileges and supports that become available.

Also in the context of the white supremist system, non-white people are encouraged to emphasize the activities of fun and games, entertainment (e.g., singing, dancing, and ball playing), religion, and sex—in other words, to become entertainment and sex machines and to develop their sense of self and personhood only through these areas of people activity. Within the same total behavior system context, white people are encouraged to develop expertise in the people activities of war, economics, education, labor, law, and politics. Of course, in a power contest, court jesters cannot compete successfully with soldiers and scholars. The court jesters become the functional inferiors.

The dominant theme in religion (irrespective of denomination) that is taught to non-whites in the white supremist system is that some force other than themselves will solve the environmental problems which they face. Invariably, the projected image and color of that force is white and not ''non-white.''

In the area of family life, in the white supremist system, the number of Black family units in which there is only one parent, who is usually female, is rapidly approaching 50 percent. Black female dominance in the Black survival unit is fostered while the system selectively emphasizes the stress-attack on Black males, thereby producing a relative Black female strength in contrast to Black male weakness.

In the same system context, the white family structure is such that male dominance is fostered. Thus, we see large numbers of white females who now wish to act like white males, including being ''liberated'' to exercise the same power that white males exercise over non-whites and doing other things that white males do, such as playing football, climbing telephone poles, etc., because they (white females) experience the white female role as being devalued in the white family dynamic.

On the other hand, there are increasing numbers of Black males who are sporting more feminine-like attire, such as braided and curled hair, high-heel shoes, earrings, necklaces, midriff tops, cinch waist pants, etc., because they experience the devaluation of the Black male role in the Black survival unit under white supremist domination.

Of fundamental important is the fact that the male attributes of strength, aggressiveness, and responsibility are fostered and emphasized in the white family, whereas female attributes (relative passivity) are emphasized for males in the fatherless or female-dominated Black family or unit. In the power contest between aggressive white males and passive Black males, the latter will not present a challenge, thus allowing for the ultimate maintenance of white supremist domination. Black males who turn out to be aggressive or assertive are jailed or placed on front lines in battlefields.

Historically, the white supremist system and culture have sought to reinforce the white male role as "the man" and the Black male role as the irresponsible "boy" or now "the baby." Techniques and methodology used to reinforce the weaker and more passive role for Black males in relationship to white males have included lynching, shooting, flogging, and actual castration.

Currently, psychological castration of Black males is carried out via television images of Black males in such programs as "Chico and The Man," "Sanford and Son," "Good Times," "The Jeffersons," and "That's My Mama," as well as in such portrayals as Flip Wilson's "Geraldine."

Of course, it is clear that these systematically programmed, dysfunctional patterns of behavior for Black males, including clowning, irresponsibility, weakness, effeminacy, and passivity, are the direct behavioral antithesis of those patterns of behavior that are needed by Black males to solve the major environmental problem of white supremist domination and Black oppression.

The absence of functional patterns of behavior which will efficiently and effectively produce a solution to the problem of Black oppression and the specific and strategic stress-attack on Black males result in widespread frustration and despair in the general Black male population. These high levels of frustration and despair lead only to further dysfunctional patterns of conduct: homicide, suicide, drug addiction, alcoholism, violence, theft, rape, wife-beating, child-abuse, and eventual incarceration.

Incarceration only further reinforces the image of Black male irresponsibility, worthlessness, dependency, and passivity. Male dependency and passivity are powerfully reinforced by encouraging homosexuality in the jail setting. Male homosexuality is the genital expression of male fear and powerlessness relative to another male.

The continuing great disparity between Black and white male unemployment and wage levels is also designed to reinforce Black male weakness and passivity in contrast to white male strength and functionality.

Black children are programmed for developing dysfunctional patterns of behavior through the imposed instability of Black family life. Also, through inadequate diet, poor housing, lack of neighborhood structural order and stability (from urban renewal programs), old schools and poor quality education, inadequate early socialization, unemployed or absent fathers, working mothers, under aged parents, emotionally immature and impatient parents, abandonment, neglect and abuse, poorly educated parents, and a lack of recreational facilities, Black children are thoroughly and adequately prepared to play their future role as functionally inferior adults in the white supremist system.

This stress-attack on Black children, indeed this violence directed against Black children, produces negative self-imagery and large-scale dysfunctional patterns of behavior in childhood and adolescence, interfering with the child's major task of learning and academic achievement, and preventing the development of self-confidence and a sense of self-worth and self-respect. This attack also prevents the child from developing appreciation and respect for others. Serious dysfunctional patterns of social conduct are seen in the constant hitting, name-calling, fighting, squabbling, cursing, and even killing of one another in gang war fashion seen in many populations of Black school-age children and youth.

In the white supremist system dynamic, Black women are taught that they are not beautiful unless they look like white women; that they are not worthy of Black male respect, protection, and support; that indeed they are to be the protectors and supporters of Black men. They are also taught to so devalue themselves that they should submit to being beaten, prostituted, and used by any and all men. They are programmed to bring into the world more children than the oppressive system will allow them to care for and fully develop if they must care for those children alone. Black women are also taught that the men who father their children are *not* always supposed to be totally prepared to support those children; thus Black women are taught and programmed to devalue the welfare and protection not only of themselves, but also of their offspring. Black women are taught in mass numbers that there is nothing wrong with being 12 or 13 or 16, and being pregnant, and that there is nothing wrong in throwing away or giving away a baby to the white supremist welfare system.

Because Black women are taught, under the system of white supremacy, to despise their offspring as well as themselves, they are simultaneously taught to despise their own reflection as seen in other

Black women. This self-rejection is seen in the many negative and destructive behaviors that Black women direct toward one another.

All of the above are but a few of the possible examples of dysfunctional patterns of behavior that are taught and programmed into Black men, Black women, and Black children by the social dynamic of white supremist domination and oppression. These dysfunctional patterns of conduct cannot and will not solve the major environmental problem confronting all Black people which is racism or white supremist domination. These patterns of conduct, inasmuch as they fail to solve problems in the environment, are examples of mental disability in the broadest and yet most specific context.

The behavior power system of racism as practiced by people who classify themselves as white, like any other system, does not seek to destroy itself or to have itself voted out of existence. Rather, it seeks to perpetuate itself by any and all necessary means, utilizing all necessary patterns of logic, thought, speech, action, emotional response, and perception in all areas of people activity (economics, education, entertainment, labor, law, politics, religion, sex, and war).

Neely Fuller has outlined the four possible behavioral responses of non-white victims of the white supremist system of power domination to that victimizing and inferiorizing process:

1. *Submission*—defined as being totally overwhelmed by the oppressing process.

2. *Cooperation*—defined as a realization that the oppressive process is self-destroying, but a willingness to go along with that process "for a better job."

3. *Resistance*—defined as full realization of how the oppressive dynamic works and a willingness to counter that dynamic only up to the point that personal comfort and life are not jeopardized.

4. *Destruction*—defined as totally prepared to face the consequences which result from continuous struggle against racist oppression, up to and including death. Fear of the racist oppressors has been fully overcome.

Whether conscious or unconscious, submission to, and cooperation with, the process and dynamic of one's own victimization and negation are the result of a negative self-image, low levels of self- and group respect and consciousness. In this context, consciousness is defined as indepth analytical awareness of exactly what is going on in the total surrounding environment as it affects the self and one's group as well as how it affects all other selves and groups. Full consciousness answers the following questions:

1. What is going on, or what is happening around me?
2. Who am I, in relationship to what is happening around me?
3. What am I, in relationship to what is happening around me?
4. Where am I, in relationship to what is happening around me?
5. What should I be doing in relationship to what is happening around me?

It should be perfectly clear that the term "mental health" cannot possibly be applied to constellations of behavior which in their social effect represent submission to, and cooperation with, one's own oppression and victimization, whether consciously or unconsciously determined. Such behaviors must logically be classified as self- and group-destructive and negating and are thus acts of mental illness or mental disability. Such behaviors solve no problems in the environment and fail to neutralize destructive environmental forces, but they do enhance survival and maximal development.

However, this writer is fully aware that from the standpoint of the white supremist oppressors and the logic of the white supremist mental health and psychiatric institutions and authorities, it is only when the oppressed (Blacks and other non-whites) are in the acts of submission to, or cooperation with, the system of racism that they gain the stamp of "mental health" from the oppressors. This is undoubtedly why many patterns of dysfunctional behavior seen in non-white populations are looked upon not as disturbed behavior or mental illness but simply as "their culture."

The white supremist oppressors, whether motivated consciously or unconsciously, will not accept or tolerate patterns of behavior (logic, thought, speech, action, emotional response, and perception in any area of life activity) which imply resistance to, or destruction of, the existing power system of racism. This holds for all areas of people activity, not only for the field of psychiatry and mental health. The reason that these guidelines must be maintained and enforced is that the system of racism (white power and non-white powerlessness) represents the entire survival mechanism for the genetic-recessive global white minority.

Thus, again, in the context of the system of racism, in its institutional mental health establishment, and in its psychiatric establishment, racism (meaning behaviors, the goal objective of which is to establish and maintain white supremist domination) as a subject for analysis, dissection, and discussion is given very low priority. Such a focus all too often stops at the level of acquisition of jobs and positions for Black and other non-white professional workers, without dealing with the acceptance of their perceptions or their understanding and recommendations.

Within the racist power system framework, any insistence on the importance of racism or focusing in depth on the dynamic of white supremacy and the color-confrontation dynamic is soon labeled with such terms as "paranoid," meaning that the non-white individual so labeled has created a fantasy or delusion about the negative factors and forces affecting his or her existence, and that in reality the total dynamic of racism as a global power system of white supremist domination does not exist. It certainly does not exist as the victims of racism analyze, experience, define, and describe it, unless those descriptions are consistent with the comfort and security of the white supremists.

Any persistent focusing on the fundamental power dynamic of racism by victims of white supremacy should indeed be viewed with alarm by racists and labeled as resistance to and possible destruction of white supremist domination, as continued observation, study, and analysis by the victims of racism may lead to a more complete understanding and thereby will, in time, lead to a successful means of neutralizing and eradicating this power system which is also a major cause of human disability.

Only through a continuing focus on the problem and dynamic of racism by the victims of racism can they begin to develop patterns of functional conduct (neutralizing conduct) in relationship to this major problem in the environment which is presently disrupting their lives and development. Only through the efforts of the victims to neutralize and effectively counter racism in all areas of life activity can they develop a positive self-image, self-respect, environmental problem solution, and thus mental health. Of course, from the standpoint of racist oppressors, resistance to, and/or destruction of, the dynamic of racism (counterracism) must be looked upon not as mental health but as some form of mental illness or mental disability.

Under any system of oppression, victims who have self-respect and seek to defend themselves are viewed as mentally disabled. Blacks have long heard about the "crazy nigger" syndrome, as applied to such figures as Nat Turner, Martin Luther King, Jr., Malcolm X, and George Jackson. All of these Black men were victims of white supremist domination. All of them demonstrated patterns of logic, thought, speech, action, emotional response, and perceptions which, if allowed to continue and carried to their logical conclusions, would have diminished white supremist power control, lessening the chance of the survival of the white phenotype. Of course, all of these "crazy niggers" who threatened white survival had to be killed, in the context of the white supremist system.

The condition described above should be contrasted with that of a white person who massacres non-white men, women, and children. Lt. Calley, accused of mass murder at Mylai, was found to be mentally healthy by psychiatrists in the white supremist system.

In clinical work, this writer has found that there continues to exist, among Black and other non-white peoples, a very deep fear of actual physical harm by the white supremist oppressors, resulting in an inability to resist effectively or to destroy the dynamic of white supremist oppression. This fear is fundamental to many of the dysfunctional patterns of behavior (mental disability) among non-white peoples in this part of the world. Such fear is only natural following the centuries of intense, high-level physical cruelty carried out by whites against Blacks and other non-whites in the course of the establishment and maintenance of racist domination. Such fear prevents the development of the will to solve the problem of white supremist domination and all other attendant problems in the environment. Blacks (as well as other non-whites) are also fearful that they cannot possibly survive and develop without the help of the white oppressors in providing and caring for them and in solving their major environmental problems.

These patterns of thought and emotional response are directly related to the fact that Blacks are being held in a state of helplessness and dependency and are being systematically prevented from actually solving all of their own problems by the oppressive dynamic exercised over the past twenty generations. Under racist domination, only whites are permitted ultimately to solve problems and to be in control.

It is a major responsibility of all Black mental health workers to bring to full consciousness in those they seek to help, this element of physical fear of the white oppressors as well as the fear of being without the white oppressors' capacity to solve problems. It is only when this double-faced, crippling fear is brought to full consciousness that it can be ultimately overcome and then resolved.

Similarly, it is essential to bring to full consciousness in all Blacks and other non-whites the negative self-images which they have been programmed to internalize in the framework of the white supremist dynamic. This negative self-image leads to self-alienation or self-hate and self-rejection. Both of these factors, fear and self-alienation, should not be allowed to be covered over by bravado or slogans of self-love, respect, and pride, or the continuous repetition of phrases such as "I am somebody." It must be made clear that as long as oppression exists, the oppressed will have low levels of self-respect, self-love, and self-pride. It is only through the dynamic and continuous process of eliminating that oppression that self-love, self-respect, and self-pride can flourish. These feelings cannot blossom fully until the oppression is totally neutralized.

The Black mental health worker also has the task of helping all Black and other non-white people to understand the exact specifics of the dynamic of racism (white supremist domination). This will answer once and for all the question all Blacks ask one another: "What's happening?" or "What's going on?" The answer is white supremist domination, and this is how it works and why it is a necessity, and this is what you must do about it.

The Black mental health worker is responsible for developing those specific patterns of logic, thought, speech, action, emotional response, and perception in all areas of people activity (economics, education, entertainment, labor, law, politics, religion, sex, and war) which will efficiently and effectively neutralize the behavior system of white supremist domination. The worker must then share this knowledge and understanding with all victims of racism who must confront daily the direct and indirect problems of racism in the environments in which they must live.

Finally, the Black mental health worker must demonstrate, through daily social practice, exercises designed to enhance Black mental health and Black self-respect, for without black self-respect there will be no belief that Blacks can indeed solve their own problems, and there will be no effort to solve one's own problems. Without the brain-work to solve one's own problems, there can be no mental health. The following suggestions are exercises in Black mental health and Black self-respect. Exercises 1 through 10 are taken from the work of Neely Fuller.

1. Stop gossiping about one another.

2. Stop name-calling one another.

3. Stop cursing one another.

4. Stop squabbling with one another and calling in the racist to settle it.

5. Stop snitching on one another to the racists for reasons of personal gain.

6. Stop being discourteous and disrespectful to one another.

7. Stop robbing one another.

8. Stop stealing from one another.

9. Stop fighting one another.

10. Stop killing one another.

11. Stop using all destructive drugs and stop selling drugs to one another.

12. Stop throwing trash and garbage around where Black people must live and work.

13. Stop referring to "the act of self-reproduction" (sex) with words of derision and disgust.

14. Stop refusing to see that skin color, in the framework of the system of white supremacy, is the major factor in the dynamics of the social environment. Stop refusing to face reality.

The development of high levels of Black self- and group-respect will be the basis for the realization that Black people *themselves* must solve all of the problems they face in the oppressive eenvironment of white supremist domination. There will also develop the will to sacrifice in order to bring about solutions to problems. The brain computer, under the influence of high levels of self- and group respect, will evolve patterns of behavior in all areas of life activity that will promote solutions to the recognized major environmental problem, which is racism.

It is also being suggested here that the major personality patterns or types which evolve among victims of the system of white supremist domination and oppression can be classified as follows:

1. The *submitting personality*—signifying behavioral manifestations of the lowest levels of self- and group respect and self-consciousness; a total pattern of helplessness in relationship to the dynamic of racist oppression.

2. The *cooperating personality*—representing a slightly higher level of self- and group respect, but one in which the objective of the behavior patterns is simply improvement of the individual's material existence under the continuing conditions of self- and group oppression.

3. The *resisting personality*—representing a higher level of self- and group respect, but because there is a fear of dying for one's beliefs and convictions, there is a willingness to cease resistance when told to do so, directly or indirectly, by the racist oppressors.

4. The *oppression-destroying* or *self-sacrificing personality*—representing the highest levels of self- and group respect, the highest levels of self-consciousness, and the highest level of character development, and thus a willingness to sacrifice one's most important possession, life itself, in order to aid in the termination of the oppression of self and the total oppressive dynamic.

Again, submission to, and cooperation with, one's own oppression are modes of behavior which constitute levels of mental illness. Resistance to, and destruction of, the oppressive process constitute, for the victims of oppression, mental health.

The statements given above constitute some of the basic premises in what this writer refers to as *counter-racist psychiatry,* the only psychiatry evolved specifically for the victims of racism in the context of the global white supremist system. For the victims of racism, it is the only psychiatry which specifically relates itself to the major problem they face in the oppressive environment and which seeks to help them to direct all of their behavior so as to effectively counter and neutralize that major problem. Counter-racist psychiatry is the only psychiatry specifically designed to elevate maximally the levels of self- and group respect among Black people essential to the solution of problems. Counter-racist psychiatry is the only psychiatry directed toward the maximal development of the genetic and constitutional potential of non-whites through the evolution of patterns of logic, thought, speech, action, emotional responses, and perception in economics, education, entertainment, labor, law, politics, religion, sex, and war that will neutralize white supremist domination.

As such, counter-racist psychiatry is the only psychiatry which is fully consistent with the major function of the human brain, which is to solve problems posed in the environment. It is degrading to the human brain to fail to teach each individual to use his or her brain computer for decoding environmental problems and attempting to produce solutions to those problems. Any other kind of instruction to human beings degrades them in relationship to their total environment and, thus, alienates them from the total environment.

It should be clear that the counter-racist conceptualization of psychiatry, mental disability, and mental health places all emphasis on (1) the nature of functioning of the brain and the nervous system which is the basis of all behavior, as well as the genetic and constitutional bases of the brain and nervous system, and (2) the total power system dynamic and the power relationships which determine the specific nature of the total surrounding social and physical environment which impacts upon the genetic and constitutional potential.

Counter-racist psychiatry does not relate to abstractions such as "love," "work," "sexual satisfaction," "feeling," "touching," or the accumulation of material possessions as signs of "success." The counter-racist conceptualization focuses on the effective functioning of the whole of the self in *all* areas of people activity (economics, education, entertainment, labor, law, politics, religion, sex, and war), in the total, evolved environment of racist oppression, to solve the problem of racist oppression or any other problem posed in future environments.

Thus, under the conditions imposed by a racist society, mental health for the victims is a matter of total functioning to produce the absolute neutralization and elimination of racism in the shortest possible time. This is the only chance to produce self- and group respect for the vast majority of the world's non-white people. This is the only chance to produce peace and harmony in contrast to the present reality of continuing war, violence, and people destruction which is necessary for white minority survival.

In closing this discussion, some attention should be directed to racism itself as a form of mental illness. Following this writer's thesis in The Cress Theory of Color-Confrontation and Racism (White Supremacy), racism (white supremacy) is viewed as having evolved as patterns of behavior needed to compensate for a sense of genetic inadequacy or genetic inferiority in the mutant albino (white) population, which, of course, was a tiny minority in a world of skin-pigmented peoples. Although racism is a behavior system which posits white supremacy and white genetic superiority, underlying this defense mechanism super-structure is a basic white alienation from the abnormal appearance of the *white-self* in a world of skin-pigmented peoples. There is also white alienation from the white-self because it can be genetically annihilated (as a genetic-recessive state) by the genetic-dominant people of color. The potential threat of white genetic annihilation is the basis for a profound level of fear felt by the whites toward all non-whites. However, this *primary self-alienation* that whites unconsciously or consciously feel toward themselves has spawned the *secondary self-alienation* that peoples of color have been taught and programmed by the whites to feel toward themselves in the presence of the super-structure ideology of white superiority.

Although this total defense mechanism produced a temporary and superficial acceptance of the white-self by whites at the psychological level while simultaneously permitting the biological survival of a mutant, genetic-recessive population, the overall effect has been to produce total violence and disharmony. In the total overview of the results of this behavioral activity and because of the necessity for the global white population to repress their negative feelings toward their appearance and then to project this negativism on the vast colored world majority toward which whites must behave aggressively and destructively, this behavior, whether consciously or unconsciously determined, must itself be classified as mental illness or dysfunctional behavior and thus, for this reason, it must be brought under control and contained.

In terms of prevention, it may in the future be possible for some scientists to develop a cure for the genetic deficiency state of albinism which, when present in an isolated collective, spawns the behavior of white survival, which is racism.

References

Fuller, N. *Textbook for Victims of White Supremacy.* 1969 (private printing).

Lasch, C. "Sacrificing Freud." *The New York Times Magazine*, February 22, 1976, 11, 70–72.

Ludwig, A. M. "The Proper Domain of Psychiatry." *Psychiatry Digest* 1 (1967).

Welsing, F. C. *The Cress Theory of Color-Confrontation and Racism (White Supremacy)*. 1970 (private printing).

4 BLACK FAMILY LIFE AND DEVELOPMENT

Robert E. Staples, Ph.D.

Circa 1977, we find that the Black family is a fluid and complex institution. Our understanding of this group has been impeded by the obtrusion of alien values and political motivations in research on the subject. Hence we have to sift through an array of literature which is in conflict in its findings and interpretation of the nature and significance of Afro-American family life. While some of the discrepancy between the Black family reality and its depiction in the social science literature may be altruistically attributed to adherence to the conventional wisdom of the times, much of it is a function of what Nobles (1974) labels ''conceptual incarceration.'' As a result the Black family's well-being is measured in terms of its statistical approximation to the white middle-class family.

It helps us little to recapitulate the history of past research. Perhaps we have already labored too long in refuting the research which generally indicts the Black family as pathological or sees it only as the darker-skinned counterpart of the white family were it not for white racism and the concentration of Blacks in the underclass of the American social structure. The alternative framework suggested by young Black scholars may be characterized as the Pan-African conceptual model. This model views the Black family in the context of Afro-American or African values and largely confines itself to presenting the strengths of Black families which are responsible for their survival. While the elaboration of Black family strengths is a necessary task, it still limits our understanding of Black family life in a dynamic society. In fact, it threatens to reimpose a conceptual incarceration upon Black scholars because, as applied, it is often a static model (Staples, 1974).

As we shall see, the Pan-African approach is most germane when we look at lower-income Afro-American families in the rural South. With the basic focus on the strengths of Black families, can we develop a holistic theory of Black family life? Or, as Lieberman (1973) poses the question: Can the model of the ethnic group rest solely, or even largely, on strengths when all human social systems have numerous weaknesses? What is required is a historical, dynamic, and process-oriented model which sees Blacks as being victims of larger, external forces but also makers of their own history. In this author's opinion, the internal colonialist framework holds the promise of such a goal. It allows us to depict the alternation between Black values which shape their family life styles and the forces in a colonial society which produce tension in the family structure (Staples, 1976).

Although not a full-blown theoretical system at this juncture, internal colonialism is a perspective that recognizes the existence of an Afro-American culture that has value (Blauner, 1970). However, it also acknowledges that in a colonial setting those cultural values of the native are constantly under attack. The colonial structure inhibits expression of the native's values by an elaborate system of rewards and penalties. More importantly it acculturates a segment of the colonized group into its own values. The interaction between the acculturation process and colonial status might be viewed as the locus of conflict between Afro-Americans and their own cultural imperatives. And it might be viewed most boldly in objective indices of family disorganization, such as male-female antagonisms, divorce, and child abuse. These are very real problems in the Black community and cannot be subordinated to our attempt to delineate the strengths of the Black family.

In our discussion of mental health and Black family life, we shall be concerned with how the family promotes emotional well-being in individuals. Our basic thesis is that the Black family has been a sanctuary which has buttressed individuals from the pervasiveness of white racism, provided needed support systems that were unavailable in other majority group institutions, and socialized and nurtured the young. This was possible as a result of Black values that related to the family. However, as the Black population has dispersed from its original location in the rural South to urban ghettos and differentiated into different class strata, new values—alien values—replaced traditional ones about the family and the role of Blacks in it. Hence culture is a dichotomous phenomenon: it enables a people to adapt to oppressive conditions, but the imposition of new institutions and value modalities can stabilize their oppression in the colonial context.

Whereas Afro-Americans were a peasant class in the rural South, their evolution into an urban people divided by subjective affiliation into socioeconomic classes was to modify their collective orientation to an individual one among some of their members. At the same time they all remain members of a colonized group with its attendant liabilities. Although taking on the values and trappings of the colonizer, they do not have the structural underpinnings of the ruling group which will compensate for the loss of their traditional values. Once they detach themselves from the emotional and spiritual support of the collective Black community, the gains allowed them under internal colonialism are not sufficient to serve as adequate surrogates. The result is a decline in the positive mental health of individual Blacks, most noticeably observed in increasing rates of psychological depression, suicide, alcoholism, drug abuse, and divorce. It is in light of such a theoretical perspective that we examine the contemporary Black family and its relationship to mental health.

Historical Reflections

There is little doubt that North American slavery was one of the harshest forms of involuntary servitude, and its impact was most vividly reflected in Afro-American culture and family life. Enough historical evidence exists to show that slave families were separated for pecuniary motives, that slave women were used as breeding instruments to produce future slaves, that males were denied their formal role as protector and provider for their families, and that slave women were often subjected to sexual asaults with impunity by men on the plantation (Frazier, 1939). But such historical accounts of slavery have misled us into thinking that the family as a unit did not exist or was not a viable institution. While it must be conceded that specific tribal languages and cultures were extinguished by slaveowners, the African ethos was not. Due to their own instinct for survival, the members of separate—and often warring—tribes reorganized as a collective community. They formed a solidary group based on the African principle of contiguity and unity. Within the context of slavery and the limited options open to them, they developed a new sense of family, and redefined their roles and the relationship between them (Nobles, 1974).

Although legal marriage between slaves was not permitted, there was a variety of socially approved and sanctioned relationships between slave men and women. These relationships were recognized as a strong emotional bond by other slaves as well as the slaveholders. Some of these slave families lived under one roof and functioned as a single family unit. While men did not have the strong patriarchal authority in the family as existed on the African continent, they were generally accorded a certain respect for the qualities of manliness they exhibited, in the form of heroic deeds, securing extra rations for the family, or making their living quarters more comfortable. The alleged matriarchy that existed during this time is described by Genovese (1974, p. 16) as "in fact a closer approximation to a healthy sexual equality than was possible for whites." Moreover, the African family had been based on a much greater equality between men and women than existed in the white family. Women had played strong roles in African society in a working partnership with their spouses (Paulme, 1963).

These relationships may not have paralleled those of ante-bellum white families, but they were consistent with the sentiments of the slave community. The notion of sexually promiscuous slaves, according to Rawick (1972), has been greatly exaggerated. For instance, few slave marriages were dissolved because of the immoral conduct of one of the partners. Due to the moral code promulgated by Baptist and Methodist churches that served the slave community, the sexual behavior of the bondsmen might be considered rather moderate if measured by our contemporary standards. The attempts by male slaves to resist the rape of their women attests to the fact that sexual relations were not taken lightly. More importantly, the slave community was reorganized as an extended family structure in which all adults looked after all children. In continuation of the African tradition, children were highly valued and cared for. After an exhausting day of laboring in the fields, slave mothers came home to nurse their children under conditions which required a great deal of physical and psychological courage. As a result of their mothers' tenderness and warmth, the children felt loved—a feeling that is deeply imprinted in slave spirituals and narratives (Blassingame, 1972).

After the abolition of slavery, there were numerous attempts by the bondsmen to establish a normal family life. Male-female bonds which existed in a de facto form were legalized. Those couples who had been separated during the slave era went to great lengths to be reunited. But the former slaves still encountered obstacles in their quest for a viable family life. Economic imperatives forced many Black men to move around the country to find work, leaving the woman to carry on many of the family functions. When families remained together, the wife often worked alongside her husband in order to obtain land and an education for their children. It was out of these economic conditions that the role of the strong Black woman was forged. This role flexibility allowed many Black families to survive the terrible travail of the post-slavery era. At the same time the assumptions about the disorganized family life of former bondsmen are counteracted by the historical evidence showing that a large majority of Afro-Americans during the period from 1865 to 1920 were lodged in nuclear families (Furstenberg, et al., 1975).

During this period Blacks represented a largely peasant class based in the rural South. The model of the family which developed during that time was one of an extended kinship system representing a number of different roles. This type of family structure also encompassed fictive kinsmen who assumed the rights and obligations of those related by genealogical bonds. As a functional kinship grouping, it provided goods and services that individual families could not have obtained by their efforts alone. In the rural South the entire Black community would take on a primary group character. As a group they maintained social control and regulated the behavior of individuals in accord with their own moral code—a code very similar to that found in African societies (Lewis, 1955).

It was this type of family structure that provided support functions for the mental health of individuals within it. By positing a categorical relationship between the nuclear family and the achievement of functional prerequisites, many behavioral scientists have labeled the Black family as a form of social pathology. Many of the social and economic functions ascribed to nuclear families isolated in separate households were in reality carried out by broader-based units related often, but not solely, by biological kinship. The anchor for this unit was a Black folk culture which might be best described as a syncretic form deriving from African values fused with orientations evolving out of the slave experience. With the security of this Black kinship network and its support functions, the individual in the family was buttressed against the harsh effects of his racial oppression. It was primarily the transition from rural areas to urban ghettos and the formation of new social classes which undermined the influence of Black cultural values and concomitantly the functioning of Afro-American families (Marshall, 1972).

At this point it should be emphasized that we are discussing the processes which have weakened the mental support function of family life among a segment of the Black population. A large number of Black people still reside in family constellations which continue to be conducive to a positive mental equilibrium. Many of the family characteristics mentioned earlier still exist in a modified form. But the trend is toward the vitiation of Black family support functions, and we need to understand the forces involved in these social transformations. The basic elements are the economic factors compounded by racial colonialism which make the establishment and maintenance of a satisfying family life a never-ending struggle for poor Blacks. As Nathan Hare (1976) has noted, the correlation between family stability and economic and racial oppression is among the highest known to social science. Among the middle-class group the acquisition of colonial society's values and the disavowal of traditional Black values removes the anchor of Black family life as a buffer against the operational effects of domestic colonialism.

The Family Life Cycle

Dating and Sexual Behavior. The research literature on Black dating and sexual patterns is sparse. Among lower-class Blacks, particularly in the South, the communal ambience brings male and female children together at an early age. The fluidity of roles accommodates the presence of children in adult fraternizing activities such as parties and other festive occasions. It is in this social context that the complementarity of sex roles is enhanced as the adults present a model to them of heterosexual relationships and sometimes give explicit instruction in the content of their future roles. Formal dating as such is uncommon since male-female interaction is more spontaneous than planned. Yet it occurs in a communal fashion as young Black children meet and romance each other through the frequent visiting that takes place between households (Halpern, 1973).

The selection of opposite-sex mates is often predicated on the personal qualities possessed by the individual, such as honesty, thoughtfulness, and respect. The more elaborate prestige-ordering system found among the middle class is not common. Women know that they cannot select men on the basis of economic criteria since few of them can obtain well-paying or even steady employment under the colonial regime. Most are prepared to assume a partnership in the family that will probably include their employment outside the home during much of their married life. Sex before marriage occurs often among this group and is not laden with feelings of guilt or anxiety. Reminiscent of African orientations, the Afro-American's attitude toward sex is that it is a natural and pleasurable activity. Although not genetically based, they possess a certain sensuality that allows them to experience sex directly in terms of a feeling rather than a cerebral experience. Ergo, sexuality is more a function of the body than the mind (Gullattee, 1971).

Sex should not be interpreted as an indiscriminate act. Sexual activity prior to marriage is invested with a great deal of meaning for the participants. And, there are frequent attempts by the female to confine her male partner to exclusive sexual relations, and vice versa. Yet there exists no rigid double standard of sexual conduct where one sex is excluded from marital consideration on the basis of past sexual history. The measure of the individual is not based on his sexual morality as much as on other standards, such as honesty and respect. Consequently, lower-class Blacks have a number of sexual options open to them without being subjected to the psychological confines of a puritanical moral code.

However, the inclination of Blacks toward natural responses to sexual stimuli has become somewhat dysfunctional in the urban setting. Due to the reluctance or inability of many Black parents to provide their children with a sound sex education, many sexually active Black females experience unwanted pregnancies (Kantner and Zelnik, 1973). In the rural South, a new birth was an asset since the child could easily be accommodated into the family. But in the urban environment, the unexpected birth of children to teenage mothers more often means an increase in high school dropouts, inadequate parenting, a risky early marriage, or welfare dependency. Some of these problems are avoided by the incorporation of the child into some aspect of the extended family. The options exercised by the middle class are not as easily available to women of the underclass. Instead they are regarded by the colonizer as being subject to unbridled carnal instincts which will only produce children who will become burdens on the public tax rolls or future delinquents. Thus these poor Black mothers are forced to participate in government-prescribed means of population control, such as sterilization.

Having internalized the dominant group's values, the Black middle class—or aspirants to that group—have adopted dating practices similar to those in the white community. Dating behavior is based on the perspectives of the dominant group which serves as their referent, and they subsequently become less responsive to the requisites of our Black folk culture. The concrete manifestation of this change in value orientations can be visibly demonstrated in the marked differences in Black dating behavior by socioeconomic position. Among the Black middle class a rating-dating system is emerging that closely approximates that of their white counterparts. The dating system takes on the character of market relations where individuals maximize their desirable attributes for bargaining in exchange for a desirable commodity possessed by a potential mate (Dickinson, 1975; Melton and Thomas, 1973).

Specifically, women seek to use the enticement of sexual relations or the possession of certain physical attributes to obtain material goods or the right kind of marriage, i.e., to a man with a high status position and income. Men, in turn, require a kind of exclusivity in their wives or girlfriends, based upon their economic hegemony as a form of control. This results in relationships based on material possessions rather than the intrinsic merit of the individual. In operation, it means the meeting of individuals who appraise each other according to their recently adopted standards of wealth and beauty. A marriage proposal will be forthcoming when the participants size up their relative merits and decide that it would be a fair exchange (Staples, 1973).

One sees the penetration of the colonizer's values in the criteria applied in the sex-role bargaining process. The women, for instance, are ranked by how closely they resemble white women in their physical appearance. One study reports that the wives of middle-class Black husbands are much lighter in skin complexion than spouses of lower-class men. And these same middle-class husbands share a more positive view of racial colonialism then their less well-off brethren (Pettigrew, et al., 1966). Rather than maintaining naturalistic, sensual attitudes toward sex, middle-class Black women use it as a tool in gaining entrance to a prestigious marriage. Since middle-class Black males have more of a double sexual standard, the women in that class must be parsimonious in their premarital sexual activity, a practice best summed up in the saying "Men won't buy what they can get free." There is ample evidence that many middle-class Black women are becoming less sexually liberated than their white counterparts (Johnson, 1974).

While adopting the values of the majority group, middle-class Blacks still must contend with the peculiarities of their colonized status. Due to the past vicissitudes of internal colonialism, the educational system has produced more female than male college graduates. In the past, when individuals were selected as mates on the basis of personal qualities, this posed no serious problem. Once their materialistic values gained ascendancy, status homogeneity became the preferred marriage. This has led to an intense competition for the available high-status males. The result has been two categories of women winding up as losers in the battle for middle-class spouses. One of them would be the present wives of these men, since some women take the position that if there are no single men available, they will go after those presently belonging to somebody else. This practice accounts in large part for the high divorce rate in the Black middle class. The other category of women who lose are those who are most dissimilar from the majority group women. They are dark-skinned women who do not otherwise fit the beauty standards of colonial society (Rosow and Rose, 1972; Jeffers, 1973).

Even the light-complexioned female is disadvantaged, as a number of high-status males turn to women of the "master race" for dating and marriage. While interracial dating is a function of a complex set of forces, it is also a result of the high-status Black male's internalization of colonial values and prestige standards. If this were not true, we would expect interracial dating to be randomly practiced among the Black population. Instead we find that most Blacks involved in this behavior are high-status Black males (Heer, 1974). As one investigator of the subject commented, "because he has a higher status now than ever before, he becomes more desirable as an object for marriage" (Porterfield, 1973). And, for males who accept whiteness *per se* as the *sine qua non* of desirability, women of the majority group become free to pick and choose. However sympathetic one may be to the individual's right of free choice in the selection of dating partners, there is little doubt that the issue of interracial liaisons has become a divisive one in the middle-class Black community (Hare, 1971).

Marital Stability

In the normative sense marriage does not appear to be a very viable institution for large numbers of Afro-Americans. The apparent trend is that fewer Blacks enter the conjugal state and more of them leave it. In 1930, husband-wife families represented 80 percent of all Black families, but fewer than 61 percent in 1973. Historically, Blacks were more likely than whites to have been once married. Recent trends indicate an increase in marriage among whites and a decline among Blacks (Glick and Mills, 1974). The reasons for these changes may vary among segments of the Black population. But a major factor is the conditions of urban life that make marriage a fragile institution among Blacks. The fact that marriage among Europeans has been rooted primarily in property relations, while colonized Blacks have been largely stripped of their ties to the land, is not an inconsequential aspect of this problem.

The Black underclass simply is prevented by internal colonialism from achieving success in marriage. Their awareness of this fact of life often prevents them from uniting in matrimony at all. Males, in particular, shy away from the institution because they do not expect to be able to support a wife and children. Only 55 percent of Black men earning less than $1,000 a year marry in comparison to 80 percent of those earning between $3,000 and $5,000. As incomes rise, so do the number of Black men who marry. The divorce statistics confirm the fears of failure among lower-class Blacks. The proportion of divorced Black men tended to decline as the amount of income increased. However, the lowest divorce rate exists among men with median incomes. A probable reason for this anomaly is the greater penetration of colonial values in the marriages of high-status Black males (U.S. Census, 1970).

In the last five years, the Black divorce rate increased from 20 to 27 percent, while it grew from 6 to 8 percent among whites (U.S. Census, 1975). This period (1970–1975) has actually resembled that of an economic depression for Blacks and compounded the normal problems they face in a racist society. As Frances Welsing (Morton, 1975, p. 171) asserts, "Ninety percent of what happens in a Black male-Black female relationship is not controlled by Black people but by the power of the social system." The system she speaks of works in a variety of ways to disrupt the marriages of Black people. It is estimated that the unofficial unemployment rate for Blacks in 1975 was 26 percent (National Urban League, 1975). With irregular employment—and low wages when employed—many Black males fear that their authority and esteem in the family is threatened. They begin to experience anxiety over their ability to meet their family responsibilities. A common response is to become hostile or indifferent toward their wives and children when rendered unable to meet family obligations.

Some Black couples have worked out their economic difficulties by the employment of both spouses, but the economic decline of the last five years has eliminated this working partnership for many of these couples. Due to the large increase of white women in the labor force, many Black women could not find jobs of any kind. In 1975, 115,000 white women joined the work force, and 34,000 Black women joined the ranks of the unemployed (National Urban League, 1975). The welfare system, ostensibly designed to assist families, often serves to break them up as intact units. A study of the relief system reported that "the intact family fares substantially worse in terms of the benefits it can receive from welfare than the female-headed family." About a third of the families studied had only pretended to break up in order to receive the higher benefits. Some wives deliberately choose the steady and higher income of the welfare system over a less reliable husband (Kihss, 1975). As one husband put it, "She says she never knows whether I can keep bringing in the food but the county is always there with whatever she needs" (Jones, 1971, p.22).

Lower-income Blacks in urban areas experienced particular difficulty in making marriages work. In rural and middle-sized communities, individuals and their marriages were more stable because they lived in an environment where marital roles took priority over the superstud character. In the South men saw stable relationships as a compliment to them, while the role of hustler and pimp became popular in the urban ghettos of the North. To a large extent hustling was a survival mechanism for some urban males, but it also reflected a change in values for those who migrated North. At any rate it was, and is, antithetical to marital stability. The longer Blacks are in the North, the more their values become transformed. Despite the disadvantages of growing up in the South, recent studies show that recent Black migrants to the North are more likely to have stable families and earn higher incomes (Long and Lynne, 1975).

As to the specific causes and nature of marital conflict among Blacks, drugs, alcohol, other women, and physical abuse are ranked as the most prevalent reasons. Most available studies show that Black wives are less satisfied with their marriages than their white counterparts (Blood and Wolfe, 1969; Renne, 1970). As income levels rise, so do the number of Blacks who are married and living with their spouses (U.S. Census, 1975). But a high income does not guarantee a satisfying marriage. The reasons may differ, but high-status Blacks have their share of marital conflicts. In high-income Black families the men complain of the financial demands placed upon them by their wives, demands which colonial society does not allow them to meet. The women protest what they call the insensitivity and sexual infidelity of their husbands (Morton, 1975, 1976). A basic problem with these high-status couples is their acceptance of colonial values relating to roles and performance in marriage. Two Black psychologists claim that Blacks who try to emulate whites have the most problems, whereas Blacks just living and making do with what they have are the most adjusted (Ford, 1973).

This probably explains why median-income Blacks have the lowest divorce rate. Not as super-oppressed as the underclass, they can surmount the economic hurdles, while their lesser acculturation to colonial values means that they do not come into conflict over such matters as male dominance or female avarice. High-status Black males often view women as property and impose rigid rules of sexual fidelity for their wives, while participating themselves in a number of extramarital affairs. As a result of finding a younger or prettier woman, they may cast their wives aside. Unlike lower-income Black males, they are more likely to marry and just as inclined to get divorced but have a higher remarriage rate. As Glick and Mills (1974, p. 10) note, the poor man experiences greater difficulty than the man of greater means in convincing a potential marriage partner to enter into remarriage with him.

Black women are often the unwitting victims of their husband's poverty and the abusive behavior it may produce, or the higher-status husband's exploitative values. Hence it is little surprise that many Black women feel that the world is passing them by and that there is little they can do about it. One survey reports that 50 percent of Black women feel that they rarely get a chance to enjoy themselves, compared to only 20 percent of the white women interviewed (Slevin, 1972). The suicide rate is also increasing faster among Black women than in any other group. A significant finding in the few studies on Black suicide is that they occur more often among married women (Velasco-Rice and Mynko, 1973).

Psychiatrists report an increase in the number of women suffering from mental depression, and a major reason for their depression, according to one survey, is concern over heterosexual relationships. As one Black woman complains: "It is hell being Black and female in this white male dominated society . . . rejection is our constant companion . . . all too often by our husbands and lovers. . . ." (Black Women's Community Development Foundation, 1974, pp. 27, 40).

The Female-Headed Household

It is rare to find the matriarchal family as part of the family life cycle. But a prevalent pattern among Blacks is entry into marriage, divorce, and the formation of a household headed by the female partner. This pattern seems to be emerging almost as the modal type of family system for Blacks. During the period from 1970 to 1974, this type of family system increased by 37 percent. It increased by only 16 percent among whites, who have a much higher rate of remarriage than exists among the Black population (U.S. Census, 1975). This racial gap in female-headed households may be narrowed if we ever get an accurate census count of Blacks. Since one-fourth of the Black population, particularly the males, was missed in the census enumeration, the number of Black female-headed households may be overstated by the undercount of Black men who may be with their families.

The data clearly indicate a close correlation between female-headed households and socioeconomic status. As income rises, so do the number of two-parent families. However, other factors are also operative. Historically, Blacks living in rural Southern areas were in intact family units. It is primarily the destructive influence of internal colonialsim that is eroding away the base of Black family life. And it is occurring in precisely those areas where Blacks have been stripped of their cultural traditions and parafamilial systems that made the family, in whatever form, a viable unit. To wit, the female-headed household is most often a product of urban conditions, of social forces which are gradually eliminating the pool of available Black men for marriage, and producing tension in Black marriages which tear them asunder. In the past the fatherless family was primarily the product of different mortality rates for Black men and women which created a large number of widows at an early age. In addition, the need of many Black men to migrate to cities to seek work meant that many families would be headed by women (Furstenberg, et al., 1975).

Under contemporary conditions the largest proportion of families headed by women is predominantly a result of two precipitating factors: the high divorce and separation rate and out-of-wedlock pregnancies. We have to look at other underlying factors to understand this phenomenon. Whites, too, have a high divorce rate but a much lower proportion of female-headed families. This difference can apparently be attributed to the much higher rate of remarriage among whites. Many Black women would also like to remarry but are unable to do so because of the low pool of available mates. There is a diminishing number of Black men, owing to a number of intersecting forces, most of them directly traceable to the functioning of internal colonialism. With 25 percent of Black males unemployed, it is not surprising to find a disproportionate number of them in prisons and the military or narcotized by drugs. But the most significant social trend is the spiraling mortality rate of Black males. While the death rates of whites and Black women declined in the sixties, the rate for Black men increased sharply. In the marriageable years of 20 to 30, Black males are twice as likely to die as white males. These deaths will usually stem from social causes (i.e., internal colonialism) such as homicide, drug addiction, suicide, and stress-producing diseases (Staples, 1973).

The other major cause of female-headed households—an out-of-wedlock birth—was not a serious problem in the past. In the South the children were easily incorporated into the extended family structure. Although such a family grouping is still prevalent—even among urban Blacks—it is in rapid decline. And the unwed mother eventually got married. Now there are fewer men available for marriage. Furthermore, the prospects of marital success with a male who cannot find work of any kind are so low as to encourage many Black women to remain single. As one government official has noted, ''When there's no job in the inner city, with everything against them, with welfare designed primarily for one-parent homes, illegitimacy and welfare are as sound a response for the poor Black girl as a shotgun marriage is for a middle-class white,'' (Malloy, 1975, p. 18).

Assumptions about the pathology of the female-headed family have often been erroneous. While not present, the biological or social father and his kin are often supportive of his family by providing services and finances to them. A female-based kin network also exists for the exchange of scarce goods and services in the form of child care, gifts, and money (Stack, 1974). However, we should be cautious lest we glorify what is essentially a pragmatic adaptation to an undesirable situation for many Black women. These one-parent families had a per capita income of $1,268 in 1973, less than one-third of the income of two-parent families headed by a white male. An overwhelming majority have incomes below the poverty level, while having more children to support than two-parent families. Almost one-half of Black children are living in one-parent homes, which has reduced 41 percent of all Black children to a subsistence standard of living (U.S. Census, 1975). Such a reality has taken its psychological toll. One psychiatrist reports his observation of numerous Black women who attempted or threatened suicide because there was no man around and they believed they were incapable of raising their children alone (Wylie, 1974).

Indications are that the one-parent family may become the majority family system for Blacks by the year 2000. The interaction between the machinations of internal colonialism and a chaotic and exploitative economy will continue to make marriage an impossibility or a fragile arrangement for many Black people. There is no inherent pathology in such a family form. Children are probably better off, psychologically, than in conflict-ridden two-parent families. A major problem, however, is the strong correlation between one-parent families and economic deprivation. But with the decline of Black cultural supports for those living in such families, the years ahead may be ones of hardship for the women and children involved. Either a renewal of old adaptive forms is needed, or new strategies must be devised to meet the problems which will eventually emerge.

Child-Bearing and Socialization

Fertility patterns among Blacks have undergone considerable modification as a result of their urbanization and differentiation. One of the most striking changes is simply the decline in their birth rate. While the Black population is still growing at a faster rate than the dominant majority group, their fertility rate actually declined at a faster pace. In the period between 1960 and 1970, white fertility decreased only by 27 percent, in contrast to 37 percent among Blacks in urban areas (U.S. Census, 1975). The nature and process of this decline are significant. Among lower-income Blacks, abortion and sterilization as well as contraceptive use contributed to the lower number of children born to Black women. Unquestionably, many Black women have voluntarily decided to limit the number of children they will have as more and more Black families fall below the poverty level. However, a number of these women—especially poor ones—are forced to reduce their families in order to get welfare or other government assistance. Despite negative Black attitudes toward abortion, the proportion of Black women getting abortions is as high as, or higher than, that of white women. Moreover, a number of cases have recently been reported of Black women being sterilized without their knowledge or consent (Gray, 1975).

The fertility rate of the Black middle class has declined to such a low point that they are no longer reproducing themselves. Their birth rate is about the lowest in the United States. Many middle-class Black couples have no children and a majority of them have only one child. A large factor in this low birth rate is the long period of the wife's employment which delays the age at which college-educated Black women bear children (Kiser and Frank, 1967). More significant is the secondary sex ratio of births to middle-class Black women. Unlike typical population trends in the United States, the majority of children born to middle-class Black families are girls. In the one study that intensely investigated this phenomenon, a sex ratio of 83:100 was found in 249 births to Black families with incomes of between $13,000 and $17,000. The reason for this sex ratio disparity is the advanced age of Black men in the middle class when they first become fathers. As the age of the father increases, so does the number of female children they sire (McKay, 1975). An obvious ramification of this sex ratio at birth is an increase in the number of Black women without available marriage partners, a problem which already exists, owing to the larger percentage of Black women who graduate from college.

Despite a host of negative assumptions about the ability of Black families to produce children with a healthy identity, we find that traditionally the extended family system provided a number of mothering figures for the child. This is in contrast to a number of middle-class white children who are prisoners of the nuclear family system. Either they receive love and approval from their parents or not at all. In general, Black children develop a healthy identity because they grow up in households where they experience love and security from a number of kinsmen and significant others, and are not stifled by the rigidity of age and sex roles which exclude them from family activities. Owing to their earlier assumption of physical autonomy, Black children demonstrate the greatest early acceleration of psychomotor development of all ethnic and racial groups (Halpern, 1973).

A number of counter-forces buttress much of the negative effect of the absence of fathers from the Black household. Within the extended family there are a number of male role models to transmit the content of masculine role behavior to male children. A number of studies found father absence not to have a particularly negative influence on the self-concepts of Black children (Rubin, 1974). Moreover, many of these "absent" fathers maintain contact with their children and carry out normal paternal functions. Stack (1974) found that a mother generally regards her children's absent father as a friend of the family whom she can recruit for help rather than as a father failing in his parental duties. Men who remain with their families have been shown to have warm, nurturing relationships with their children, concurrently providing for their children's economic and social development (Lewis, 1975).

Notwithstanding their positive aspects, Black socialization practices have changed over time and space. In the lower-income Black urban ghettos, there is an increasing tendency on the part of Black parents to abuse their children (Gil, 1971). This is a result of the tensions produced by poverty conditions and the lack of community control over the antisocial behavior of Blacks in urban settings. Inadequate parenting, especially by teenage and one-parent families, has contributed to the arrogance and negativism emerging among Black youth. The formation of youth gangs and the beatings of elders, children, and other Blacks are manifestations of this problem. This is atypical behavior for Black youth and dissimilar to the values of the Black community. But the values these youths are adopting are often taught them by forces outside their community. They are socialized into the values of the colonizer through the medium of the schools, television, movies, and radio. These are values built on materialistic strivings, the use of violence, and individualism (Staples, 1975).

The Future of the Family

In this discussion of Black family life we have presented a mixed view of its functioning. This should not be seen as another treatise on the pathology of Black family life, but rather as a balanced and dynamic perspective which reflects the evolution of the Black family over time and space. It is not that the family is no longer a strong institution, but that a more truncated form has emerged as Blacks moved to the cities and differentiated into various socioeconomic classes. Many Blacks continue to find support for their needs and aspirations within the warm environs of the family. However, an increasing number of them have ceased to find the kind of family life they are allowed to have very satisfying. The most pronounced trend we see is the tendency of many Blacks not to enter marriage at all and to abstain from bringing children into the world.

We have already described the conditions that have shaped the Black family into its present form. The operational effects of an internal colonial order were much more destructive once Blacks moved into the cities where they could not maintain the cohesiveness and sense of "peoplehood" they had known in the South. It is probably no coincidence that the rate of marital break-up is significantly greater for Blacks born and living in Northern areas than for those who migrated from the South. In the case of the middle-class Black, the role he adopts will be determined partially by his acceptance or rejection of the values of the majority group. He is not as susceptible to the destructive influence of economic forces as those consigned to the underclass. The adoption of rules and values consonant with those held by the colonizer inevitably brings him into conflict with the cultural traditions of Black people.

What exactly is the status of the contemporary Black family? It would appear that the trend is toward attenuation of its traditional structure. In a period when one-fourth of Black men are out of work and Black family income has declined to 56 percent of white family income, a stable, gratifying family life becomes difficult to sustain. Without the cultural supports that have allowed them to transcend those economic forces in the past, Blacks have retreated into a variety of other family forms. Among the visible manifestations of these changes are increases in Black singlehood, female-headed households, homosexuality, and interracial marriages. Underlying many of these transformations are changes in the white family and the emergence and acceptance of women's liberation ideology and alternative family life styles. None of the aforementioned changes needs to be regarded as negative *per se*. However, they are concomitants of urban poverty, crime, suicide, and mental dislocation among Blacks.

In summary, the Black family is dialectically linked to the functioning of internal colonialism. The relationship between changes in the economic order and Black family functioning is quite clear. What is not understood is that culture is a two-edged sword: it can act as a mechanism for survival or as an apparatus of control. To the extent that Blacks forsake the family and the role they must play in it, the greater will be their vulnerability to the destructive forces of racial colonialism. Diffused groups of people who are detached from their cultural roots are powerless to resist the forces of oppression that they must eventually encounter in a society which is based on race and class exploitation. The family represents the basic collectivization of the Black community and contains within it the potential for Black survival in a world composed of the colonizers and the colonized.

References

Black Women's Community Development Foundation (ed.). *Mental and Physical Health Problems of Black Women.* Washington D.C.: B.W.C.D.F., 1975.

Blassingame, J. *The Slave Community.* New York: Oxford University Press, 1972.

Blauner, R. "Black Culture: Myth and Reality." In N. Whitten and J. Szwed, (eds.), *Afro-American Anthropology: Contemporary Perspectives*, pp. 347–366. New York: Free Press, 1970.

Blood, R., and Wolfe, D. "Negro-White Differences in Blue Collar Marriages in a Northern Metropolis." *Social Forces* 48 (1969): 59–63.

Dickinson, G.E. "Dating Behavior of Black and White Adolescents Before and After Desegregation." *Journal of Marriage and the Family* 37 (1975): 602–608.

Ford, J. "Black Men and Women: Deteriorating Relationships." *Los Angeles Sentinel,* March 1, 1973, C13.

Frazier, E.F. *The Negro Family in the United States.* Chicago: University of Chicago Press, 1939.

Furstenberg, F.; Hershberg, T.; and Modell, J. "The Origins of the Female Headed Black Family: The Impact of the Urban Experience." *Journal of Interdisciplinary History* 5 (1975): 211–233.

Genovese, D. "The Slave Family: Women—A Reassessment of Matriarchy, Emasculation, Weakness." *Southern Voices* 1 (1974): 9–16.

Gil, D. "Violence Against Children." *Journal of Marriage and the Family* 33 (1971): 637–648.

Glick, P., and Mills, R. "Black Families: Marriage Patterns and Living Arrangements." A paper presented at the W.E.B. Dubois Conference on American Blacks, Atlanta, October 1974.

Gray, N. "Sterilization and the Black Female: An Historical Perspective." In Black Women's Community Development Foundation (ed.), *Mental and Physical Health Problems of Black Women*, pp. 80–90. Washington, D.C.: B.W.C.D.F., 1975.

Gullattee, A. "Black Sensuality." *Essence* 2 (1971): 28–31.

_____ (ed.). *The Black Family: Fact or Fantasy?* Washington, D.C.: National Medical Association, 1972.

Halpern, F. *Survival Black/White.* Elmsford, New York: Pergamon Press, 1972.

Hare, N. "Will the Real Black Man Please Stand Up." *Black Scholar* 2 (1971): 32–35.

_____. "Division and Confusion: What Happened to the Black Movement?" *Black World* 25 (1976): 20–33.

Heer, D. "The Prevalence of Black-White Marriage in the United States, 1960 and 1970." *Journal of Marriage and the Family* 36 (1974): 246–259.

Jeffers, T. "The Black Woman and the Black Middle-Class." *Black Scholar* 4 (1973): 37–41.

Johnson, L. "Premarital Sex Attitudes and Behavior: A Comparison with Midwestern and Scandinavian Whites." Ph.D. dissertation, Purdue University, 1974.

Jones, J. "Father's Side Can't Compete With Welfare." *Los Angeles Times* March 26, 1971, 22.

Kantner, J.F., and Zelnik, M. "Contraception and Pregnancy: Experience of Young Unmarried Women in the United States." *Family Planning Perspectives* 5 (1973): 21–35.

Kihss, P. "New Study Says Relief System Penalizes Intact Families Here." *New York Times,* June 15, 1975.

Kiser, C., and Frank, M. "Factors Associated with the Lost Fertility of Non-White Women of College Attainment." *Milbank Memorial Fund Quarterly* 65 (1967): 427–449.

Lewis, D. "The Black Family: Socialization and Sex Roles." *Phylon* 36 (1975): 221–237.

Lewis, H. *Blackways of Kent.* Chapel Hill: University of North Carolina Press, 1955.

Lieberman, L. "The Emerging Model of the Black Family." *International Journal of Sociology of the Family* 3 (1973): 10–22.

Long, L., and Lynne, R. "Migration and Income Differences Between Black and White Men in the North." *American Journal of Sociology* 80 (1975): 1391–1409.

Malloy, M. "The Black Kid's Burden." *National Observer,* November 15, 1975, 1, 18.

Marshall, G. "An Exposition of the Valid Premises Underlying Black Families." In A. Gullattee (ed.), *The Black Family: Fact or Fantasy?* pp. 12–15. Washington, D.C.: National Medical Association, 1972.

McKay, R. "One-Child Families and Atypical Sex Ratios in an Elite Black Community." A paper presented to the American Association for the Advancement of Science, New York, 1975.

Melton, W., and Thomas, D. "Instrumental and Expressive Values in Mate Selection of Black and White College Students." A paper presented to the American Sociological Association meeting, New York, 1973.

Morton, C. "Mistakes Black Men Make in Relating to Black Women." *Ebony* 30 (1975): 170–175.

National Urban League Research Department. *Quarterly Economic Report on the Black Worker* 2 (1975): 1–8.

Nobles, W. "Africanity: Its Role in Black Families." *Black Scholar* 5 (1974): 10–17.

Paulme, D. (ed.). *Women of Tropical Africa.* Berkeley: University of California Press, 1963.

Pettigrew, P. et al. "Color Gradations and Attitudes Among Middle Income Negroes." *American Sociological Review* 31 (1966): 365–374.

Porterfield E. "Mixed Marriage." *Psychology Today* 6 (1973): 71–78.

Rawick, G.P. *The American Slave: From Sundown to Sunup.* Westport, Connecticut: Greenwood, 1972.

Renne, K. "Correlates of Dissatisfaction in Marriage." *Journal of Marriage and the Family* 32 (1970): 54–67.

Rosow, I., and Rose, D. "Divorce Among Doctors." *Journal of Marriage and the Family* 34 (1972): 587–599.

Rubin, R. H. "Adult Male Absence and the Self Attitudes of Black Children." *Child Study Journal* 4 (1974): 492–506.

Stack, B. *All Our Kin: Strategies for Survival in a Black Community.* New York: Harper & Row, 1974.

Slevin, J. "Money Woes Felt by Black Women." *Washington Post,* April 3, 1972, D12.

Staples, R. "The Black Dating Game." *Essence* 4 (1973): 40, 92–96.

_____. *The Black Woman in America.* Chicago: Nelson-Hall, 1973.

_____. "The Black Family Revisited: A Review and a Preview." *Journal of Social and Behavioral Sciences* 20 (1974): 65–78.

_____. "To Be Young, Black and Oppressed." *Black Scholar* 7 (1975): 2–9.

_____. *Introduction to Black Sociology.* New York: McGraw-Hill, 1976.

U.S. Bureau of the Census. 1970 Census of Population, *Marital Status.* Vol. 11–4C, Table 9. Washington, D.C.: Government Printing Office, 1971.

_____. *The Social and Economic Status of the Black Population in the United States, 1974.* Washington, D.C.: Government Printing Office, 1975.

Velasco-Rice, J. and Mynko, L. "Suicide and Marital Status: A Changing Relationship." *Journal of Marriage and the Family* 35 (1973): 239–244.

Wylie, F. "Suicide Among Black Females: A Case Study." In Black Women's Community Development Foundation (ed.), *Mental and Physical Health Problems of Black Women,* pp. 121–125. Washington, D.C.: B.W.C.D.F., 1975.

5 THE CHILD: YOUNG, GIFTED, AND BLACK

Pearl L. Rosser, M.D.

The continuation and future of any race or people are dependent upon its children. Black children are therefore our most precious possessions, our Black jewels, our Black gold. They are our links to the future and the keys to the survival of the race.

Black children today are among the smartest, most creative, most imaginative, most industrious, most able, and most gifted people on earth. They are not the strange, innately violent, hard to teach, hard to reach, deviant and amoral characters so often portrayed by deficit/deviant-oriented models. As parents and as communities, we all too often permit this ability, gift, potential, imagination, and energy to die, or to be squandered, in our failure to meet adequately the Black child's needs from conception through adolescence. It is our responsibility as Black people to guarantee the Black child's optimal growth and development physically, emotionally, socially, and intellectually.

Population Statistics and Infant Morbidity and Mortality Rates

In the census, Black people made up 11 percent of the total population of the United States. This percentage should continue to increase since, of the 15 million Black people in the U.S., approximately one-third are children under 16 years of age. Similarly, 15 percent of all children in the country under the age of 5 are Black. Though birth rates declined for both Blacks and whites between 1957 and the early seventies, the birth rate for Blacks remained about one and a half times that of whites (16.7 babies per thousand population for whites; 25.4 babies per thousand population for Blacks) during that period. Today, birth rates are again on the increase for both races. Black babies and children, however, face numerous hazards and handicaps which often prevent their survival as well as their arriving at the desired goal of physically sound, mentally alert, individually capable, and socially well-adjusted adulthood.

The infant mortality rate for Blacks is almost twice that for whites. Infant death in any population is an indicator of the level of health hazard to which that population is exposed. A high infant mortality rate reflects the existence of circumstances hostile to life in the environment, such as illness, overcrowded living conditions, faulty nutrition, poor conditions for birth, and poor health care and/or prenatal care. For many women poverty is a lifelong condition, not a sudden circumstance of adulthood. The competencies of women as child-bearers are often influenced by the environment in which they have grown up long before they have begun to reproduce.

Infant mortality rates indirectly suggest the rate of survival with increased risk of damage to the survivors, for the killing conditions of life are frequently the disabling ones for those who survive. Infants of the socioeconomically disadvantaged (of whom a disproportionate number are Black), both those who live and those who die, are excessively exposed to these conditions.

Growth and Development

"Growth" and "development" are terms frequently used interchangeably. However, there are differences implied in each term. Growth serves to emphasize changes in size, while development denotes progressively greater facility in functioning. Growth in terms of size results from cell multiplication and is a continuous process which follows a predictable pattern. This process moves with biologic time and links the many physical, chemical, metabolic, and developmental components of the body into functional units. Development, on the other hand, denotes qualitative changes; changes in the complexity of structure which make it possible for functioning to progress at increasingly higher levels. Just as disease represents an absence of health, adequate growth in the child represents the presence of health.

Relatively few studies have been published on growth in North American Black children. Some of the most outstanding studies to date have been provided by the Department of Pediatrics at the Howard University College of Medicine. In 1950 and 1962, Scott and his co-workers described the growth pattern of North American Black children under 1 year of age, and in 1969 published results of a study of growth beyond infancy (Scott, et al., 1950; Verghese, et al., 1969). Contrary to earlier reports, the 1950 study showed that there was no statistically significant difference between Black and white infants in growth patterns for weight and stature during the first year of life. The 1969 study also demonstrated that there was very little difference in growth patterns (height and weight) between Black and white children after the first year of life in the sample studied.

In order to understand growth and development, it is well to discuss the changes that take place in terms of the life cycle of childhood.

The life cycle of the child may be divided into the following periods:

1. *Prenatal*—conception to birth.
2. *Neonatal*—first 4 weeks after birth.
3. *Infancy*—age 1 month to 1 year.
4. *Preschool or early childhood*—age 1 to 6 years.
5. *Prepuberal or late childhood*—age 6 to 10 years.
6. *Adolescence*—age 10 to 20 years.

At birth the infant's only tools for dealing with the world are simple ones—sucking, grasping, listening, looking, vocalizing, and moving the limbs. It is through these simple processes that he receives information from the world and affects both physical objects and people. Through a repeated interactional process of acting and observing the consequences of his actions, his simple tools become modified, and he gradually builds up a whole set of strategies for coping with more and more complex and difficult tasks. It is these strategies which constitute intelligence.

Below the age of 4 years, the number one socializing force for the child is the family. The family is the most sensitive, important, and enduring element in the culture of any people. Whatever else its role, its most important function must be to ensure the survival of its people. The most valuable institution for the survival of Black people is, therefore, the Black family.

Optimal growth and development of Black children are dependent upon the cohesiveness and strength of the Black family and the community to which that family relates. Recognition and utilization of the strengths of Black families and Black communities are crucial in preparing the Black child for the impact of the larger non-Black society on his life.

Birth through Adolescence

Between birth and 5 years, when the family serves as the number one socializing force, there are twelve basic tasks that all children must learn, whatever their race, creed, or color. These tasks are as follows:

1. Gain increasing control over the body's regulatory and physiologic mechanisms, gross motor development, and coordination.
2. Come to see oneself as a special and important person who is able to cope with life successfully.
3. Acquire the ability to care about other people and feel that they care and can be counted on when needed.
4. Learn to learn from what is seen, heard, and felt.
5. Learn how to use the large muscles to walk, run, and dance, and small ones in the hands to explore, fit things together, and build.
6. Learn about relationships between shapes, sizes, and positions in space; to solve problems by doing and by thinking.
7. Learn to use and understand language to express immediate needs as well as fantasies, experiences, ideas, plans, feelings, hopes, and dreams.
8. Develop a wide range of ways of communicating with others, not only through written and verbal language, but also through gestures, expression, and cooperative work and play.
9. Satisfy the curiosity and desire to explore.
10. Learn to appreciate one's own feelings and express them in appreciative and constructive ways.
11. Learn how to relate to other people and to understand their needs and feelings.

12. Move from a position of total dependence to that of an increasingly more independent, self-sufficient, and capable individual.

In most Black families, just as in most other American families, the mother is the major socializing agent for her preschool children. Consequently, she continually functions as a teacher in their everyday interactions, or lack of same, whether she is aware of her teaching role or not. Differences among mothers in their teaching techniques, including language, motivation techniques, ability to interpret the child's responses, and success in giving appropriate feedback in reaction to these responses, affect not only the degree to which children learn the intended message or meaning, but also their motivation and the kinds of learning strategies and habits they develop.

The period between 5 and 8 years is one of relatively slow growth, but it is an important time for development. It is during this period that significant motivation occurs in thinking, understanding, feeling, and social interrelationships. It is during this period that the child is called upon to leave the security of the home to enter the competition of the outside world. At this age, the school represents that outside world where the child must begin to live increasingly independently and to look outside the home for standards of behavior and goals. This transition is often anxiety-provoking for both the child and the parents. The child, unable to meet the newly imposed standards, may learn for the first time the sense of failure. This may lead to feelings of rejection, lowered self-esteem, and distorted self-concept which frequently result in acting-out and hostile behavior. It is during this age period that basic attitudes, values, ways of working and relaxing, and coping skills and strategies become solidified. The basic personality does not change much from this point on, although important experiences later in life may tend to modify its expression.

Adolescence is a time of rapid growth and development. It has its beginnings at about age 10 in girls and about age 12 in boys. Puberty occurs during this period of adolescence and signifies the development of the secondary sex characteristics in boys and girls and the onset of the menarche in girls. The body matures physically, and the ability to procreate is established. Parental influence is perhaps greatest in early adolescence and puberty. As the teenager matures and enters late adolescence (age 16 to 20 years), the influence of parents decreases and peer influence increases.

Delayed Development

Delayed development and mental retardation occur in Black children just as in all other groups. However, before jumping to such diagnostic conclusions, extreme care must be taken to evaluate carefully what is true *pathology* and what is *cultural difference*. An IQ test alone will not make this differentiation and should never be used alone for this purpose. A child who has not had the benefit of an interdisciplinary medical and behavioral assessment has not had an adequate evaluation of the etiology of his developmental delay and easily becomes prey to mislabeling and subsequently to the abusive practice of educational mismanagement.

The diagnostic assessment must include prenatal, perinatal, and postnatal information. Details of all childhood illnesses should be obtained, including the age of the child at the time of the illness as well as the symptoms, severity, course medications, and care provided. The developmental history should include details of adaptive, personal-social, language, and motor development. Family-social history must include detailed information regarding family constellation, cultural background, specific interpersonal family dynamics, and socioeconomic stresses. The academic history should include observations regarding school behavior as well as academic progress and achievement. School records, including samples of school work and test results, should be available, and a first-hand look at the home and school environment should be undertaken.

Psychological evaluation is a component of the behavioral assessment and should include behavioral observations in a variety of settings, measures of complex visual-motor-perceptual functioning, an assessment of personality characteristics, and indices of learning styles. Information derived from testing should be presented with much less emphasis on scores (than is the usual common practice and much more emphasis on individual strengths and weaknesses, with descriptive and prescriptive recommendations for teaching.

Language evaluation is also a component of the behavioral assessment and should include a detailed examination of speech and language behavior, articulation, voice quality, and both the expressive and receptive aspects of language. An educational evaluation is best conducted by an educational diagnostician and should include a complete analysis of academic abilities as well as levels and methods of skills acquisition.

The Environment

Every individual is born with a genetic potential (inherited potential). It is important to understand that no "genes or traits for intelligence" have been identified and that as far as genetic pool and race are concerned, most humans are created equally. The environment can either enhance or retard the development of one's genetic potential. Genes will respond to the environment only in the manner in which the environment enables them to do so. The same genes under different environmental conditions will produce quite different results.

The infant and young child, whether born healthy or not, are vulnerable to both the hostility and beneficence of the environment. Children who live in poverty tend to live lives which are physically destructive as well as intellectually depressing. They are exposed to poor food, poor housing, poor sanitation, and poor medical care, and their homes are frequently devoid of toys and games for stimulation of cognitive skills development.

Hostile inputs from the environment result in the following facts of life for many low-income families in addition to the high infant mortality rates already cited:

1. The incidence of premature births (among which neurological and physical disorders are 75 percent more frequent than in full-term babies) is almost three times as great among low-income women as among other groups of women.

2. Forty-five percent of women delivering in public hospitals have received no prenatal care. Avoidable complications of pregnancy (such as prematurity and toxemia), which are often the harbingers of disabling conditions in children, soar in this group.

3. A child from a low-income rural or urban family is 15 times more likely to be diagnosed as retarded than is a child from a higher-income family. This is a fault of nurture (environment), not nature (genes).

Of those environmental factors having a profound effect on growth and development, nutrition is one of the most serious. Inadequate food, both in quality and quantity, and both prenatally and post-natally, represents one of the most obvious and dramatic of the causes of low survival rates and poor growth developmental performance among economically deprived populations.

There is an intimate association between poor nutrition and disease. The "diet of poverty," which tends to be high in carbohydrates and low in proteins, results in a high incidence of nutritional anemia. Poor nutritional status promotes infection, and infection in turn depresses an already poor nutritional status. Nutritional stress may also produce apathy and irritability in the child, thus depressing normal curiosity and desire for exploration.

Overcrowded housing and living conditions, inadequate heating and ventilation, poor facilities for storage of food, and inadequate washing facilities all increase the occurrence of infections, particularly upper respiratory, gastrointestinal, and skin infections, in children of the socioeconomicaly disadvantaged. Crowded, poorly equipped kitchens, poor electrical connections, badly lighted and unstable stairs, and neighborhoods with heavy traffic all contribute to an increased occurrence of accidents.

Additionally, there is a high incidence of poisoning secondary to poor supervision of toddlers, poorly secured cleaning materials, and poorly stored medication (prescribed and non-prescribed). Where children live in dilapidated old buildings with peeling paint and falling plaster, the incidence of lead poisoning ("ghetto malaria") increases. One lead-based paint chip the size of a fingernail, eaten daily for 3 months, can turn a bright, happy 2-year-old child into a human vegetable; more can kill him (Chisolm and Maloney, 1974).

In addition to perpetuating poor health, poverty perpetuates learning failure. Poverty and educational failure thus become mutually reinforcing conditions. The likelihood of being caught up in this cycle of poverty and failure is disproportionately high for minority groups in this country. Children from different socioeconomic levels have historically had, and continue to have, very dissimilar opportunities for early social and psychological experiences and a quality education. Moreover, styles of child-care differ greatly. So different are these early experiences and styles of care that children of the poor often arrive at school age with neither the experiences nor the skills believed to be necessary for immediate success and achievement in the school setting. For many children the educational battles are either won or lost during the first 6 years of life.

What can parents do to assist the child in the development of skills for academic success? Keeping in mind that the foundations for academic success are laid during the first 4 years of life when the family serves as the major socializing agent, it becomes important that parents:

1. Teach children the verbal and perceptual skills needed in order to learn to read and to bolster their sense of self. This is not the job of the school alone.

2. Establish skill in auditory discrimination.

3. Promote a sense of order, beauty, and safety in the physical environment as well as a sense of discipline.

4. Provide physical activity for the development of gross and fine motor skills and coordination.

5. Encourage the child's innate curiosity and delight in discovery.

6. Enhance learning skills (cognition) by providing appropriate stimulation to all the senses: touch, smell, and taste as well as sight and hearing.

7. Provide opportunities for the child to solve problems and make decisions.

To be able to teach these skills effectively, parents must have "parenting know-how," in other words, parenting skills. There is a significant difference between parenting and parenthood, and this difference must be understood. Parenthood is a biological, and sometimes legal, phenomenon. Parenting, on the other hand, is learned behavior and not necessarily a natural phenomenon. It should not be assumed, therefore, that because individuals have babies (parenthood), they understand the art of parenting.

External environmental influences are sometimes reflected in the strikingly early time at which some parents seemingly become ineffective in providing parental control and emotional support for their children. This sometimes happens when the children are only 5 or 6 years old, but more often occurs when they are 11 or 12. For the most part, these are loving parents who have educational aspirations for their children. What is needed is knowledge and clarity as to how children obtain projected goals, and what skills they as parents must possess in order to motivate their children. Loss of parental control and emotional support seems to be related to the degree of optimism or pessimism that parents have about the future of their families. Consequently, in socioeconomically deprived families, lack of confidence and optimism emerges as one of the most insidious and eroding processes affecting child-rearing.

The Culture

The immediate family and environment give the child his earliest feelings about himself. At long last Blacks have come to view Black childhood and Black family life in their rightful perspective—as a source and reflection of Black culture and consciousness and as a resource for the larger, majority society in this country. There can be little doubt that Black culture exists and that the ways of life for Blacks in America are different in major respects from those of whites. There are, of course, similarities, but there are indeed differences, and these differences should be used to the Black child's advantage.

A review of the strengths of Black people reveals that the most dominant characteristics are strong kinship bonds, a sense of related-ness, and a quest to understand and support each other. Black people also have a strong work orientation and a high achievement orientation with a desire to learn, to get ahead, and to conquer. Blacks are a deeply religious people. They have a strong sense of community and tend to be motivated more by a spirit of cooperation than by competitiveness. These resources, characteristics, and strengths, which have helped Blacks to survive as a people, should continue to be firmly incorporated into the socialization of Black children.

Most Black parents, considering both economic and social circumstances, do a good job of child-rearing, but there is room for improvement. Black parents have a long history of teaching children pride and self-respect. However, various media presentations, especially television and films, sometimes hinder this effort. Black exploitation films tend to emphasize self-defeating violence, and many popular records and television shows glamorize negative images. Children need to be exposed to positive role models and the positive side of their heritage as often as possible.

The goal of child-rearing and socialization of the Black child must be to produce competent, confident individuals—people able to *be,* able to *know,* able to *do,* and above all able to *think.* It is a challenge to teach the child to be Black and proud in a white-oriented society. Black children must never be permitted to use oppressed status as an excuse for inferior achievement or for undesirable personal characteristics. Dedicated Black parents, as well as Black teachers, are needed to assure this optimal outcome, for next to parental attitudes, teacher attitudes and teacher expectations are two of the most significant factors influencing the Black child's self-concept.

Different perceptions of the child's rights have led to a variety of child-management styles. Approaches to child-rearing range from overly strict to overly permissive ones. The former approach is based on a strong perception of the parent's right to exercise authority or power over the child. Its emphases are on constantly restricting, setting limits, demanding, commanding, and expecting certain behavior and obedience. It is based on creating fear of the parent and of authority. The latter approach stresses the avoidance of setting limits. It does not condone punishment and authoritarian methods and discourages restricting or demanding certain behaviors of the child as well as commanding and expecting obedience. Since parenting and child development are not taught to the majority of parents today, they simply rely on the same styles of rearing their children and dealing with problems in the family as were used by their parents, their grandparents, and their great-grandparents. All of these techniques may not fit the reality of today's situation, although they may have been most appropriate at another point in time.

An *awareness* of how children mature and what affects their emotional, psychological, and social development, coupled with an awareness of the strengths of Black families, the strengths of Black children and communities, and the destructiveness of racist attitudes and actions, is needed for effective parenting in today's world. The message of the responsibilities of parenthood and parenting, and the social, economic, and moral commitment that must accompany both, must get across to our young people. In this age of liberal birth-control information, couples do not have to become parents unless they really want to. And unless they are willing to make the social, economic, and moral commitment needed, perhaps their children could be served best by remaining unconceived. Once a decision is made to bring a child into the world, an irrevocable debt is owed to that child. That debt includes the following:

1. The basic necessities of life—food, clothing, and shelter—regardless of how rich or how poor the family might be.

2. The right to an education. This includes a responsibility to create a climate for education in the home that motivates the child toward learning and helps him to conquer the basics of reading, writing, and arithmetic. Television is by far one of the most destructive influences on the establishment of good study habits in the home.

3. A sense of pride—pride in race and pride in self. The Black child must be given by his parents an honest knowledge of who he is, where he came from, and where he is going. They must teach him about Black heroes, accomplishments, and strengths, for some segments of the larger society will see to it that he learns about negative models and weaknesses. A Black child with a firmly established sense of pride in himself can survive wherever he goes.

4. Respect. A child deserves to be respected as an individual and as a person in his own right. Children must be permitted the right to speak, think, question values, and solve problems for themselves.

5. Love. Parents owe their children love. In the hostile, racist-oriented society in which we live, Black children need special assurance that their parents love them and want them, and that this love is *unconditional*, with no strings attached.

The Social System

Schools. The school is the second most important institution in the socialization of the Black child—second only to the family. Next to parents, teachers play the most important role in the formation of a positive identity. No attempt at reaching and teaching Black children can hope to be successful unless the attitude of the teaching staff and the administration is both optimistic and enlightened, and unless new approaches are not only accepted but welcomed. Unfortunately, too many teachers and administrators continue to believe and perpetuate the myth that Black students are inferior to their white counterparts and are unable to learn. It is hardly surprising that Black children surrounded and overwhelmed by such feelings of inferiority are frequently unmotivated to learn.

Too many schools are failing our children by inappropriate intervention techniques, inappropriate teacher expectations, or worst of all, no expectations at all. As has been demonstrated time and again, when teachers have low expectation levels for their children, the children seldom exceed the expectation. Many white teachers are openly rejecting and antagonistic, while others overcompensate by not expecting enough of Black children. Too many teachers, Black and white, do not set limits because they are afraid. Consequently, too many Black children are in educational trouble. Their energies are not being channeled to gain school and work skills and to accept the responsibility for the full development of self, future family, or the Black community.

As a result, the cycle of educational failure, joblessness, poverty, and frustration is set into motion. Frustration in attempts to break this cycle seems to contribute greatly to the high incidence of drug addiction, alcoholism, and incarceration of Black males between the ages of 16 and 25. It is important for educators of Black children to realize that unlike the rapidly industralizing economy of the nineteenth and early twentieth centuries, our present automated economy has little need for the talents the uneducated have to offer—strong backs and clever hands. Rather, we have an increasing need for trained minds, educated judgments, and conceptual skills.

Underlying many of today's academic and social intervention programs is the assumption that the manners, customs, and characteristics existing in the Black child's home and environment (i.e., his culture) are inferior and need to be replaced with the Anglo-Saxon cultural ideal. A preponderance of educational dogma is based on the Anglo-Saxon ideal, with learning styles and modes emanating from this supposed standard. If a child possesses a different style and mode, he is viewed from a deficit/deviant model as "culturally deprived," in need of "compensatory education," or, more brutally, as "mentally retarded." Consequently, Black children are subjected to "cognitive stimulation," "language development," and "behavior modification," all based upon the assumption that they have no unique cognitive style, no language that is expressive and communicative, and that their behavior is obnoxious.

No longer should we accept ideologies growing out of the deficit/deviant model, which stereotypically characterize Black children as having inefficient verbal communication skills, disruptive-maladaptive behavior patterns, disidentity, inability to delay gratification, and a sense of hopelessness. Instead, the characteristics which the Black child brings to the school should be fostered. These characteristics include:

1. The spontaneity, problem-solving ability, and creativity which exist and grow even under severe limitations of environment.
2. The nature and effort of peer collective, a major socializing agent for the urban Black child.
3. Cognitive and affective styles which permit the development of extensive non-verbal communication processes.

A culturally determined educational environment for the Black child would therefore include:

1. Recognition and utilization of the preferred mode of communication of the child, while at the same time teaching new communication skills.
2. Utilization of the child's perferred mode of relating (e.g., personalized directions from adults).
3. Incentive motivation based on the child's incentive preference (may be cooperative, not competitive).
4. Utilization of the child's preferred mode of thinking, perceiving, remembering, and problem-solving.

The curriculum would include:

1. Materials and content that are related to the real-life situation of the child involved.
2. Emphasis on doing and approaches to learning that require active physical participation.
3. Emphasis on multiple-level learning materials.
4. Manipulative materials which provide for discovery of basic number concepts.
5. Utilization of dancing, rhythm, and music as an approach to learning.
6. Utilization of more concrete objects to enliven the more traditional abstract approach to teaching.
7. A multisensory approach to learning.

8. Peer group teaching and learning.

9. Peer group support.

10. Emphasis on child-parent-teacher motivation designed to raise the level of expectation on the part of the teacher, increase participation on the part of parents, and provide pleasure and reward in learning for the child.

Black parents and communities have an obligation to see to it that schools, segregated or integrated, instill in the Black child a sense of competence, a knowledge of worth, a feeling of dignity, a sense of mastery, a desire to acquire technical skills as well as professional skills, and a quest for achievement. The notion that the existence of racism excuses incompetence and mediocrity in the performance of Black children must be dispelled, for such a notion does nothing more than support the doctrine and practice of racism.

Tests and Filters. Intelligence testing, aptitude testing, and achievement testing have become big business in America. These three types of testing are firmly entrenched in the American way of life both on an individual level and on an institutional level. Such testing can, and often does, become an attack on poor, Black, and other minority group children. It is important to understand that none of these tests can in fact effectively measure the intelligence or learning capacity of poor, Black, and other minority group children.

Of the three types, intelligence testing appears to have the most abusive affect on the child, for it is the IQ test score that is used to mislabel and subsequently to justify the educational mismanagement of large numbers of Black children. What do commonly used intelligence tests measure? In Black, poor, and other minority group children, they certainly do not measure intelligence. For the most part, they measure the degree to which an individual's background matches the Anglo-cultural pattern of American society. Unfortunately IQ tests measure everyone by an Anglo yardstick. The more anglicized a non-Anglo child is, the better he does on an IQ test.

The most common incorrect notion about the IQ score is that it magically indexes inborn and unchangeable mental capacity. As one noted Black psychologist observed, testing Blacks in order to ascertain their potential (with past and present instruments) is often no more scientific than the Gypsy practice of reading tea leaves (Green, 1974).

You can prove almost anything with present test instruments if you juggle items for sex, skill, or culture. Thus it is frighteningly easy to pin a ''retarded'' label on an individual if an ''IQ-only'' definition of retardation is used.

Ethnic groups, and in general those of low socioeconomic status, are the most likely to be penalized by an ''IQ-only'' definition of retardation. Seventy-five percent of all persons identified as mentally retarded in America are found in isolated and impoverished urban and rural slums. In the majority of cases this diagnosis is based on an IQ score alone. Is such labeling more a matter of convenience than of actuality and, if so, are there not sociopolitical implications? To label poor, Black, and minority group children in such a manner sentences them to a life without opportunity.

Such labeling is in effect a self-fulfilling prophecy, for the label becomes a trap confining many poor and minority students within the vicious cycle of educational failure, joblessness, and poverty. Doomed to an inferior education, often on the basis of one inappropriate test, the child steadily falls further and further below his peers, motivation disappears, and defeatism leaves its indelible mark on the child's self-esteem and self-concept. The usual result is that the individual drops out of school to join the ranks of the uneducated, unskilled unemployed. Thus test results serve to reinforce social roles.

Proponents of IQ testing argue that the tests themselves are not the problem, but rather that the problem is one of interpretation and use of information. It seems naive and impractical, however, to place the burden of racial relevance in interpretation totally in the hands of the myriad psychologists who administer IQ tests. The fact is that per-centage-wise, despite lip-service to a recognition of the limitations and bias inherent in present intelligence test instruments, most psychologists still tend to lean toward standard and traditional ways of interpreting and scoring. This is usually done because of (1) lack of time to interpret from a Black perspective, even if the skill to do so is present; (2) the examiners' own middle-class orientation, whether Black or white; and (3) institutional pressures for strict interpretation.

Test misuse is one of the worst forms of child abuse. Minorities have a right to cry conspiracy since it appears that IQ data are being used to label certain biosocial groups as inferior and to perpetuate the status quo socially, educationally, and economically. Black parents and communities owe it to Black children to limit the influence of unfair testing on their lives. Parents have the power to demand, and the obligation to seek, a role in determining testing policies and procedures in their local schools as well as nationally, both legislatively and through the courts.

Special Mental Health Considerations

Adoption. Adoption as a means of creating families is openly accepted in American society today. In Black families, the concept of the family as a unit based on ties of affection and on performance of the child-rearing roles was accepted long before it came into vogue in the larger society. For generations Blacks have automatically "raised" and "kept" the children of relatives and friends alike. For the most part these were informal adoptions which were accepted as a matter of course without the legal hassle and red-tape associated with today's institutionalized adoption process.

In the interest of the continued survival of the race, Blacks must get back to these traditional feelings of kinship and more openly accept the children of relatives and friends when situations call for this. It is imperative that Black children be spared the often devastating experiences of the child welfare system. Black communities can go a long way in improving the quality of life for Black children by embracing the guidelines formulated at the May 1973 National Black Parent Convention, held in New York and sponsored by the Council of Independent Black Institutions. A few of these guidelines are given below:

1. To have a feeling of love and responsibility for all Black children, be they one's own biological descendants or not. (The extended family is a traditional part of our African heritage.)
2. To teach what is right and what is wrong.
3. To respect Black children and demand respect from them.
4. To produce harmony, stability, and an atmosphere of trust and love in the home.
5. To provide opportunities for learning and instill a sense of pride by teaching our past and present history.
6. To establish and perpetuate those moral attitudes and values which will add to the child's personality and character—virtue,

knowledge, temperance, patience, godliness, brotherliness, kindness, and charity.

7. To develop a deep inner love that flows over and around the Black child to form a shield of protection, guidance, wisdom, and strength.

8. To assume the responsibility for cultivating the development of Black youth.

9. To be a model of the intellectual, emotional, and moral discipline necessary to the child's understanding of, relationship to, and responsibility for the total Black experience—past, present, and future.

10. To help every Black child develop the skills to survive.

Transracial Adoptions. White families do Black children a disservice in adopting them *unless* they can teach the Black child to be Black and proud in a white, racist-oriented society. Many white families cannot meet this basic requirement. If the motive for adoption is to rescue the Black child from his Blackness, or if it is one of pity, the child's mental health will almost surely suffer.

Black social workers in this country have voiced strenuous objections to the practice of transracial adoptions. It is important that the mental health needs and welfare of the Black child be given priority consideration over the adopting couple's single desire to have children.

Day Care. It is important for the Black community to promote community institutions which support family life and help children to fulfill their potential. Quality day care for the infant, preschool, and school-aged child, when it is family-focused and family-oriented, is one such institution which can be of invaluable assistance in meeting these objectives. Because many parents must work to make ends meet, they must find someone else to care for their children for a part of the day. Also, mothers who do not work often need day care as a means of improving their parenting skills.

Quality day-care programs should include at least two basic features: (1) they should add to and strengthen the kind of care and guidance provided by parents, and (2) they should aim at providing the child with experiences which encourage healthy growth of body, personality, and intellect. Day-care programs hold the potential for bringing children of all ages and adults together in activities that are fun and that improve the quality of the child's life.

There are several types of day care, the most common of which are (1) the day-care center, and (2) family day care. Family day care is the care of a child in the home of another family. The activities in the family day-care home tend to be a bit more informal than in the day-care center. Many parents seem to prefer the family day-care home for the infant and very young child, though many day-care centers also provide service to children of these age groups.

Both types of programs should be readily available in Black communities. Whatever the type, the principal objective must be to provide the Black child with the kind of care which is essential for his or her best social, emotional, and intellectual development.

References

Chisolm, J. Jr., and Maloney, L. R. "Lead Poisoning: Man-Made Epidemic." *Urban Health,* 3 (1974): 68–72.

Green, R. L. "The Danger of 'Intelligence Tests.' " *Ebony* 29 (1974): 68–72.

Scott, R. B.; Cardozo, W. W.; Smith, A.; and Delilly, M. R. "Growth and Development of Negro Infants." *Pediatrics* 37 (1950): 885.

Verghese, K. P.; Scott, R. B.; Texieira, G.; and Ferguson, A. D. "Studies in Growth and Development XII: Physical Growth of North American Negro Children." *Pediatrics* 44 (1969): 243.

6 THE BLACK ADOLESCENT

Thomas A. Gordon, Ph.D.

Our youth now love luxury. They have bad manners and contempt for authority. They show disrespect for their elders and love idle chatter instead of exercise. Children are now tyrants—not servants of the household. They no longer rise when elders enter the room. They contradict their parents, chatter before company, gobble up their food, and tyrannize their teachers.

Socrates
450 B.C.

The Young Adult

The Flow. Whence come these "young adults"? Not merely social thinkers, but many a parent has wondered aloud this very question. Whence do they spring and where are they going? With what heritage, legacies, skills, movements, and hoped-for potential? Nature provides each species with a life code for its own duplication and survival. What aspect of the human code do these "young adults" harbor or suggest? Where do they fall within the cycle of life subsumed under nature's grand design? What is the "flow" pushed onward and perpetuated through them? Of what consequence is their presence to the improvement and fulfillment of the human endeavor?

It may be instructive to begin with basics—first principles from which to view humanity in perspective—with youth as one phase in the human pattern with all its cultural variants. The universe is immense, orderly, and structured within finite cycles of existence. This principle holds for the physical world and for animals and humans. The universe is unmistakably large and patterned: no one aspect of the design is so great and consequential as to surpass the whole; yet no part is without merit in the grand scheme that seemingly connects everything to everything else. In fact, the sheer energy alone we humans channel into history, philosophy, religion, and science attests to our enduring capacity to "wonder" at the full breadth and depth of the universal scheme.

On a small scale, the cellular interdependence of a plant, animal, or embryo depicts this grand design: order, energy, matter, cycle, object in relation to other object, small system in relation to larger system, growth and decline, continuum after continuum of existence. At a larger level, pause to consider the sun. The sun is our star, but it also reflects the same universal design (Rosenfeld, 1976). Without the sun there could be no life as we know it. Yet the sun is but one of hundreds of millions of stars in the lens-shaped galaxy we call the Milky Way. Moreover, instead of being in the galactic center, as was once believed, it is actually located out near the edge of the lens, about three-quarters of the distance from the galaxy's core. Now the Earth and the other planets orbit the sun within a finite time frame. Similarly, the entire solar system revolves around the hub of the galaxy in a majestic, orderly swing that takes some 200 million years.

This galaxy of ours is one of a "local cluster" of galaxies—there are millions of such clusters—and the light from our closest neighboring galaxy takes 2 million years to reach us. Thus our sun, while essential to earthly life, relates to a larger scheme of connection. From a cosmic perspective, it is barely more than a lightspeck beaming on the outskirts of a minor galaxy. It has a finite cycle of existence. Now about 5 billion years old, it beams life-sustaining energy to Earth, having nearly reached the prime of its own middle age. At some future time, the sun's cycle will draw to a close. Such is the pattern or order of growth/decline, appearance/disappearance, and matter/energy relation recognizable as basic in nature's design.

Human life reflects this order, interdependence, and finite span, too. After youth comes age, then decline and death—all recognizable junctures on a life continuum punctuated somewhat earlier by conception, birth, and the childhood years. Our cultural groundings and needs constrain the mileage we humans can make of the youthful years, though every human group demands and expects certain kinds of returns from its young. In the preindustrial East, the youthful years may coincide with fairly rigid commitments to labor, sex-role initiation, marriage, the military, and other demanding pursuits (Grinder, 1963; Haley, 1976; Kenyatta, 1965). In the technological West, the youth time-frame imposes different demands, typically more openly permitting flexible exploration of choice, delay of commitment, and continued education rather than fixed work and marriage goals or acceptance of other major responsibility (Adams, 1969; Brim and Wheeler, 1966; Erikson, 1950; Evans, 1970; Winter and Nuss, 1969). Whether East or West, however, the "young adult" years represent a critical juncture of transition, improvement, and self-definition. Youth—in terms of even one life and certainly relative to all the lives and life cycles of the universal scheme—is barely more than a cosmic lightspeck. Still, on the other hand, it is integral to the fulfillment of the human life plan.

Youth and Human Endowment

Let us consider youth in terms of man's special endowment and potential. Like all life forms, human beings are a part of nature's grand scheme and respond to the demands of the systems or environments which operate around them. To be alive is to be responsive and open to adaptation. Mankind is also consequential: every human act has echoes, ripples, repercussions, and effects for today and for the future. Man is educable; he communicates and learns from his interdependence with nature and his connection to others of his kind (Bateson, 1973; Fuller and Marks, 1973). This last feature of special endowment affords mankind the use of tools and symbols which strengthen his responsive abilities and augment his consequential powers. Man not only adapts, but also demonstrates enormous capacity to control and alter his surroundings. Being educable, man can discover; he can seek out and focus on the lessons of events, on rules and principles, on the inter-accommodation of smaller principles to larger ones, and on countless aspects of nature's lawful design. With the capacity to discover and "know" comes potential application or utility—with each tiny effort in the direction of discovery fueling mankind's learning storehouse, the refinement of his approaches to discovery itself, and the delivery of more effective applications. Because of our biological and social endowment, we are increasingly able to perceive the world around us and our own shortcomings, moving on to do something about them.

Most importantly—for our consideration of youth in the human cycle of life—mankind's educability and understanding can be shared and need not begin anew with each problem situation or subsequent generation. Human beings do pass on their biological and cultural heritage—reducing the likelihood that any single generation will have to start from scratch or truly remake the wheel. The life of one human is itself a cycle, but always in a series of greater cycles and experiences transpiring on a much larger time-frame. Generation follows generation, and through successive generations the particular cultural grouping of which any one youthful life is an integral part evolves, grows, prospers, and develops. In this way, human groupings are able to derive enormous, even *exponential advantage from the accumulation of experience across time.* Think of it: one youthful human life—barely a cosmic lightspeck—except that this same youthful life can be viewed at another level as there, in place, stationed, and ready to absorb and add to the generational flow of biogenetic and cultural treasures, the wellspring from which the entire grouping is intended to derive advantage.

Mankind, then, can preeminently profit from his past—from all he has studied, experienced, and applied before—and prosper from the assistance of others now remote from him in time and place. In the West, Euro-American man consciously and selectively slants history and orchestrates a massive technology of computers, media, and transportation devices to locate and apply knowledge treasures from his past or spatially remote present. In the East, by contrast, Afro-Asian man draws upon and shares in a community of ritual, oral, and ancestral ties through which are transmitted the valued collective treasures defining his likely enemies, enduring supports, and all that is of import, thus ensuring continuance of the cultural line. Such is the net gain cultures accumulate from the experiences of others, living and dead. Mankind can learn and teach; he can help and be helped so long as he appreciates that the cycle of one life is biogenetically and socially interwoven with those of many others. While in some ways fragile relative to the agility and strength of larger animals, mankind's special endowment permits this order of appreciation and makes us all potentially powerful and effective.

Under nature's scheme, then, man's special potential permits a special, permanent heritage—one of cumulative experience. Over the long view and snail's pace, geologic history attests to our human capacity to evolve and grow and prosper from the accumulated experiences of simpler species, themselves moving toward greater complexity. Even more strikingly, the last few hundred years have provided us with evidence of quantum leaps in what we have been able to discover about our world by pooling our knowledge and building on the foundations of previous explorers. And whereas it is generally agreed that humanity has changed little genetically in the last 6,000 years, it cannot be denied that even in the last 60 years human beings have developed, stretched and changed their minds and social modes drastically, often with alarming speed and effect. There can be no question: human life is organized for *connection, evolution,* and *cumulative gain.* Let us examine to what ends the Black American has been able to activate this natural potential inherent in our human endowment.

The Concept of Adolescence

Adolescence Among Animals. The animal world acknowledges a youthful, adolescent, juvenile phase in the cycle of life (Devore, 1965; Eaton, 1976; Lorenz, 1967). For animals born immature and helpless it corresponds to a time between early life dependency and full adult stature and privilege. It is always a period of practice, imitation, improvement, and transition. During the juvenile phase, the animal assumes new powers and interests, according to the puberty/mating schedule for its species. The juvenile animal can be seen participating in a number of activities critical for later adult functioning and the survival of its species: (1) reduced close proximity with adults, (2) exploration and mobility in the terrain, (3) food-gathering, (4) peer contact, (5) play-fighting, (6) sex practice and play, (7) grooming, and (8) defensive posturing and maneuvering against a host of perceived threats. The key consideration here, though, rests not so much with the particular juvenile behaviors of any particular animal species as with the integral value and place of "adolescence" in many sectors of the animal world.

Species survival requires an orderly transition from early life dependency. For species survival really depends upon the orderly replenishing of the pool of species adults. It is the adults, by and large, who must ultimately defend and replenish the entire grouping. From biogenetic heritage the juvenile/puberty animal assumes new urges and powers, displays new postures and behaviors, imitates more appropriately, and thereby strengthens its "renunciation" of early life dependency. Still this "adolescent" renunciation is tied to strong social moorings: the juvenile/puberty animal does not assume or misread its new urges and capabilities for license to do as it wishes. The animal world is organized socially in terms of hierarchies of power and status (Devore, 1965; Wilson, 1972). In the wild, at least, the juvenile animal invariably responds to the dominance relations of its grouping and regulates its movements accordingly.

What does this social heritage or organization accomplish or ensure? Put simply: species survival and cumulative gain. The animal world seems to store its accumulated lessons around the right balance of closeness-distance, dependence-autonomy, approach-avoidance, initiative-respect, and play-reality in its dominance orderings. The "adolescent" animal's commerce with choices—to run or fight, practice mounting, stay close to the den or nest, explore but within sight of adults, play and tease vs. actual defending—is phased in with due regard for the overall dominance patterns. In this way the juvenile/puberty animal does not suddenly "break way" from early life into some pattern that is strange, alien, and potentially dangerous for the species. Rather it retains much proximity and contact with species adults throughout the juvenile period. Adults watch its movements and communicate their pleasure or displeasure as required. Exploration and sexual activity are phased in, but never indiscriminately. The juvenile peers practice adult posturing, but respect the real limits prescribed by their ties to a larger community net. The experiences of the species over long time-frames have established the advantage of the dominance hierarchy. Species survival is much too critical to jeopardize—hence the orderly absorption and direction of the animal "adolescent" into the scheme for the larger grouping.

The Afro-Asian View of Adolescence. Like all animals, humans tend to use the youthful, adolescent, puberty period for practice, imitation, improvement, and transition from early life dependency. Of course, for humans, the social heritage and organization—and accompanying social "meanings" of adolescence—are even more critical than for animals. We have seen that instinctively and socially animals respect their communication nets, dominance hierarchies, and connections to the species grouping. Adolescence *per se*—new urges and powers notwithstanding—does not "break" the presence of species community and connection. And there is considerable species advantage to the overall preeminence of community relative to the urgings of any one member, whatever its life cycle phase.

In the Afro-Asian East, community is also preeminent. Community membership (ancesters included) is the foundation for existence (Haley, 1976; Jung, 1958; Kenyatta, 1965). For most of Afro-Asian history, the prevailing theme has been community/connection/continuity. Aloneness was news; true uniqueness was feared; isolation was punishment. Change was orchestrated carefully to preserve the best aspects of tradition and ensure the orderly transmission of accumulated wisdom. The child grew amidst reverence for community and kind: he sang and heard tales of his cultural line; he offered devotions to his ancestors and the unseen realm beyond himself; he coordinated his efforts and accomplishments with others; he shouldered small sex-role tasks; he learned to identify enemies and friends; he felt the security of an extended family and the communal blanket of protection.

In the East, the young adult does not "break" with childhood any more than animal species do. True enough, the Afro-Asian youth must explore and experiment with new urges and roles, negotiate new sexual and public status, consolidate peer bonds, and take steps to settle into a work and family situation of his own. Still the critical consideration in the Eastern view remains the community focus or preeminence. Community legitimately supersedes any personal upheaval or desire that may be experienced by any one member of the larger whole. The community protects its long-term survival by phasing, channeling, and absorbing the adolescent's energy into predictable and productive options. The Afro-Asian adolescent does not "free" himself. He does not break away from the community/connection/continuity of his childhood. Rather his community teaches him that true "freedom" unfolds with the full appreciation of one's inextricable bonds or "constraints" in community.

Community survival and prosperity are too precious to jeopardize. For this reason, Afro-Asian societies tend to organize themselves around powerful rituals, such as puberty initiation rites and experiences, to encourage community—rather than personal—control of the "young adult" urges and aspirations. In this way, the community can honor the need for juvenile encounter with transition, improvement, and self-definition without risking "break-away" assaults on its most cherished ideals or future vitality. The Afro-Asian adolescent is free only to continue the membership, heritage, and cultural line. His connections to the whole provide the courage and clarity he will need to practice and assume adult responsibilities. His ritualistic involvements are not haphazard, destructive, or even voluntary. The options to "grow up" or not to "grow up" are not left to him. Because they emanate from community and involve large segments of the person's familiar world, these ritual involvements further solidify the adolescent's ties to the whole. Greater connection leads to greater security and clarity, especially of self-knowledge and the movements required of all adult members if the community is to stay afloat and well.

In this regard the elevated incidence or prevalence of mental neurosis, psychosis, disturbance, and illness in modern times is historically peculiar to the non-Afro-Asian world. Afro-Asian people have tended to live pretty much in harmony with their surroundings and at peace with themselves and at least their own immediate kind. The sense of community/connection/continuity is a prerequisite for this kind of peace. It takes clarity of membership and courage to establish this peace and hold it. In the East, enormous cumulative advantage—and much emotional well-being—is apparently *stored* in community, connection, and continuities across time. The community simultaneously safeguards and unveils this "truth" to the adolescent in the care and *collective attention* it brings to regulating the entire "young adult" phase. The community demonstrates its unalterable bond to the child and the weight it places on successful "adolescent" transition by simply structuring the key adulthood options in terms of what is best for the whole, not the particular child.

In this way the community protects the *integrity* and *continuity* of its *cumulative experience*. The community also conveys—by its *presumed initiative* in structuring the "adolescent" transition experiences—an important "truth" so often ignored or lost in the West. Children tend to feel strongly what key adults feel strongly. And they will grow to feel most secure when they can distinguish what ideals and behaviors are most important for the key adults in their lives. Such security is particularly evident when the key adults are not only consistent and clear, but actually reorganize their energy to guide the young into the behavior modes and status conditions that support the community ideals. Rather than risk destructive insecurity, the Afro-Asian community disallows youth development as falling under the province of each youth or even each dyadic parenting cell. Instead the community builds on the trust of the child's earlier connections to the whole, holding out collective attention/intervention as the bedrock premise of life. During puberty the community's heavy involvement in ritualistic experience further illuminates and imprints the cherished ideals. The rituals themselves also delineate the critical "next steps" or pathways that reduce ambiguity and uncertainty around the attainment of full membership as adults. Sound youth development hinges on both the presence of cherished ideals and the reality of adult support and supervision of the young. The individual adolescent self must function in concert with the collective selves. The true community says this message best in the structured initiatives of its adults through their supervision and control.

The Euro-American View of Adolescence. In the West, Euro-Americans have fashioned a way of living grounded in key bedrock assumptions largely contrary to Afro-Asian experience. The Western mode or perspective—with awesome applications for mental illness and adolescent stress—teaches us a reality of individual aspiration, material accumulation, technological complexity, frantic upward mobility, and the rhetoric of personal liberty. In the West the nuclear family—now often streamlined to one male, one female, 1.9 children, or even fewer people resources—bears the brunt of the primary child socialization work. As with animals and in the East, the Western child experiences new urges and powers during the adolescent phase: he practices, imitates, explores, experiments, consolidates, learns, and better defines himself as do all children throughout the world.

The major difference, East vs. West, rests not with the physiology and new demands of adolescence, but with the West's conceptualization and cultural response to the "young adult" phase. To the Western frame, largely owing to our psychoanalytic leanings, the juvenile phase is fairly uninterpretable without reference to "storm and stress," upheaval, individual identity-seeking, personal rebellion, adolescent disruption, and other images of the young as foolish, *disturbed,* or *disturbing.* These images are powerful in our culture, drawing substance from countless media works and relations and (mostly urban) realities with troubled youth or youth in trouble. In fact, these images hold true for many young adults in the West. The unsettled question remains whether they hold true inevitably, as if by force of natural law. This writer disagrees and believes that the adolescent stress presumed in the West to be inevitable is really more reflective of our culture's failure to appreciate the power of community. Without benefit of clear ideal and incorporative ritual, we expect the young adult and his family cell to find their own station and way.

In the West, the Euro-American really expects to produce healthy, happy children under the auspices of the nuclear family. This assumption is preposterous: an adult dyad cannot and never will provide sufficient nurturing, communicative, and recuperative powers to meet the full needs of young children.

In the industrialized West, the culture asks the nuclear family to protect and nurture the child. At the same time the imperatives of the technological West undermine the familial and ecological supports so essential for any real child protection and nurturance. Above all, the nuclear family is oriented primarily to the world of industrial work. Its size, aspirations, and loose connections to other people resources represent structural features much more consistent with modern geographical and upward mobility than with rearing healthy children. Moreover, the true emancipative/regulatory function of the family—appropriate "renunciation" of childishness, phasing in age-appropriate responsibility—is rendered nearly impossible by the *way* the nuclear family treats its children and the *duration* of their stay in its care.

Technology provides certain standards of material advantage; it also requires certain orders of expertise and education. In the technological West, the Euro-American feels the presence of the material standards and seeks to provide his children with as much material comfort as his credit and socioeconomic condition will allow. The nuclear family, organized for mobility, provides its children with "things" and "events" and "accelerating" experiences, but relatively little community or connection. We are "child-focused" in "what" and "how much" we give to children, but typically poor architects in building incorporative networks for their wider connection and support. Television and public day care are the West's rejoinder to Eastern community and connection.

Lastly, the nuclear family typically functions in the child-care domain over a very long time-frame. We physically, emotionally, and economically support our children until they are completely educated and established. In the technological West, the education and establishment process can take a very long while (Goethals and Klos, 1970; Goodwin, 1974; Sadock et al., 1976). To compound matters, the West has no clear puberty/initiation involvement or demarcation—all of which can contribute to considerable "storm and stress" around the young adult's self-definition, personal strengths and liabilities, and overall direction. Except for certain provincial pockets, selected rural instances, and among its "old-line" higher strata, the Euro-American nuclear family pattern prevails. Without benefit of community, the Euro-American West has mustered little socio-structural protection against the myriad stormy upheavals peculiar to young adulthood.

Black America

The picture is troubling. Of Afro-Asian heritage, Black Americans still cling to dimly appreciated visions of community/connection/continuity. Still, inevitably, the Western ways and imperatives have taken their toll. In our will to survive, we have been responsive and adaptive, learning the ways of this environment and accumulating advantages within its terms. Naturally, there is a price associated with our stay in the West. And the Black American adolescent feels the weight of this mixed lineage and membership.

Two factors loom large: slavery and technology. Black Americans are descendants of Afro-Asian people brought to the West as slaves. Despite chattel emancipation, considerable vestiges of the old master/slave and slave/slave relations remain intact. The scars are there and the emotional wounds barely healed beneath the surface. To this day, Black people enjoy little real power within the terms of the material and technological West. Sadly, we, the descendents of slaves in the West, function emotionally as one would expect of any "slave": we chew up people and property and "fresh starts" that cannot be replaced. Scheming and dreaming, we mimic the lifestyle of Euro-Americans and spout the rhetoric of individualism and personal comfort. We downplay our Afro-Asian roots and "self-destruct" at a moment's notice or with any trivial discord (Fanon, 1967; Staples, 1975). We eat what Euro-Americans have taught us to like, rather than what will add dimension to our growth. We aspire to the prosperity and mobility of Euro-Americans. Such are the workings of slavery and other conditions of massively brutal disparities in power.

Slavery is key. Still, technology in the West cannot be overlooked for one instant. Technology uproots, changes, replaces the old with the new, converges people and styles, and creates pressures for everything to become more like everything else. Rapid transportation converges old distance barriers. Communications media converge frames of reference, drawing people from distant places into the same ideas, images, and experiences in ways never before possible. The great levelers and homogenizers—media messages and images—enter the lives of rich and poor, white and Black, young and old. More than 99 percent of American households have at least one television set. In Philadelphia, there are more homes with at least one TV set than there are homes with telephones or even indoor toilets! The advance of technology alters the terms of consciousness and living, bringing nations together and reducing differences between the experiences people share (Boorstin, 1972; Goffman, 1967; Toffler, 1970, 1974).

Slavery itself has been brutal and its emotional legacies alien and devastating to Black people. Even so, the crushing momentum and seeming inevitability of technology in the West raise an equally horrible specter. Black Americans run the risk of becoming just as much a part of the Americanization experience as Euro-Americans. After long decades of servitude it is as if the homogenizing pressures within the West will finally force or permit Blacks to embrace the same level of individual aspiration, material accumulation, technological complexity, frantic upward mobility, and the rhetoric of personal freedom as do Euro-Americans. Nothing could be more destructive to our emotional well-being than to become so many "homogenized" Americans.

Black Americans: Empirical Sketches. In the late sixties, I began to study the process of "homogenization" empirically (Gordon, 1974). In Detroit, I spent long hours following, observing, and interviewing young, Black adolescents in their homes, streets, and schools. I probed their feelings about their youthful "status." I watched their movies and listened to their music. I charted the course of their "demands" and "questions" to the world of adults. I noted their perceptions of "enemies" and "supports," of self-definition, courage, and needs for systemic change. I recorded their strategies of engaging and utilizing adults to help to negotiate their interests. Looking back on this research, I will never forget the frightening impact of "homogenization" on the significant adults for these children. Only a select segment of the youth population had developed the right balance of homogenized traits to attract and hold strong Black adult support. The upwardly mobile and gifted children—in terms of honor grades, sports, and school ROTC—marshalled nearly all of the adult supervision and support. The silent majority and vocal young "militants" depressed or frightened most of the Black adults into reactive posturing or plain withdrawal. In the end, it was the young, fresh-out-of-college, white liberals who reorganized their time and energy to lend guidance to the young, Black children. Irony of ironies, the young whites fought hard to resist their own Americanization, openly flouting established convention and at times passing drugs to the Black children in mock defiance of the "System." Sadly, the Black faculty and parents had really "given up" on the apparently "immobile" Black youngsters, turning their energy and cumulative insights to what they considered more promising pursuits, namely, the continued march toward incorporation into the American Dream. America had not been oppressive beyond measure, so long as they could glimpse a more mobile future, a wee bit closer to the driver's seat. A structural retreat had developed: collective Black adult guidance had stepped aside in abdication to make room for explicit encouragement of the fastest young runners in the homogenization race.

In the early seventies, I again focused on the homogenization process and the Black American adult—his beliefs, his aspirations, and supervision approaches with the young (Gordon, 1974). I was particularly interested again in the progressive onslaught of homogenization and penetration of America's ideal images and guiding assumptions in the child-rearing practices of Black people. I decided to concentrate on the American conceptualization of rights and personal liberties inalienable to us all. I chose the domain of children's rights. In Philadelphia there had already been some heated disputes over the child's right to set school dress codes and to seek confidential advice without parental consent. At the same time, the sixties had rekindled in many the American theme of inviolable rights for all citizens under the banner of democratic thought. This prompted a question: How might the culture's ideas and imagery about appropriate rights for children show through in the beliefs and styles of selected Black parents?

A 90 percent Black public housing project in Philadelphia served as a target site for the study of Black adults' views of children's rights. I interviewed 50 project children (mean age: 9 years; range: 8 to 12 years), and 50 project adults (mean age: 32 years; range: 18 to 77 years). The sample was all Black, with 13 adult males and 37 adult females. In addition I followed up the initial interviews with in-depth sessions with 8 members of the original sample pool. In an effort to compare the responses of Black parents and prospective parents, I mailed paper-and-pencil questionnaires to over 200 Black college students to probe their views on the subject of children's rights. The study was conducted during the winter months of 1974—January through March. Prior to

January, I had developed our interview schedule designed to probe the "rights" theme along several dimensions of "self-supervision." The schedules permitted the parents and prospective parents to voice their approval or disapproval of the "child's basic right" to supervise his own (1) body care, (2) daily habits and routine, (3) information search or verbal expression, (4) resolution of conflict, (5) personal privacy, and (6) exposure to media. I asked, Does the child have a basic right to (1) know the reasons parents make the rules they do? (2) be heard when he has opinions to express? (3) privacy for his personal mail? (4) choose the programs he watches on TV? (5) choose the movies he attends? (6) choose the music he hears? (7) help decide the medicine he takes? and (8) decide the schedule for when he sleeps?

Without listing the details of the findings, the overall patterns across parents, prospective parents, and children clearly supported my original suspicions about the penetration and homogenizing influence of American ideals within the domain of Black parenting concerns. Not surprisingly, it has always been extremely difficult to live in America and remain emotionally critical and unassimilated. The study samples displayed sentiments of moderate to high acceptance of the child's right to self-supervision. The democratic ideals of the child's right to know, be heard, enjoy privacy, and have access to adult explanation were accorded high support. Surprisingly, given Black samples, the liberal trend on the approval of the child's right to choose his own mate (irrespective of race) held for all respondents. Not surprisingly, the child's command over potentially dangerous medicines and his free movements outside the "safe" home perimeter were deemed highly inappropriate. The child's self-supervision of food intake and exposure to media ranked moderately high in terms of parental approval. The adults seemed fairly comfortable with the concept of children's basic rights and in real life attempted to be supportive of their children's self-supervisory efforts. In fact, the in-depth sessions and field observations proved that for some areas—food selection and media fare—the parents' basically liberal views gained in the liberal direction when actual parenting behavior was observed. In these instances the young children ate and enjoyed whatever food and media they pleased, largely because these pleasures were available, fun, accessible, the "in-thing" to do, and outside the supervision priorities of the Black adults. Needless to say, youth choice without adult supervision is a poor foundation for development.

These empirical sketches serve to remind us that very few Black

Americans are positioned in this society so as to protect themselves from the massive influences of Western ideals. In a mobile society the people grow closer in outlook as they aspire to upward mobility. In a democratic society the people grow closer in their rhetoric and practice of democratic ideals, even if the attendant homogenization process adds nothing constructive to their overall parenting mission. In America homogenization will isolate and individualize, because these are part of the guiding assumptions of the Western world. The Black nuclear, mobile, selfishly aspiring family cannot match the adolescent/youth storm-and-stress upheavals any more than can their Euro-American counterparts. Youth development flourishes amid community, connection, and continuity.

Black Americans: Social and Training Needs. Over half of the American people today are 28 years of age or younger. Even the oldest of these, now conscious of their membership in the technological West, have few powerful memories before Vietnam, the civil rights movement, Black Power, Watergate, Chappaquiddick, the assassination of the Kennedys, and the disgrace of Richard Nixon. In terms of continuity and integration with cumulative experience, they are truly a young sector. In terms of community and connection, they have emerged from fractured nets of support. What do they need and where might they be headed in the last of the seventies? What can they hope to improve or fulfill within the human endeavor? Of course, young people will define many of their own directions with or without our adult approval. They will head this way and then the other, make political and economic choices with their special flair and intensity, then swing back the other way again. They will retain much of their idealism and zeal for exploration. They will move toward strong peer affiliations and fashion identities from the exchanges and intimacies they share with others. I believe, however, that above all young people need strong adult systems to make it through their "storm." Mankind has always paid homage to the importance of adult support nets in the training of youth. Still, true guidance implies that a society organizes its people resources in ways that do in fact guide. True guidance suggests adult initiative—time, rituals, and supervisory interaction. Nature's design calls for adult commitment in the child-care scheme. It takes sustained adult community, continuity, and connection to raise healthy, productive children.

For Black America the ultimate challenge will be to rebuild the adult networks of support. To care is to guide, to protect and use the age connections, to "hold out" together long enough to pass on the cumulative advantage. This supervisory, transmission process is the business of the "old" in any society in the world. I am optimistic. I feel the adult networks of support can take form again and will flourish as we understand nature's grand design and the force of community, connection, and continuities across time. In the West, slavery shackles our collective potential. Technology converges and homogenizes, diffusing cultural legacy and cumulative gain. Individualism promotes isolation and separate accomplishment. Materialism distracts. Mobility targets our aspirations along extremely narrow paths. We are told our young are "free" today more than ever: the "choices" before them for identity-formation are said to be richly "varied" and "promising." Such is the stuffing of the American Dream. No people can survive who will "give up" their young to the illusionary promise of full homogenization in this scheme.

Reality intrudes. The realities for Black youth are stark in comparison to the prevailing myth structure (Staples, 1975). The "promised" quality schools and jobs are thinly scattered: approximately 65 percent of America's Black teenagers are unemployed and about 50 percent of all Black labor force dropouts are teenage and male. While many young adults are losing jobs or dropping out of the educational area, the crime and gang statistics in the Black community continue to display alarming patterns. Most of the victims of the "slave's" self-destructive orgies and property assaults are other Blacks. The largest number of thefts and crimes against persons have been committed by Black males under 24 years of age. A majority of all homocide victims last year were Black, and the perpetrator of the crime typically was a young Black male aged between 20 and 24 years. The number one cause of death among Black males 15 to 30 years of age is homicide. The cities are nightmare death traps. In Detroit the homicide rate among Black males is so high that the average life expectancy among Black males actually declined nearly 3 years in the last decade. In 1972, Black inmates made up 42 percent of the nation's jail population. Most of them were young, poorly educated, low-wage earners or unemployed prior to arrest. Some 51 percent were under the age of 24. Among those prisoners sentenced to death, 50 percent of them were Black. Within that group of Black death-row prisoners, 35 percent were under 24 years of age compared to only 9 percent of the whites. The years of slavery and the residual scar tissue bring forth their inevitable toll—mostly on our own. Still, the Dream persists.

Within Black America our approach to vice and entertainment is nothing short of insane (Key, 1974). Alcohol, drugs, and nicotine are distributed at will through our own social networks, right on down to youth gangs which in some cities have organized in the elementary grades. These addictive substances not only confuse and conquer, but also serve as poor substitutes for the natural security we miss when there are few strong adult nets and adult-supervised incorporation rites. Our rituals of courtship, marriage, heterosexual access, and sexual transaction gouge and destroy. In some instances they would put most carnivores and predators in the wild to shame (Lopez, 1976).

The "slave," schemer and scavenger, chews up his own kind—male and female alike. In some cities more than half of all Black births are from Black teenagers aged between 15 and 19. Should these young mothers be unable to find work, as is likely, they will pay in dependency on the debilitating doles of welfare. Our family life—once extended within vast networks of support—has become fractured by the twin evils of modernity: poverty *and* affluence. Age gradations/hierarchies hold no special honor. Marriage is going, going . . . gone. It has lost its status as social dogma, while divorce has lost its stigma. We experiment with the "new" forms and promised "pleasures," but most are variations on the same "nuclear" theme—mobility and individual aspiration at the expense of community, continuity, and lasting connection.

We must remember that the animal world draws upon its hierarchies of dominance and status to order its social exchange, regulate its youth endeavors, and promote the survival of the whole. In the Afro-Asian East, the conventional wisdom insists upon the steady intervention of community and reverence for its hierarchy and tradition as the building blocks of sound youth development. Still, in the technological West, Black Americans supervise themselves and their own nuclear kin, leaving the rest to media, disco, streets, and the shifting promises of the Dream.

In many ways it is *painful* to survey the Black experience in the West. We claim no territory; we cannot protect and provide for what is rightfully ours. We own few schools to teach and share our heritage and cumulative gains. We beg and barter in the world of work. Black male, black female: too often we court and conquer, get over, get off, get down, break up, break out, and move on. Our youth rituals depress rather than establish our collective presence. At age 13, we compete by fighting for turf; at 17 we compete by partying, fashion design, and dependency on the feelings of chemically induced euphoria.

We often depend on chemicals, rather than people networks, for feeling wholesome and complete. The pain continues. We rebel against the hurt and aloneness. The pain continues. We smash authority. We rebel for the sake of rebellion. We grow inward, insecure, more afraid to *risk* community, continuity, and connection. It is even painful to say these things, but these are the harsh realities that bear witness to our spiritual and social needs.

We must begin to teach each other and the young the "cumulative insights" and healthy strategies for living to meet our present needs. Reality intrudes. The pain—personal and collective—simply will not subside on its own. The youth of Black America feel this reality and pain. It is a pain so pervasive that it renders personal and collective peace impossible. Not TM, est, the Human Potential Movement, the gurus of Esalen, Hare Krishna, Moonies, *Ms.,* Superfly, disco, cool Fonz, J.J. (Dyno-mite), Ike Hayes, Fred Sanford, Geraldine, Deep Throat, alcohol, Motown, SuperBowl XIII, Charlie's Angels, snuff flicks, child pornography, narcotic substances, nor any other "trinket" of the West can make the pain subside. No "trinket" can transform pain into peace. Such is the endeavor of interdependent living under nature's grand design. Community, continuity, and interdependent connection are the prerequisites for human peace.

It falls to Black adults to rekindle the ties, rebuild the nets, supervise the settings, and order the energy of the young. Our cue comes from the Afro-Asian East. Lasting emotional rejuvenation and collective regeneration—what we are calling real pain "release"— cannot occur without benefit of community, continuity, and connection. Give us the clarity to understand true interdependence in nature's scheme. Give us the courage to work to establish what we clearly see. In this time the youthful ones are feeling their varied *pain* and seeking a lasting version of special *peace.* When the young feel and seek, the old must exemplify and instruct. Community, continuity, and connection represent the only unequivocal response. Community . . . continuity . . . connection: taken together, these reflect the price that life exacts for granting *peace.* The people who know them not know no release.

References

Adams, J. *Understanding Adolescence*. Boston: Allyn and Bacon, 1969.

Bateson, G. *Steps to an Ecology of Mind*. New York: Ballantine, 1973.

Boorstin, D. *The Image: A Guide to Pseudo-Events in America*. New York: Atheneum, 1972.

Brim, O., and Wheeler, S. *Socialization After Childhood: Two Essays*. New York: Wiley, 1966.

Devore, I. (ed.). *Primate Behavior: Field Studies of Monkeys and Apes*. New York: Holt, Rinehart & Winston, 1965.

Eaton, G. "The Social Order of Japanese Macaques." *Scientific American* 235 (1976): 97–106.

Erikson, E. *Childhood and Society*. New York: Norton, 1950.

Evans, E. (ed.). *Adolescents: Readings in Behavior and Development*. Hinsdale. Illinois: Dryden Press, 1970.

Fanon, Franz. *The Wretched of the Earth*. New York: Grove Press, 1967.

Fuller, R., and Marks, R. *The Dymaxion World of Buckminster Fuller*. Garden City, New York: Anchor, 1973.

Goethals, G., and Klos, D. *Experiencing Youth: First-Person Accounts*. Boston: Little, Brown, 1970.

Goffman, E. *Interaction Ritual*. Garden City, New York: Anchor, 1967.

Goodwin, R. *The American Condition*. Garden City, New York: Doubleday, 1974.

Gordon, T. "Communication and Political Order: Child Management Implications." Unpublished manuscript, University of Pennsylvania, Philadelphia, 1974.

Grinder, R. (ed.). *Studies in Adolescence*. New York: Macmillan, 1963.

Haley, A. *Roots*. Garden City, New York: Doubleday, 1976.

Jung, C. *Psyche and Symbol*. Garden City, New York: Doubleday, 1976.

Kenyatta, J. *Facing Mt. Kenya*. New York: Vintage, 1965.

Key, W. *Subliminal Seduction*. New York: Signet, 1974.

Lopez, B. "Wolf Kill." *Harper's* (August 1976): 25–27.

Lorenz, K. *On Aggression*. New York: Bantam Books, 1967.

Rosenfeld, A. "Star of Stars." *Saturday Review* (October 30, 1976): 13–15.

Sadock, B.; Kaplan, H.; and Freedman, A. *The Sexual Experience*. Baltimore: Williams & Wilkins, 1976.

Staples, R. "To Be Young, Black, and Oppressed." *Black Scholar* 7 (1975): 2–9.

Toffler, A. *Future Shock*. New York: Bantam Books, 1970.

_____ (ed.). *Learning for Tomorrow: The Role of the Future in Education.* New York: Vintage, 1974.

Wilson, E. "Animal Communication." *Scientific American* 227 (1972): 52–60.

Winter, G., and Nuss, E. (eds.). *The Young Adult.* Glenview, Illinois: Scott, Foresman, 1969.

7 THE BLACK ADULT AND THE WORLD OF WORK

David L. Ford, Jr., Ph.D.

Introduction

One of the most pressing issues with which America is faced today is that of the industrial work culture and its effects on the attitudes toward work of those persons employed in business firms. Concern with this issue has resulted in a number of research studies in such areas as satisfactions and/or need deficiencies of managerial and blue-collar employees (Schwab and Cummings, 1970), union-management relations (Miller, 1966), work group processes (Likert, 1961, 1967), and superior-subordinate relationships (Bowers and Seashore, 1966) to name but a few. The topic of job satisfaction has received a good deal of attention in the scientific literature, owing largely to the concern of behavioral scientists and administrators for the "quality of work life," which job satisfaction is assumed to reflect. However, recent studies have not only focused on job satisfaction *per se,* but also on the broader issues of workers' attitudes in general and their reactions and affective responses to job characteristics and the work environment in particular. The importance of work attitudes can be seen by noting that negative work attitudes of a work force may result in high absenteeism, high turnover, and other dysfunctional forms of behavior, such as low performance, sabotage, and tardiness.

This chapter will explore the world of work of the adult and examine those factors related to work which have been found to contribute to positive and negative attitudes and outcomes on the part of the workers in general. However, a particular focus of this paper will be upon the Black worker in a predominantly white work environment and how this affects his or her job attitudes and performance. We will also examine certain factors which might be inherent in the Black worker which also contribute to certain work outcomes, depending upon the nature of the work situation. Finally, the implications of our analysis for the future behavior of Black workers in organizational settings are discussed.

From a definitional point of view, our discussion in this chapter will be focused on those persons 18 years of age and older who are employed at least on a part-time basis in business organizations or in the public sector. The majority of our discussion will center on persons employed at both the operative and managerial levels in organizations and will not consider those persons who may only work occasionally or who are too young to understand and appreciate the complexities of work life.

Formal Organizations

Formal organizations are created to carry out tasks that are either impractical or impossible for individuals to accomplish by themselves. In accomplishing these tasks the organization's management is guided by desired outcomes on the one hand and cause/effect relationship on the other (Thompson, 1967). Formal organizations, by definition, are those which are deliberately established and goal-seeking (Bobbitt, Brienholt, Doktor, and McNaul, 1974). For example, business concerns are created to make profits for their owners.

The variables necessary to achieve desired outcomes for the organization are generally identified through management's knowledge of cause/effect relationships. For example, if a supervisor *believes* that there is a relationship between a worker's output (desired effect) and the amount of money a worker receives (cause), he will use money as a means of increasing worker output. However, management's knowledge of cause/effect relationships regarding organizational variables is far from complete.

The concepts of organizational effectiveness and efficiency are important considerations for the organization if it is to maintain its existence. Effectiveness is achieved when the organization achieves its desired outcome. Efficiency, on the other hand, is not so simply defined. Generally, it is taken to mean how well resources are being used to produce output and is often expressed as a ratio of work input to work output. However, organizations are not simply machines, and the mechanical definition of efficiency applies only in certain limited cases.

More appropriately, if organizations are viewed as cooperative systems, we need to view efficiency as the organization's ability to offer inducements to organizational participants which are just sufficient to elicit their contributions, which, in turn, are used by the organization to generate inducements (March and Simon, 1958). Therefore, the way an individual perceives the relationship of organizational inducements to his individual contributions (I/C ratio) may have important consequences for how motivated he is in terms of participating in the organization's goal-directed activities (Bobbitt, et al., 1974). Ideally, for the individual, his I/C ratio should be greater than or equal to 1. From the organization's point of view, the most desirable I/C ratio is 1 or less. The greater it is above 1, the less efficient we can expect the organization to be, other things being equal.

Functional and Dysfunctional Aspects of Organizations. If organizational actions were deterministic, i.e., if the outcomes or consequences of organizational processes were completely predictable, given the structure and objectives of the organization, the problem of organizational design would be very simple in principle. It would be limited to selecting the structure that promised to lead most efficiently to the organization's objectives.

Traditional theories of organization have generally treated organizations as deterministic. Consequently, the problem of structure has been their major focus. The outcomes of organizational *processes,* however, are not deterministic and thus not always predictable. *Unanticipated* consequences of organizational action occur in every organization. Whether anticipated or unanticipated, these consequences may be functional or dysfunctional with respect to the goals and objectives of the organization. Consequences are said to be *functional* when they contribute to the efficient attainment of organizational objectives. On the other hand, if a consequence interferes with the attainment of the objectives, it is said to be *dysfunctional.* Very often it is observed that individuals have personal goals that are different from—even in conflict with—the organization's goals. It is possible, therefore, for an organizational activity to result in consequences that are dysfunctional for certain members' goal achievement but functional for recognized organizational objectives. Of course, the opposite could also happen.

We mentioned in the introduction several examples of dysfunctional consequences embodied in worker behaviors when organizational processes do not lead to individual goal achievement, namely, negative work attitudes (i.e., dissatisfaction, absenteeism, turnover, and low performance). A greater understanding of the antecedents and causes of such behaviors and consequences can be gained by examining the nature of the organizational climate relative to the world of work. This is done in the sections which follow.

The World of Work

Organizational Climate. Organizational climate refers to a set of attributes which can be perceived about a particular organization and/or its subsystems and that may be induced from the way that organization and/or its subsystems deal with its members and its environment (Hellriegel and Slocum, 1974).

Organizational climate also embraces the enduring qualities of an organization's internal environment that distinguish it from other organizations which (1) result from the behavior and policies of members of the organization, especially top management; (2) are perceived by members of the organization; (3) serve as a basis for interpreting the situation; and (4) act as a source of pressures for directing activity (Pritchard and Karasick, 1973). The reader should note that organizational climate as used here refers to *practices* in the organization, not feelings of the individual members or some general emotional or attitudinal "tone" which might exist within a group or throughout the organization. Measures of organizational climate most commonly used include the following (Bowers, Franklin, and Percorella, 1973):

1. *Human resources primacy:* the extent to which the most important resources and assets of the organization are seen to be the members, their talents, knowledge, skills, and commitment.

2. *Communication flow:* the extent to which information flows freely, quickly, and accurately in all directions (upward, downward, and laterally) through the organization.

3. *Decision-making:* the extent to which decisions are made at those levels in the organization where the most adequate and accurate information exists, are based on all available know-how, and are made by participative processes.

4. *Motivational conditions:* the extent to which conditions (people, policies, and procedures) in the organization encourage or discourage effective work.

5. *Lower-level influence:* the extent to which non-supervisory personnel and first-line supervisors have some way or influence over matters affecting their organizational lives.

To a large extent, the role expectations that organizational members hold are determined by the broader organizational context. Factors included in the organizational context that influence role expectations and pressures experienced by any particular organizational member are organizational structures, size, number of status levels, products produced, formal reward system, and functional specialization and division of labor, to name a few. These factors are the organizational antecedents of roles (Kahn, et al., 1964). Personality factors of the individual also influence role episodes between role senders and focal persons. Additionally, the variables identified by Bowers and co-workers (1973) as measures of organizational climate probably should be included in those organizational factors that are assumed to influence roles. We prefer to take this broader view of organizational antecedents of roles since, as we noted in the definition of organizational climate above, climate refers to the relatively enduring qualities of an organization's internal environment which act as a source of *pressures* for directing activity.

Role Perceptions and Organizational Stress. The literature on role theory suggests two constructs describing role perceptions: role conflict and role ambiguity. Role ambiguity describes a situation in which there is inadequate role sending, that is, when lack of agreement among role senders produces sent expectations that contain logical incompatibilities or that take inadequate account of the abilities and needs of the focal person (Schuler, 1975). This is essentially a situation in which information is lacking or not communicated in the role episode. Role conflict is a simultaneous occurrence of two or more sets of pressures such that compliance with one would make compliance with the other more difficult (Kahn, et al., 1964). Role theory hypothesizes both role conflict and role ambiguity to be negatively related to job performance and job satisfaction.

Perhaps one of the best descriptions of the concepts of role conflict and role ambiguity is given by Kahn and his co-workers (1964) in their book *Organizational Stress*. Role conflict and role ambiguity are seen as two forms of stress which affect an individual's existence in an organization. As the authors note, one of the dominant trends of our time is the increasing importance of large-scale organizations in shaping individual and social life. One of the great inherent needs of any organization is dependability of role performance on the part of its individual members. With a high degree of dependability is associated a tremendous influence of the organization over member behavior.

The first step in linking the individual and organization is to identify the individual in the total set of ongoing relationships and behaviors comprised by the organization. The key concept for doing this is *office*, by which is meant a unique point in the structure of interrelated offices and the pattern of activities associated with them (i.e., organizational space). The set of activities associated with each office constitutes the *role* to be performed by the person occupying that office.

A person's *role set* consists of those offices in the organization which are directly related to him by virtue of the work-flow, technology, and authority structure of the organization. Also included in a person's role set may be people who are related to him in other ways, e.g., persons within or outside the organization who are concerned with his behavior in his organizational role (friends, relatives, "significant others," etc.). The members of a person's role set depend upon his performance in some fashion, and they develop attitudes and beliefs about what he should and should not do as part of his role. The prescriptions held by members of a role set are designated as *role expectations*. When these expectations are communicated, they become the *sent role*, and the members of the role set are designated as *role-senders*.

The acts which are engaged in in the process of role sending are actually attempts directed toward the focal person and designed to bring about conformity, on the part of the focal person, with the expectations of the senders. Thus such acts become *role pressures*, the requirements and demands that are actually communicated to the focal person. The *received role*, as opposed to the sent role, consists of the focal person's perceptions and cognitions of what was sent and may or may not correspond to the sent role. The degree of correspondence depends on the properties of senders, receivers, substantive content of the sent pressures, etc. (Kahn, et al., 1964).

While the sent role is the medium through which the organization communicates to the person the "shoulds" and "shouldn'ts" associated with his office, it is the received role which has the immediate influence on the focal person's behavior and is the immediate source of his motivation to role performance. Role behavior, therefore, is the behavior which results through the focal person's responses to role pressures as conditioned by his received role. Role behavior, however, is defined as behavior which is systemically or organizationally relevant, and the focal person performing the behavior is a member of the system and accepted by other members of the system.

As noted above, *role conflict* results from different members of the role set holding quite different role expectations toward the focal person. At any given time they may impose pressures on him toward different kinds of behavior. To the extent that these roles pressures give rise to role forces within him (i.e., psychological forces of some magnitude and direction), the focal person will experience psychological conflict.

There are several forms which the role conflict may take. *Sent role conflict* is defined as the simultaneous occurrence of two or more sets of pressures such that compliance with one precludes or makes difficult the compliance with the other. This is analogous to *intersender conflict* in which pressures from one role sender oppose pressures from one or more other senders, for example, a foreman caught between the vice-like pressures for close supervision as dictated by his superiors and looser supervision as demanded from his subordinates (Kahn, et al., 1964). Another type of role conflict is *intrasender conflict* in which different prescriptions and proscriptions are sent from a single member of the role set to the focal person that are oftentimes incompatible.

A third type of role conflict is *person-role conflict,* which occurs when the needs and values of a person and the demands of his role set are in conflict. A fourth type of role conflict is *interrole conflict* in which the role pressures associated with membership in one organization are in conflict with pressures arising from membership in other groups. The one common, major characteristic of all four of these forms of role conflict is that members of a role set exert role pressures to change the behavior of a focal person. These pressures may be so great and varying in number at times that the resulting conflict is that of *role overload.*

To summarize, the origins and consequences of role conflict can be depicted as shown in Figure 1. This role episode consists of contradictory role expectations (box I) giving rise to opposing role pressures, or role conflicts (box II). These opposing role pressures induce in the focal

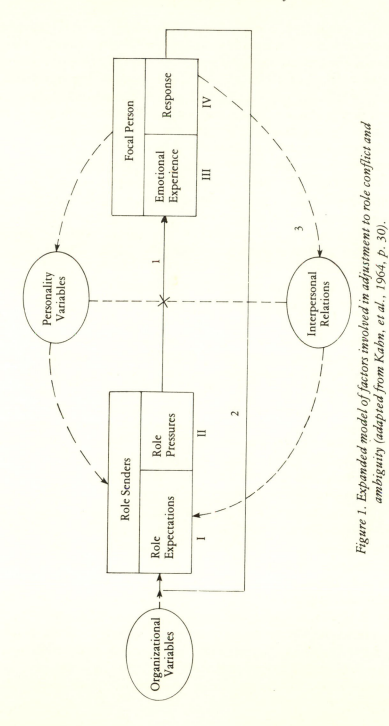

Figure 1. Expanded model of factors involved in adjustment to role conflict and ambiguity (adapted from Kahn, et al., 1964, p. 30).

person an experience which has both perceptual and cognitive properties generally resulting in the following effects on the emotional experience (box III) of the focal person: intensified internal conflicts, increased tension associated with various aspects of the job, reduced satisfaction with the job and various aspects of it, and decreased confidence in supervisory personnel and upper management as well as a decrease in the confidence in the organization as a whole (arrow 1).

The strain experienced by the focal person leads to certain adjustive (or maladjustive) coping responses, e.g., social and psychological withdrawal evidenced by a reduction in communication (box IV). The responses of the focal person are observed by those exerting the pressures, and their expectations are correspondingly adjusted (arrow 2). Finally, when conflict is present in one's role, this tends to undermine his relations with his role senders and weaken the bonds of trust, respect, and attraction (Kahn, et al., 1964) (arrow 3). Data to support these consequences were reported by Kahn and co-workers (1964) and are based on an intensive study of role conflict and ambiguity. They suggest that role conflicts are costly for the organization as a whole, in terms of a decrease in the effectiveness of coordination and collaboration within and among its parts, and also costly for the focal person in emotional and interpersonal terms.

Although we have dealt at length with role conflict, the other kind of organizational stress—role ambiguity—is certainly a large and real component of the psychological stress experienced by organizational members. Role ambiguity is conceived of as the degree to which certain required information is available or unavailable to a given organizational position. The ambiguity of a given position may result from the fact that required information which is needed by the focal person for adequate role performance, i.e., in order to conform to the role expectations held by members of his role set, is not available anywhere in the organization. Or the information may be available at some point in the organization but not in the role set of the focal person. In a number of instances the required information is available in the role set but is not communicated to the focal person, for example, as when subordinates withhold information from an untrusted superior. If the communication processes between a pair of persons are unclear, if any message is garbled or fragmentary, or if several role senders communicate contradictory messages regarding the same event, the result will often be uncertainty and confusion. This latter form of ambiguity links the concept closely to that of role conflict (Kahn, et al., 1964).

To summarize, a focal person must have certain information for adequate role performance. He must know what is expected of him: the rights, duties, and responsibilities of his office, as well as certain means-end knowledge. In addition, he needs to know what kinds of behavior will be rewarded or punished, the nature of the rewards and punishments, and the likelihood of their occurrence, information about opportunities for advancement, about respect and acceptance by others, etc. To the extent that this information is lacking and/or not communicated to the focal person, role ambiguity is certainly very likely to occur. Again, as with role conflict, role ambiguity is costly to both the individual and the organization.

Other organizational processes and conditions related to organizational functioning which have an impact on the degree of role conflict and ambiguity experienced by persons in organizations include supervisory and peer leadership practices, group processes, work group effectiveness, goal integration, cooperation/competition, reward systems, and conflict resolution processes, to name but a few. These organizational processes and conditions have been shown to be important factors related to the effectiveness of organizational functioning (Likert, Bowers, and Norman, 1969; Bowers, 1973; Bowers, Franklin, and Percorella, 1973). Therefore, we assume that these factors, along with those components of organizational climate noted above, are included in the organizational factors which serve as organizational antecedents of roles, as diagrammed in Figure 1.

The relationships between employee role conflict and role ambiguity and job satisfaction, propensity to leave the organization, and perceived threat and anxiety are well documented (House and Rizzo, 1972; Rizzo, House, and Lirtzman, 1970; Greene and Organ, 1973; Tosi, 1971). However, results from recent studies suggest that role conflict and role ambiguity are not always negatively related to job satisfaction. Tosi (1971) found that role conflict and job satisfaction were negatively related but found no relationship between role ambiguity and job satisfaction. Hamner and Tosi (1974), House and Rizzo (1972) and Rizzo and co-workers (1970) found significant negative relationships between role ambiguity and job satisfaction but no relationships between role conflict and job satisfaction.

These inconsistent results between role conflict and job satisfaction and between role ambiguity and job satisfaction have been reconciled by Hamner and Tosi (1974), who suggest that the inconsistencies are based on the employee's level in the organization. They indicated that the nature of positions at higher levels of an organization is primarily one of solving unstructured problems and tasks, thereby making role ambiguity a more crucial source of stress and dissatisfaction than role conflict. Additionally, role ambiguity is more stressful than role conflict at the higher organizational levels because employees at these levels retain the power and discretion to obtain additional resources, make organizational structure changes or divisions of responsibility, change the rules and procedures, or generally reduce the sources of role conflict if they so desire (Kahn, et al., 1964). Therefore, the presence of role conflict should be of less concern to higher-level employees than should role ambiguity because they have less influence over the sources of the latter.

Positions at lower levels of the organization have low levels of discretion, autonomy, and variety and are well understood by the incumbents, thereby making the need for reducing role ambiguity less important than the need for reducing role conflict (Hamner and Tosi, 1974). Kahn and co-workers (1964) suggested that in lower-level positions role conflict is more stressful and dissatisfying because the employee is more dependent on the supervisor and has little power to influence him. The employee's inability to cope adequately with role conflict when he is highly dependent on his supervisor should thus lead to dissatisfaction with the job.

Based on these rationales developed by Hamner and Tosi (1974) and by Kahn and co-workers (1964), Schuler (1975) conducted a study in which role ambiguity was hypothesized to have a greater negative relationship than role conflict with job satisfaction and performance for employees at higher levels in an organization. In addition it was hypothesized that role conflict would have a greater negative relationship than role ambiguity with job satisfaction and performance for employees at lower levels in an organization. Schuler's results supported the hypothesized relationships with job satisfaction but not with performance. In fact, the results of previous research indicate that the reported relationships between performance and role perceptions are inconsistent. Green and Organ (1973) have reported significant negative relationships between role ambiguity and role conflict and job performance ratings. In addition, House and Rizzo (1972) reported negative relationships between role conflict and role ambiguity and performance; however, Tosi (1971) found no relationships between those role perceptions and performance.

Hall's (1972) study of role conflict coping behavior is of particular interest here because it is concerned with the development of a theoretical model of coping behavior. In particular, Hall's study focused on the types of conflicts faced by married women as the result of multiple-role performance, the strategies used for coping with these conflicts, and the varying degrees of satisfaction to be gained from different strategies. Although the study focused on multiple roles of college-educated women in the work force, the results of the study are also applicable to married males today, in light of the changing values and norms surrounding the "appropriate" roles for wives and husbands.

A generalization of the hypothetical model of multiple roles and identity components presented by Hall (1972) is shown in Figure 2. Identity is denoted as a person's perception of himself as he relates to

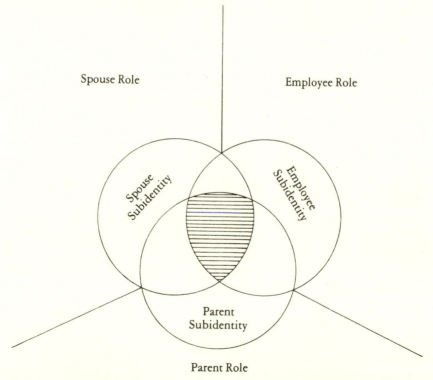

Figure 2. Hypothetical model of multiple roles of a married individual (after Hall, 1972, p. 472).

his environment, and the term subidentity refers to that aspect of the total identity engaged when a person is behaving in a given role (Hall, 1972). The model shown in Figure 2 suggests how each subidentity might compete for its share of a person's total identity if the amount of overlap between the subidentities were small. Hall noted that the numerous subidentities of women often present a clear example of chronic role conflict. The major problem a woman faces is the conflict arising from multiple roles (interrole conflict), rather than from conflicting expectations within a particular role (intrarole conflict). However, Kahn (1969) has reported results which suggest that the latent problems of multiple roles emerge for men as well, especially if they have to enact them simultaneously.

Hall suggests three types or levels of coping behavior corresponding to the three levels of role process described by Levinson (1959): structurally imposed demands, personal role conception, and role behavior. The first type of coping (Type I), termed structural role redefinition, is a strategy by which the person attempts to alter external, structurally imposed expectations held by others regarding the appropriate behavior of a person in his or her position. The critical feature of this approach is that it involves dealing directly with environmental transmitters of the structurally imposed demands, actively attempting to alter (reallocate, reduce, reschedule) these demands and coming to an agreement with the role senders on a new set of expectations (Hall, 1972). The second type of coping (Type II) involves changing one's personal concept of role demands received from others, i.e., personal role redifinition, as opposed to trying to change the environment. Actual behavior or the objective expectations of others may not change, but seeing one's own behavior or the external expectations in a new light may lead one to attempt to reduce the amount of conflict actually experienced (Hall, 1972). The third type of coping (Type III) is reactive role behavior, which entails attempting to improve the quality of role performance so that one can better satisfy all of the demands of one's role senders. Implicit in this latter type of coping behavior is the assumption that one's role demands are fixed and unchangeable and that the person's main task is to find ways to meet them. This thus involves a passive or reactive orientation to one's roles (Hall, 1972).

Hall identified sixteen strategies for coping with role conflicts which are distributed across the three categories of coping behavior. These are presented in Table 1. Hall's results suggested that Type-I and Type-II strategies for coping with role conflict are positively related to the

Table 1. Coping Strategies for Role Conflicts*

Type of Coping	Coping Strategy
I. Structural Role Redefinition	A. Eliminate (or add) particular activities within roles. Do not give up or add entire role, only certain components of it.
	B. Role support from outside role set. Employing outside help to assume certain role activities.
	C. Role support from member of role set. Receiving help from role senders (usually in family) in performing activities necessary to meet role demands.
	D. Problem solving with role senders. Collaborative redefinition of roles. Moral support from, or problem solving with, role senders in deciding how to resolve role conflicts.
	E. Integrate roles. Increase overlap among roles in a way that each contributes to the other.
	F. Change societal definition of person's roles. Changing general social expectations as opposed to the expectations of specific role senders.
II. Personal Role Redefinition	A. Establish priorities for roles or within roles. Rank activities in order of importance.
	B. Partition and separate roles. Devote full attention to a given role when in that role. Attempt to minimize simultaneous overlap of roles.
	C. Overlook role demands or reduce standards. Choose not to meet certain role demands.
	D. Change attitudes toward roles or develop a new attitude which helps reduce conflicts.
	E. Eliminate roles. Withdraw from entire role area.
	F. Rotate attention from one role to another. Handle each role in turn as it comes up.
	G. Develop self-interests. See personal interests as valid source of role demands.
III. Reactive Role Behavior	A. Plan, schedule, organize better. Increase efficiency of role performance.
	B. No conscious strategy. No attempt to control role demands or own responses. Passive orientation toward role conflicts.
	C. Working harder to meet all role demands. Do all that is expected. Work harder, devote more time and energy inputs to role performance.

*Adapted from Hall (1972), pp. 478–479.

satisfaction of married women with their roles; Type-III strategies were
negatively related to satisfaction. The reasons for the latter finding were
related to the fact that Type-III behaviors are *defensive* rather than
coping behaviors. In a similar vein, Anderson (1976) has shown that the
use of what he calls Class-I coping or problem-solving mechanisms
(similar to Hall's Type-I) is related to high job performance, while the
use of Class-II or emotional-defensive coping mechanisms (similar to
Hall's Type-III) seems to inhibit performance at high levels of stress.

This section has included a discussion of role perceptions and
organizational stress. A model for coping with role conflict was also
discussed. The thrust of the discussion has been directed toward the
responses of the individual to the stresses imposed by the external
(organizational) environment. We now turn our attention to a consideration of some factors *within* the individual which may have
dysfunctional consequences in terms of job-related stress.

***Personality Variables, Individual Differences and Reactions to Job
Characteristics.*** Recall from Figure 1 that personality variables affect role
episodes. Several researchers have examined the effects of certain individual difference variables as moderators of the relationships between
role conflict, role ambiguity, and job satisfaction (Johnson and Stinson,
1975); job performance and job satisfaction (Steers); and task
characteristics and job satisfaction (Wanous, 1974). Johnson and
Stinson (1975) demonstrated that need for achievement (n-Ach)
moderated the relationships between intersender role conflict and satisfaction and between task ambiguity and satisfaction, while need for
independence moderated the relationship between intersender conflict
and satisfaction. In their study Johnson and Stinson found that the
relationship between intersender conflict and satisfaction is more
negative for subjects with a high need for achievement and subjects
with a high need for independence than for subjects low in these
characteristics. These results also indicated that the relationship between task ambiguity is more negative for subjects with a high need for
achievement than for those with a low need for achievement.

Steers (1975) investigated the effect of n-Ach on the job performance–job attitude (satisfaction) relationship among a sample of
first-level supervisors. It was hypothesized that a positive relationship
would be found between job attitudes and performance for high n-Ach
subjects and that no such relation would be found for low n-Ach
subjects. The hypothesis was supported by the data.

Wanous (1974) found that higher-order need strength is the best of three individual difference variables in moderating the relationships between job characteristics and specific job facet satisfaction and overall job satisfaction. The Protestant work ethic and urban/rural distinction were less effective as moderator variables.

Several recent studies have examined the effects of organizational stress from the standpoint of specific personality variables of the workers. That is, given a particular set of job demands (role expectations) and a particular personality type, how do the two combine to determine the human ability to cope with job stress? This question was the focus of a recent study by Caplan and Jones (1975) which examined the role of Type-A personality in the relationship between work stress and psychological and physiological strains. The study capitalized on the impending 23-day shutdown of a large computer facility at a university. Because the shutdown occurred at a time during which the usage was to be at peak load (end of academic term), this provided a situation for studying the effects of high work load. It was expected that many users might experience a great deal of ambiguity in deciding how to complete their work most efficiently in the time remaining prior to shutdown.

Caplan and Jones distinguished between objective and subjective forms of stress, where the former is measured independently of a person's environmental perceptions; the latter form of stress relies on self-reporting. Kraut (1965) had demonstrated that subjectively measured role conflict, compared to objectively measured conflict, was a better predictor of job-related tension. Similarly, French and Caplan (1972), in a study of the relationship between quantitative work load and cardiovascular response, found that subjective ratings of work load, compared to objective tallies by observers of each person's phone calls, office visits, and meetings, etc., were better predictors of heart rate. Generally, it was how the person viewed the work, rather than its objective amount, that mattered the most. Therefore, subjective quantitative work load and role ambiguity were chosen for study by Caplan and Jones because both appeared to be salient features of the computer shutdown.

Additionally, based on the results of previous laboratory research (Sales, 1969, 1970) and cross-sectional research (Caplan, 1971) which suggest that personality interacts with job stresses to determine the well-being of employees, as well as results which have found the predictive association of Type-A personality with coronary heart disease (Roseman, Friedman, Straus, Jenkins, Zyzanski, and Wurm, 1970), Caplan and Jones believed that Type-A persons should be the most strongly strained by the effects of a job stress such as an impending computer shutdown because they are more involved in their work and more persistent than persons without Type-A traits (Type B). That is, the Type-A personality is hard-driving, persistent, involved in his work, has a sense of time urgency, and is oriented toward leadership and achievement; Type-B personality characteristics are considered to be the opposite (Caplan and Jones, 1975).

Measures of stress (subjective quantitative work load and role ambiguity), personality, and psychological strain (anxiety, depression, resentment) were assessed by questionnaires during the last 3 days preceding the announced computer shutdown (Time 1) and 5 months later (Time 2). In addition, a 30-second reading of heart rate was taken of each respondent at the time of completion of the questionnaires in both instances. The relationships between changes in stress and changes in strain from Time 1 to Time 2 were examined by Caplan and Jones. The respondents served as their own controls.

The results indicated that there were clear changes in strain from Time 1 to Time 2, such that anxiety, depression, and resentment were significantly lower at Time 2 than at Time 1. Heart rate was also significantly lower at Time 2 than at Time 1. Subjective quantitative work load tended to be the highest at the time of the shutdown. The changes in subjective quantitative work load from Time 1 to Time 2 were positively correlated with changes in anxiety-tension. In turn, changes in anxiety-tension were positively associated with changes in heart rate and in general anxiety covaried with stress to a greater degree than did either resentment or depression. Changes in role ambiguity were positively correlated with changes in anxiety. The more interesting results included the fact that there was a tendency for the relationship between changes in anxiety and heart rate to be higher for the Type-A than for the Type-B persons. The relationship between changes in subjective work load and changes in anxiety was higher for the Type-A persons than for Type-B persons as well. The authors concluded that stress does indeed have its greatest effects on strain in the hard-driving, involved Type-A person (Caplan and Jones, 1975).

We have purposely reviewed the study by Caplan and Jones because it is one of the more recent studies to examine systematically several issues related to the mental health of organizational inhabitants. Their findings were consistent with earlier published data by Gurin, Veroff, and Feld (1960) in the national survey study, *Americans View Their Mental Health*. In reviewing the findings of Gurin and his co-workers, Caplan and Jones noted that job involvement, which is characteristic of the Type-A personality, is both a blessing and a curse. According to Caplan and Jones, Gurin, Veroff, and Feld found that the higher the status of people's occupations, the more involved they were in their work. While these highly involved persons presumably obtained greater emotional and intrinsic rewards from their successes, they also paid a greater psychological price when they faced prospects of failure in their work roles (Caplan and Jones, 1975).

From a practical point of view, employees with Type-A traits should be of great value to organizations interested in productivity and achievement. The findings of Caplan and Jones, as well as the research of others cited, suggest that employees having Type-A personality traits may contribute to their organizations, *but at some cost to their own mental and physical health*. This is an important point for this chapter as well as this entire volume on mental health. While the organization in which a person works can contribute dysfunctionally to an individual's mental health, so too can the individual, particularly if he or she possesses the kinds of traits and characteristics most often sought by organizations, i.e., achievement-oriented, highly motivated, and hard-working.

In the same vein as the Caplan and Jones (1975) study, Rogers (1975) and Ogilvie and Porter (1975) have discussed the need to give increased attention to stress-induced coronary heart disease and its increasing toll in the lives of American men in the middle-age group. Their discussions suggest an interaction of organizational and Type-A personality factors which contributes to this state of affairs, particularly among American executives. In particular, Ogilvie and Porter note, in their discussion of the "paradox of achievement," that people equate the only valid form of self-acceptance with achievement, yet while they may obtain a certain level of achievement, their self-acceptance does not change. That is, the usual symbols of personal success for the executive (e.g., key to the executive washroom, parking privileges, private secretary, expense accounts, and remunerative rewards) do not really contribute to genuine feelings of accomplishment or human worth, i.e., self-acceptance. Ogilvie and Porter suggest that the executive caught up on the "treadmill to oblivion" should undertake an objective self-evaluation and self-critique and actually confront the truth as to the relationship between achievement and the human needs that are met by such achievement. In particular they suggest that the executive or manager ask himself the following question (Ogilvie and Porter, 1975, p. 18):

> Can your executive or managerial role contribute positively to any of the following?
> 1. Your sense of being a meaningful and valued human being.
> 2. Your sense of being a loved and loving person.
> 3. Reassurance that you are sexually successful.
> 4. Proof that you are a good, a successful husband or wife.
> 5. Reassurance that you are more acceptable son or daughter.
> 6. Proof that your existence has contributed in some positive way to the existence of your fellow man.

Perhaps it would be well for the person with Type-A personality traits to take the above self-examination. While persons in organizations may be able to do very little about the organizational factors that contribute to stress, it certainly is within their power and control to modify their own predispositions and behaviors such that individually contributed factors of stress are reduced—in other words, a move toward Type-B behavior, free of pressing conflicts with time or other persons and generally without a chronic sense of time urgency.

Organizational Stress and Black Professionals. While some conflicting results concerning worker responses to job situations among blue-collar Blacks have been obtained in recent research studies, the general indication is that they are generally less satisfied overall than whites with their work situation. However, with regard to specific facets of their jobs, blue-collar Blacks have been shown to be more satisfied than whites in some instances. The generality of the former finding is more pronounced for white-collar and professional Blacks relative to whites. The discussion below will focus primarily upon professional Blacks in organizations and their responses to organizational environments. The discussion is not intended to be detailed. The interested reader is referred to Ford (1976), which contains a number of studies concerning worker response of blue-collar and white-collar Blacks to their work environments, in comparison to whites.

Several recent articles have been concerned with the plight of Black professionals in organizations and have pointed up wide disparities between the career success and work experiences of Black professionals and those of their white counterparts. Fields and Freeman (1972), for example, noted that as late as 1972, there were still certain inequities that Black professionals faced in terms of access to "equal opportunity" in industry, education, and government. They noted that Blacks usually find themselves at the low end of the totem pole relative to career growth when compared with their white counterparts. They also noted (p. 84):

> Three major factors contribute to slow upward mobility for black professionals as compared with white professionals: (1) blacks enter jobs at lower salaries than whites; (2) promotion is slower for blacks; (3) as a group, black professionals eventually plateau in the corporate hierarchy.

Bramwell (1973) concurs with the conclusions of the Fields and Freeman study that business corporations have not convinced their Black professionals that equal opportunity exists by noting that "black professionals . . . have all the vaunted ingredients of success. They should be more successful than their equivalent white partners. But such is not the way of the world. The fact is that the black rarely reaches his goal of 'success' " (Bramwell, 1973, p. 24).

Perhaps one of the most damaging criticisms of the nature of organizational life and employment of Black professionals is given by Taylor (1972a). He notes the effects of discrimination and organizational stress on the careers and aspirations of Black executives in large corporations. The subjects of his study were Black American executives (BAE) in the *"Fortune* 500" companies. The purpose of the study was to determine what the climate is like for Black American executives and how they respond to the direct and indirect effects of the executive suite. Among the hypotheses of the study which were, for the most part, verified by his results were the following (Taylor, 1972a, p. 91):

1. Because of specific on-the-job events or actions indicative of white racism, BAE's experience a variety of psychological defenses that serve as the starting point for several behavioral patterns for black and white executives.
2. Despite the racial climate in the executive suite, the BAE will reflect more liberal philosophies toward racial integration, brotherhood, etc. than blacks in general. The BAE will therefore experience considerable conflict between being a member of a racial minority and a corporate representative of the management majority.

Taylor's findings included the fact that Black executives find that the organizational structure is a source of pain through which they suffer many injustices. The jobs and relationships within the organizational structure were not as fulfilling and rewarding as one would expect. Moreover, organizational dynamics which give rise to organizational changes, rivalry, role ambiguity, self-doubt, and increased responsibility are experiences of Black as well as white executives, but the former often are at a disadvantage because they have usually traveled a different career path to the executive suite—a path that did not necessarily provide the experience and confidence that comes from working one's way up in the system. In the terms suggested by Hall (1972) and discussed above, Type-I coping behaviors or structural role redefinition would be an appropriate coping strategy for executives in this situation—to the extent that it was possible.

Other sources of psychological stress, strain, and frustration for Black executives in American corporations, which Taylor notes, are white racism and the practice of programming Blacks for failure. One example which Taylor relates is the following (Taylor, 1972a, p. 96):

> In two organizations two BAE's had opportunities to attend an advanced management training program. Both men had supervisors who had never attended, and one of them thought such programs were a waste of time and money. The blacks were discouraged from attending the programs and were informed their work was good and that they would move along without the formal management training. One of the men discovered months later that he had missed a promotion because, in part, his supervisor included on his evaluation a note that the BAE was not interested in improving his management ability. The other executive experienced a similar disappointment and subsequently transferred to another division.

Very often, coping responses of Black executives experiencing such treatment included avoiding contact with other white managers or trying to please whites in order to compensate for any prejudice. A few of the Black executives reported behavior which suggested that at times they would try to conceal their identification with certain kinds of Black ideologies and identify with white executives. Thus these executives find it is in their best professional and personal interests to abandon overt behavior that is characteristically "Black" and to embrace overtly the behavior of their white peers, i.e., the adoption of white roles (Taylor, 1972b). In general, Taylor notes in another article related to his study that it is unrealistic and *psychologically unhealthy* for some Blacks to strive sincerely for and expect to receive promotions leading to top managerial positions in these companies (Taylor, 1973).

While these findings of the Taylor study may come as a surprise to some people and perhaps not to others, there have been other studies reported in the recent scientific literature which indicated that the above findings are indeed valid. Richards and Jaffee (1972), for example, in a race-related leadership study investigating potential differences between Blacks and whites, hypothesized that Black supervisors possibly must display a different pattern of behaviors in order to be seen as effective as their white counterparts, simply because they are Black and under close scrutiny by whites. Their study was a laboratory study involving Black and white students in supervisory positions. Richards and Jaffee found that the behavior patterns of Black and white supervisors were indeed different. Black supervisors who were rated by whites were perceived to emit few behaviors related to being an effective supervisor. Whether the evaluations were due to possible racial attitudes and biases of the white raters is not known, as the authors did not include Black raters of the Black supervisors in their study. The behaviors of white subordinates who were supervised by Blacks were found to impede the effectiveness of the Black supervisor. It thus seems that the racial composition of work groups is a factor specifically affecting leader-subordinate behavior.

Several recent race-related studies conducted in the military have also indicated that there are differences in perceptions between various racial and/or ethnic groups. Parker (1974) reported a study of differences in organizational practices, preferences, and felt racial discrimination by race and racial composition of work groups in the Navy. The findings of this study indicated that there is little evidence of differences in organizational practices by races among Blacks and whites. However, differences do occur when the racial composition of work groups is examined. Respondents in work groups whose supervisor is of the same race view the conditions in the organization better than those whose supervisor is of a different race. Differences in organizational preferences were also found, with Blacks being more concerned about having a job with different characteristics than whites, especially a job which is firm in its economic rewards. When felt racial discrimination on the job was examined by race, Parker found that Blacks clearly felt more discrimination than whites and those of other races. He noted, however, that this difference may reflect felt or perceived differential treatment by the Blacks in the Navy or aspects of work life not measured, or similar treatment of Blacks and whites may be differentially interpreted by the two racial groups.

Another study by Hill and Fox (1973) was conducted in the Marine

Corps and investigated Black and white Marine squad leaders' perceptions of racially mixed squads as part of an overall study of leadership effectiveness. In particular, one focus of this study concerned perceptions that Black and white supervisors have of their Black, white, and Puerto Rican subordinates. Interestingly enough, the results seemed to indicate that white squad leaders gave proportionately more reprimands to their white subordinates than to Blacks, but also gave them proportionately more praise. Moreover, they gave their Black subordinates proportionately better performance ratings than they gave their white members. There were no differences in responses when Blacks were compared to Puerto Ricans or Puerto Ricans contrasted with whites. These findings, somewhat contrary to those of the Parker study, raised some interesting questions for the authors, one of which was: "Could it be that white squad leaders were maintaining a certain 'distance' from their black subordinates and were handling them with 'special care'?" (Hill and Fox, 1973, p. 36). They concluded that the higher performance ratings for Blacks by their white supervisors would seem to indicate this. However, an issue which the authors failed to address was the possibility that superior performance ratings of Blacks given by whites were indeed indicative of superior performance on the part of Blacks relative to whites, as opposed to being simply indicative of a "handling with kid gloves" approach.

Slocum and Strawser (1972) found that Black CPAs assigned more need importance to lower-level needs (security, safety) and had more need deficiency in other aspects of their work than their white counterparts. O'Reilly and Roberts (1973), in a hospital study involving only females, found that whites were consistently more satisfied with most aspects of their jobs, although the differences seemed to diminish for persons in lower job levels. Furthermore, satisfaction with promotion accounted for a significantly greater proportion of the overall job satisfaction variance for whites at higher professional levels than for Blacks at the same level.

Milutinovich (1976), in still another study investigating whether cultural-ethnic differences have any important influence on work attitudes of minority and white workers, found that with the exception of Blacks having lower satisfaction with supervision than whites, no consistent differences in job attitudes were found between the white and minority workers in his study. However, when his sample was stratified by job level and other socioeconomic variables, differences did emerge. Blue-collar Blacks had more positive, and white-collar Blacks more negative, attitudes toward their job than their white counterparts respectively. This latter finding for white-collar Blacks is consistent with other findings relative to job satisfaction of Black professionals in organizations.

In summary, the results of these race-related studies in the military and in business and industrial organizations seem to suggest that race and the racial configuration of work groups make a difference in the kinds of experiences organizational members encounter and the degree of satisfaction associated with their work situation.

Consequences of Dysfunctional Organizational Experiences. Perhaps we should make a point here that while the above studies have tended to show negative outcomes for Black professionals in terms of their organizational life and employment, not all Black professionals experience such negative outcomes. The work situation of many Black professionals is both rewarding and satisfying, and many of them compete on an even basis for the fruits and rewards accruing to good job performance. Moreover, the negative experiences noted above are not limited to Black professionals; there are some white professionals for whom the same scenario could be played. For example, Connor and Fielden (1973) talked about unproductive middle-management self-sitters consisting primarily of white managers (not many Blacks are in higher middle-managerial levels) and what can be done about them. Burack and Pati (1970) found obsolescence a major problem for managers with blocked mobility. Furthermore, in recent studies in the area of correctional manpower, Pati (1973, 1974) found that Blacks and whites at operative as well as professional-level positions encounter difficulty in finding jobs and blocked mobility in their career patterns not because of their race but because of their past record. Those of us who work closely with industry can't help but find that many white professionals are not progressing in the management hierarchy, while some Blacks are being promoted not because of their race but primarily because of their competence.

However, for the most part, the good and happy stories for Blacks are often not told, and the negative white experiences within the white structure are not placed in perspective within the framework of discrimination or do not seem to get widely reported. Regardless of this, it can be safe to say that in spite of progress, Blacks in particular, and minorities in general, seem to have worse organizational disillusionment than their white counterparts.

While we have not specifically attempted to relate each research finding and outcome to the two forms of organizational stress which we discussed in the earlier sections of this chapter, i.e., role conflict and ambiguity, the serious reader no doubt will be able to do this for himself or herself. Such things as being programmed for failure, loss of racial identity, overt signs of racism, being more qualified than their white superiors, and lack of support are all influenced by, and result from, the expectations communicated to the Black professional by organizational members of his role set. Very often these expectations are contradictory and confusing to say the least.

Taylor (1972a) observed a comment made by Dr. John MacIver, director of psychiatric services for the U.S. Steel Corporation, relative to Black and white managers (p. 92): "It is disquieting to me that from this group of basically competent and well adjusted people, 43 percent say they have been hurt careerwise by organizational changes and 31 percent expect to be hurt in the future." A startling fact is that the hurt experienced by these managers is not only psychological, but also may have physiological manifestations as well in the form of hypertension. It is a well-acknowledged fact that the danger of hypertension is even greater in Blacks than in whites. Blacks are about three times more likely to have moderately severe hypertension than are whites (*Ebony*, June, 1974).

Although the cause of hypertension, commonly known as high blood pressure, is not known, it is generally accepted that hypertension is affected by age, race, sex, smoking, obesity, and social factors (*Ebony*, June, 1974). It is perhaps safe to assume that organizational and work factors could be added to this list of factors that affect hypertension. Indeed the recognition of the dysfunctional consequences and dangers that the organizational setting may have on the individual has resulted in a major research study of hypertension control in organizational settings, under the auspices of the Program for the Improvement of Worker Health and Well-Being, undertaken jointly by the Institute of Labor and Industrial Relations at the University of Michigan and Wayne State University. Dimensions of "occupational" stress to be considered in this study include aspects of the work environment (work area, temperature, co-workers, safety, etc.), aspects of the job (diversity of tasks and responsibilities, decision-making, opportunities for promotion, etc.), and aspects of supervision (flexibility, work influence and supervision, friendliness, etc.) Erfurt and Foote, 1974). While results of this study are not available as yet, a plausible hypothesis would be that high blood pressure in Blacks is significantly related to the types of jobs they hold as well as the kinds of conditions under which they work.

If we juxtapose the present discussion with our earlier discussion of the Caplan and Jones (1975) findings, it seems plausible to expect that the most negative results to be found from the Michigan/Wayne State study will be for Black workers. In particular, an intuitively appealing hypothesis would be one which posits that the incidence of hypertension among Black professionals in organizations would potentially be higher among those who are known as "high achievers." Owing to the fact that in many instances Blacks have had to be much better than their white counterparts in order to get ahead in their organizations, it is reasonable to suspect that those who have been successful could easily be identified as Type-A personalities. The requirements for success just about dictate that such individuals have Type-A personality traits. The unfortunate thing is that these issues have received no attention from behavioral scientists relative to Black professionals in organizations. Caplan and Jones (1975) suggested that while persons with Type-A personality traits may contribute to the attainment of organizational goals, they do so at a cost to themselves. Whether or not these costs offset the value of the employee's productivity is a worthy scientific question apart from any moral considerations, as Caplan and Jones observe. However, more importantly, this writer feels, immediate attention to the issues raised here should be given in order to determine the nature and extent of these mental and physical "costs" to Blacks in organizations. We address this matter further in our conclusions below.

Conclusions

Persons in responsible (management) positions in organizations must accept the idea that work can adversely affect both the mental and physical health of many workers through what has become known as "job stress." Very generally, this term conveys a sense of the employee's unhappiness with his work (McLean, 1976). McLean (1976) notes that rather than the blatant and obvious, the stressors that may stimulate mental disorder and produce unhealthy behavior in individuals have their origins in, or are associated with, the emotional aspects of the job or work environment.

The study, *Work in America,* published by the Department of

Health, Education and Welfare in 1973, concluded that improvements in the quality of working life hold out opportunities for actually stimulating healthy behavior. The study's authors also noted, however, that various aspects of work account for many factors associated with heart disease, hypertension, and other health problems, including a high correlation with symptoms of mental disorder (McLean, 1976).

According to McLean (1976), two factors help to determine whether a specific stressor will produce symptoms: the *context* in which an interaction takes place and the particular *vulnerability* of the individual at the time. The context—social, physical, or environmental—may be as broad as an economy or as small as a family unit; a context can also be set by management policy or practice. On the other hand, the individual's vulnerability to specific sources of stress is even more important than the context in determining reaction to factors in a work environment. The enduring personality characteristics of a person are major elements in determining the dimensions of vulnerability. Additionally, however, vulnerability varies with other factors, such as age, occupation, occupational level, and education.

A reconsideration of the studies by Caplan and Jones (1975), Rogers (1975), Ogilvie and Porter (1975), Johnson and Stinson (1975), and other studies cited earlier in conjunction with the discussion of McLean (1976) should help us to begin to see that worker reactions to psychosocial forms of stress depend upon both the context of the situation and the vulnerability of the individual. With respect to the latter, persons who display Type-A personality characteristics may very well be more vulnerable to stress than those persons who don't. Additionally, an implication in our discussion prior to the beginning of this section is that race may interact with other factors to increase the vulnerability of Blacks to sources of stress. Therefore, it becomes imperative for Blacks in particular to develop ways and means of reducing vulnerability and improving the factors that make up the context of organizational interaction.

The methods of coping with the role conflict as outlined by Hall (1972) can serve as a starting point for improving the organizational context and/or making organizational life more bearable. Granted, these approaches are probably more useful on an individual level. McLean (1976, p. 47), on the other hand, has suggested four broad categories of ways to help persons cope with stress on the job. These categories are primarily concerned with broader, more collective efforts that involve more than just the single individual, and illustrate the varying level and quality of activity possible in support of occupational mental health:

1. *Policy considerations.* This category considers the social responsibility of organizations for the health and well-being of those they employ. Organizational policies should reflect the social concern of work organizations.

2. *Legislation.* One legislative approach that could foster the coping mechanisms of the individual would be specifically to require the establishment of "social indicators" as part of the monitoring process of a work organization. As such, measures of job satisfaction and the psychosocial climate of an organization would ultimately be related to specific legislative guidelines.

3. *Education and training.* The emphasis here would be on imaginative educational systems whereby organizations assumed responsibility for specific "applications education" following a person's broad, basic education. In addition it has been suggested that lifetime guidance systems be established as well as greater emphasis on making persons aware of the psychosocial work factors.

4. *Programs of individual support.* These approaches would involve specific programs designed to provide clinical support for more successful coping with occupational stress, e.g., educating supervisory personnel in specific health principles and the techniques of referral to programs such as occupational health and counseling.

At a practical level, it is extremely important to understand the interrelationships of job stress, performance, and coping behaviors. In that members of society are subjected to ever-increasing stress levels from various sources, the "management" of stress is a critical area, especially with regard to performance. Several authors have offered suggestions for coping with stress, i.e., McLean (1976), Hall (1972), and Anderson (1976). The decision is not one of determining which approach is best, but rather of resolving to undertake an approach.

One technique that is gaining ever-increasing popularity among executives in high-stress positions is that of transcendental meditation (TM). Anecdotal evidence available to this writer indicates that Blacks especially have not begun to realize the benefits of TM as much as they possibly could. Since Black people have historically been a spiritual people, the utilization of prayer and meditatiion has been an integral part of their lives for many years. Therefore, the potential benefits to be gained from incorporating two 20-minute meditation periods in the workday are enormous.

As America takes stock of itself in the wake of the bicentennial celebration, it would do well for all concerned to assess the *meaning* of work and its purposes for all who engage in this endeavor. We have attempted in this chapter not to present the solution to all the ills, but rather to raise the pertinent issues for debate and future research and study. Like the child at play, the adult in the world of work should be able to experience the situation without tremendous hazard to his physical and mental health. Hopefully, this chapter and the remainder of this volume will aid our pursuit of this worthwhile goal.

References

Anderson, C. R. "Stress, Performance, and Coping Behaviors: Intervening Mechanisms in the Inverted-U Relationship." *Journal of Applied Psychology* 61 (1976): 30.

Bobbitt, H. R.; Brienbolt, R. H.; Doktor, R. H.; and McNaul, J. P. *Organizational Behavior: Understanding and Prediction.* Englewood Cliffs, New Jersey: Prentice-Hall, 1974.

Bowers, D. G. "OD Techniques and Their Results in 23 Organizations: The Michigan ICL Study." *Journal of Applied Behavioral Science* 9 (1973): 21–43.

Bowers, D. G.; Franklin, J. L., and Percorella, P. A. "A Taxonomy of Intervention: The Science of Organizational Development." Unpublished technical report, Institute for Social Research, University of Michigan, 1973.

Bowers, D. G., and Seashore, S. "Predicting Organization Effectiveness With a Four Factor Theory of Leadership." *Administrative Science Quarterly* 11 (1966): 238–263.

Bramwell, J. "The Black Professional Today: The Multidimensional Human." *Contact Magazine* 3 (1973): 22–24.

Burack, E. H., and Pati, G. C. "Technology and Managerial Obsolescence." *MSU Business Topics* 18 (1970): 49–56.

Caplan, R. D. "Organizational Stress and Individual Strain: A Social Psychological Study of Risk Factors in Coronary Heart Disease among

Administrators, Engineers, and Scientists." Unpublished Ph.D. dissertation, University of Michigan, Institute for Social Research, 1971.

Caplan, R. D., and Jones, K. W. "Effects of Work Load, Ambiguity, and Type A Personality on Anxiety, Depression, and Heart Rate." *Journal of Applied Psychology* 60 (1975): 713–719.

Connor, S. R., and Fielden, J. S. "RX for Managerial 'Self Sitters.' " *Harvard Business Review* 52 (1973): 113–120.

Department of Health, Education and Welfare. *Work in America.* Cambridge, Massachusetts: M.I.T. Press, 1973.

Erfurt, J. C., and Foote, A. "Hypertension Control in Organizational Setting." Unpublished manuscript, Institute of Labor and Industrial Relations, University of Michigan, 1974.

Fields, C. L., and Freeman, E. S. "Black Professionals: The Gap Is Not Closing." *MBA* 6 (1972): 73, 78, 82, 84.

Ford, D. L. *Readings in Minority Group Relations.* La Jolla, California: University Associates, 1976.

French, J. R. P., and Caplan, R. D. "Organizational Stress and Individual Strain." In A. J. Marrow (ed.), *The Failure of Success.* New York: Amacom, 1972.

Greene, C., and Organ, D. "An Evaluation of Causal Models Linking the Received Role With Job Satisfaction." *Administrative Science Quarterly* 18 (1973): 95–103.

Gurin, G.; Veroff, J.; and Feld, S. C. *Americans View Their Mental Health.* New York: Basic Books, 1960.

Hall, D. T. "A Model of Coping With Role Conflict. The Role Behavior of College Educated Women." *Administrative Science Quarterly* 17 (1972): 471–485.

——————. "Equal Opportunity + Low Support = Discrimination." Paper presented at the Sixth National Meeting of the American Institute for Decision Sciences, Atlanta, Georgia, October 1974.

Hamner, W. C., and Tosi, H. "Relationship of Role Conflict and Role Ambiguity to Job Involvement Measures." *Journal of Applied Psychology* 4 (1974): 497–499.

Hellriegel, D., and Slocum, J. "Organizational Climate: Measures, Research and Contingencies." *Academy of Management Journal* 17 (1974): 255–280.

Hill, W. A., and Fox, W. M. "Black and White Marine Squad Leaders' Perceptions of Racially Mixed Squads." *Academy of Management Journal* 16 (1973): 680–686.

House, R. J., and Rizzo, J. R. "Role Conflict and Ambiguity as Critical Variables in a Model of Organizational Behavior." *Organizational Behavior and Human Performance* 7 (1972): 467–505.

Johnson, T. W., and Stinson, J. E. "Role Ambiguity, Role Conflict, and Satisfaction: Moderating Effects of Individual Differences." *Journal of Applied Psychology* 60 (1975): 329–333.

Kahn, R. L. "Stress from 9 to 5." *Psychology Today* 3 (1969): 34–38.

Kahn, R. L.; Wolfe, D. M.; Quinn, R. P.; Snoek, J. D.; and Rosenthal, R. A. *Organizational Stress: Studies in Role Conflict and Ambiguity.* New York: Wiley, 1964.

Kraut, A. "The Study of Role Conflicts and Their Relationships to Job Satisfaction, Tension, and Performance." Ph.D. dissertation, University of Michigan, 1965 *Dissertation Abstracts* 26 (1965): 7476.

Levinson, D. "Role, Personality, and Social Structure in the Organizational Setting." *Journal of Abnormal and Social Psychology* 58 (1959): 170–180.

Likert, R. *New Patterns of Management.* New York: McGraw-Hill, 1961.

————. *The Human Organization.* New York: McGraw-Hill, 1967.

Likert, R.; Bowers, D. G.; and Norman, R. "How to Increase a Firm's Lead Time in Recognizing and Dealing With Problems of Managing Its Human Organization." *Michigan Business Review* 21 (1969): 12–17.

March, J., and Simon, H. *Organizations.* New York: Wiley, 1958.

McLean, A. A. "Job Stress and the Psychosocial Pressures of Change." *Personnel Psychology* 53 (1976): 40–49.

Miller, E. "Job Satisfaction of National Union Officials." *Personnel Psychology* 19 (1966): 261–274.

Milutinovich, J. S. "A Comparative Study of Work Attitudes of Black and White Workers." In D. L. Ford (ed.), *Readings in Minority Group Relations.* La Jolla, California: University Associates, 1976.

Ogilvie, B. C., and Porter, A. L. "Business Careers as Treadmill to Oblivion: The Allure of Cardiovascular Death." *Human Resource Management* 13 (1975): 14–18.

O'Reilly, C., and Roberts, K. H. "Job Satisfaction among Whites and Non-Whites: A Cross-sectional Approach." *Journal of Applied Psychology* 57 (1973): 295–299.

Parker, W. S. "Differences in Organizational Practices and Preferences in the Navy by Race." Unpublished technical report, Institute for Social Research, University of Michigan, 1974.

Pati, G. C. "Ex-Offenders Make Good Employees." *Public Personnel Management* 2 (1973): 424–428.

Pritchard, R. D., and Karasick, B. W. "The Effects of Organizational Climate on Managerial Performance and Job Satisfaction." *Organizational Behavior and Human Performance* 9 (1973): 126–146.

Richards, A. S., and Jaffe, C. L. "Blacks Supervising Whites: A Study of Interracial Difficulties in Working Together in a Simulated Organization." *Journal of Applied Psychology* 56 (1972): 234–240.

Rogers, R. E. "Executive Stress." *Human Resource Management* 14 (1975): 21–24.

Rosenman, R. H. et al. "Coronary Heart Disease in the Western Collaborative Group Study: A Follow-up Experience of 4½ Years." *Journal of Chronic Diseases* 23 (1970): 173–190.

Rizzo, J. E.; House, R. J.; and Lirtzman, S. I. "Role Conflict and Ambiguity in Complex Organizations." *Administrative Science Quarterly* 15 (1970): 150–163.

Sales, S. M. "Organizational Roles as a Risk Factor in Coronary Disease." *Administrative Science Quarterly* 14 (1969): 325–336.

――――――――. "Some Effects of Role Overload and Role Underload." *Organizational Behavior and Human Performance* 5 (1970): 592–608.

Schuler, R. S. "Role Perceptions, Satisfaction, and Performance: A Partial Reconciliation." *Journal of Applied Psychology* 60 (1975): 683–687.

Schwab, D., and Cummings, L. "Employee Performance and Satisfaction with Work Roles: A Review and Interpretation of Theory." *Industrial Relations* 9 (1970): 408–431.

Slocum, J., and Strawser, R. H. "Racial Differences in Job Attitudes." *Journal of Applied Psychology* 56 (1972): 28–32.

Steers, R. M. "Effects of Need for Achievement on the Job Performance-Job Attitude Relationship." *Journal of Applied Psychology* 60 (1975): 678–682.

"Stresses and Strains on Black Women." *Ebony* 24 (1974): 33–40.

Taylor, S. A. "The Black Executive and the Corporation—A Difficult Fit." *MBA* 6 (1972a): 8, 91–92, 96, 98, 100, 102.

――――――――. "Action Oriented Research: An Application of Organizational Behavior Methodology to Black American Executives in Major Corporations." Proceedings of the Thirty-Second Annual Meeting of the Academy of Management, Minneapolis, August 1972b, pp. 13–16.

――――――――. "A Funny Thing Happened on the Way Up." *Contact Magazine* 3 (1973): 14–16.

Thompson, J. D. *Organizations in Action*. New York: McGraw-Hill, 1967.

Tosi, H. "Organizational Stress As a Moderator of the Relationship Between Influence and Role Response." *Academy of Management Journal* 14 (1971): 7–20.

Wanous, J. P. "Individual Differences and Reactions to Job Characteristics." *Journal of Applied Psychology* 59 (1974): 616–622.

8   MENTAL HEALTH OF THE BLACK AGED

Brin Hawkins, Ph.D.

Overview

Two hundred years ago, life expectancy at birth was about 38 or 39 years, so that the older population numbered about 50,000, or 2 percent of the total. By 1900, there were three million older Americans, aged 65 and older, comprising 4 percent of the total population, or every twenty-fifth American. In 1975, over 22 million older persons represented approximately 10 percent of the total population of the United States, or every tenth American. Blacks represent only 8 percent of elderly Americans, approximately 1.6 million persons, and only 7 percent of the Black population, although the total Black population in America today is close to 12 percent. This phenomenon is easily understood in light of the fact that growing old for the masses of Black people has not progressed at the same rate as that for whites (20 percent).

Men in general experience a shorter life expectancy than women, but both men and women in the Black community have a life expectancy that is at least 7 years less than that of whites. The shorter life expectancy is generally attributed to the low socioeconomic status of Blacks in America, and the concomitant factors related to physical and emotional stress experienced over a lifetime in the struggle for survival.

In recent years, a few major studies have focused on the complex and compound problems related to being old, Black, and poor in America. In 1964, the National Urban League explored the *double jeopardy* status of the Black elderly, boldly asserting: "Today's aged Negro is different from today's white because he is a Negro . . . and this alone should be enough for differential treatment. For he has, indeed, been placed in double jeopardy, first by being Negro, and second, by being old. Age merely compounded those hardships accrued to him as a result of being a Negro.''

In 1971, Dr. Inabel Lindsay prepared a report for the Senate Committee on Aging on the *Multiple Hazards of Age and Race.* She was able to document significant levels of deprivation for the Black elderly in all major areas of living. She found that ''the majority of [Blacks] over 65 are less well educated, have less adequate income, suffer more illnesses and earlier death, have poorer quality housing and less choice as to where they live and where they work, and in general, have a less satisfying quality of life.''

In the progressive 1970's, the unique stresses and strains which confront the Black elderly have not been alleviated. In fact, in some areas, the problems have been aggravated by an inflated economy and a highly mobile and youth-oriented society, which encourages the maintenance of the nuclear family and frequently excludes aging grandparents.

There is no doubt that income is the most pervasive concern of the Black elderly. It influences the quality of their lifestyle in virtually all other areas, including housing, transportation, health care, and more indirectly, social relationships. The gradual decline of the financial and emotional support of the extended family is also very important, but an area in which the Black older person seems able to cope with much greater resiliency than is commonly believed.

Positive mental health for the elderly is frequently defined very generally as a state of ''well-being'' and is measured by the level of social adjustment and personal satisfaction experienced by individuals as they grow old, lose traditional roles of the young, and accept new roles appropriate to the later years. Old age does not occur overnight. It requires a period of transition, which does not always flow smoothly. For some individuals it is a pleasant period of slowing down, of sharing thoughts and experiences with family and friends, of learning new and different things about themselves and the world around them, of growing old ''gracefully.'' For others it means unwanted wrinkles, periodic aches and pains, forced retirement, widowhood, diminished sexuality, loneliness, and fear of death. The experience of growing old is further degraded by a society that perceives older persons as senile, unproductive, sickly, cantankerous, and feeble. It cannot be denied that some unpleasantness accompanies the aging process, but many of the nemeses of old age are more myth than reality, more environmental than biological, and more social than psychological.

It is a fact that 86 percent of older persons have one or more chronic health problems, but 95 percent are able to live in the community, leaving only 5 percent in institutions. It is a fact that brain damage from cerebral arteriosclerosis and senile brain disease is a real problem, probably causing 50 percent of cases of mental disorder in old age, but according to Dr. Robert Butler (1973), noted psychiatrist and gerontologist, "senility" is excessively used by doctors and laymen alike to explain the behavior of the elderly. He further states that "senility" is an especially convenient tag put on old women by doctors who do not wish to spend the time and effort necessary to diagnose and treat their complaints, which in fact may be related to emotional responses such as depression, grief, and anxiety. It is also a fact that some of the most productive and creative persons in history and modern times did not reach their pinnacle of success until old age. It is therefore very important to keep in mind the fact that old people are a very heterogeneous group and should be considered as such in any exploration of their behavior and circumstances. More specifically, all old people are not alike, whether they be Black or white, and each individual will experience the aging process differently, although some patterns are commonly seen. Some of the major patterns and circumstances that influence the mental health of elderly Black persons will be discussed in the following section.

Good adjustment to the aging process and the loss and/or changing of roles are very much related to such factors as economic security, congenial and attractive living arrangements, and support and affection from family and friends. In the absence of such resources and supports, the elderly, regardless of race, are more likely to experience isolation, depression, hopelessness, and very little, if any, personal satisfaction. The high incidence of poverty, increased susceptibility to debilitating physical disease, loss of status in a youth-oriented society, and personal losses of friends and family that increase with advancing age are all factors that contribute to the vulnerability of this age group and to the pressing mental health problems that they experience. What, then, is the potential for the Black aged to experience positive mental health in America, where frequently old age is the climax to a lifetime of social and economic indignities?

Economic Stress Factors

Income. Older persons have half the income of the younger population. In 1974, 50 percent of families headed by an older person had incomes of less than $7,200. The median income of older persons living alone was $2,956, compared to $5,862 for a younger person living alone. The Black aged are disproportionately represented among the aged poor. In 1975, 52.9 percent of the Black elderly population was classified as poor, compared to 25 percent of the white elderly. Elderly Black women as a group were even more disadvantaged with 70.8 percent living in poverty. Many of the white aged become poor as a result of loss of earnings following retirement. The majority of the Black aged were poor as young people and become poorer in old age. Aged Blacks are much less likely to have good retirement plans and pensions, and until recent years they were employed in unskilled and domestic jobs that were not even covered by Social Security. Since January 1974, over one million elderly poor and disabled persons have been added to the Social Security rolls through the Supplemental Security Income (SSI) program, which replaced state welfare assistance. SSI guarantees a minimum income of $167.80 for individuals and $251.80 for couples. It is apparent that the average social security income is below, or very near, the poverty line and is the only source of income for 85 percent of the Black elderly receiving benefits.

Housing. The quality of housing occupied by the elderly has not improved significantly over the past 10 years. Elderly persons occupy 32 percent of the substandard housing in the United States because it is all they can afford. If they are homeowners, the costs of taxes, utilities, and repairs are equally burdensome. The Senate Committee on Aging reports that the average older poor person spends 45 to 90 percent of his income on housing expenses, depriving himself of adequate food, medicine, and personal items. As in other areas, the Black aged suffer even more, with 60 percent of them occupying substandard units. Furthermore, the Black aged are more vulnerable to the strains and stresses found in the inner city because they are forced to live there in greater numbers. Blacks have shown a dramatic migration to the inner city urban areas since 1950, when 43 percent of the Black population over age 65 lived in rural areas, compared to 24 percent in 1970. Today over 60 percent of the Black aged reside in the cites. Golant (1975) predicts that the growth of the Black elderly in the inner cities will continue, as a natural process, as the younger Black population grows old. At the same time, the white elderly are becoming increasingly dispersed in suburban areas.

The inner city is not kind to the elderly. They must endure the noise, dirt, smog, and social tension of the ghetto. In a study of "geriatric ghettos" in Philadelphia, Lawton (1971) concluded that "it was not an easy life for older people. They were prime targets for purse snatchings, armed robberies, mugging, rape, and murder, which kept fear alive among the elderly residents." Similar findings are reported by Hawkins (1976) in a study of elderly Black tenants living in public housing located in the inner city and the suburbs. The inner city tenants reported high levels of fear, reluctance to leave their apartments, and feelings of isolation. The suburban tenants felt more secure and comfortable, and moved freely around the neighborhood. The residential environment plays a major role in the social adjustment of older persons. The research data indicate that improved living conditions are associated with improved social functioning (Jackson, 1972), while poor living conditions contribute to physical and psychological impairment for both Black and white older persons (Lowenthal and Frier, 1967).

Health Care. Spiraling health care costs are also a major worry to older Americans, who spend more of their budgets on health care, proportionately, than does any other age segment. As expected, Blacks spend significantly less on health care because of limited income. They report fewer physician's visits, less preventive care, and more self-diagnosis and self-treatment (Lindsay, 1971). Unfortunately, they also experience a higher incidence of heart disease, high blood pressure, and other chronic conditions related to a lifetime of heavy labor, frustrations, and poor nutrition. The results of poor health care are evident in mortality rates which are twice as high for the Black elderly, in the 55 to 64 age group, as for the white elderly. Results are also evident in the mental health of the poor Black aged, which is influenced by physical health more than by any other single factor (Thompson, 1971).

Contrary to popular belief, Medicare is not meeting the major health care needs of older people. In 1974, Medicare paid only 38 percent of the health bills of the elderly, inasmuch as it does not cover eyeglasses, hearing aids, dentures, physical checkups, and some prescription drugs. Medicare has closed the gaps in some states, but benefits are currently being cut back drastically as a reaction to economic inflation. In addition, the recent exposure of wasteful spending and fraud in Medicare-Medicaid reimbursement raises many questions about the quality of the care that is being provided under these programs.

National health care legislation has been, and will continue to be, a major political issue while the older American suffers. In the meantime "alternative" approaches to hospitalization and institutionalization such as home health services, day-care programs, and foster-care homes are widely supported but "still fight an uphill battle for recognition in our Federal Policy," according to the Senate Committee on Aging.

Social and Psychological Stress Factors

Isolation and lack of social contact and communication can be as physically debilitating as health dysfunctions and may lead directly to emotional breakdown. The older person who has lost family, friends, and satisfying social roles may lose the will to eat, to participate, and eventually the will to live. These stresses are compounded for a large number of Black elderly who are left without the necessary economic and personal resources to maintain an active and meaningful social life. Social contact frequently requires travel, or a telephone, or even writing skills. Many Black elderly are immobilized by lack of bus fare, taxi fare, and access to automobiles. They are further handicapped by the fact that 35 percent of the Black elderly do not have telephones, compared to 10 percent of the white elderly, and 70 percent of the Black elderly compared to 30 percent of the white elderly in a national survey indicated some difficulty with written correspondence as a result of a very low level of educational attainment (Rubenstein, 1971). As a result of the above, 35 percent of the Black elderly and only 11 percent of the white elderly reported infrequent contact (over a year) by phone and letter with children and siblings.

The household situation of the Black elderly is also potentially depressing. Almost 70 percent of the Black elderly are widowed, compared to 50 percent of the white elderly. Women predominate as survivors in both races, because of the higher mortality rates for men in general. Although well-adjusted older persons are usually able to compensate for loss of a spouse with new roles and new relationships, the data also indicate that older persons living with a spouse are more socially active and integrated as a result of the security and support they receive in the marriage relationship (Hawkins, 1976; Lawton, 1975). It is also interesting to note that the Black extended family is more myth than reality for half the Black elderly in this country. Less than 50 percent of the Black elderly live in an extended family situation. The others live alone or with one other person, relative or non-relative (Butler, 1973). It is commonly believed that older persons are happiest in the extended family setting. And some of them are. Others who are forced into congregate family housing as an economic necessity may experience a loss of privacy, independence, and even identity. In some cases, they must carry on the energy-consuming household work for larger families and care for young children at an age when the older person's health is poorest, energies are lowest, and the need for less stress is greatest. In fact the majority of Black elderly in the Hawkins (1976) study expressed preferences for living with a spouse, living alone, or being part of a "companion" household (with one other adult). A very small minority indicated a preference for living in an extended family household where their major role was that of grandparents. Almost all of the respondents, however, indicated a desire to maintain close contact with family and friends. Butler (1973) suggests that human contact and human support in the housing environment are major mental health needs in old age, but we need to develop more group-living alternatives in which the elderly do not lose their self-esteem and sense of independence.

As we grow older, it is inevitable that death becomes a constant companion. Friends and family who are peers also grow old, and sick, and die. Grief becomes a common emotional expression in old age. Butler (1973) defines the primary purpose of grief as "adaptive emotion which helps us to accept the reality of the loss of significant and loved people and to find ways of filling up the emptiness caused by the loss, through identifying with a new style of life and new people." Very little empirical data exist which are focused on the grief of the Black elderly, but some assumptions can be made about how they handle their grief.

The Black elderly as a group have shown amazing fortitude in the face of overwhelming deprivation. Their strength may be attributed to a lifetime struggle for survival and/or their very close involvement with the church. Regardless of the reason, the majority of them have been able to compensate for their losses in a very positive and healthy manner. There is evidence that they have a strong capacity for establishing new relationships with friends and neighbors that take on greater importance for them than relationships with relatives who live far away or do not maintain frequent contact. The Black elderly, in the aggregate, do not participate in formal clubs and organizations to the extent that the white elderly do, but they are involved to a much greater extent in church activities, which are very important to their social integration and mental health. Those Blacks who are involved in formal clubs and organized activities experience a much higher level of morale (Hawkins, 1976). Rubenstein (1971) supports the conclusion that belonging to, and participating in, social organizations is even more important for Blacks than whites, because of a greater need for social and emotional supports. He suggests that in all probability, older Black people, harassed and restricted by discrimination, injustice, uprooting, and living conditions and patterns derived historically from slavery, may have experienced separation and isolation from the mainstream of society, i.e., secondary institutions. Therefore, they may receive greater satisfaction from this involvement because to them it represents acceptance and a freedom to participate.

It is apparent that the total population of elderly experience multiple psychosocial stresses which influence their mental health, but the poor and the Black elderly are much more vulnerable to the stresses of old age. The potential for physical and emotional breakdown is much greater when they can no longer cope with the "overload" of stresses, regardless of how well-adjusted or "strong" they may appear to be. The results of sustained stress are evident in the fact that the Black elderly reflect "a higher degree of sustained unhappiness" (Rubenstein, 1971). It matters little that the "official" suicide rate for older whites is three times that for older Blacks. The fact that they choose to endure and "keep the faith" does not suggest that they suffer any less from the experience of being old and deprived, but that they choose a less dramatic form of protest. In fact, suicide more broadly defined might easily include alcoholism, drug abuse, starvation, and self-imposed isolation, all of which are commonly seen in the elderly Black population.

Support Systems

In earlier times, life expectancy was much shorter than it is today, but the society was also better prepared to care for those who did live to experience old age. Modern society has only recently begun to "plan" for the inevitable and unique needs of old age, and we still have a long way to go before we develop public policies, programs, and institutions which provide appropriate resources and supports.

Currently, we have only two major public policies related to aging in America: the Social Security Act of 1935 and the Older Americans Act of 1965. Social Security was not designed to provide a comprehensive income protection and security program, but rather it was considered a supplement to savings and pensions. For this reason, it *does not* and *cannot* provide adequate economic support for the poor elderly who depend solely on Social Security, including the majority of the Black elderly. The Senate Committee on Aging is painfully aware of the inadequacies of Social Security and has made several significant recommendations that would raise the level of assistance to abolish poverty among older Americans. The Committee has also made recommendations to close the gaps in service in Medicare coverage, to limit the ever-increasing costs of Medicare, and to expand benefits to include more health-related services than are presently covered. An additional concern is the overwhelming focus of Medicare coverage on hospital-related services, rather than alternatives to institutionalization, such as home health services and outpatient care, which are substantially less expensive and more desirable to many older persons. The elderly, like the young, prefer to remain in their own homes, rather than be prematurely or unnecessarily institutionalized, which has proven to be a traumatic experience for the ill aged, leading frequently to severe depression, and even an early death, in some cases (Blenkner, 1965; Lieberman, 1967).

The Older Americans Act of 1965, as amended, provides the most comprehensive federal funding for aging programs in the United States. The Act was a giant step for this country, but "forty to fifty years behind the aging programs of other countries in the Western World." The major provisions of the Act include funds for (1) community planning, social services, and model projects (Title III); (2) training and research in the field of aging (Title IV); (3) multipurpose senior centers (Title V); (4) nutrition programs (Title VII), and (5) volunteer service programs, i.e., Foster Grandparents, Senior Companions, and Retired Senior Volunteers Programs. These programs have been well received and contributed a great deal to the quality of life and the mental health of older Americans. As would be expected, however, in a society that devalues old age, federal appropriations are comparatively "skimpy," limiting seriously the overall impact of the program on the total population of elderly persons. Title III and Title VII have probably had the most direct and significant influence on the mental health of Black aged recipients. Title III provides for services that enable many older persons to continue to live independently, instead of being institutionalized at a much higher public cost. Title VII provides low-cost, nutritious meals for the elderly in congregate settings where they have an opportunity to socialize and obtain rehabilitation and social services. The nutrition program, in particular, has been widely supported because of the close relationship between poverty, poor nutrition, and poor health. This program has also appealed to the elderly who are not poor, but poorly nourished as a result of isolation and/or depression which destroys the incentive to prepare a meal and eat alone.

The issues related to institutionalization of the Black aged take on a more complex twist than those related to the white aged. Blacks comprise less than 3 percent of the residents of nursing homes and homes for the aged, which remain largely segregated (Butler, 1973). As a result of this discriminatory practice, aged Blacks who need mental *or* physical health services for chronic conditions are usually committed to mental hospitals as the only alternative for care (Jackson, 1972). Frequently, these older persons could remain in their own homes or in the homes of relatives, if supportive home and community health services were available. In 1975, Title III provided such supportive services as counseling, homemaker services, home health aides, and day care to 1.7 million older Americans, including Blacks, who might otherwise have been institutionalized—where in most instances the philosophy of treatment is custodial rather than therapeutic. There is no doubt that many more older people could benefit from the services funded under Title III, if the federal budget provided for the expansion of these services. Older Black people, in particular, would benefit since these services offer a "reprieve" from the state hospital and hope for improved health functioning in the community.

It is impossible to discuss support systems impacting on the mental health of older persons without considering housing, which has already been identified as a major problem area for the elderly. The housing problem, in its most basic and traditional form, can be defined as one of finding ways to assure an adequate living environment for people too poor to pay market prices for decent housing. The Black aged appropriately fall into this category. The major housing resource for the poor Black aged is public housing, which was authorized for elderly persons in the Federal Housing Act of 1956. It is estimated that over 400,000 elderly persons reside in public housing in the United States, with 50 to 90 percent of the residents being Black elderly in the large metropolitan areas. In Washington, D.C., the residents of public housing for the elderly are 98 percent Black. A second resource for the Black aged has been low-cost housing developed by private non-profit organizations in the Black community with federal loans. In recent years, housing construction in both these areas has come to a halt, although new legislation has been introduced to increase funding for elderly housing and rent supplements. It is estimated that over five million units are needed to meet the needs of older Americans for decent housing. We are far from reaching that goal.

A very special area of interest is the alternative of "congregate housing," which is a residential environment which incorporates shelter and the services needed by elderly persons who are functionally impaired but not chronically ill. This housing arrangement enables them to maintain a semi-dependent lifestyle and avoid placement in institutions as they grow older. This is a common problem in public housing as old tenants grow older and the natural deterioration of age begins to restrict their activities. An increasing number of public housing agencies are faced with the fact that they must evict these older tenants who can no longer sustain basic chores of shopping, cooking, cleaning, or administering simple, but required, medical care. Over three million persons could benefit from congregate housing with services. If the services are not provided, all of these persons could be forced into nursing homes or mental hospitals unnecessarily (Donahue, 1975). There is little doubt that the demand for residential living with basic services will increase dramatically within the next decade, given the fact that the older population is growing faster than any other age group. Similarly, the Black aged population should experience significant growth in the next few decades as the middle-aged Black population, which is healthier, better educated, better nourished, and less isolated, begins to close the life expectancy gap between Blacks and whites.

Final Comment

Growing old in America is not generally perceived as the fairy tale experience portrayed by such cliches as the "golden years," and the "twilight of life." On the other hand, it does not have to represent the misery and deprivation that is experienced by aging persons who are poor and Black. The natural process of aging brings with it discomforts that are both physical and emotional, but the older person who is financially secure, physically healthy and comfortable, and socially integrated is much better prepared to cope with the aging process. Evidence of physical and mental well-being in the later years is very apparent in retirement communities around the country, on the sands of Miami Beach, and in the homes of the "middle-class" Black elderly. If all older Americans are to be assured comfort and security and a lifestyle that promotes positive feelings about their dignity and self-worth, it is imperative that the federal government make a commitment to aging programs that is realistic rather than token. Above all else, there is a need for the development of new attitudes toward aging and older persons—attitudes which recognize that older Americans have a zest for living, a level of appetites, and the right to their full satisfaction comparable to that of their younger counterparts—attitudes which fully recognize the rights of older persons to freedom of choice as first-class American citizens.

References

Blenkner, M. "Environmental Change and the Aging Individual." *Gerontologist* 7 (1965): 101–105.

Butler, R., and Lewis, M. *Aging and Mental Health*. St. Louis: C. V. Mosby, 1973.

Donahue, W. "Adequacy of Federal Response to Housing Needs of Older Americans." *Testimony before the Senate Committee on Aging,* October, 1975.

Golant, S. "Residential Concentrations of the Future Elderly." *Gerontologist,* 2 (1975): 16–24.

Hawkins, B. "Social Participation of the Black Elderly in Two Communities." Unpublished Ph.D. dissertation, Brandeis University, 1976.

Jackson, H. "Alternatives to Institutional Care for Older Americans." Presented to the Conference on Alternatives to Institutional Care, Duke University, June 1972.

Jackson, J. "Social Impacts of Housing Relocation Upon Urban Low Income Black Aged." *Gerontologist* 12 (1972): 32–42.

Lawton, M. "The Aged Resident of the Inner City." *Gerontologist* 7 (1971): 277–283.

——————. "Housing Characteristics and the Well-being of Elderly Tenants in Federally Assisted Housing." *Journal of Gerontology* 30 (1975): 601–607.

Lieberman, M. "Relationship of Mortality Rates to Entrance to a Home for the Aged." *Geriatrics* 16 (1967): 515–519.

Lindsay, I. "The Multiple Hazards of Age and Race: The Situation of Aged Blacks in the U.S." Senate Committee on Aging, 1971.

Lowenthal, M., and Frier, M. "The Elderly Ex-mental Patient." *International Journal of Psychiatry* 13 (1967): 103–106.

National Urban League. *Double Jeopardy: The Older Negro in America Today*. New York: National Urban League, 1964.

Rubenstein, D. "The Social Participation of the Black Elderly." Unpublished Ph.D. dissertation, Brandeis University, 1971.

Senate Committee on Aging. "Developments in Aging: 1975 and January through May 1976." (Most of the statistical data in this article were taken from this reference and the U.S. Census Supplements.)

Thompson, G. "Adjustment in Retirement: A Causal Interpretation of Factors Influencing the Morale of Retired Men." Unpublished Ph.D. dissertation, Brandeis University, 1971.

9 FUNCTIONS OF THE SOCIAL NETWORK IN THE BLACK COMMUNITY

*Thomas A. Gordon, Ph.D., and
Norman L. Jones, M.A.*

Function—network—community. An old African proverb comes to mind: "If in the course of his journey a man does not know where he is going, then swiftly he travels nowhere and any road will take him there." As is so often the case in human endeavor, we need a good beginning—a road map or strategy for spotting the key guideposts—if we are to get anywhere at all. Understanding Black people—their health and mental health—is really no different. For here, too, the alternative to the map, marker, or way of viewing the world is typically continued involvements with costly expenditures of energy, traveling down one false path or another.

Function—network—community. It is important to map the full terrain, but to keep our markers simple and useful. A "function" refers simply to a specific duty, act, or essential "purpose" for which an entity or system is organized to deliver or perform. In terms of common body performance, we are likely to say that the function of the eye or vision system is to enable the organism to see; the function of the digestive system is to enable the organism to utilize food nutrients; the function of the ear is to enable hearing and assist in regulating body equilibrium, and so on. The human body discharges an enormous range of functions, as do other living and non-living systems in the universe.

A "network" refers simply to a connection or intermingling of entities or systems—typically in ways that permit functioning or work that goes beyond the capability of one entity alone. A network, then, permits the amplification of work via the alignment of separate entities or systems, considered distinct for reasons of separation in time, distance, or useful convenience. A piece of cloth or fabric embodies a network of threads. A transportation network—whether Pony Express or Amtrack—regulates the flow of passengers and freight across vast distances via an interlocking arrangement of hardware and stations. A power network might consist of hundreds of miles of lines, arranged to regulate the flow of electrical energy and information required to meet the needs of persons in diverse locations. A communication network represents an indispensable array of interconnecting devices, designed to provide citizens with vital information and entertainment. The radio and television broadcasting networks, for instance, enjoy almost constant and instantaneous communication with billions of people, scattered across oceans and terrain, who will always know and feel and share some of the same ideas and information, but will in all probability never encounter each other face to face.

Obviously, as in the example of communications, the interlocking features of a network need not be entirely visible to enjoy considerable influence and binding power. A network requires merely a context, entities, pathways for connection, and codes or rules of design for enabling the whole arrangement to function or do work. A single source-receiver combination is a minimal network; a context with many sources, branches, and destinations forms an elaborated network. Effective networks hinge on resourceful design. That is, effective networks tend to optimize the capacity of their components, regulate the load, pace the transmission, and stabilize the whole assembly in times of distraction or stress. The design represents the code which permits the assembly to survive demands and adapt successfully.

A people network operates similarly. A social network assumes a social context or setting, people, options for contact and exchange, and shared understandings about the proper terms for sustained interaction. Every community has a variety of formal and informal "networks" which "function" to regulate the flow and intercourse of its people. A community, then, operates via its physical and social hardware, way stations, and connecting encounters. It represents the pool of people who may be considered as operating under the presence of demonstrably common assumptions, symbols, sentiments, habits, needs, and interests. A community is often demarcated by such tangible criteria as geographic occupancy, language, income, education, value tradition, and religious affiliation. Ideally, for example, we would expect to detect the felt presence of community quite readily among a grouping of people who live on the same land, speak the same language, work and study with roughly equivalent gains, and practice the same value beliefs. Anthropology attests to the worldwide reality of community in this vein of shared physical and social experience.

With Black Americans the presence of true community, whether physical or social, can be only spoken of symbolically. Our survival and growth has been conditioned within a context and over a number of years of considerable duress. Many of the old ways and shared understandings have been lost or gradually supplanted by other terms for living. The differences among us are evident. On many issues, real differences in geography, education, income, occupation, and the like make for pronounced differences in sentiment and behavior. On other matters, however, the differences appear to be less significant. Our historical relation to white people and present circumstance tend to override a host of apparent differences, particularly around the common "stakes" involved in our securing life and limb, property and privilege, and dignity. To be Black is to "feel" and "know" that one's access to privilege and dignity is fundamentally delimited by color and its meaning within the American frame—whatever the education and income, nuances and differences among us some would hold up to view.

Black homogeneity, no; some Black community differences, yes. But the accumulated weight of the American experience presses heavily, forging for certain categories of concerns a real, however often denied, feeling of common destiny and community. At times it is useful to say the words "Black community" to call attention to our legacy and interdependence. Where there are variations among any people, the key consideration is never simply to deny or applaud the differences. Rather, we ask: "What difference does the difference make?" America's resounding answer seems to be that for a wide range of themes the differences among Blacks do not count for much. The Black community thus remains a reality experience and binding force—for us and the rest of the world.

Function—network—community. Our concern in this chapter is community health and survival. To define community is to highlight what it is supposed to be. By so doing, we project a standard from which the realities of Black community life may be compared. The gap between the standard and the reality speaks to our needs. Briefly, a community operates within the design of its networks and institutions to sustain the physical and social life of its members. Food, clothing, shelter, and currency for barter and exchange are physical necessities. In addition a community is intended to provide productive work assignment or niches for its members (role), an environment suitable for the transmission of skills and values (socialization), and the experience of validation, both personal and surrounding the worth of one's own kind (identity). Furthermore, a community hinges on the presumption of mutual aid and interdependence. The terms "member," "stranger," "guest," "outlaw," "outcast," and the like reflect the power of community conventions governing access to privilege and mutual aid. Lastly, a community—not always in words, but in its priorities, taboos, and rituals—becomes the storehouse of cultural wisdom and cumulative experience. Each new generation cannot remake the wheel or rediscover the entire set of strategies for extracting advantages from the environment. A community must store the lessons, retell the principles, and exemplify the applications, if each generation is to profit and regenerate from the wealth of the last.

The function of social networks is to fulfill the requirements of community. A true community enjoys institutions and networks designed to perpetuate and enhance the life chances of its members. It provides living space, employment, things to wear, settings where people can relax, value reinforcement, and protection from undue intrusions from the wider world. The networks condition the *pace* and *quality* of social exchange, offering up settings and customs within which people can learn how to meet various problem situations and accumulate advantage. In this vein it is worth noting that the old authority and tasks, once the province of intact family networks, have fallen in modern times to a host of other formal and informal arrangements—from street action settings and entertainment to communications media to a string of "agencies," "disciplines," and "therapies" geared up to lighten and reduce distress. So often the community accumulates little real advantage, owing to the special agendas as well as the alien and uncoordinated nature of many of these non-familial nets. A community which relies on "outside" institutions to ensure its growth and survival is fortunate when it profits from the experience. More often than not, it is perilously close to cooptation or debilitating control.

Ideally, in terms of the life cycle, the human offspring is intended to be born and nurtured within community settings that are consistent with his family outlook and desires, where those who supervise the health and education of the young are in close communication with the relevant parents. Children should play in safety and mingle with other children well before school age. Children should enjoy the love and concern of adults across different generations, returning appropriate recognition and respect. Teachers and parents must collaborate in planning for the child's exposure to training and values. Peer affiliations must build on the foundations of home and school with adults supporting peer expressions of responsibility and movement toward maturity. The community condones the regulated interaction of males and females, drawing upon cross-generational wisdom in assisting young adults to sift through courtship and career developments. All adults should demonstrate clear investments in community survival. They must anchor behavior within some frame of values; they should move freely across extrafamilial contacts; and they should welcome communication with children. With declining strength and productivity, the older adults, nevertheless, ought to retain considerable status. Their cumulative experience provides the backdrop for important community decisions; their presence becomes integral for the care and inspiration of the very young.

In order to build a strong community, one capable of approximating the kind of support outlined above, it is essential to develop trustworthy formal and informal nets. The overlapping and interlocking network design ensures that the family receives multiple and ongoing attention to its life-cycle demands. The key overarching consideration involves values, power, and people. The stability and orchestration of social networks proceed from some set of value positions. Power implies the community's capability to protect its value frame. And people are the instruments who must in the final analysis interpret and apply the values, coordinate the power, and deliver the services which will make the difference between community survival and deterioration.

As researchers and consultants, the authors have noted persistent evidence of the importance of the value position/power/people consideration. Educational arenas, for instance, are notorious for claiming "objectivity" and "comitment to skills," while projecting raw value positions at every turn. Young, liberal, white teachers are especially prone to bring sentiments to class around the Black child's needs that are wholly inconsistent with the views of parents. The tenor of the sixties highlighted an elaborate mythology about the deprivations and inadequacies of Black children, Black parents, and Black communities.

Young, liberal, white teachers tend to retain much of the assumptions of this "victim deficiency" mythology in their encounters with Black families. Whereas older whites are often extremely "hard" on "deprived" Black children and "give up" early on training them, young, liberal whites tend to be extremely lenient on "deprived" youngsters and overly concerned with meeting their every whim and desire. Young liberals often have views of physical punishment that diverge sharply from those of Black parents. To feel that there is never an excuse for hitting a child often puts the teacher and parents at odds. In such instances the presumptive ability of Black parents to rear and nurture their children is often called into question. The teacher patronizes or scapegoats or avoids the parents. The parents are often defensive and impatient, however well-intended the teacher's value position. Such teachers, not respecting the value frame and power of Black parents, always communicate their feelings and contempt.

Eventually, the child, parents, and major segments of the community take notice of the negative feelings and respond in kind. Where there is low respect or trust across home and school, the child always pins the gaps in value consistency and the real clout his parents can wield. He knows when teachers are misguided about his culture and his needs or when his parents are relatively powerless to command respect from others. The tensions around home-school conflicts bear on the child's mood and learning. The end result is a "no-win" condition—the child always loses. Ideally, then, a community seeks to deploy its people and power in ways that reduce the incidence of value conflict and confusion for the young.

With this exploration of ideal community, let us return to the real-world Black community to analyze the actual functions of its social structures. Again, "Black community" is used here as a social and experiential marker—where the years of injustice, instability, and powerlessness have provided the backdrop and basis for our coming together and feeling common bonds. Heterogeneity notwithstanding, Black people do mix and mingle under the terms of shared social and symbolic experience. We share the people and value roots; we share the relative powerlessness within the American frame; we share the legacy of dislocations and strains; we share the enclaves, institutions, and networks that regulate social exchange; we share the ties and social supports. In fact, for most matters, North or South, Black people share so much in the way of cumulative understanding and social currency that the logistical problems associated with something like moving people or ideas or goods across Black collectivities are almost always easily manageable.

We share the rituals, greetings, tastes, smells, styles, speech, and manners that permit this order of social commerce. In this sense, our geographic proximity and isolation accentuate, rather than perfectly depict, the common bond. Certainly we "know" that, by and large, most "real" Black people live under marginal incomes and privilege over here or there, in this ghetto or the next, on that "side of town." Geography counts. But we also "know" that America constrains these boundaries and other options, and that wherever Black people live or travel, we are likely to be experiencing America in some of the same socially negotiable ways. Blacks do not always operate within clearly demarcated living boundaries. The Black community always operates within social legacy, irrespective of physical boundary and proximity. Relationship supersedes proximity and flows from the acknowledgment and binding force of our wider common condition.

Unfortunately, the real-world Black community is a far cry from the interlocking people/power/value supports evidenced in the ideal. The Black community faces a fundamental problem of social organization and network design; that is, the community is organized without the power to protect its people or values. It is organized for self-destruction or what Fanon, in *The Wretched of the Earth,* called "collective auto-destruction." At best, it is organized for survival and gratification, seldom-sustained productivity, and accumulated advantage. At worst, it is organized for sheer predatory abuse. Popular myths are revealing: we often hear slogans and expressions about Black life that tend to suggest that Black communities are somehow "chaotic," "unpredict-able," "random," or "disorganized."

On one level, the words are accurate in that they describe what the "insider" and "outsider" must feel at times watching the parade of Black community events. On another level, however, the expressions are misleading: the Black community is highly organized, identifiable, and predictable. Ask any Black child over 5 years of age what he "knows" about his world, and he will speak about the people, problems, predators, power brokers, idols, tastes, music, aspirations, sexual mores, cash flow, squabbles, crime patterns, church influences, and sports options of his community, drawing parallels for nearly any Black community in the country. Why? How? Where are these lessons stored? What are the formal and informal institutions and settings that preserve them? What is the carry-over of this kind of exposure? The answers point to community network design.

The Black community networks, conditioned by years of relative powerlessness, are neither randomly operating nor crumbling all around us. The physical dwellings of our communities may be crumbling, but the social networks are fairly well intact. In the North the "promise" of jobs, escape from the farm, glamor and gratification pulled Blacks away from one set of social connections to another. Looking back it is clear that at first "ghettos" or "Black enclaves" held out "glamor," but ultimately they condemned Black families to extremely depressing and debilitating living conditions. Fewer Blacks are migrating North; if anything the migration trend is reversing as more Blacks are returning to the South.

It is true that Black people do not enjoy full power, North or South. But even with "Jim Crow" segregation, Black people in the South never bore the burdens, pace, isolation, crime, crowding, insecurities, and dislocations of the Northern urban centers. Southern Blacks enjoyed some degree of productive capability and "local" autonomy, if over no more than their "piece of land" or "section of town." Before the desegregation plans of the sixties, Black people in the South, for instance, "ran" or managed the Black schools. Under these conditions, a school provided much more than classroom instruction: it cultivated a considerable array of informal social networks through which Black youngsters passed and attracted community support. After years of desegregation, the strains and changes in this network array are troubling many Black adults who initially favored integration. School morale, teacher authority, discipline, "grapevine" understandings and communication lines between Black parents and Black teachers, Black role models in positions of competence and authority, the Black child's opportunities to attract "after-class" attention, excel in sports, be a majorette, or act in a school play—all of these are shifting drastically under integration.

The productive potential of the South is still there, however, awaiting full utilization of Black people's traditional ties to land and home ownership, church and extended family, skilled craftsmanship and agricultural experience. The Northern Black enclave, by and large, is simply not geared up to sustain productive output, massive self-restoration, or uplift. Its rituals and relevant settings, payoffs and penalties, crime patterns, violence and mutual abuse, interpersonal codes and styles, and its visible supports for predatory vs. cooperative living teach lessons of desperation and sheer survival. Of course, Black people in the South continue to find some of these same survival conditions present, but the long-standing association of epidemic social ills with the urban North still seems to hold true. North or South, Blacks are individually and collectively attempting the adaptations to ensure at least survival—and more where possible. Full productivity must await a different order of power and social network design.

Survival Settings

A close look at the network of social supports and critical settings within the Black community reveals considerable detail about our productive potential and survival adaptations. The Black community is attuned to *social relationship* and is organized for *gratification* and social experience. A patchwork of clubs, organizations, fraternal orders, church-work associations, aid societies, night spots, playgrounds, and recreational areas dot the Black community, providing a context and "havens" for socialization and relaxation. Most individuals and families frequent a regular setting or several places principally to exchange information and ideas and to interact with others like them in comfortable surroundings. These places may include large institutions with formal task and social mandates, like the church, or they may range more informally from clubs and concert halls to local bars and street-corner conglomerations.

Few Black persons are surviving who are unattached to these or similar social support settings. Quite often the settings are explicitly charged with service and relief commitments, having grown out of the historical needs to counter specific community ills. Churches and charitable groups, elite social clubs, neighborhood associations, chartered lodges, and fraternal and fund-raising orders fall into this category. Here the explicit charge and structure of the setting provide a continuing rationale for the process of coming together and deriving gratification from the exchange.

Another category of support settings involves those which downplay productive output and instead explicitly promote the full incorporation of Black community members into the gratification/relaxation/entertainment theme. Black people tend to congregate, not just in churches and clubs, but in lounges and bars, "juke-joints" and night spots, luncheonettes, playgrounds, parks, street corners, and porch stoops, merely to experience the presence of other people who look and feel the way they do. Thousands of such places flourish throughout the country because they provide invaluable connections and gratification for the people who pass through them. They are critical to the survival patterns—and hence the health and mental health—of Black people.

Let us remember that body and spirit require nourishment. In this sense, a person's favorite tavern is much more than an afterwork "watering hole." Alcohol relaxes, but the setting itself is a communication experience. The same is true of other key settings: a pool hall is only secondarily used for the rules of the game; a barbershop or beauty salon is not just a place where one's hair is groomed; a concert hall is not just for listening. With the bar (as with the pool hall, barbershop, and street corner), the setting is organized primarily as a relaxation preserve where men can "unwind" and talk about things in a personal manner with friends and acquaintances. The seating is comfortable; the mixtures of music and drink are soothing and stimulating; the *pace* seems to be all one's own.

For a few dollars more, there are disco and night club arrangements, offering dance and professional entertainment. Where is the survival value in these settings? They provide gratification and tension release, to be sure. Social connection is also a dominant theme. In fact, it is terribly misleading to say cavalierly (as social scientists often do) that Black people frequent these settings and indulge in potentially destructive habits like drinking and narcotics use merely because they are "alienated" or "unattached." On the contrary, the very people who indulge regularly over time are actually the ones who might be considered most "attached" and incorporated into the prevailing norms and direction images of the community. It is almost impossible not to sample the pleasures and "goodies" of these settings if one's whole scheme for self-definition, connection, and gratification is anchored within this social frame.

The Black community's social networks also are designed to enhance enormous information exchange and instrumental learning. If intelligence may be summarized as the capacity to understand the contours and constraints of an environment and negotiate advantages within it, these social networks provide extensive information, process-ing training and reinforcement for young and old alike. A street corner is "turf" for roving bands of young males whose identity is organized around gang activity. It is also where community members come to learn and hear, to see and be seen. Young boys and girls "check out" the styles and tastes around them; relay information about parties, clothes, tall tales, and other exciting happenings; and fine-tune the images of appropriate adulthood they will carry for life.

In Philadelphia the street corner is awake and bustling at 7 A.M. each day, and the bars are flourishing! There is a tavern on almost every corner. Where is the need? People are exchanging greetings and socially cohesive gestures: they "slap five" and ask, "What's happening?" as a way of plunging into the topics of the day. The talk moves back and forth from one tale to another, across legal thresholds and proper language, stopping here and there on people and things that are im-portant to the speakers and listeners.

By age 3 or 4, the Black child may know these settings well, but still at some distance. By age 9 or 10, he may be thoroughly proficient in how to walk, talk, cuss, fight, lie, smoke, drink, mock adults, idolize gangsters, dress, steal, play numbers, and write graffiti—all socially negotiable skills in most Black communities. The dilemma is that the street corner provides essential nourishment for the physical and emotional needs of community members. It offers respite from the white world; here people can "come together," "pass through," or "stop in" and engage familiars without reference to the "man" or white demands. In this sense the corner, like the taverns, pool halls, and playgrounds, bolsters the individual's social connections and fulfills critical survival needs.

The problem comes in translating this order of survival activity into its parallels in sustained productivity and collective gain. The bridges are not yet in place. The *idols* of young children are those people who adopt the habits and life style of "predatory survival" and "glamorous consumption." Community uplift is of low priority. Accordingly, the social props and settings and rituals which sustain sheer gratification and survival tend also to prepare young Black children to assume the same types of roles that they have seen community adults play all along. Here, the potential for perpetuating long-term mutual abuse—inherent in the gratification ethic—appears to undercut the value of current Black community social network design. The survival and gratification ethic *per se*—without strong, intervening group values—builds up its own following, but there is every likelihood that future generations will function as part of the community problem rather than part of the solution.

Unfortunately, survival still comes first: the sixties ethic of Black consciousness and group achievement has been stilled by the calming, personal mobility message of the seventies. Some people are boning up, keeping up, and "making it" relative to personal goals; others are content with surviving at levels of minimal pain. One seventies norm among Black youngsters is to use the "pleasures" of the community networks not just to "get high," but to maintain nearly constant euphoria by "staying high." Drug distribution and use have long been common occurrences within the Black community network design. The support settings have long functioned to introduce, idealize, and train the young to deal with drugs. Dope is still big business, and these same nets are functioning to attract even younger, elementary-age cohorts to the "pleasures" of induced euphoria. The survival and gratification ethic addresses the child's immediate need to feel a part of what his familiars are doing, while simultaneously paving the way and justifying the worst kind of spiraling self-destruction.

Identity and Health

Mental health is contingent upon power: in the best of worlds, a healthy community marshals its resources and deploys its full range of power to protect its value frame and orchestrate successful adaptations. Black mental health suffers to the extent that Black people find themselves relatively powerless to protect themselves, their communities, or their values. Still, people do press on with survival and draw gratification and connection wherever and whenever it is socially available. People need to validate the worth and existence of themselves and their own kind. This is the essence of the process of feeling positive about oneself and consolidating one's identity. The problem comes with the historically low status of Black people in the American context. The wider society projects negative images about Black capabilities, whether community or personal. The message is a classic double-bind or "no-win" condition: be white, come close; stay Black, get back. A community struggles to protect itself from this level of emotional intrusion.

Historically, the Christian church represents the dominant bulwark, protector, value anchor, and identity source in the survival struggle of the Black community. It provides the "coming together," the nurturance and haven; it speaks to Black issues and needs; it delivers education, relief, and service; it opens its facilities for political and community use; it strengthens invaluable connections across family units, age groupings, and role and class divisions. Before the intrusion of recent secular trends, the Black middle class and huge segments of poorer Blacks viewed the church as the very heart of the community social fabric. The church lifted the spirit; it encouraged participation and release; it provided identity with powers larger than oneself; it directed the energies and talents of believers into constructive work. Secularism notwithstanding, the Christian church is still one of the most attractive and productive settings in the Black community. Like all religious institutions, it has the capacity to orchestrate an enormous range of formal and informal incentives and occasions to seal one's personal identity and promote collective goals.

The use of the wider term "religious" is deliberate, because identity and health require connection, though not necessarily Christian church connection. Over the last two decades, the Black community has witnessed the strong identity pull of several non-Christian religions, most notably Islam as interpreted by the teachings of the Nation of Islam. The Nation of Islam, under the Honorable Elijah Muhammad, and with considerable charismatic impetus from Malcolm X and Muhammad Ali, has attempted to carve out an identity for poorer Blacks with a tremendous staying power that combines productive output and personal zeal. The Nation attempts to meet its members' needs internally. It provides a broad umbrella of protection, a value frame, clearly demarcated male/female roles, defined settings for child growth and learning, and special observances and symbols (e.g., Savior's Day) for highlighting group identity. Its social networks are tied to political goals and special targets that span a wide order of settings—from prisons and factories to street corners, schools, bars, and other places formerly considered hopeless for constructive incorporation and identity development.

It is instructive to watch Black community religious institutions at work, attracting and holding people for purposeful action. The congregations acknowledge shared realities, shared understandings, and shared pain. The larger society denies Black people access to many kinds of privilege and identity options, holding them fast to their own communities and forcing them to deal with whatever family or peer supports they can muster. Frustrated, angry, tense, mistrusting—all these terms describe Black people at some point in their cycle of inter-actions with the larger society. What can be done with the inevitable dislocations and tensions? There is always the prevailing ethic of sheer gratification and survival. We have examined some of the self-perpetuating, self-defeating properties of this survival theme. What is the one ingredient needed to move beyond survival alone? It would appear to be "productive purpose," the overlay of the assumption that survival *per se* is not enough, that the future belongs to those who iden-tify themselves with power, productive output, and the taking in hand of their destiny. The extended family system aside, no other Black community setting comes close to matching the Black religious ones for bringing together connection, gratification, and purposeful action for community gain. Healthy people need to feel a part of some power larger than themselves; they need to be productive and to enjoy their relations and accomplishments. In this view, the healthy community is designed to function in ways that build in connections, not merely in the service of gratification, but in alignment with productive action.

Presently, the Black community offers up an enormous range of connections that are gratifying, but few that hold out the possibility of sustained productivity. The religious institutions bring together large numbers of people who find it both comfortable and necessary to define their lives in terms of zeal and work. The numbers themselves are important, as are the participatory climate and capacity for high feeling found in the religious sector. People, when linked together, can provide extremely coercive emotional experiences for each other. In this sense the participatory emotions of religious experience are mesmerizing and potentially available for constructive work. An everyday counterpart of this emotional intensity can be viewed in the pulling power of large crowds such as might frequent an athletic event, a movie, or a live entertainment performance. Any casual observer of live performances or film audiences will note that Black people tend to respond emotionally according to the pull of the crowd elements present. We talk to our movies and to each other in the theater as the film plot develops. We move in time with the live performances and often experience states akin to religious frenzy. It is not coincidental that Isaac Hayes is called "Black Moses." The parallels to religious experience are striking throughout his performance. The connection and gratification are evident. What is missing, to move beyond the level of sheer gratification, is the constructive channeling toward purposeful action. Survival demands and gratification come first in the Black community. Yet, ultimately, survival can be transcended only when one's happiness is grounded in joining up in relationships to do just that—to transcend sheer survival.

The Future

The Black community network design strains at times under the weight of sheer survival demands. No immutable law gives any guarantee of even continued survival. After all, we know, for instance, that approximately two-thirds of all known animal species are now extinct. There is a lesson here for man. The future belongs not to the isolate, but to those who heed the call of mutual aid and interdependence and who devise nets for collaborative work. Under conditions of extreme duress, finite resources, food or water scarcity, or emotional intensity, it is not uncommon to find animal species which gradually succumb to their deprivations as they lose sight of their potential for purposeful action. In one sense a human assembly is no different: it perishes beyond certain limits of duress; it grinds to a halt under debilitating competition and confusion. Yet, in other ways, a human community has the distinct advantage of high collaborative capacity and the potential to use cumulative experience to counter its current strains. It can adapt to scarcity; it can share the resources; it can regulate and siphon off the intensity of the emotional load. All of this is possible, but there are no guarantees.

The Black community must draw upon the knowledge and lessons stored in its *relationships* and social network *design*. Some orders of connection and social commerce have proven to be strengthening; some categories of settings have shown their power to bind human energy in constructive, uplifting endeavors. The extended family has developed the linkages of mutual aid and interdependence. The religious orders have built bridges across social divisions and found channels for utilizing the potential of many diverse settings, clubs, groups, and persons. Survival and gratification *per se* cannot accomplish this. Both the extended family and religious structures recognized this principle too: they have been organized to deliver work and to view membership as always requiring validation in constructive action.

In response to our separate exclusion, we often ignore the advantages of collaborative ties. Black people spend considerable energy in defining one category of Blacks as "out" and themselves exclusively as "in." This process represents a kind of "territorial imperative" that feeds on the narrowest criteria for entry and privilege. Philadelphia, for instance, is a city of rigid class, clique, and neighborhood boundaries. In the past the social networks of Blacks of higher status have decisively excluded other Black people on the basis of gradations of skin color, money, professional background, and the like. The parallel among the young is found in street-corner gang activity. Philadelphia is notorious for the sheer volume of its organized gangs; within the gang arena, young Black males are joined in perpetual conflict with other Black youth over something so narrowly exclusive as a corner. The Black youth also learn the harsh realities of street life: how to prey and defend against predators, how to use drugs, and how to study crime as a career. The lesson is simply that the Black community cannot afford unwarranted exclusion. The linkages await cultivation.

It is difficult to establish social bonds if fear and the assumption of scarcity prevail. Mental health requires the bond which itself requires the trust to risk the encounters to make it grow. If the adults fear the risk, the children will feel the missing support and will not risk being "swallowed up" either. The young ones will seize the territorial imperative with a vengeance and eventually rule out the old. There is power in the recognition of shared experience, shared pain, shared tradition, and shared outlook on responsible action. When Black people understand this principle, they will once again devise settings, units, institutions that function to their collective gain. They will span the present divisions, identifying with the sense of shared experience and shared cultural condition. They will forego sheer survival. They will deny the ethic of territorial exclusion and predatory abuse. They will reunite the families; they will rekindle the ideal and cumulative advantage of community itself. They will understand that survival and gratification are not enough. Community implies the higher call to set in motion the processes of interdependence and responsible production. The real-world Black community awaits commitment to this higher call. The challenge is inclusion and sound production—to connect and construct, to light the candle bringing in a new and better day.

References

Arasteh, A. R. *Toward Final Personality Integration*. New York: Wiley, 1975.

Benge, R. *Communication and Identity*. London: Bingley, 1972.

"The Black Church." *Black Scholar*. 2 (1970): 13–26.

Brown, C. *Manchild in the Promised Land*. New York: Signet, 1965.

Chestang, L. "The Child Welfare System." Unpublished paper. Annual Convention, Black Child Development Institute, Washington, D.C., 1974.

Clark, K. *Dark Ghetto*. New York: Harper & Row, 1965.

Drake, S., and Clayton, H. *Black Metropolis*. New York: Harcourt, Brace & World, 1970.

Duhl, L. (ed.). *The Urban Condition*. New York: Simon & Schuster, 1963.

Easton, D. *A Systems Analysis of Political Life*. New York: Wiley, 1965.

Fanon, F. *The Wretched of the Earth*. New York: Grove Press, 1968.

Forde, D. *African Worlds*. New York: Oxford University Press, 1970.

Inose, H. "Communication Networks." *Scientific American* 227 (1972): 116–128.

Liebow, E. *Tally's Corner*. Boston: Little, Brown, 1967.

Scanzoni, J. *The Black Family in Modern Society*. Boston: Allyn & Bacon, 1971.

Swingle, P. *Social Psychology in Natural Settings*. Chicago: Aldine, 1973.

Waters, F. *The Book of the Hopi*. New York: Ballantine, 1971.

Watzlawick, P.; Beavin, J.; and Jackson, D. *Pragmatics of Human Communication*. New York: W. W. Norton, 1967.

10 THE IMPACT OF ECOLOGICAL INFLUENCES ON THE MENTAL HEALTH OF URBAN BLACK COMMUNITIES

Lewis P. Clopton, Ph.D.

Introduction

The interdependence of man and his environment is the focus of human ecology. Determining the relative influences of environmental or contextual factors on human behavior and social organization is compounded by the diversity of environmental factors and their interactions over space and time. Often these interactions result in behavioral consequences not predictable or explainable in terms of linear or additive reasoning.

Consider, for example, the finding that parents residing in high-rise apartments find it difficult to monitor or intervene in their children's recreational activities (Mitchell, 1971). A simple extrapolation of this finding would predict that the intensity and incidence of this concern are positively related to the intensity of residential development. There are a number of reasons to doubt this, however. In fact many diverse influences, including attributes of the social and cultural environment as well as the physical attributes of proximity, determine the nature of parent-child relationships (Srole, 1972). Thus not all families in high-rise apartments are concerned with decreased parental control, nor does household proximity to play sites guarantee increased parental influence on child activities.

The science of human ecology is particularly relevant to an assessment of the consequences of urban living on the mental health of Blacks. The number of Blacks in urban communities has grown phenomenally in the recent past. While direct comparisons of the available statistics are tenuous, primarily because of counting biases and urban definitional changes (Clawson, 1971, pp. 13–30.), the number of Blacks residing in places defined as urbanized by the U.S. Bureau of the Census has increased from 6.8 million in 1950 to 17.49 million by 1970. (As defined in the census, an urban area consists of at least one city with a minimum population of 50,000 and contiguous densely settled areas.) Over the same period the Black non-urbanized population decreased from 8.2 million to 8.0 million. By 1970, the nation's Black population was more urbanized than its non-Black counterpart: 69 percent for Blacks and 62 percent for whites (U.S. Dept. of Commerce, 1969; 1974). If concern for the impact of urban environments on human health behavior has consequences for anyone, American Blacks must surely be first priority.

A Classification of Ecological Factors

Characterizing the contextual phenomena which influence human behavior is an ambitious undertaking. Contextual or environmental factors can, however, be classified by both the medium of the stimulus and the scale on which influences are elicited. With respect to the medium of an environmental variable, three modes can be identified: physical, social, and economic. (Often economic factors have been used as intervening variables in explaining the interrelation between physical and social processes.)

Physical factors are those which are primarily experienced through our senses. These physical elements of the environment usually occupy space, although the amount of space disposed by some factors may be infinitesimally small. Alternatively, these factors can be distinguished by their ability to affect physical well-being directly, as when sounds of extremely high frequency are inaudible to human beings and yet can damage the organs necessary for hearing.

Physical factors can be further subclassified by whether they are naturally occurring or are the intended or unintended result of human effort. The first are usually referred to as factors of the natural environment, while the latter are referred to as factors of the built environment. While human ecology has historically tended to underemphasize the natural environment as a stimulant of human behavior, there is an increasing realization of its importance. Man in the process of creating a built environment alters the natural environmental relationships. To the degree that features of the natural or built environment condition human behavior by inhibiting or facilitating specific forms of response, these factors are important from a human mental health perspective.

Some aspects of the physical environment may occasionally direct behavioral responses, while others may affect behavior indirectly. Such is the case, for example, with various kinds of air pollutants on urban populations. A high concentration of sulphur dioxide in the air does not elicit a direct behavioral response. Continued exposure, however, under conditions which produce sulphuric acid (e.g., high humidity) may result in irritation of the respiratory system. The latter does result in behavioral responses which may be involuntary, as when one coughs or sneezes to reduce congestion, or voluntary, as when one moves or alters activity to avoid or reduce exposure.

Many human ecologists have discounted the direct impact of physical ecological variables on human behavior (Mitchell, 1971). Proponents of this view hold that attributes of the physical environment set wide boundaries within which the more important and relevant aspects of behavior are determined by non-physical factors. Underlying this position was the theoretically unsound form of some early ecological research which correlated various attributes of the urban physical environment, usually housing conditions or density variables, with social, behavioral, or health variables and equated high correlation with causality. It is only recently that many of the long-term consequences of physical environmental conditions for human physical health have been determined. More recent yet has been the concern for mental health impacts. Much remains unanswered, but there are some findings of relevance to the mental health of urban Black residents which will be explored subsequently.

Social environmental factors are those which characterize human interaction and organization on an intellectual, as opposed to senusal, basis. Usually these phenomena are treated as attributes of communities or aggregates of individuals (Michelson, 1970, p. 19). Choosing communities as the unit of analysis, social ecologists emphasize the relative homogeneity of culture, values, and social structure within communities, as opposed to their relative diversity between communities. The structure and form of interaction within the community is the focal point in the social ecologist's analysis of the urban context. Individual and group behavior are then explained and analyzed in terms of intragroup culture, shared expectation and interdependency, and intergroup competition, dominance, accommodation and adaptation.

As opposed to physical ecology, which tends to emphasize the deterministic nature of the discrete environment, social ecology tends to emphasize process. Aspects of the social relations and organizational context influence individual or group change in certain directions. The influences of this social environment as conditioned by individual or group response and other forces instigate a set of unequally likely responses and results.

Economic forces have played an important role in ecological theory, although they are seldom considered as independent factors in themselves. Economic forces represent the degree of control over critical and unequally allocated resources. The most frequently encountered economic ecological variable is income.

It is sometimes useful to distinguish between wealth, or the degree or resource control at any specific time, and the flow or change of wealth over time as illustrated by income. The behavioral consequences of wealth and income may not be the same. Thus it may be expected that housing expenditures are more closely related to permanent income expectations over a period of years (a measure of wealth) than to immediate income (Aaron, 1972). Similarly, social class and status are the product not only of current position and income, but are also the cumulative effect of past experience and socialization as conditioned by wealth.

In addition to differences in medium, ecological variables vary by the scale on which they impact behavior. Some factors exert their influence on a localized or individual level. On this scale two individuals identical in all other respects except with regard to the variable in question would be expected to exhibit behavioral differences attributable to the significant variable. Distinct from factors which impact on a limited scale are those which influence large numbers of persons over large spatial areas simultaneously. Bank lending policies, for instance, impact on the decisions of a large number of property owners simultaneously, although not always similarly, concerning property improvements.

Unlike differences in the medium of ecological factors, scale differences vary on a continuum. This has caused some difficulty in the analysis of ecological factors, for it has added the question: Over what scale should ecological relationships manifest themselves? This scale of effect is important in that it determines the predominance and significance of the effects and the appropriate scale for intervention. It should be noted that many early ecologists were not concerned about effectuating change in the human environment. Their charge was only to explain and understand the interrelatedness of men with their environment, especially the urban environment. But Black researchers cannot afford such passive standings vis-à-vis their communities. For to assess the significance of urban environmental factors on the mental health and welfare of Black residents is meaningless if it is not useful in improving that condition.

The Significance of Urban Housing Patterns

Few decisions simultaneously affect an overall range of environmental influences as does the locational decision of the household. When deciding on an individual unit in which to reside, the household at the same time avails itself of the physical, social, and economic amenities and liabilities which proximity and accessibility distribute spatially. With respect to urban Black households, the segregated pattern of residential areas and the spatial allocation of ecological influences are of critical importance.

Evidence of racial and ethnic segregation in urban residential areas is obvious and well documented (Kain, 1973). An analysis of census materials, or a review of recent urban demography (United States Census Bureau, 1969), reveals that Black residential areas are clustered in older, relatively dense settlements contiguous with the central business districts of the city. At a higher level of aggregation, it is noted that Blacks reside in the central sections of metropolitan areas as opposed to the more recently developed suburban communities on the periphery of the urban area (Kain, 1973). The central city–suburban distinction is important because the governmental jurisdictions which provide local services (e.g., schools, police, public housing, municipal hospitals, and mental health districts) and collect tax revenues are more frequently than not coterminal with central city boundaries. To the extent that public services are not provided equally across jurisdictional boundaries, the boundaries are important determinants of local environmental conditions.

One anomaly of urban development in the United States is that the most accessible and presumably most valuable urban locations are occupied by households with low income and social status. This is in contrast to pre-industrial societies in which the most valuable sites in and near the city center are occupied by more wealthy tenants (Sjöberg, 1960). Two or three not totally inconsistent theories have been proposed to explain this occurrence.

Early urban theorists noted that cities develop radially from the central hub of business and economic activity outward (Burgess, 1925). Such a developmental scheme mandates that newer, more recent development takes place on the periphery of existing development. Areas of close proximity to the central business district are therefore characterized by older development than are those at a greater distance from the center. With increasing age, the physical amenities packaged in the housing unit decline relative to those of new housing, and in- creasing maintenance costs are incurred in the upkeep of the unit. These two factors result in a decreasing demand for the aging stock of housing with resultant declines in selling and/or rental costs (Lowry, 1960). Since low-income persons, Blacks in particular, have limited housing budgets, they occupy this "low-cost," older housing stock in the urban center.

While this aging theory of urban development has many short- comings, the most notable of which is that it ignores supply and discrimination considerations, it does capture some of the reality of urban Black residential patterns. Blacks do tend to occupy the older, more deteriorated stock of housing in the urban core.

An alternative theory for Black residential patterns has been proposed more recently by urban economic theorists (Alonso, 1964; Muth, 1961, 1969). Here it is noted that the intensity of land development and the allocation of land to various uses is essentially an extension of agricul- tural economics. Land, it is argued, is a relatively fixed commodity, the value of which is derived essentially from its productivity. Urban land highly accessible to the urban core is potentially more productive be- cause of its access and correspondingly more valuable than less accessible sites. This higher productivity mandates higher land values which, in turn, precipitate more intense development in the urban core. Potential residents, it is noted, consider both the cost of space and the cost of travel in location decisions (Alonso, 1964; Muth, 1961, 1969). Those of lower incomes, including Blacks, wish to minimize commuting cost, which mandates conveniently close locations. Further, low-income individuals, wishing to economize, purchase less space than their higher-income counterparts. They, therefore, are less sensitive to the price of space since they purchase little and tend to settle in the intensely developed, i.e., high-density, urban core. The primary contribution of this theory to our analysis is that it confirms another observation of urban Black residential patterns, namely, high density.

Yet a third explanation for the spatial development of segregated urban residential areas is offered by Walter Firey (1947). Firey's analysis, which until recently has been ignored by many human ecologists, implicitly considers the role of social values in the determination of urban residential patterns. In an analysis of the role of sociological factors in the development of the Beacon Hill section of Boston, Firey concludes that economic factors alone would result in the demolition of low-intensity residential development and redevelopment to more intensive uses. This did not occur, according to Firey, because of the cultural values of Beacon Hill and Boston residents and the sentimental and symbolic value they attached to the site. Firey thus concludes that culture and culturally determined values are significant factors in the urban development process. Following Firey's line of reasoning, culturally determined values may play a significant role in the evolution of Black residential areas in the urban space.

Each of these theories posits the importance of a particular ecological set of variables in explaining urban residential patterns, and by implication, the residential segregation of urban Blacks. The synthesis of these individual ecological factors and their cumulative implications for the mental, and physical, health of urban Blacks exceeds in total effect their simple aggregation.

Older housing units frequently predate the promulgation of local housing codes and ordinances legislated to institute minimum standards for health and safety. Structural integrity, fire retardation, the use of lead-based paints for interior wall surfaces, emergency access, and adequacy of ventilation are just a few of the concerns which housing codes and ordinances address. Where older units are not in compliance with minimum acceptable standards, the safety and well-being of occupants are jeopardized. Individual residents of such units are continually exposed to potentially injurious or incapacitating personal harm, and, as a result, must maintain a constant surveillance and alertness as to these hazards. The result is inevitably a heightened level of stress with behavioral adaptations as mediated by personalities and social influences. The effect of stress and the variety of adaptive behaviors in the presence of stress are examined subsequently.

In the case of lead-based paints there are direct physical and mental health dangers to children which may not be evident immediately where consumption of paint chips is limited but continued over a period of time. The resultant learning retardation and defective mental adjustment are irreversible. Poor ventilation and the continual surveillance necessary in the face of fire hazards can precipitate such stressful conditions that normal patience and tolerance are decreased with important effects in social relationships and interactions. This is a critical concern in many urban ghettos where noxious gases emitted by defective heaters and the constant danger of fires have increased to the point that even normal sleep is interrupted.

With age the costs of building and equipment maintenance and upkeep increase. The failure to maintain housing results in increased exposure to extremes in the weather and unsafe and unsanitary facilities. Housing studies reveal a high correlation between the incidence of respiratory infections, childhood diseases, minor digestive diseases, infectious and non-infectious skin diseases, household accidents, and housing inadequacy (Schorr, 1970). Undoubtedly personal hygiene and sanitary practices, along with increased communicability because of high density, must be considered before attributing causality to the physical aspects of the housing package.

There is evidence, from controlled studies, that improved housing reduces the incidence of health problems among relocated residents (Schorr, 1970). This reduction in health problems is most likely due to a number of factors. The adequacy of protection from natural environmental factors, such as extreme temperatures, undoubtedly reduces the incidence of respiratory infections and other health problems resulting from complications. Additionally, the improved condition of sanitary facilities and appliances reduces the frequency of infectious diseases and accidents. Most notable, however, may be the improved self-perception, stress reduction, and personal sense of efficacy which residents experience with improved housing (Schorr, 1970). Wilner and co-workers (1962) noted an improved general morale among relocated residents. This may account for an increased willingness of relocated residents to undertake the maintenance of their units.

John Cassel (1972) has noted that the housing unit and its niegh-borhood affect the residents' perception of self and commensurately play an important role in susceptibility to infectious and non-infectious diseases.

Density as an Ecological Factor in Black Mental Health

Few physical variables have been as thoroughly considered for their impact on human mental and physical health as housing density and crowding. Largely because it is relatively easily quantified (i.e., the number of persons or households per unit area) and is a pervasive aspect of urban life, population density as an ecological phenomenon is the subject of a voluminous amount of literature. The fact that urban Blacks reside in relatively high-density communities under conditions of crowding merits a consideration of density on Black mental pathology.

As an index of housing characteristics, density is unsurpassed in terms of its recognized signifance. The presence of scalar considerations and the complexity of human response and adaptive behavior in the presence of high densities and crowding are important in the con-sideration of their importance. There is a prevailing view that crowding and high residential densities are injurious to human health. But the scale on which these factors are considered has significance for these findings. With respect to the individual housing unit and household, there is little solid evidence that the available amount of space per person, or density *per se,* has permanent effects on physical or mental health (Schorr, 1970). What does appear to be significant at this micro-level is the arrangement of space to provide physical conditions con-ducive to household and individual pursuit of activities, and the perception of available space as being limited or crowded (Stokols, 1972).

This crowding phenomenon has been examined in relationship to the psychological development of children. In these studies it has been concluded that the lack of privacy and space for insular activity can adversely affect the development of a sense of individuality and proficiency at activities requiring individual effort and privacy (Schorr, 1970). Children find it difficult to study and sleep in environments where interference cannot be excluded.

These observations are particularly important where Blacks are tenants rather than owner-occupants of their residences. Tenants, as a rule, are limited in the degree to which they can petition and modify the configurations of their dwelling units. Thus, even where there is adequate space in the aggregate, the inability to structure and arrange the space can result in crowding phenomena. At least one recent study of youths in highly crowded environments found that the parents of these youths encouraged them to spend time outside the house (Mitchell, 1971).

The impact of crowding is not limited at this scale to its effects on children. Crowding is a generator of stress which, if continued, necessitates adaptive behavior to alleviate the stressful condition or its effects (Stokols, 1972). The specific form of adaptive behavior is conditioned by personality, culture, and the nature of stress-generating agents. To the extent that some forms of adaptive behavior or environmental modification to relieve the stressful effects of crowding are not available to the individual, the range of adaptive behavior is proportionately reduced. Thus, as opposed to partitioning space within the unit, the Black tenant may resort to spending less time at home in an effort to mitigate the stressful effects of crowding. Alternatively, members of the family or household may engage in confrontations and even violent and antisocial behavior as frustration mounts in the presence of an inability to control or moderate a stressful, crowded environment.

Glass and Singer have noted that adaptation to stress can affect mental disease and general emotional adjustment (1972). Thus, even where initial adaptive behavior reduces the immediate level of stress, the consequences for a wider range of social and emotional interactions and experiences may be detrimental.

High densities on a neighborhood or community scale have been associated with a wide range of mental and physical disorders similar to those noted previously for poor housing (Schmitt, 1966). As in the case of poor housing and interior crowding, high exterior densities occasion adaptive behavior, contingent on the range of available options. For Blacks this range of options is limited by housing segregation and economic circumstances which effectively rule out locational changes. The result is often that adaptation is played out on an emotional and behavioral level within the immediate environment. These adjustments do little to relieve the environmental problem of high densities and may, in fact, magnify the initial stressful situation. Crime, violence, and many aspects of street life may be the manifestation of attempts to adjust to the stressful effects of high-density living.

With increased densities the number and diversity of stimuli demanding and competing for individual attention increase. The ability of individuals to receive and process inputs is limited, and as this limit is approached, increasing selectivity is exercised as stimuli are filtered, blocked, or disregarded. The result is an increase in insularity on the part of individuals living in high-density, highly stimulating environments (Milgram, 1970). It has been noted that Blacks often appear indifferent, or even callous, to a number of factors and influences which impact the conduct of life and events in urban areas. This may be a form of adaptive behavior to reduce the stress of stimulus overload in the city.

Cities are places where many diverse persons and activities congregate to transact business, communicate, interact, and produce. It is precisely the advantages of high-density and concentration in facilitating communication, exchange, and interaction which account for the existence of urban agglomerations. The ability to support a diverse range of cultural and economic activities is dependent on the existence of demands capable of supporting such activities. Many Blacks who have migrated to the city have done so precisely because of the range of employment and the social, cultural, and educational opportunities anticipated with urban membership. To the degree that such expectations become reality, the deleterious effects noted above can be outweighed by the mental and emotional benefits of self-effectuation and realization. Unfortunately, inadequate educational and skills preparation in rural communities, which leaves the rural migrant ill-prepared for urban life and the realities of racial segregation and class discrimination, has resulted in the failure of urban Black migrants to realize many of their aspirations for urban life. Leo Srole has noted that if Black populations were excluded in comparisons of the incidence of stress-related mental disorders between rural and urban areas, there would be relatively small differences between rural and urban incidence (1972). When Blacks are added, due to the relatively higher incidence of stress and the mental conditions which result among urban Blacks, rural and urban comparisons show a higher incidence of mental problems in urban areas. If accurate, Srole's observations are ominous for the health and welfare of urban Blacks.

Economic and Institutional Barriers to
Black Residential Mobility

Among the prevailing features of urban development since the Second World War have been the increasing concentration of Black households in inner cities and the migration of white households, and recently economic activity and employment, to suburbs on the urban fringe (Neidercorn and Kain, 1973; Mills, 1972, chapter 6). These trends have a number of ominous consequences for urban Black populations.

Suburban growth has been a consequence of a number of factors and policies. Increasing wealth and the availability of housing finance promoted by VA and FHA mortgage programs have increased the effective demand for single-family housing. Urban expressway and freeway systems constructed during the last 40 years have made suburban areas increasingly accessible by automobile in an era when automobile ownership skyrocketed. The low relative cost of suburban property and the amenities of open space, high-quality schools, and natural environmental factors have all enhanced the desirability of suburban locations.

Unfortunately, the option of a suburban residence was not, and is not, equally available to Blacks and whites. To the extent that Blacks historically have suffered discrimination in labor markets and given the fact that VA and FHA mortgage finance and guarantees were openly denied to potential Black homeowners throughout the fifites (Aaron, 1972), the ability of Blacks to purchase single-family homes was stifled. During the sixties and seventies many suburbs have institutionalized, in local zoning and land use controls, the exclusion of minorities and low-income families from suburban residence. This exclusion has included restrictions against multifamily housing, minimum lot sizes of half an acre or more, and a number of developmental standards which increase the minimum cost of suburban housing to the point that all but a few Blacks are excluded. To be sure, these exclusionary controls are rationalized on a number of grounds, including the fiscal costs of providing public services and environmental quality. In fact, their effect has been to deny the suburban residential option to Blacks and the poor in general.

With an increasing number of employers relocating to the urban fringe, the exclusion of Blacks from suburban residence has taken on added significance. Lower land costs and the utilization of land-intensive technologies and production methods have encouraged industrial development in suburban areas on the urban fringe. Retail and commercial enterprises have followed their middle-class patrons to the suburbs. The result is that an increasing number of viable employment opportunities are inaccessible to inner-city Blacks. Getting to and from suburban employment frequently necessitates an automobile, since low-density suburban areas cannot support extensive systems of public transit. The available public transit accommodates the commuting needs of the suburban resident to and from employment in the central business district (CBD) of the city. The highest service levels are for incoming travel in the morning and outgoing trips in the evening rush hours. Inner-city Blacks commuting to suburban jobs travel opposite to the dominant commuter flow and have lower levels of commuting service as a result (Kain, 1964). This assumes that Blacks are knowledgeable about, and can obtain, suburban employment, but a number of factors mitigate against such knowledge. Very often suburban employers advertise only in suburban newspapers, and even more frequently knowledge of potential employment is contingent upon the propagation of information through relatives and friends. To the degree that proximity influences friendship and availability of information, denial of suburban residence influences employment opportunities. In a study of Black unemployment and residential segregation in the 25 largest standard metropolitan statistical areas (SMSA), Kain and Quigley (1972) found that the greater the number of suburbanized employers, the greater the incidence of Black unemployment. This factor was second in importance only to overall SMSA unemployment in arriving at an explanation of Black unemployment.

These observations concerning the effects of Black residential segregation and changing urban structure on the employment accessibility of Blacks are supported by journey to work patterns in the nation's metropolitan areas. Forty-three percent of Black workers, as opposed to 29 percent of white workers, used public transit for commuting. On the other hand, fewer Blacks utilized private automobiles for commuting (54 percent for whites, 44 percent for Blacks). A smaller proportion of Black than white workers actually worked in the central city (75 and 80 percent respectively); and relatively fewer Blacks had short journeys of 30 minutes than their white counterparts (28 and 49 percent respectively). On the other hand, 21 percent of Black workers, as opposed to 11 percent of whites, commuted in excess of 1 hour. In addition, Blacks paid more for transportation and earned less than their white counterparts. Among the unemployed, 65 percent of the Blacks and 52 percent of the whites had no available automobile (Council on Municipal Performance, 1975).

The importance of gainful employment and income to the individual and social welfare of all persons cannot be overemphasized. In their absence or inadequacy, individuals and households are forced to rely on alternative income sources such as public assistance, welfare, or criminal activity. The stigma attached to reliance on public assistance and the inability to alter by individual action the limitations imposed by societal constraints lead to increased frustration and pessimism among those affected. Antisocial behavior of a criminal or violent nature is reinforced to the degree that such actions lead to positive results in terms of income as opposed to labor force participation. The inability of the head of a household to provide for the needs of the family unit strains family relationships and structure. The incentive to work is decreased among urban Blacks to the degree that lower wages and higher commuting costs, relative to those of whites, result in lower real wages and income for Blacks.

The institutionalization of urban residential segregation has adverse environmental effects other than limiting Black employment opportunities. The jurisdictions of local governments are coterminous with the boundaries of central cities and suburban incorporated areas. The potential of local governments to provide public services is dependent on the amount of taxable wealth within the local jurisdictional area. Local public services such as education, police and fire departments, public housing and health, and public transit are dependent on local revenues for financing. As middle-income residents and economic activity have migrated from the central city, the taxable wealth of cities has not kept pace with the cost of public services. The primary source of local government revenues is the property tax, and with new housing, and commercial and industrial expansion increasingly concentrated outside the central city, assessed property values and tax revenues have not kept pace with the cost of local government services (Mills, 1972). The result is that central cities increasingly are faced with severe budgetary constraints and find it necessary to reduce public service provisions. Many local public services, such as education, are important in eliminating the cumulative effects of poverty and constrained opportunity. Others, such as police, fire and health services, are essential in the maintenance of public health and welfare. To the degree that these are provided at reduced levels in the central city, the ultimate result is an unproportionate reduction in the welfare of urban Blacks.

References

Aaron, H. *Shelters and Subsidies: Who Benefits from Federal Housing Policies?* Washington, D.C.: The Brookings Institution, 1972.

Alonso, W. *Location and Land Use.* Cambridge, Mass.: M.I.T. Press, 1964.

Burgess, E. W. "The Growth of the City: An Introduction to a Research Project." In R. E. Park and E. W. Burgess, (eds.), *The City.* Chicago: University of Chicago Press, 1925.

Cassel, J. "Health Consequences of Population Density and Crowding." In R. Putman, (ed.), *People and Buildings.* New York: Basic Books, 1972.

Clawson, M. *Suburban Law and Conversion in the United States: An Economic and Governmental Process.* Baltimore: Johns Hopkins University Press, 1971.

Council on Municipal Performance. "City Transportation." *Municipal Performance Report* 1 (1975): 10.

Firey, W. *Land Use in Central Boston.* Cambridge, Mass.: Harvard University Press, 1947.

Glass, D. C., and Singer, J. E. *Urban Stress: Experiments on Noise and Social Stressors.* New York: Academic Press, 1972.

Kain, J. F. "Coping with Ghetto Unemployment." *Journal of the American Institute of Planners* 35 (1964): 80–83.

——————. "Effect of Housing Market Segregation on Urban Development." In J. Pynoos et al., (eds.), *Housing Urban America.* Chicago: Aldine, 1973.

Kain, J. F., and Quigley, J. M. "Housing Market Discrimination, Homeownership, and Savings Behavior." *American Economic Review* 62 (1972): 263–277.

Lowry, I. S. "Filtering and Housing Standards: A Conceptual Analysis." *Land Economics* 36 (1960): 362–370.

Michelson, W. H. *Man and His Urban Environment: A Sociological Approach.* Reading, Mass.: Addison-Wesley, 1970.

Milgram, S. "The Experience of Living in Cities." *Science* 167 (1970): 1461–1468.

Mills, E. S. *Urban Economics.* Glenview, Ill.: Scott, Foresman, 1972.

Mitchell, R. "Social Implications of High Density Housing." *American Sociological Review* 36 (1971): 26.

Muth, R. *Cities and Housing.* Chicago: University of Chicago Press, 1969.

_____. "The Spatial Structure of the Housing Market." *Papers and Proceedings of the Regional Science Association* 7 (1961): 207–220.

Niedercorn, J., and Kain, J. *Suburbanization of Employment and Population, 1948–1973.* Rand Corporation, P-2641, January 1975.

Schmitt, R. C. "Density, Health and Social Organization." *Journal of the American Institute of Planners* 32 (1966): 38–40.

Schorr, A. L. "Housing and Its Effects." In H. Proshansky et al. (eds.), *Environmental Psychology: Man and His Physical Setting.* New York: Holt, Rinehart & Winston, 1970.

Sjöberg, G. *The Pre-Industrial City, Past and Present.* Glencoe, Ill.: Free Press, 1960.

Srole, L. "Urbanization and Mental Health: Some Reformulations." *American Scientist* 60 (1972): 576–583.

Stokols, D. "A Socio-Psychological Model of Human Crowding Phenomena." *Journal of the American Institute of Planners* 38 (1972): 74.

U.S. Bureau of the Census. *The Social and Economic Status of Negroes in the United States, 1969.* Current Population Reports, Series P23, No. 29, 1969.

U.S. Department of Commerce, Bureau of the Census. *Statistical Abstract of the United States.* 1969, 1974.

Wilner, D. et al. *The Housing Environment and Family Life: A Longitudinal Study of the Effects of Housing on Morbidity and Mental Health.* Baltimore: Johns Hopkins University Press, 1962.

11 THE ORGANIZATION OF MENTAL HEALTH SERVICES DELIVERY

Audreye E. Johnson, D.S.W.

Introduction

Organizational involvement and concern is not new to Blacks. With the establishment of the Philadelphia Free African Society on April 12, 1787, Richard Allen and Absalom Jones took "the first wavering step of a people toward a more organized social life (Bennett, 1969). Such organized endeavors were necessary within the context of a hostile society (Drake, 1940). The systematic exclusion of Blacks from free and open participation in the wider society has been, and continues to be, the basis for the efforts of Blacks to cope on their own. Of paramount importance in the exclusion of Blacks has been racism: *"The race problem in America was a deliberate invention of men who systematically separated Blacks and whites in order to make money"* (Bennett, 1975).

Racism is the systematic exclusion of a people from societal participation, psychosocial and economic, based on color; using oppression and discrimination to ensure prejudice of people and institutions against those of color, formally and informally, by any means possible. The behavior resulting from exclusion policy is both individual and institutional racism. From individual and institutional racism emerges administrative racism. This type of racism is the overt or covert collusion of either board, executive, supervisor, or staff in not committing resources to serve those of color, or it may be expressed in discriminatory hiring or training practices. Administrative racism is affected by informal as well as formal communication.

Though racism has not always been a factor for Blacks in America, it soon became the predominant way of life and invaded all levels of society, its people, and its institutions. Carmichael and Hamilton (1967), among others, have put the case thus:

> By 'racism' we mean the predication of decisions and policies on considerations of race for the purpose of *subordinating* a racial group and maintaining control over that group . . . Racism is both overt and covert. It takes two, closely related forms: individual whites acting against individual blacks, and acts by the total white community against the black community. We call these individual racism and institutional racism . . . Institutional racism relies on the active and pervasive operation of anti-black attitudes and practices. A sense of superior group position prevails: whites are "better" than blacks; therefore blacks should be subordinate to whites. This is a racist attitude and it permeates the society, on both the individual and institutional level, covertly and overtly . . . institutional racism has another name: colonialism.

It was against this backdrop of sentiment, superiority and inferiority, that the policies and institutions of America were forged. And, of course, mental health services and institutions were very much affected. Thus, those mental health services which deigned to include Blacks were separate and, of course, unequal.

Organization of Mental Health

People form organizations and resultant institutions in the face of need. When society does not, or cannot, automatically provide within its structure for all people, designated structures spring from individual and concerned action toward meeting the unmet needs. Fragmented efforts directed toward different groups of people—adults, children, the blind, prisoners, the mentally ill, etc.—were singled out for such specialized attention on the part of certain others within the society. One of the foremost pioneers in improving patient care in the area of mental health was Dorothea L. Dix (1802–1887).

Early Development of Service. Hospitals for the insane were among the first organized efforts toward providing for the mentally ill. However, emphasis was upon reform of the individuals and not the societal institutions which might have been contributors. While there was recognition of the possibility of environmental influences, attention was directed toward an environment in which the individual could change and thus adjust to the society. The push for the involvement of government on the local, state, and federal level, however, was within the context of provision of service to those who were considered "people."

The Constitution of the United States of America, which was adopted in 1787, was still the abiding guide for the provision of service to people.

> [The Constitution] . . . recognized slavery by (1) counting five slaves as three persons for determining taxes and representatives; (2) providing for the return of fugitive slaves fleeing to other states; and (3) restricting for 20 years congressional interference with the African slave trade (Toppin, 1969).

Therefore, the provision of services for people did not include Blacks. The slaves were expected to be cared for by their owners, and free Blacks were left to their own devices, except in a few instances. Thus, those in the vanguard of providing care to the mentally ill were influenced by the prevailing ideation of the time about Blacks and other minorities. These minority groups were not thought to be afflicted by the stresses and strains of their environment, "being less emotionally sensitive and . . . thereby protected from the strains of progress (Prudhomme and Musto, 1973). Dr. Thomas S. Kirkbride, a noted mental hospital superintendent, argued forcibly for the segregation of patients, which included segregation by race. That famous crusader and reformer, Dorothea L. Dix, was highly influenced by Dr. Kirkbride's advice:

> His views were followed with care in the establishment of the federal model institution, the Government Hospital for the insane, or, as later known, St. Elizabeth's. . . . St. Elizabeth's opened its doors in 1855 (Prudhomme and Musto, 1973).

The model mental institution, St. Elizabeth's, true to the doctrine of separation of the races, built a special cottage for Blacks. This segregationist arrangement was not discontinued until the 1950s. While the first half of the nineteenth century saw the establishment of mental health services, they were instituted under the existing practice of exclusion of Blacks from development and participation, and were segregated.

Prior to the Civil War, Blacks were thought not to be affected adversely by mental stress and strain, inasmuch as they were "uncivilized" and "inferior." After the war, emancipation was seen as adding undue stress for which Blacks were not prepared:

Rarely considered by writers on the subject were other factors which might account for an increased enumeration of the mentally ill such as changing patterns of health service delivery or a rising utilization of health services by groups such as Blacks (Prudhomme and Musto, 1973).

The emancipation of Blacks did not bring about a change in status for the newly freed or for those already free. Indeed, much effort was extended to keep the newly freed Blacks under the control of the old regime. This was done through the enactment of the "Black Codes" passed in many states. Thus mental health activity prior to and after the Civil War was carried on within the confines of established patterns of racism. Those leaders concerned with the care of the mentally ill, individual reformers as well as the medical profession, were not likely to go against the existing patterns of the society. The Association of Medical Superintendents of American Institutions for the Insane, which was the forerunner of the American Psychiatric Association, discussed the situation but took no direct action toward change.

Concerns for Service Delivery. Reflection upon the course of events which led to the establishment of mental health services and the action taken to meet this end permits observations as to the viability of organizations engaged in mental health services. While such concerns can take a broad view, of interest to this discussion is the way Blacks were, and are, affected. The following observations can be considered about organizations from a Black perspective:

1. Frequently the needs of the entire constituent population are not met.
2. Frequently organizations and their resultant institutions are not definitive as to their function(s).
3. Frequently specialized organizations and institutions do not select priorities which will enable service delivery to the constituency.
4. Frequently provider organizations and those in need of service have different options and ideas as to the service need.
5. Frequently provider organizations are not in communication with service users as to what their function(s) should be.
6. Frequently provider organizations do not view the user as capable of making a contribution to the service delivery.
7. Frequently there is distrust between the provider organization and users. Thus there is little congruence between providers and users in their perceptions of need and remedy.

Some selected organizational service models will be explored as to their strengths and limitations from a Black perspective. Several basic areas of concern arise as to the dimensions of mental health organizations:

1. What are the Black perceptions of the organizations?
2. To what extent are Blacks involved in the design and delivery of services?
3. Do Blacks have expectations of these organizations?
4. What impact do Blacks think such organizations have upon their lives, and the Black community as a whole?

Blacks are the largest minority within America, a conservative estimate of well over 22 million persons. Thus the mental health field would do well to concern itself with the needs for service of this group as well as for others. Not only in magnitude, but in content of ideation and action, the Black viewpoint is significant. Exclusion, segregation, and benign neglect are, therefore, not only immoral, but cannot be tolerated for the good of society.

Organizational Theory and Mental Health

The ways in which people tend to deal with the stresses of society are varied. Merton has indicated five modes of individual adaptation: conformity, innovation, ritualism, retreatism, and rebellion (1968). Obviously, since people make up groups and are the formers of organizations and institutions, the typology might be explicated beyond individuals. Thus it can be seen that people in concert often utilize these modes of adaptation as they struggle to master the complexity of societal conditions. When people act together to alleviate pressures in a formal manner, seeking mutual achievements, such activity can be characterized as formal organization. This has been pointed out above in relation to the efforts directed toward providing for the mentally ill. Of course, a major element which has been a part of such organizational endeavors has been racism, which has resulted in the systematic exclusion of Blacks.

As in all other institutions, the mental health field has its formal organizations. These organizations have a hierarchical structure which in most instances is dominated by the providers of service. There is little in the way of user or consumer input. Such organizations are linked with the other organizations within society, and do not stand in isolation. Thus, as social systems, they are concerned not only with internal, but also with external considerations of their purpose and function, especially as these relate to the larger society.

> Institutions are fairly stable social arrangements and practices through which collective actions are taken. Medical institutions, for instance, marshal talents and resources of society so that health care can be provided. Medical institutions include hospitals, research labs, and clinics, as well as organizations of medical people such as doctors and nurses. The health of all of us is affected by general medical policies and by established practices and ethics. Business and labor, for example, determine what is to be produced, how it is to be produced, and by whom and on whose behalf products will be created (Knowles and Prewitt, 1969).

The classical theory of organization was expounded by Max Weber in his theory of bureaucracy in 1921. Since that time others have taken his work and developed it further. Essentially, Weber concerned himself with the make-up of organizations which he described as having hierarchy, order, rationality, and impersonality (Weber, 1947). In this view the organization, not the individual, was of most importance. A later conception of organizations, promoted by others (Agyris, 1962; Caplow, 1964), emphasized the individual member of the organization and not the organization itself as being of importance. Additionally, there is the explication by Blau and Scott (1962) of Merton's theory of function and dysfunction in organizations.

The make-up of an organization is influenced by its personnel as well as its goals. As Merton (1968) has pointed out,

> the social functions of an organization help determine the structure (including the recruitment of personnel involved in the structure), just as the structure helps determine the effectiveness with which the functions are fulfilled . . . in a phrase . . . structure affects function and function affects structure.

Many organizations form for the best interests of those they plan to serve, and proclaim the mass participation of their members. However, they tend toward hierarchy and elitism. Michels (1970) notes this by indicating:

Organization implies the tendency to oligarchy. In every organization, whether it be a political party, a professional union, or any other association of the kind, the aristocratic tendency manifests itself very clearly. The mechanism of the organization, while conferring a solidity of structure, induces serious changes in the organized mass, completely inverting the respective position of the leaders and the led. As a result of organization, every party or professional union becomes divided into a minority of directors and a majority of directed.

Mental health organizations have managed to have high goals in the service of mankind, yet there is domination by mostly one segment of society. There has not been the opportunity for full participation by Blacks, nor, until very recently, has there been much concern expressed about this lack of involvement and participation. Those most active in mental health—psychiatrists, social workers, nurses, and psychologists—have maintained a firm grip upon the reins of control of the organizations and institutions geared toward mental health service delivery. They have ostracized or granted only limited access to Blacks. The service centers, whether hospital or clinic, public or private, have been segregated and have had very little input from Blacks. And the education of Blacks has been limited and at times almost nonexistent. Blacks were not taken into these structures for training, and the care given to them was of the "Jim Crow" nature—separate and unequal. Stinchcombe (1965) has noted the impact of history and tradition on organizational development. Thus the values of the organizers are important.

Those on the inside of organizations have tended to protect their "turf" from invasion by that group already defined by their society as inferior. Thus those on the inside have been considered superior and have made efforts to maintain their status. Through the professions to which they belong, these providers have maintained a monopoly and engaged in restraints of trade. Caplow (1964) indicates what an organization does and what it is: as a *social system*, it has a collective identity, a program of *activity*, and a method of membership replacement. Additionally, Caplow's (1964) framework of organizational ideology and function can be seen as relevant to mental health organizations:

> An organizational ideology has a double function. On the one hand, it rallies members in a common cause, reinforces their commitment, and creates psychological barriers against desertion by tying their affiliation to organizational loyalties and values. At the same time, by linking the

organization's practical goals to wider purposes shared with outsiders, an ideology provides ways of wooing allies and isolating enemies.

Those who staff the mental health organizations have tended to carry with them their values from the wider society. Often, these values have superseded their concern for the care of those in need of mental health services. The impact of the people who belong to organizations has been given only limited attention. The interaction that such people have with each other and within the organization is important. As Hall (1972) has pointed out,

> Traits of individual organizational members which would appear to have significance for the organization have been surprisingly ignored. There have been relatively few examinations of the role of minority group members . . . such as Blacks, women, or Indians, in the organization and reciprocally, of the impact of organizational life on the minority group members.

The interaction and socialization which occur among organizational members have importance for the functions of the organizations. Etzioni (1961) has noted the effect on control of such interaction. Though he calls for more study in this area, he does highlight differences which are a party of culture and the impact on hierarchy:

> There are, however, two sets of factors which surely significantly affect organizational control on which there is little systematic information— one is difference in cultural and social contexts. . . . Secondly, much more is known about control of lower-ranking participants than of high-ranking ones, and, clearly the control of the higher ranks is at least as important.

Additionally, Reissman (1958) points out:

> The concept of role offers a valuable tool for the study of bureaucracy in at least two important ways. First, it serves to focus upon the basic content and processes in the bureaucratic situation through the individual involved. . . . Secondly, it serves to synthesize information gained from other relevant areas.

Mental Hospitals: Public and Private. In the nineteenth century, hospitals for the "insane," as they were then called, sought to provide a different atmosphere for the mentally ill. It was thought that the stresses of society contributed to their condition and that providing the proper atmosphere would be conducive to recovery. However, by the

1880s, it was apparent that the change of environment was not providing the cure expected. Care was mostly custodial rather than rehabilitative.

The states began to take some responsibility for the establishment of mental hospitals prior to the initiation of programs by the federal government. The utilization of hospital facilities in the early part of the nineteenth century was mostly by those who could afford to pay for the care. Those not having the financial resources were cared for in their communities or in the local almshouses. The latter part of the nineteenth century saw a change in this direction with the states making provisions for the care of the mentally ill. Private care continued to be available and was made use of by those in a financial position to meet its cost.

For the most part, the federal government did little in the care of the mentally ill. St. Elizabeth's hospital was their model care center, but President Pierce's 1854 veto of land grants for the mentally ill checked the extent of federal involvement. State hospitals continued to fill and become overcrowded. Between 1845 and 1945 nearly 300 of such facilities were built. Added to this was the segregation of the races which was the prevailing pattern of treatment. Those Blacks in need of care, when it was available to them in their communities, were provided little in the way of services. Because of the attitudes of the providers toward Blacks, little of their life concerns were dealt with, and they suffered, perhaps even more than others, from custodial care at the public level. Few of the private institutions admitted Black patients.

Except for the people employed in menial tasks within these institutions, Blacks were not likely to experience care from other Blacks. Few Blacks were being trained in the care of the mentally ill, whether in the private or the public sector (Prudhomme and Musto, 1973). These barriers to training and utilization of Black providers in the mental health facilities continued until well after World War II.

Kramer and co-workers point to the lack of adequate measurements on statistics related to mental disorders of Blacks and other minorities, and utilization of mental health facilities. They also point out deficiencies in dealing with mortality and morbidity rates, and census data as well. Noted also is the "sparse data available on the prevalence of mental disorders in the United States, not only for minority but also for majority groups" (Kramer, Rosen, and Willis, 1973).

Data related to mental illness cannot be considered in isolation from other institutional data or racist practices within the society. For instance, Black youth are more likely to be sent to juvenile court for infringement of rules and regulations, while youth of the dominant society will usually be remanded to their parents. The same is true in the case of the adult offender. The Black male is more likely to be sent to jail, while the male of the dominant society might be sent for treatment to a mental health facility. The interlocking racist systems of society—housing, politics, economics, etc.—converge in the treatment of Blacks, affecting mental health and mental illness, and thus the utilization of these facilities.

> . . . racist practices affect the composition and characteristics of the noninstitutional population by removing persons with various types of behavioral problems, diseases, disabling conditions, and social and economic characteristics from the noninstitutional and the institutional setting at disproportionate rates. The removal rates (i.e., rates of institutionalization) and the durations of stay are not equal among the different age-sex-racial-socioeconomic classes of the population or among the various states (Kramer, Rosen, and Willis, 1973).

Additionally, it is pointed out that

> Racist attitudes and practices can influence . . . life-style, value system, health status, use of psychiatric facilities, use of institutions other than mental hospitals, differential use of diagnositc criteria, and diagnostic labels (Kramer, Rosen, and Willis, 1973).

While there is some knowledge of the negative influences of racism on the utilization by Blacks of public and private mental health facilities, there is little extensive awareness of the kinship bond in the coping patterns of Blacks. Nor have the various institutions within the Black community, established in the face of rank order discrimination, been fully examined as to their viability in having an impact on Black mental health and mental illness. Additionally, the Black culture, which was forged out of a combination of African, European, and American experiences, has not been examined for its contribution and relationship to Black mental health. The paucity of exploration of these variables dominates Black use of mental hospital facilities. Until they are explored, there will continue to be problems in determining incidence, prevalence, and use.

> Most state departments of mental health collect data on patient movement by race, but very few publish tabulations of these data in their

annual reports (NIMH 1970). Publication of such data would add considerably to our knowledge of racial differences in patterns of use of mental hospitals, clinics, and community mental health centers (Kramer, Rosen, and Willis, 1973).

Data which are available, though limited, do indicate a higher admission rate and use of facilities by Blacks. However, as this information is subsumed under the category of non-white admissions, which includes other minority groups, a true picture cannot be obtained. This difference, however, cannot be evaluated meaningfully without consideration of some of the factors noted above which relate to the racism of the society, as well as the significance of such things as Black culture, institutions, and kinship bonds.

Community Mental Health Centers. The quest for improved, more accessible care of the mentally ill was a gradual process which culminated in the passage of Public Law 88–164 in 1963, the Community Mental Health Centers Act. The first funds for centers were awarded in 1965. The events leading up to this change in the institutional pattern of care for the mentally ill, which for the first time got massive federal support, have been noted by Bloom (1973). He points to three major developments.

> First, the field of psychopharmacology began its current period of rapid growth with the development of new tranquilizing drugs for the care of the mentally ill. . . .
>
> The second development was the inauguration of the philosophy of the therapeutic community . . . that therapeutic potential resided in patients as well as staff and that by forming a democratic community within the hospital of patients and staff that could take advantage of these therapeutic potentials, the effectiveness of psychological treatment could be increased. . . .
>
> The third development was the phenomenon of geographic decentralization in large state mental hospitals.

Other associated developments which preceded the Community Mental Health Centers Act were the National Mental Health Act of 1946 (Public Law 79–487); the establishment of the National Institute of Mental Health, as provided in this law; the Mental Health Study Act of 1955 (Public Law 84–182), which created the Joint Commission on Mental Illness and Health; a decrease in the number of persons in state hospitals; Congressional appropriation of funds for the National Institute of Mental Health to finance demonstration projects; and a concerned President John F. Kennedy, with a mentally retarded sister.

Following passage of the 1963 Community Mental Health Centers Act, which authorized construction of facilities, were a number of amendments to the act which dealt with personnel for staffing, types of care, extension of funding, special grants for specific types of service, and consideration to poverty areas. Since that time centers have been established in all the states and territories of the United States—392 centers as of 1973, according to the National Institute of Mental Health.

The basic policy format of Community Mental Health Centers was to provide a comprehensive, coordinated program of mental health services (for 75,000 to 200,000 persons) which would be located in one or more facilities in the community. The stated purpose was to provide a varied range of accessible and coordinated services to help prevent mental illness and to treat the mentally ill. This was to be accomplished by the provision of what were termed the five essential services:

1. *In-patient care*—treatment to patients who need 24-hour hospitalization.

2. *Out-patient care*—for patients (individual, group, or family therapy) while permitting them to live at home and go about their daily activities.

3. *Partial hospitalization*—either day care for patients able to return home in the evening, or night care for patients able to work but needing further care, and usually without suitable home arrangements. Care might be both day and night and/or weekend.

4. *Emergency care*—available psychiatric service at any hour around the clock in one of the three forms given above.

5. *Consultation and education*—provided by the Center staff to community agencies, professional personnel, and other community groups.

Additional services for a comprehensive program which could be made available were diagnostic and rehabilitative services; precare and aftercare; training, research, and evaluation; and special services for children, elderly citizens, alcoholics, and the retarded. To operationalize the Community Mental Health Center idea, social-structural change was called for "(1) incorporating different people into the same structure, or (2) incorporating the same people into different structures" (Mayer, 1972).

Quality mental health services had long been out of the reach of minorities in this country, who are at the bottom of the socioeconomic ladder. For the oppressed Black, the poor, and other minority groups, the promise of Community Mental Health Centers had to be looked at with an arched brow—Was it for real? It would be necessary to prove the availability of care regardless of race, color, or creed, but also regardless of socioeconomic status. As Gil notes, the constraining variables of beliefs, values, ideologies, customs, and traditions were present which would influence resource development (provision of services), status allocation (providing the necessary personnel to perform the task), and rights distribution (right to services) (1973).

The previous exclusion and the need for legitimation of the program would have to be considered. Care would have to be exercised as to the imposition of values which ignore existing value screens.

Community Mental Health Centers were, and are, proclaimed by some as a panacea. They were influenced by the social responsibility of the civil rights movement of the sixties, which signaled a change in the direction of mental health services. Yet, as Panzetta has noted, the cornerstone of services was traditionally based; only the Consultation and Education Services were truly innovative (1971). The medical model remained, and conflict ensued as to community-based providers.

It was not until the Act was amended in 1970 that special grants were made for Consultation and Education Services. Service was to be available to the poor, but if the Center could not afford the provision of service without cost, they could charge. Prevention was to be a major factor. Gerald Caplan, among others, had been promoting the need for preventive care for years (1964). The people of the community were to be in on the planning, demonstrating democracy at work within a medical setting. Yet the basic tools for implementing the ideals were not available: resources of staff, money, awareness of community, and sensitivity to Blacks, the poor, and other minorities. Once again the racism of the society was at work.

The 1974 *U.S. Statistical Abstracts* delineates the course of treatment facility used by patients. This does not indicate that Community Mental Health Centers have readily taken in a number of patients, but shows patients distributed through other care methods (see Table 1).

Table 1.

Mentally Ill Patients, by Type of Treatment Facility,
1955 to 1971

% Distribution

Year	Hospitals, Inpatient	Outpatient Psychological Services	CMHC	Day Treatment
1955	77.4	22.6	NA	22.6
1965	59.4	40.6	NA	40.6
1967	52.9	47.1	3.1	44.0
1969	47.0	53.0	8.1	44.9
1971	42.6	57.4	15.4	42.0

Per 1000

Year	Hospitals, Inpatient	Outpatient Psychological Services	CMHC	Day Treatment
1955	1,296	379	NA	397
1965	1,266	1,071	NA	1,071
1967	1,659	1,480	97	1,383
1969	1,678	1,894	291	1,603
1971	1,721	2,317	623	1,694

Data are not now available for a definitive evaluation of Community Mental Health Centers. Bloom (1973) thinks that the impact has been very important:

> . . . if the trend toward the democratization of decision-making continues, the health and welfare of Americans cannot help but improve.

On the other hand, it is said that the lack of a mechanism for input and output data leaves uncertain "whether mental illness represents an area of improvement or a growing problem" (Bellak and Barten, 1975, p. 3).

Blacks have not seen Community Mental Health Centers as innovative meccas of service for them. Some would say that Blacks have not been educated to use these services. However, there are, perhaps, some other more important issues facing the Black community, such as jobs, physical health problems, housing, and the general oppression of society in that Blacks are the last hired and the first fired. Moreover, the usual societal attitudes of providers toward Blacks have been a factor. Community Mental Health Centers have not proved that they really have the best interest of Blacks at heart; democracy has not been seen at work. Until there is consideration of these variables in conjunction with the provision of mental health services, the gap will continue. Communication is absent on basic needs. The lip service to consideration of Blacks and other minorities has not been followed through with definitive action. Little has been done by the mental health providers and planners to address themselves to the interrelationship between mental illness and other societal institutions. Protests that they are on the side of right and that they are liberal often masks the basic anti-change attitudes of the mental health professionals. The exclusion of Blacks from participation in planning and delivery of services remains.

Health Maintenance Organizations. The cost of medical care to the average individual is prohibitive for any long-term illness. Also, for many Americans, even a short-term illness can be catastrophic. The free-market system has not operated in such a way that all can equally participate. Most people do not have the funds to tide them over a period of illness, nor can many even afford systematic medical checkups to maintain good health standards for themselves. While there have been some efforts at alleviating costs through the establishment of neighborhood health centers, this has not been widespread or comprehensive in meeting the need. Yet health care continues to grow as a major big business, now costing about $80 billion per year.

There have been public and private efforts to mitigate the cost of health care. Additionally, there has been growing concern over the years on the part of all segments of society as to the need to take action in this regard. However, the steps have been incremental, fragmented, and far from comprehensive. The battle has raged over whether health care cost is a private or a public responsibility. For the most part, the private sector seems to have carried the day, even though the cost of privately sponsored programs is too great for the average person. The majority of Blacks, who are economically disadvantaged, are even more adversely affected in their ability to pay for adequate health care.

The many efforts now being made in Congress to do something about the cost of health care in this country spring from a middle-class social perspective. Thus the question arises as to the extent of impact upon Blacks should one of the bills, or a compromised version, be passed. Comprehensiveness, quality administration, accessibility, benefits, universality, accountability, financing, cost, and use can be questioned in each instance, but especially whether these variables productively affect Blacks.

Moving in concert, the private health industry and the medical profession staved off for many years the passage of a health insurance program. However, they no doubt would deny overt collusion. At this point, many think that there might be a change, for the opposition has diminished, though it has not died.

> The lack of opposition to substantial health care legislation is being predicted because almost all other institutional groups that have serious interests in the health care delivery system have apparently foresworn generalized opposition for the strategy of supporting, and in some cases, originating, particular legislative proposals they can live with (Weeks, 1974).

Blacks do not control or participate equally or proportionately in the private or public sectors of the health plans of this country. Granted that it has been necessary, as in other areas of life, for Blacks to establish institutions in the areas which excluded and/or discriminated against them, their ownership and influence in such areas are limited, notwithstanding the important contributions of such concerns as North Carolina Mutual and Universal Life Insurance Companies. Thus, whether there is a national insurance plan of public or private sponsorship, unless Blacks are more involved, continued overt and covert racism can influence the enactment of such programs.

Public responsibility in the area of health insurance has no doubt taken a forward step with the passage of the Title IX amendments to the Social Security Act, involving Medicare and Medicaid. Yet there is continued debate as to how much should be done by government in the area of health insurance. However, there is an obvious need for equal consideration to all of the people in regard to health. This reflects the need to take into consideration the other excluding factors in society which adversely affect the participation of some of its members. The health of the country cannot and should not continue to be geared toward a privileged few.

Though it may be difficult to operationalize, the definition of health as provided by the World Health Organization—"a state of complete physical, mental and social well-being, not merely the absence of disease or infirmity"—should be given serious consideration. Those areas influencing physical and mental health need to be given far more attention. For Blacks the residual effects of slavery, racism, economic and political disenfranchisement, housing, aging, and a host of other variables need to be considered consciously in terms of their influence on health conditions. It is also necessary to consider these factors in relation to other groups; however, it must be noted that the dominant population usually considers its vested interests of which it is already in control, and in which it freely participates. Moreover, in the health area.

> What social policy has to deal with are not choices between opposites, but the selection of mechanisms situated at some point on the continuum between the traditional polar positions: private vs. governmental and voluntary vs. compulsory (Donabedian, 1973).

Health should be a right and not a privilege, yet this country has not set up the mechanism for a national health policy, but rather goals which have had the input of different groups. A national health plan can change this state of affairs, or it can continue the fragmentation. The direction it will take awaits the action of Congress, which will react to the pressures of the constituency.

The fragmented involvement of government in health has been considerable but not well-coordinated. Ventures to provide better health have been directed from a public health concept. There have been many different efforts on the part of government which relate to health insurance. Workmen's compensation, in 1911, dealt with an insurance principle. Not too long after that, several state commissions were set up to study health insurance. During this period, 1915–1919, the American Medical Association also set up a study committee in this area. Interestingly, this professional committee concluded that there was a need for a compulsory insurance system to reach the needy. The first national health insurance bill was introduced in Congress by Senator Robert Wagner of New York in 1943. But, by this time, the medical profession had done an about-face relative to health insurance, maintaining that such a plan should be in the private sector, and lobbied extensively against national health insurance. Taking up the concept of Senator Wagner, President Truman, in 1945, presented elements of a national health insurance program to Congress. This was met with opposition. It was not until 1965 that the major step of passage of Medicare and Medicaid was made. In the interim, the Hill-Burton Act, providing some federal support in the health area, had been enacted.

Currently there are a number of measures being discussed for a national health insurance plan. These are sponsored by the private and professional sectors as well as by Congress. These proposals differ in terms of their comprehensiveness, accessibility, and cost, among other considerations. There is a good deal of similarity in the quality control features of the Professional Standards Review Organization (PSRO). This would be an advisory board of health standards. Obviously, composition and participation become crucial factors for Blacks in PSRO. Additionally, cost, accessiblity, and comprehensiveness cannot be ignored either.

Regardless of the proposal, it becomes apparent that the value system of the dominant society is highly influential in each. The availability of any plan to Blacks will be dependent upon a number of interlocking factors related to what might be characterized as "bio-psycho-socio-economic" considerations. However, it should be noted that none of the various proposals effectively reaches all segments of society. Even though the plan that eventually gets through Congress will not be a panacea, any step may well evolve toward meeting the health maintenance needs of society.

Neighborhood Health Centers. The 1960s saw the beginning of a number of community-based, federally sponsored programs. One of the programs provided for the Neighborhood Health Centers which emerged from the "Great Society" impetus of President Johnson. This program was originally sponsored by the Office for Economic Opportunity. Not only did it propose to provide health services to a neglected segment of the population, the poor, but it also provided that such services would be centered within the community of the consumers. One of the very different ideas of this and similar programs of the sixties was,

> the charge . . . that the community, that mass of committed, un-committed and most different people, become involved in the planning and operation of such programs . . . the proposed guidelines for . . . programs . . . [were embodied in the] adage, *maximum feasible participation* (Johnson, 1970).

However, the base of service continued to be quite traditional with the same disciplines providing service. There was an effort toward using staff persons who were residents in the neighborhoods. In addition, advisory boards were set up supposedly to enable the community residents to participate to a greater extent in the service of their communities. This was to be *maximum feasible participation.*

The health needs of the poor had been documented over and over again, and the relationship of economic plight and health had also been acknowledged. The thrust was to bring services to the places where the need existed, where the people were, and where the action was.

> Basic to the concept of neighborhood health centers is a belief that health services for the poor are generally inadequate; that they are based on outmoded concepts reflecting a poor law tradition which is no longer consistent with the more democratic concept of trying to integrate the poor into the mainstream of society with equal access to essential services. It is believed that these outmoded concepts have tended to perpetuate services which are insufficient, of poor quality, inaccessible in time and place, impersonal, fragmented, and lacking in continuity. The doctor-patient contact under such circumstances is not conducive to establishing a therapeutic relationship essential for successful treatment of many types of illness. That the poor show rates of disease, disability, and premature death which are different from those of the rest of the population may be due in part to the nature of prevailing health services. The neighborhood health centers are proposed as a solution to the problem of inadequate health services to the poor. They are to correct prevailing shortcomings by effecting new organizational patterns which will involve changes in traditional attitudes as well as practices (Office of Economic Opportunity, 1968).

The solution proposed was good, but the implementation was problematic. The people to be served were poor and lived within a particular geographic area with various social handicaps of housing, limited education, nutrition, etc. Based on the above proposals, Neighborhood Health Centers had the goals of:

1. a location in the community which is easily accessible
2. a location which is attractive, which can give a sense of warmth and caring
3. an approach which will allow needs to be met on the premises, without a lot of back and forth in delivery of service
4. the provision of quality service, utilizing qualified personnel at all levels
5. coordinating services for the best delivery system, so that different disciplines complement service needs
6. integrating the services within the community, thus it will not be isolated from the community and its other needs
7. concern for the totality of the person as he relates to self, family, community and society (Johnson, 1970)

The value screens of the service providers have contributed to the difficulty in implementation of Neighborhood Health Centers. Centers exist all over the country, and the problems they have faced have been related to the providers' willingness to work toward the solution proposed. In those instances in which the providers could not substantially alter their value system and/or accept the value system of the consumer there were problems. This failure to adapt meant that the providers could not allow community participation and engage in practices of individual, institutional, and administrative racism. The needs of the community were not related to the operation of the center. To Blacks the non-implementation was another in a series of broken promises. Action—not words—was needed, and when this did not materialize, neither did cooperation.

Coordination became a key word in service delivery (Johnson, 1970). This called for bringing together not only the service deliverers, but also the institutions, within and without the community, and the people of the community, coupled with consideration of the associative problems of daily living which confronted them. Only when such an arrangement is consciously sought can a climate of respect and exchange of ideas and concerns be achieved in which both sides are considered equal and neither will want to assume superior or inferior roles.

Prevention. Great strides have been made in the public health sector in preventing various communicable diseases. Effort has also been extended toward prevention in mental health (Caplan, 1964). However, the imprecision of the disease entity has led to limited success. Prevention is usually thought of in terms of primary, secondary, and tertiary measures.

With the use of chemotherapy, there has been some improvement in controlling mental illness and the length of hospital stay. However, other factors which might be causative in relation to mental illness in Blacks have not been given much attention. The conditions under which Blacks live have not been explored. There is a paucity of information as to the relationship between racism and mental health. Data are not available on hospital admissions or outpatient visits which have as their direct cause racism. Nor have the resultant conditions of racism affecting life-style, family relationships, housing, and economic condition been explored in this connection.

Primary prevention which calls for getting at the root problem before manifestation calls forth the most concern. There is some question as to whether we have the knowledge and the ability to do this. Moving in to help people know about causative factors and helping them to deal with these are not easy tasks. The number of variables which might cause mental illness in a person is not finite. However, prevention might possibly alleviate some causes but not all. If effort is not directed to deal with those factors which are known to be causative because the area is difficult to deal with, then failure is admitted before beginning. Means of communicating which are already known still need to be improved. Also, there is the need to begin the research needed to investigate other areas which can be causative. Beyond research there is the need to make conscious efforts to eliminate racist oppression by recognizing the interrelationship between individuals, institutions, and society in making racism possible.

While there are a number of facilities available to treat mental illness by secondary prevention, not all people have easy access to these facilities. Access is not only physical proximity, but willingness and ability to accept the treatment available. The "medical" beliefs of the user are not likely to be taken into account. It is not unusual for Black consumers to believe that the state of their mental health or illness is associated with "roots and herbs." There are some who seek out persons with a knowledge of folk medicine to provide them with help, and they often receive relief (Snow, 1974). This cultural derivitive should be understood. In order to be successful, secondary prevention must not isolate the consumer from his accustomed life-style or fail to show an appreciation of it.

Secondary prevention, which seeks to treat the cause of illness, control influencing factors, and return the consumer to functioning, must include an awareness of the supports of the community. These supports may well differ from those usually considered, but are no less viable. Just as a family member might be used, so must the "medical" belief system of the consumer.

Tertiary prevention seeks those resources of the community which will be remedial in nature. The support system of the Black community can be found not only in the family, but in the church, social clubs, and other community sources. The communal nature of the Black culture lends itself to such utilization in a constructive manner. Often these support systems have previously been in operation and have delayed the onslaught of illness. It is not unusual for non-blood-related persons to be available and instrumental. Consideration for these resources needs to be weighed and utilized for the improvement and continued functioning of the consumer.

Community Mental Health Centers, which have a component of service to be directed toward prevention, consultation, and education, have not given much attention to the prevention aspect of their task. This service is usually considered an indirect one with little measurement potential. The more traditionally based services have received most of the attention in service delivery. Funding, too, has been difficult for this unit. Going out into the community is a feature of this service which is not readily accepted as a means of consumer care. The task is hard and, in spite of Caplan's efforts, not easily implemented. The means of such service have to be adjusted to the community in need, and require broad-based community as well as institutional support. Additionally, this service calls for a different utilization of staff that is not engaged in the one-to-one relationship.

An Organizational Model for Black People

The selected models of mental health delivery which have been reviewed all have optimal goals. The goals, however, are not always directed toward all of the people. Blacks are not usually addressed from their experiences, but rather from the experiences of others. The organizations and members who carry out the functions are not likely to be Black or to have an appreciation of the Black experience. These organizations tend to follow the Weber model of hierarchy, rationality, impersonality, and order. While it is true that chaos cannot prevail, this does not mean that organizations cannot have a humanistic approach. The blending of the two approaches with thought-out purpose and goals might well lead to a more productive organization.

This type of organizational blend is what Bennis calls the organization of the future (1969). In such a coming together, there would be a place for the collectivity as well as the individual. Rationality and emotionalism would co-exist. Consideration would be given to the interface which exists between the consumer's contextual life-style and experiences within his or her own culture, as well as those experiences outside of that culture. Hence, there would be opportunity for both concrete and intangible expressions of the world as it is.

It is not the name of the various organizations which should be changed, but rather the "game" which is played. The game of implementation, as currently practiced, leans toward, and gives more emphasis to, the dominant society's view. The dominant society's connection with, as well as responsibility for, maintaining certain ritualistic behaviors which enhance a status system of superior and inferior must be addressed. In doing so, there will be freedom for both sides.

An organizational model for Blacks will take into consideration the racism which exists in organizations, facilities, and professions which relate to health care at the internal level, and will also show an awareness of the external forces of racism. The distribution of health care will then be viewed as a right and not a privilege.

Knowles and Prewitt (1969) have concluded that health institutions are racist. They state:

> This racism seems a powerful indictment of a system of medical care which (1) is capable of offering part of its population the best health care in the world, but (2) has the ultimate responsibility for providing health care for everyone in a country that believes all men have certain inalienable rights to life . . . there is not a uniform system of health care to analyze, but rather a very complex series of independent institutions which must act together to provide health care.

The eradication of racism within the health field will require conscious, concerted action at many levels. Not only must Blacks be served in a manner which will be to their best interest, but there must be recognition of the many factors which influence that interest. Training opportunities must be made available not only in medical and other professional schools, but also within the many health care facilities. What is needed is not a token for affirmative action compliance, but an open system of acceptance. Seen as important are Black role models for identification which cannot now be present because of the limited number of trained Black personnel. Recognition that Black destiny is intertwined with that of others is only a partial realization—the dominant group's destiny is intertwined with that of Blacks. Each has a heritage within this country which can and must be expressed. This is a struggle which has not ended.

> If there is no struggle, there is no progress. Those who profess to favor freedom, and yet deprecate agitation, are men who want crops without plowing up the ground. They want the ocean without the awful roar of its many waters (Douglass, 1857).

References

Books and Pamphlets

Axinn, J., and Leven, H. *Social Welfare: An American History Response to Need.* New York: Dodd, Mead, 1975.

Argyris, C. *Interpersonal Competence and Organizational Effectiveness.* Homewood, Illinois: Dorsey Press, and Richard D. Irvin, 1962.

Bell, G. (ed.). *Organizations and Human Behavior: A Book of Readings.* Englewood Cliffs, New Jersey: Prentice-Hall, 1967.

Bellak, L. and Barten, H. (eds.). *Progress in Community Mental Health,* vol. 3. New York: Brunner/Mazel, 1975.

Bennett, L., Jr. *Before the Mayflower: A History of the Negro in America, 1619–1964,* rev. ed. Baltimore, Maryland: Penguin Books, 1969.

_____. *Confrontation: Black and White.* Baltimore, Maryland: Penguin Books, 1965.

_____. *The Shaping of Black America.* Chicago: Johnson, 1975.

Bennis, W. G.; Benne, K. D.; and Chin, R. (eds.). *The Planning of Social Change,* 2nd ed. New York: Holt, Rinehart & Winston, 1969.

Billingsley, A. *Black Families in White America.* Englewood Cliffs, New Jersey: Prentice-Hall, 1968.

Blau, P. M. *Exchange and Power in Social Life.* New York: Wiley, 1967.

_____. *The Dynamics of Bureaucracy: A Study of Interpersonal Relations in Two Government Agencies.* Chicago: University of Chicago Press, 1955.

Blau, P. M., and Scott, W. R. *Formal Organizations: A Comparative Approach.* San Francisco: Chandler, 1962.

Bloom, B. L. *Community Mental Health: A Historical and Critical Analysis.* Morristown, New Jersey: General Learning Press, 1973.

Bracey, J. H., Jr.; Meier, A.; and Rudwick, E. *Black Nationalism in America.* Indianapolis: Bobbs-Merrill, 1970.

Caplan, G. *Principles of Preventive Psychiatry.* New York: Basic Books, 1964.

_____. *The Theory and Practice of Mental Health Consultation.* New York: Basic Books, 1970.

Caplow, T. *Principles of Organization.* New York: Harcourt, Brace & World, 1964.

Carmichael, S., and Hamilton, C. V. *Black Power: The Politics of Liberation in America.* New York: Vintage Books, 1967.

Comer, J. P. *Beyond Black and White.* New York: Quadrangle Books, 1972.

Coser, L. A. *Greedy Institutions: Patterns of Undivided Commitment.* New York: Free Press, 1974.

Donabedian, A. *Aspects of Medical Care Administration: Specifying Requirements for Health Care.* Cambridge, Massachusetts: Harvard University Press, 1973.

Douglass, F. West Indian Emancipation Speech, August 1857.

Dowd, B. (ed.). *Some Dimensions of the Formal Organization: A Reader.* New York: MSS Information Corporation, 1972.

Drake, S. C. *Churches and Voluntary Associations in The Chicago Negro Community.* Chicago: Work Projects Administration, 1940.

——————. *Race Relations in a Time of Rapid Change: Report of a Survey.* New York: National Federation of Settlements and Neighborhood Centers, 1966.

Drake, S. C., and Cayton, H. R. *Black Metropolis: A Study of Negro Life in a Northern City,* rev. ed., 2 vols. New York: Harcourt, Brace & World, 1970.

Etzioni, A. *A Comparative Analysis of Complex Organizations.* New York: Free Press, 1961.

——————. *Complex Organizations: A Sociological Reader.* New York: Holt, Rinehart & Winston, 1962.

Evaluation of Neighborhood Health Centers: A Plan for Implementation. Washington, D.C.: Office of Economic Opportunity, 1968.

Gil, D. G. *Unravelling Social Policy.* Cambridge, Massachusetts: Schenkman, 1973.

Hall, R. H. (ed.). *The Formal Organization.* New York: Basic Books, 1972.

Kahn, R. L., and Boulding, E. (eds.). *Power and Conflict in Organizations.* New York: Basic Books, 1964.

Katz, D., and Kahn, R. L. *The Social Psychology of Organizations.* New York: Wiley, 1966.

Knowles, L. L., and Prewitt, K. (eds.). *Institutional Racism in America.* Englewood Cliffs, New Jersey: Prentice-Hall, 1969.

Lewin, K. *Field Theory in Social Science.* New York: Harper, 1951.

Lipset, S. M. et. al. *Union Democracy.* Glencoe, Illinois: Free Press, 1965.

March, J. G. *Handbook of Organizations.* Chicago: Rand-McNally, 1965.

Mayer, R. R. *Social Planning and Social Change.* Englewood Cliffs, New Jersey: Prentice-Hall, 1972.

Mayo, E. *Human Problems of an Industrial Civilization.* New York: Macmillan, 1933.

Meier, A. and Rudwick, E. *The Making of Black America: Essays in Negro Life and History.* New York: Atheneum, 1969.

Merton, R. K. *Social Theory and Social Structure,* 3rd ed. New York: Free Press, 1968.

Olsen, M. E. (ed.). *Power in Societies.* New York: Macmillan, 1970.

Panzetta, A. F. *Community Mental Health: Myth and Reality.* Philadelphia: Lea & Febiger, 1971.

Stein, H. D., and Cloward, R. A. (eds.). *Social Perspectives on Behavior: A Reader in Social Sciences for Social Work and Related Professions.* Glencoe, Illinois: Free Press, 1958.

Toppin, E. A. *Blacks in America: Then and Now.* Boston: Christian Science Monitor, 1969.

Weber, M. *Theory of Social and Economic Organization.* (Talcott Parsons, ed.) New York: Oxford University Press, 1947.

Weeks, D. A. *National Health Insurance and Corporate Benefit Plans.* New York: The Conference Board, 1974.

Willie, C. V.; Kramer, B. M.; and Brown, B. S. (eds.). *Racism and Mental Health.* Pittsburgh: University of Pittsburgh Press, 1973.

Woodward, C. V. *The Strange Career of Jim Crow,* rev. ed. New York: Oxford University Press, 1966.

Articles in Books

Argyris, C. "Individual Actualization in Complex Organizations." In G. D. Bell (ed.), *Organizations and Human Behavior,* pp. 208–217. Englewood Cliffs, New Jersey: Prentice-Hall, 1967.

Bennis, W. G. "Changing Organizations." In W. G. Bennis; K. D. Benne; R. Chin (eds.), *The Planning of Change,* 2nd. ed. New York: Holt, Rinehart & Winston, 1969.

Blau, P. M., and Scott, W. R. "The Concept of Formal Organization." In G. D. Bell (ed.), *Organizations and Human Behavior,* pp. 77–81. Englewood Cliffs, New Jersey: Prentice-Hall, 1967.

Drake, S. C. "Folkways and Classways within the Black Ghetto." In A. Meier, and E. Rudwick (eds.), *The Making of Black America: Essays in Negro Life and History,* pp. 448–454. New York: Atheneum, 1969.

Etzioni, A. "Organizational Control Structure." In J. G. March (ed.), *Handbook of Organizations.* Chicago: Rand-McNally, 1965.

Hall, R. H. "Professionalism and Bureaucratization." In R. H. Hall (ed.), *The Formal Organization,* pp. 143–163. New York: Basic Books, 1972.

——————. "The Impact of Internal Factors on Organizations." In R. H. Hall (ed.), *The Formal Organization,* pp. 49–53. New York: Basic Books, 1972.

Kramer, M.; Rosen, B. M.; and Willis, E. M. "Definitions of Mental Disorders in a Racist Society." In C. V. Willie; B. M. Kramer; and B. S. Brown (eds.), *Racism and Mental Health,* pp. 353–459. Pittsburgh: University of Pittsburgh Press, 1973.

Michels, R. "The Iron Law of Oligarchy." In M. E. Olsen (ed.), *Power in Societies*. New York: Macmillan, 1970.

Miller, G. A. "Professionals in Bureaucracy: Alienation among Industrial Scientists and Engineers." In R. H. Hall (ed.), *The Formal Organization*. New York: Basic Books, 1972.

Ordway, J. A. "Some Emotional Consequences of Racism for Whites." In C. V. Willie; B. M. Kramer; and B. S. Brown (eds.), *Racism and Mental Health*, pp. 123–145. Pittsburgh: University of Pittsburgh Press, 1973.

Pettigrew, T. F. "Racism and the Mental Health of White Americans: A Special Psychological View." In C. V. Willie; B. M. Kramer; and B. S. Brown (eds.), *Racism and Mental Health*, pp. 269–298. Pittsburgh: University of Pittsburgh Press, 1973.

Pinderhughes, C. A. "Racism and Psychotherapy." In C. V. Willie; B. M. Kramer; and B. S. Brown (eds.), *Racism and Mental Health*, pp. 61–121. Pittsburgh: University of Pittsburgh Press, 1973.

Prudhomme, C., and Musto, D. F. "Historical Perspectives on Mental Health and Racism." In C. V. Willie; B. M. Kramer; and B. S. Brown (eds.), *Racism and Mental Health*, pp. 25–57. Pittsburgh: University of Pittsburgh Press, 1973.

Reissman, L. "A Study of Role Conceptions in Bureaucracy." In H. D. Stein, and R. A. Cloward (eds.), *Social Perspectives on Behavior: A Reader in Social Sciences for Social Work and Related Professions*. Glencoe, Illinois: Free Press, 1958.

Stinchcombe, A. "Social Structure and Organizations." In J. G. March (ed.), *Handbook of Organizations*. Chicago: Rand-McNally, 1965.

Thomas, C. S., and Comer, J. P. "Racism and Mental Health Services." In C. V. Willie; B. M. Kramer; and B. S. Brown (eds.), *Racism and Mental Health*, pp. 165–181. Pittsburgh: University of Pittsburgh Press, 1973.

Articles in Periodicals

Johnson, A. E. "The Delivery of Social Work Services in the Black Community." *Black Caucus Journal* 1 (1970): 36.

Jones, T. "Institutional Racism in the United States." *Social Work* 19 (1974): 218–225.

Rabinowitz, H. N. "From Exclusion to Segregation: Health and Welfare Services for Southern Blacks, 1865–1890." *Social Service Review* 48 (1974): 327–354.

Scott, C. S. "Health and Healing Practices among Five Ethnic Groups in Miami, Florida." *Public Health Reports* 89 (1974): 524–532.

Snow, L. F. "Folk Medical Beliefs and Their Implications for Care of Patients." *Annals of Internal Medicine*, July 1974.

12   REFLECTIONS ON PUBLIC POLICY AND MENTAL HEALTH*

Theodis Thompson, Ph.D.

Introduction

The role of public policy in the provision of mental health services is boundless. An understanding of how mental health care is organized, structured, financed, and distributed throughout the American society is a necessity in order to avoid the perceived continuous government boondoggle of mental health in this country (Musto, 1976). When the myriad issues pertinent to public policy are applied to the Black community, the need for an exposition on the topic is more germane. Unfortunately, this chapter will not elaborate on such a concept as Black public policy. It is the author's view that public policy is public policy—whatever that is.

Often the issue of using the research and evaluation strategies of white researchers is questioned vis-à-vis the development of our own (Black) methodologies, techniques, and approaches. The challenge to the use of any mechanism to predict, explain, or destroy concepts, constructs, models, ideologies, etc., is for the Black researcher, teacher, policy-maker, planner, and entrepreneur to utilize their (white) parameters to extrapolate every resource for the short-run and long-run benefits to the Black community. Granted, there is a need (and efforts are being made) to develop research instruments and modalities based upon the Black experience, and Black norms and standards.

The objectives of this chapter are to reflect on selected aspects of public policy from an administrative perspective by (1) defining traditional concepts and approaches to the study of public policy, (2) exploring policy issues in the field of mental health, (3) discussing some

*The author would like to acknowledge the assistance of Mr. Larry Schwartz and Ms. Wanda Horne Flurry in the preparation of this chapter.

legal aspects of mental health, and (4) reiterating a planning approach to mental health services in the Black community.

Public Policy and Decision-Making

It has become commonplace among behavioral and social scientists to lament that so many of their basic terms are vague, or at least lacking in clearly understood content. Consequently, the literature of political science abounds in definitions of "public policy," and like other such terms as "system," "power," and "mental health," a great deal of time and effort have been spent seeking to hone the details of its definition. Although such activity undeniably has value in clarifying issues and debate, it seems that sooner or later almost everyone gives in to the urge to define "public policy" and does so with varying degrees of success according to his critics. Nevertheless, a number of influential political scientists have noted that the range of disagreements concerning "policy" is not really that great.

Public policy is not a new concept for those interested in politics. Philosophers of politics from Aristotle onward have demonstrated concern about the policies pursued by government, but their investigations have never centered around policies *per se,* but rather on the institutions and structures of the governments which make and execute them.

Wasby (1970, p. 253) has pointed out that difficulties in definition originated in the distinctions and emphasis drawn between public administration and political science. Others (Jones, 1970) argue about the change from traditional to "modern" behavioral political science.

Traditionally, a hard and fast dichotomy was drawn between "policy" and "administration"—policy being made by the legislative branches of government and implemented by the executives. "Stress on this distinction was reinforced by belief in the doctrine of separation of powers between legislative, executive, and judicial branches, as well as by the jointly held ideas that politics was corrupt and administration was neutral" (Wasby, 1970, p. 417). These assumptions and the subsequent attempts to depoliticize government services soon brought the recognition that this distinction was much too simplistic.

The discovery that policy and administration are not at all disparate, but rather intimately related, brought about a concern for policy development to students of public administration. Their principal concerns in this regard have been the development of policy within the administrative organs of government, although this has extended to include the development of policy in legislative and judicial branches of government as well.

Definitional problems also exist along with the changing concepts of public policy. David Easton's (1953) definition referred to policy as "the authoritative allocation of values for the whole society" (p. 129). This phrase is one of the most widely used. It implies that governmental actors make policy in authoritative decisions, referring to what government *does* as distinguished from the decision-making process.

Another view of policy would confine the usage of policy (especially social policy) to broad issues or general questions—not the detailed choices within that framework. In this case, it would consist of broad authoritative rules, "the boundaries of which are ill-defined, but the content of which is rich" (Boulding, 1973, p. 3).

Thirdly, policy is often spoken of as being objective-oriented. It becomes an action or set of actions calculated to achieve a goal or purpose. Laswell and Kaplan (1950, p. 71) refer to "a projected program of goals and practices." This view proceeds from the assumption that all political behavior can always be understood in terms of a set of policy goals, including the methods (or means) by which they are achieved. These views are all combined in Carl J. Friedrich's (1963, p. 79) definition:

> A proposed course of action of a person, group or government within a given environment providing obstacles and opportunities which the policy was proposed to utilize and overcome in an effort to reach a goal or realize an objective or a purpose . . . It is essential for the policy concept that there be a goal, objective or purpose.

Most students of politics tend to concur that there is a difference between specific decisions or actions and policy (a general program of action or statement of principles). Thus we can see that policy is an abstract term to be approached holistically through *patterns* of discrete acts.

Dye (1972) summarizes this discussion by stating that whether performing "regulative, organizational, distributive or extractive" tasks, public policies are simply "whatever governments choose to do or not to do" (pp. 1–2). There is a rough accuracy to the approach, but it does not take into consideration that often there are discrepancies between what government decides to do and what actually is accomplished.

With its departure from the institutional approach to governmental activities, behavioral political science led to a concern for policy processes. Adept at identifying and defining the processes and behaviors associated with government, behavioralists provided better insights into the social and psychological reasons for certain kinds of political activities. However, the approach "described the processes by which public policy was determined, it did not deal directly with the linkages between various processes and behaviors and the content of public policy" (Dye, 1972, p. 2).

Today, more concern than ever is being shifted to the "description and explanation of the causes and consequences of governmental activity" (Dye, 1972, p. 3). This policy orientation involves the investigation of "authoritative outputs from the political system, actions aimed at affecting those outputs, and the goals or purposes or interests at stake in authoritative decisions" (Salisbury, 1968, p. 153).

Implications of Public Policy

The existence of the concept of public policy indicates several things about the nature of the social system. Firstly, policy is goal-oriented. It is purposive rather than a random or chance occurrence. In modern political systems, public policies cannot generally be said to *just happen.*

Secondly, as we have already stated, policies consist of courses or patterns of decisions by governmental officials rather than discrete acts. In this sense acts usually fall into categories of relatively congruent intent—policies not only involve decisions to pass laws, but also subsequent decisions to implement, fund, and enforce them.

Stated intent is often a poor guide to the real intent of policy. If a rule is made or a law enacted but no provision is made for its implementation, then policy can hardly have been said to change due to the passage of the rule or the law.

Thirdly, policy can be either positive or negative in form. Positively, it may create or amend a government rule or action; negatively, it may involve a decision not to do anything—not to create or amend a government rule or action. A non-decision can also have policy consequences.

Finally, it is generally true that public policy is based on law and can be authoritative—carrying legal, potentially coercive sanctions.

Theories of Decision-Making for Public Policy

Almost as often as they indulge the urge to define key terms, many political and social scientists concern themselves with the development of models, theories, approaches, and concepts for analyzing public decision and policy-making. Although it often seems that more energy is expended in theorizing about public policy than in actually studying policy, such theories give direction to political inquiry.

The Rational-Comprehensive Theory. Rationalism sets up policy as the mode of efficient societal goal achievement. Thus it is supposed that any sacrifice in one or more values required by a policy is more than compensated for by the attainment of other values. Dye (1972) likens it to the concept of efficiency—the ratio between valued inputs and valued outputs (p. 27).

In his book *Public Policy-Making Reexamined,* Dror (1968) notes the prerequisites for national decision-making. He argues that public actors must know all the values of society and their relative importance, and all the alternatives and their consequences. They then must calculate the ratio of achieved to sacrificed values for each alternative and select the most important alternative.

All of this adds up to the suggestion that the values of society as a whole can be completely identified, weighted according to importance, and acted upon. An implicit assumption is that perfect knowledge about the decisions, their alternatives, and future impacts is in the hands of the appropriate actors at all times. It also assumes that the decision-making actor or apparatus is intelligent and predisposed to rational action.

With these rather considerable assumptions, there has been a great deal of criticism directed at the rational-comprehensive model. Braybrooke and Lindblom (1963, p. 48) contend that defining the problem is often a major difficulty for the decision-maker in that he is seldom faced with concrete kinds of problems, especially with regard to social programs.

Another difficulty with this model is that it presupposes superhuman moral and intellectual feats on the part of the actors involved. Lack of time, difficulty in collecting information on all relevant alternatives, and an inability to predict all the future consequences of a decision usually frustrate attempts at rational analysis.

There are problems with the view of the rational-comprehensive model as value-maximizing as well. It is argued that values are not easily separated out from many situations and that decisions must often be made among conflicting, as opposed to competing positions, the differences between which cannot be assessed or weighed in terms of the importance to the whole society. Even if it were possible, some argue, the decision-makers would not be disposed to choose options in a purely objective, non-partisan manner anyway.

Finally, large investments in existing programs and policies, known as "sunk costs," often prevent policy-makers from reconsidering alternatives which were foreclosed by previous decisions. For example, Washington D.C.'s Metro subway system has become expensive beyond all previously conceived imagination. At this point, "sunk costs" would prevent major reroutings of the subway to conform with demographic changes since it was planned and to make its services available to those people who display the greatest need for its services.

The Incremental Theory. Charles E. Lindblom has been the foremost philosopher of incrementalism. He first presented his theory as a criticism of rationalism, which he felt inaccurately described the manner in which public actors make decisions. Contrary to the rationalists, he argues that the decision-makers are constrained by time, intelligence, and cost from identifying and passing on the full range of options and their foreseeable consequences. The incremental process is best described as follows:

1. Decision-makers consider only *some* of the alternatives for dealing with a problem, and these differ only marginally from existing programs.

2. For each alternative only a limited number of important consequences are evaluated.

3. Decisions are essentially remedial—geared more toward the social "fix" than to the promotion of the future social goals.

4. There is no solution for a problem or decision which must be made other than by the concurrence of a number of analysts who see it as a means to an end.

5. Decisions are made to be politically expedient, for agreement comes easiest when the items in dispute are only increases or decreases in budgets or modifications of existing programs. Thus no one's "core" values are threatened.

Lindblom proceeds from the premise that in pluralist societies such as the United States, the decision-makers find it easier to continue existing programs rather than engage in overall policy planning toward specific societal goals. Incrementalism is geared to yield acceptable, conservative, programmatic decisions.

Mixed Scanning. Amitai Etzioni (1967) has forged a meeting point between these diametrically opposed views of decision-making. Although he agrees with the criticisms leveled at the rational approach, he sees the shortcomings in the incremental theory as well. Etzioni points to the emotional reaction which incrementalist theory stirs, because its acceptance lacks the ability to propagate social innovation, thus fixing for some time the status of those at the bottom of the social ladder. Incrementalism reflects the needs of society's special interests to the neglect of the underprivileged and unorganized.

Etzioni proposes mixed scanning as a compromise between the rational and incremental approaches which would be situation-specific. Although he has never clearly enunciated the implications of the method, he points up the fact that different decisions may require different decision processes. As Anderson (1975, p. 15) interprets it, "the greater the capacity of decision-makers to mobilize power to implement their decisions, the more scanning they can realistically engage in; and the more encompassing is scanning, the more effective is decision-making."

Theories of Policy-Making

Political scientists have proposed a number of theories of public policy-making, each representing a different way of viewing politics. We will briefly examine the major theories—each with a unique outlook, each with its own set of strengths and weaknesses.

Systems Theory. Public policy may be viewed as the response of a political system to demands arising from its environment. Easton (1965) has done much of the important work in systems theory. He defines the political system as being composed of those identifiable and interrelated institutions and activities in a society that make authoritative decisions or allocations of values which are binding on the whole of society.

Inputs are received into the political system in the form of both demands and supports. Demands are the claims people make on the political system; supports occur when people conform to policy decisions. The environment consists of all those conditions and events which are external to the boundaries of the political system. The outputs are the authoritative allocation of values—public policy. It is recognized that outputs have a modifying effect on the environment and the demands and supports generated therein. This is the concept of feedback.

Systems theory is limited by its highly general nature—it says nothing about how policy is actually made within the system, but it *is* a useful aid in organizing our information about policy formation. It directs attention to the effect of the environment on policy and *vice versa,* shows how the characteristics of the political system affect the content of public policy, and helps to identity the characteristics of the political system which enable it to function and preserve itself over time.

Computer modeling, a mathematical extrapolation from systems theory, has recently begun to come into its own through the work of Jay Forrester at the Massachusetts Institute of Technology (1969). Using many of the principles of systems theory, Forrester has been investigating the nature of complex social systems. Although computer modeling is still a rough tool, it is an exciting new approach to social problems. Complex systems, it proposes, are high-order, multiple-loop, nonlinear-feedback structures; social systems are ultimately related to the interaction between positive and negative feedback processes. Also, such systems are counter-intuitive. We are used to thinking in first-order, negative-feedback loops.

Group Theory. The group theory of public policy contends that group struggle is the central organizing force in social interactions. If groups are collections of individuals, then the contention, interaction, and struggle among them for claims on other groups in the society is the essence of politics.

A corollary of this assumption is that public policy, at any given time, will reflect the interests of dominant groups. As groups gain in power (or wane in power), public policy will adjust itself to the changes in favor of those with the greater influence.

David Truman's study, *The Governmental Process* (1971), explains group theory at great length. Under this system, the prime task of government is to manage group conflict by establishing the ground rules, arranging and enacting compromises among groups, and subsequently enforcing them.

While certainly focusing on one of the major dynamics of policy formulation, especially in pluralist societies like the U.S., group theory seems to overstate the power of political interest groups and to understate the independence of actors in political institutions, as well as the impact of ideas and other (outside) institutions.

Elite Theory. Dye and Zeigler (1970) provide a good discussion of elite theory. This approach regards public policy as the values and preferences of a governing elite, carried out by public officials and agencies. Policies flow downward from the elites to the masses, not the other way around.

Dye and Zeigler provide a summary of elitism (1970, p. 6):

1. Society is divided into the few who have power and the many who do not. . . .
2. The few who govern are . . . drawn disproportionately from the upper socioeconomic strata of society.
3. The movement of non-elites to elite positions must be slow and continuous to maintain stability and avoid revolution. Only non-elites who have accepted the basic elite consensus can be admitted to governing circles.
4. Elites share a consensus on the basic values of the social system and the preservation of the system.
5. Public policy . . . reflects . . . the prevailing values of the elite. Changes in public policy will be incremental rather than revolutionary.
6. Active elites subect to relatively little direct influence from apathetic masses. Elites influence masses more than masses influence elites.

Elite theory does focus on the role of leadership in the making of policy. Whether elites rule with little influence from the masses is the object of some debate among political scientists. Although this elite theory is widely shared, it cannot be proved by assertion alone. Some suggest that it may have greater utility in explaining the behavior of totalitarian or dictatorial states than that of pluralist republics.

Institutionalism. The study of government institutions is one of the oldest concerns of political science. As mentioned earlier, it was once one of the only theories of politics. Although it receives less attention now than previously, it is not an unproductive approach. An institution is a set of regularized patterns of behavior which exist over time. These regular patterns of behavior can certainly affect policy and are never neutral in intent or action.

Institutionalism has sought to describe in detail the procedures and structures of decision- and policy-making, but little was done to explain how institutions actually operated (as opposed to how they were supposed to operate), to analyze policy outputs from institutions, or to discover the relationships between institutional structure and public policy. In sum, institutions can have a great impact on policy and should not be ignored in an analysis; neither should analysis be performed without concern for the dynamics of politics.

Evolution of Mental Health Policy

Stimulated by interest and funding from the federal government, the field of mental health has been rapidly changing over the last 30 years. In this section we will seek to describe, using the traditional institutional mode of analysis, the historical evolution of mental health policies in the United States. (When describing the problems of mental health services in the Black community, we will attempt a more in-depth analysis of the mental health policy system, but for now, a descriptive mode of analysis will suffice in analyzing the historical strengths and weaknesses of mental health policies.)

Mental health workers and scholars tend to divide its history into two periods: before and after World War II. For those with even the most cursory knowledge of the history of mental health, the reasons for this should be obvious. The advent of World War II marks not the beginning of mental health policy, but the rapid increase in the number and types of health personnel involved in the mental health profession as well as the interest of the federal, state, and local governments in funding and operating mental health facilities.

Mental health is as old a problem as physical health. Societal methods of caring for the mentally ill and providing mental health services have followed no consistent developmental pattern; in fact, they have been erratic. Concern for mental health goes back to the earliest records of human activities. The early Egyptians, for example, attributed mental illness to evil spirits and wrote about senile and alcoholic behavior as many as 1500 years before Christ. In the Old Testament of the Bible there are accounts of madness, such as the alternating maniacal and depressed attacks from which King Saul suffered, ending in his suicide (Overholser, 1975, p. 3).

These "Divine Vistations" grew up alongside the work of sixth-century Greek philosophers who were paying considerable attention to the problem of mental illness and developing theories which are not altogether unlike those of modern psychiatrists. Pythagoras described the functioning of the brain as the central organ of intellectual activity. Hippocrates described several types of mental disorder which he called phrenitis, mania, and melancholia (Overholser, 1975, p. 3).

Along with the many theories of mental illness went a plethora of prescriptions for its cure. Some prehistoric cavemen allegedly punched holes in the skull to release demons causing mental illness in afflicted individuals' brains. Connery (1968, p. 3) comments on such practices:

> Some were psychic, such as hypnotism and incantations. Others were mechanical, such as Rush's tranquilizer chair. And still others were medicinal, including weird potions concocted of ewes' bladders or lizards' eyes or gantweed and cropleek, perhaps steeped in ale or holy water. One prescription required a potion to be drunk on nine successive mornings out of a church bell. . . .

Mental Health Policy in America—The Historical Perspective

Albert Deutsch's work, *The Mentally Ill in America* (1949), has provided the standard historical review of the treatment and care of the mentally ill in the United States. He notes that in the colonial period, the mentally ill were confined in jail cells, often in chains. It was often a source of amusement to taunt them or exhibit them as sideshows in a circus.

The Pennsylvania General Hospital of Philadelphia was established in 1756 by the Society of Friends as the first institution in the U.S. attempting to emphasize treatment and care as opposed to confinement. The first public institution was established in Williamsburg, Virginia, in 1773. Not another state hospital was founded until Kentucky did so in 1824, some 50 years later.

In the 1790s, a Frenchman named Philippe Pinel advanced a new theory of treatment for the mentally ill consisting of a minimum of restraint and a maximum of intelligent understanding and sympathy. The treatment, known as "moral management" or "moral treatment," was slow to be adopted in the U.S. It was described in 1811 as involving

[The removal of patients] from their residence to some proper asylum; and for this purpose a calm retreat in the country is to be preferred . . . Have humane attendants who shall act as servants to them; never threaten but execute; offer no indignities to them, as they have a high sense of honor . . . Let their fears and resentments be soothed without unnecessary opposition . . . The diet ought to be light, and easy of digestion but never too low. When convalescing, allow limited liberty; introduce entertaining books and conversation. [Deutsch, 1949, pp. 91–92]

In essence, moral treatment was based on the assumption that psychiatric problems could be cured if the patient was treated in a considerate fashion, if his interest was stimulated, and if he was kept actively involved in life. In essence, treatment was associated with re-education.

Unfortunately, change was not to come quickly. Although moral treatment was adopted at most of the established institutions throughout the world, there were few therapeutic hospitals, and most of the mentally ill received no better treatment than previously. Moral treatment was a right of the affluent; other patients were treated as the equals of the destitute poor.

Dorothea Dix was perhaps the most militant crusader for improving the care of the mentally ill. A retired schoolteacher, she was asked to teach a Sunday school class in an East Cambridge, Massachusetts, jail in the winter of 1841. There she was shocked to find that mentally ill persons were locked in unheated cells because of the widely held belief that they were insensitive to cold (Connery, 1968, p. 13). For the next 40 years she traveled around the country seeking to rally influential people to support humane treatment for the mentally ill. The thrust of her message was the removal of the insane from local jails and county poorhouses and their placement in hospitals built and operated by the states.

Ironically, the reforms of Dorothea Dix have become today's orthodox practice and themselves have become the object of reform—returning the concern of mental health to the community level once more, with assistance from the federal and state governments.

Centralization of control at the state level was accompanied by the construction of new state facilities which helped in relieving overcrowded conditions and allowed the gradual transfer of mental patients from local jails—white mental patients, that is. Most Black patients remained in jails. At the Worcester State Hospital in Massachusetts, a landmark social institution founded in 1833, separate facilities were constructed for the races, and a brick shop was remodeled to provide quarters for Blacks. Similar separation was common practice, both North and South, as it was believed to be better for treatment purposes (Grob, 1966, p. 50). In 1863, the American Freedman's Inquiry Commission discovered, upon researching the matter, that most institutions, both private and state, did not accept Blacks, and where they did, only a few were accepted.

In the nineteenth century, racist theories of mental illness were carried over from general societal values. Theories developed in an interesting manner to explain the relatively low numbers of Blacks and Indians afflicted with mental illness as compared with whites. The relatively low rates of insanity among people of color were generally attributed to the security of slavery or the dull strength of the uncivilized. After emanicipation, the reported number of mentally ill Blacks began to climb, according to white accounts (Witmer, 1891, p. 20).

> Previous to their emancipation, the health and morals of the slaves were carefully preserved . . . Since their liberation, through overindulgence, exposure and ignorance of the laws of health, many have suffered from . . . insanity. Untutored in a knowledge of the world, and without a sound philosophy or a religion deeper seated than the emotions to sustain them in adversity, many minds have failed under the constant strain of their advancing civilization.

Life was harsh for unskilled immigrants who began arriving on U.S. shores in the 1840s. The misery of the industrial working class from among such groups often resulted in strange and disorganized patterns of behavior. The combination of unfamiliar cultural patterns and bizarre behavior led to growing feelings among society at large that the mentally ill should be physically removed from the community. As a result, increased demands were made upon existing mental hospitals to take them. In sum, what had happened is that along with the Industrial Revolution, increasing immigration and urbanization, societies became less able to cope with deviant behavior.

The federal government remained largely unconcerned with the problems of mental health until 1917, when, after the passage of the Selective Service Act, the Army became concerned about the mental fitness of its draftees. The War Department's Surgeon General was given a Division of Neurology and Psychiatry to screen recruits and bar from enlistment all those suffering from some recognizable form of mental illness and to treat those already in the service. After the First World War these activities were continued, and long-term treatment of service personnel became a task of the new Veterans Administration (Connery, 1968, p. 15).

In 1930, a Division of Mental Hygiene was established in the Public Health Service. Besides doing some research in the mental health field, the Division did some work with federal prisoners and was involved with studies of drug addiction. But it was not until 1946 that the U.S. began to treat mental health as a problem of *public health*.

Since World War II. During the Second World War, the enormous task of screening draftees and the large number of psychiatrically disabled soldiers brought about great changes in the government's attitude toward mental health. Almost two million men were rejected by the armed forces because of mental problems when the war began; testifying before Congress, Selective Service System Director General Hershey noted that as of August 1, 1945, "somewhere around 4,800,000 men ages 18 to 37 [were] rejected for the armed forces . . . 856,000 . . . for mental diseases . . . 235,000 . . . for neurological cases . . . 676,000 for mental deficiency" (Connery, 1968, p. 16).

The publicity given to the number of psychiatric casualties and the large manpower loss due to the number of those screened out for mental health reasons provided a boost for the development of public policy in relation to mental health. In 1946, Congress passed the National Mental Health Act, which created the National Institute of Mental Health. NIMH started with a budget of 9 million dollars in 1950; in 1975 it had reached $404 million.

The National Mental Health Act required each state to designate a "mental health authority" which would plan for and disburse grant-in-aid funds for the state.

Although there were significant advances in the U.S. in mental health research following World War II, very little of this gain was transferred to mental hospitals in the early fifties (Mechanic, 1969, p. 58). By 1955, the most concerned government officials no longer believed that large institutions could effectively deal with mental health problems. The issue of community mental health was receiving a great deal of attention and was motivated both by a desire to reduce hospital populations (and thus costs) and by a belief that such measures would be of great therapeutic value.

In 1955, Congress passed the Mental Health Study Act, which created the Joint Commission on Mental Illness and Health. The Commission's report, *Action for Mental Health,* was released in 1961. It argued for more funds for basic research in mental health and new programs for the care of patients with mental health problems, including smaller "community" mental health programs and mental health clinics.

In the end, President John F. Kennedy threw his weight behind many of the Commission's proposals in the great debate that ensued. The concept of community mental health, which Kennedy endorsed, took the viewpoint that mental illness is not inherently different from the larger range of psychological differences in each community. The harmful aspects of the custodial/hospital environment had become generally recognized, as had the disparity of access to treatment between rich and poor (Mechanic, 1969, p. 60).

The system of community mental health which has emerged since that time emphasizes outpatient care and hospitalization for short periods—and then only when necessary. This system has both advantages and disadvantages. While much of the program has been put into effect, the services provided to patients are "sporadic and fragmentary, and frequently the burden that had been the hospital's has been shifted to the family" (Mechanic, 1969, p. 63).

Mental Health and Public Policy

In addition to the public policies involving treatment for the mentally ill, governments must also decide on when, and the means by which, the mentally ill should be removed from the community after they are perceived as being in danger or are threatening danger. Also, policy must be established setting the conditions and standards for the competent performance of the responsibilities of citizenship.

There are difficulties in establishing a clear-cut and coherent policy pertaining to the identification, etiology, and care of mental illness and mental health because the issues remain cloudy in the professional community. As a result, confusion and lack of agreement also reign in official procedures. Although, for legal purposes, society has seen a need to define mental illness and health, mental competence, fitness to stand trial, and dangerous behavior, because behavioral knowledge of such concepts is deficient, their application becomes ambiguous and inconsistent (Mechanic, 1969, p. 121). However, there seems to be considerable societal consensus that even though experts cannot agree on such concepts, policy-makers must attempt to grasp them, for these are issues to which they cannot remain oblivious.

The discussion here draws heavily upon the excellent analyses provided by Allen, Ferster, and Rubin's *Readings in Law and Psychiatry* (1975), Kittrie's *The Right to be Different* (1971), and Mechanic's *Mental Health and Social Policy* (1969).

Every society has rules to which it expects individuals and groups to adhere. In most societies it is expected that a large majority of the citizens will conform to the rules most of the time. It is also expected that there will always be some nonconforming individuals and groups. While law is generally viewed as an instrument for decreasing nonconformity, it also sets the general framework defining criminality and deviance. Subsequently, the amount of deviation in any given society will depend on the range of behavior which it seeks to control (Kittrie, 1971, p. 3).

Although this approach—criminal law sanctions—has been the traditional tool of the state in recent years, the U.S. has utilized ever increasingly the model of social controls described as " 'civil,' 'therapeutic,' or *'parens patriae'* (a term derived from the English concept of the King's role as father of the country)" (Kittrie, 1971, p. 3). *Parens patriae* focuses to a greater extent on the physical, mental, or environmental problems of offenders than on his or her guilt or innocence of any particular offense: in such a role, society supposedly plays a parental, reforming, healing, socializing role, decreasing deviant behavior through treatment and therapy.

Because of the peculiar role which the state allegedly plays under *parens patriae,* the individual was not supposed to require protection from the state, as has long been recognized in criminal legal affairs. However, as more people are ever more subject to *parens patriae* (criminal law has been in the process of divesting the health, mental health, and other health-related fields in favor of this approach, probably with the object of searching for less judicially cumbersome and more individualized and informal programs of control), emphasizing therapy, rehabilitation, and prevention, as opposed to punishment, there have grown up whole series of proceedings and sanctions in the gap between civil and criminal law. Kittrie notes that the Supreme Court has directed a great deal of attention in recent years to the rights of the individual and the protection of due process in criminal affairs.

The historical roots of divestment can be found in fourteenth-century England, when it was decided that insane murderers could be exempt from criminal responsibility for their actions. But the more meaningful manifestations of this process began in the early nineteenth century, when it became widely felt that the nonviolent insane should be institutionally and conceptually distinguished from the common criminal. With this process of divestment came concerns for prevention instead of suppression of criminal activities—a sense of punishment designed to fit the individual appropriately and a recognition that *mens rea* (intent of wrongdoing) simply is inappropriate in certain cases.

Involuntary Hospitalization

One of the biggest legal problems before the "therapeutic state" has been the involuntary hospitalization of those considered mentally ill. Who is mentally ill? The discussion above makes it clear only that it is difficult to say with certitude. Nevertheless, all 50 states have laws providing for the commitment of the mentally disordered (given certain circumstances) on the assumption that some patients may constitute a threat either to themselves or others.

Although Virginia enacted a law providing for the involuntary commitment of mental patients in 1806, the process of involuntary incarceration remained largely informal until the mid-nineteenth century. It became immediately a matter of considerable public concern. In 1845, Massachusetts Supreme Court Chief Justice Lemuel Shaw set the precedent that individuals could be restrained only if dangerous to themselves or others and only if restraint would be conducive to restoration (Mechanic, 1969, p. 125). This became the cornerstone of most state statutes; however, even then it was evident that although such statutes were instituted to protect "normal" and "sane" individuals, they simultaneously deprived citizens of their civil liberties.

The criteria for involuntary commitment have progressively broadened over the last century. This has developed under the belief that the prospective patient's "need for treatment" is a state of affairs sufficient in and of itself to justify treatment (commitment). In most states the question of need has superseded commitment of only the "dangerous"; the laws of the various states are by no means uniform.

The mentally ill are not the only people subject to involuntary commitment. The mentally deficient or defective—ill due to congenital conditions—have also been the inmates of state mental institutions. Here the powers of the state are so broad that in not a single state are the results of test scores required in determining whether deficiency is great enough to justify commitment.

Until recent years there have been few limits on the powers of the states to apply vague commitment criteria to those with mental health problems. In both the Fourteenth Amendment to the Constitution (the right to "due process" of law) and the traditional common law guarantees against law "void for vagueness," concern for application has come almost exclusively in the area of criminal cases. Such legal guarantees have not been so stringently applied in civil cases involving mental commitments, when patients have had their cases passed on, often without the benefit of counsel. The vagaries of commitment criteria have rarely been challenged in the courts, but when challenged, they are usually upheld (Kittrie, 1971, p. 70).

Despite the diversity in the laws of the states, the procedures for involuntary hospitalization can be divided into three basic groups—courts, administrative tribunals, and the hospitals themselves. The most common commitments in the United States are for an indeterminate amount of time, although in the last 20 years the trend has been toward temporary or observational hospitalization—ordered frequently with a minimum of formalities and obtained on medical certification only, but often for indeterminate amounts of time.

In sum, the trends and pressures for adopting new, effective, and more humane procedures will continue in mental health-related areas. Most states have attempted to reform their laws to stay astride advances in the problems of mental illness. These efforts have been only partially effective, because the necessary physical and professional resources have been lacking. As a result, those interested in keeping flexibility and informality (to make the treatment fit the patient) have been only partially satisfied with the progress to date; those concerned with the civil liberties of the individual have become alarmed (perhaps justifiably) by the watering down of procedural safeguards.

Current issues in due process for those with mental health problems subject to involuntary hospitalization include time to prepare (right to prior notice of the proceedings initiated for commitment); an opportunity to be heard (right to a hearing and to be present at it); trial by one's peers (right to a hearing, including the right to a jury trial); and guaranteed assistance of counsel (as with a criminal case, the subject's entitlement to an attorney perhaps appointed by the state, if he or she does not have access to a private one).

Competency to Stand Trial. It is often recognized by the courts that persons charged with crimes are, under certain circumstances, incompetent to stand trial. This is based on the belief that a defendant must assist counsel in the preparation of his or her case for the defense. If the patient lacks the capacity to understand the proceedings, owing to mental illness or deficiency, a trial would, *ipso facto,* deprive the defendant of his or her rights.

It is difficult to assess the state of the law with regard to incompetence in terms of the substance of concepts used. Similar to the commitment process, the nature of the law is used for a variety of situations confronting the community; in many cases it provides for the indefinite detention of the person deemed incompetent. Such detention may be for life, even though incompetence to stand trial has no bearing on whether the individual was guilty of any crimes and might pose a clearcut danger either to the community or to the defendant or plaintiff (e.g., Szasz, 1961).

Insanity as a Defense. Over the years, a number of decisions and rules have been made to govern the culpability of an individual believed to be insane when committing a criminal act. Certain assumptions, not always consistent, have been made concerning the nuances of the words in the rules.

The basic grounds for such maneuvers have been that treatment is more meaningful and effective in response to deviant behavior than is imprisonment. Some (Szasz, 1961, for example) have stated that given the poor quality of mental health care and the stigma associated with it, hospitalization is not necessarily more humane or useful than imprisonment.

We have already discussed the various opinions among psychiatrists about the concept of mental illness. Furthermore, mental illness is a limited concept, applicable only to a small number of individuals. On the other hand, it is a general concept, and almost everyone in some sense is mentally ill. Although such uncertainty is permissible in the therapeutic community, it is insupportable in the legal community, where "equality" is of such great concern.

The role of the psychiatrist in the insanity defense is difficult because the very nature of the case shifts the burden of determining responsibility on to him, rather than to judges and juries. The role of the psychiatrist is mostly one of informing the lay persons, who must ultimately make the determination as to whether insanity is a legal defense.

As important as the insanity defense may be, it can be considerably clarified by firm public policy which ensures the rights of the defendant and the meaningfulness of legal labels (Mechanic, 1969, p. 143). A more resolute public policy stance on the legal issues involved in the insanity defense (for the determination of sanity is ultimately a social judgment) could wipe away many of the inconsistences in present practice.

The Mental Health Law Project. The Mental Health Law Project (MHLP), located at Suite 300, 1220 19th St., N.W., Washington, D.C. 20036, (202) 467-5730, is "an interdisciplinary public-interest organization devoted to protecting the legal rights of the mentally handicapped (and those so labeled) and improving conditions for their care, treatment, education and community life." It publishes a quarterly *Summary of Activities,* which can be obtained free of charge. Sponsored by the American Civil Liberties Union, the American Orthopsychiatric Association, and the Center for Law and Social Policy, MHLP is primarily an organization of attorneys involved in test-case litigation.

The activities of the MHLP take place all over the country; members have successfully sued over the right to treatment (and to refuse treatment) and protection from harm, deinstitutionalization and rights in the community, doctor-patient confidentiality, and patient-worker rights, and have participated in criminal justice cases. As a result of its widely publicized success, the project has attracted a number of foundation donors interested in supporting the aims of public-interest law.

The MHLP has participated in two recent cases which have been particularly successful. In the *O'Connor v. Donaldson* case, the Supreme Court ruled in the patient's favor. The decision was based upon the constitutional right to liberty, holding that nondangerous patients held in custodial care have a right to release. This put new limits on the ability of the state to hospitalize its citizens involuntarily.

A case presently receiving attention in Washington, D.C., is a suit charging that patients at St. Elizabeth's Hospital have a right to proper treatment. Since the quality of treatment at the hospital has been found to be substandard, the suit seeks to compel the creation of better facilities with appropriate means of treatment, or the forced release of up to one-half of the patients presently hospitalized there.

In general, MHLP, like other public-interest groups, seeks (1) procedural reform, and (2) reform of criteria for social intervention. In the mental health field this translates into the guarantee of rights to those dealing with the mental health care system, and puts curbs on activities of the state, both in terms of when it can act and of what it does once the decision to intervene has been made.

Changing Trends. Kittrie (1971) notes that for many years, "the therapeutic state" has heavily and uncritically relied on expert judgment, often relinquishing its own roles in favor of the experts. This trend is changing (pp. 408–409).

> It is . . . a sign of maturity for the therapeutic experiment that we finally dare test its precepts in our judicial forums . . . Ill-defined, multi-purposed, and expert-reliant throughout much of its history, the therapeutic state is slowly being fitted into more carefully delineated molds. As one reviews the developments . . . it soon becomes clear that . . . legal scrutiny is the tool which is increasingly being utilized both for the preservation of individual liberty and for the necessary audit of societal fulfillment vis à vis the therapeutic promise.

Selected Mental Health Legislation

In the period immediately following World War II, it became a well-known fact that a large number of Americans had to be excluded from military service, owing to mental illness or alleged clues to mental disorders which would impair their functioning in a combat situation. After a long series of hearings on the subject, Congress became convinced of the need for an active national mental health policy.

The first major step was Public Law 79–487, adopted on July 3, 1946. The National Mental Health Act was an amendment to the already existent Public Health Service Act. As given in Section 2, its stated purpose was:

> . . . the improvement of the mental health of the people of the United States through the conducting of researches, investigations, experiments, and demonstrations relating to the cause, diagnosis, and treatment of psychiatric disorders; assisting and fostering such research activities by

public and private agencies, and promoting the coordination . . . and application . . . training personnel in matters relating to mental health and developing and assisting States in the use of the most effective methods of prevention, diagnosis, and treatment of psychiatric disorders.

The most significant aspect of PL 79–487 was that it formally included psychological disorders in the schema of national health problems. For the first time in U.S. history, mental health was recognized as a national problem, with implications almost as important as physical health, and so recorded in public law. One of the ways in which this recognition was granted was the authorization of an initial appropriation of $7.5 million for the building and equipping of the National Institute of Mental Health (NIMH).

The first years of NIMH were undoubtedly inauspicious. In the years thereafter it became a matter of concern among both specialists and lay personnel involved in the field of mental health that little progress was being made in terms of the quality of care given to those with mental health disorders, despite the upgrade in status which the field had received. On July 28, 1955, Congress passed PL 84–182, the Mental Health Study Act, which established the Joint Commission on Mental Illness and Health. After studying the problems and opportunities posed by the field for almost five years, the Commission's report, *Action for Mental Health,* was delivered to President Kennedy in 1961. Among its conclusions the Commission endorsed a major change in federal policy—the hotly contested concept of community mental health centers.

As is the case with any other commission, the significance of its recommendations went only as far as the willingness of politicians to implement them. The recommendations of the Joint Commission were tactfully vague, offering the appropriate decision-makers the widest latitude for action.

Two years later, on February 5, 1963, President Kennedy sent a message to Congress on mental illness and mental retardation which outlined the new philosophy of offering mental health treatment in a comprehensive manner in the patient's own community:

. . . the Federal Government has recognized its responsibilities to assist, stimulate and channel public energies in attacking health problems. Infectious epidemics are now largely under control. Most of the major diseases of the body are beginning to give ground in man's increasing struggle to find their cause and cure. But the public understanding, treatment and prevention of mental disabilities have not made comparable progress since the earliest days of modern history.

There are now about 800,000 such patients in this Nation's institutions—600,000 for mental illness and over 200,000 for mental retardation. Every year nearly 1,500,000 people receive treatment in institutions . . . Most of them are confined and compressed within an antiquated, vastly overcrowded chain of custodial State institutions. The average amount expended on their care is only $4 a day—too little to do much good for the individual, but too much if measured in terms of efficient use of our mental health dollars.

I propose a national mental health program to assist in the inauguration of a wholly new emphasis and approach to care for the mentally ill . . . If we launch a broad new . . . program now, it will be possible within a decade or two to reduce the number of patients now under custodial care by 50 percent or more. Many more mentally ill can be helped to remain in their own homes without hardship to themselves or their families. Those who are hospitalized can be helped to return to their own communities. All but a small proportion can be restored to useful life. We can spare them and their families much of the misery which mental illness now entails. We can save public funds and we can conserve our manpower resources. . . .

The combined impact of the Commission's report and the President's message provided the impetus for the enactment of the Community Mental Health Centers Act on October 31, 1963 (Title II of PL 88–164). The Act authorized federal grants for the construction of public, nonprofit community mental health centers (CMHCs)—$35 million for the fiscal year ending in June 1965, $50 million for 1966, and $65 million for 1967. Part 54.212 of the Act described the projects, essential elements of comprehensive mental health services, and program requirements for these new entities.

In the years since the enactment of the Community Mental Health Centers Act, the legislation has been updated and amended a number of times. For example, PL 89–105, passed on August 4, 1965, provided grants to aid in the initial cost of staffing centers with the necessary professional and technical personnel. Known as the Mental Retardation Facilities and Community Mental Health Centers Construction Act Amendments of 1965, "Section 224 of the law authorized appropriations for community mental health centers in the amounts of $19.5 million for fiscal year 1966, $24 million for 1967, and $30 million for 1968 (see Table 1).

The Mental Health Amendments of 1967 (PL 90–31) were passed by

Table 1.

Appropriations for Community Mental Health Centers

Fiscal Year Ending (June)	$ (millions)
Assistance for the acquisition and construction of CMHCs	
1965	35
1966	50
1967	65
1968	50
1969	60
1970	70
1971	80
1972	90
1973*	100*
1974	20
Assistance for the development and staffing of CMHCs	
1965	00
1966	19.5
1967	24
1968	30
1969	26
1970	32
1971	45
1972	50
1973*	60*
1974	49.1

* Beginning at this point it became difficult to sort out the kinds of expenditures made for the different kinds of programs, especially due to the great interest in resources for drug-abuse programs at the time.

Congress on June 24, 1967. These made federal funds available through 1970 for the acquisition, construction, and staffing of community mental health centers.

Because of the decentralized nature of the community mental health centers' programs, there was much discussion about the nature of services that they might render in addition to those required by statute. Since mental health care was becoming community-defined and controlled, it was also suggested that mental health and mental illness were value-laden terms which could be best determined in each community. At the same time, the problems of alcoholism and drug abuse were receiving a great deal of public attention as issues which combined both physical and mental health components.

The Alcoholic and Narcotic Rehabilitation Amendments of 1968 added new sections "C" and "D" to the Community Mental Health Centers Act. Passed by Congress on October 15, 1968, PL 90–574 provided federal grants for the construction and staffing of facilities for the prevention and treatment of alcoholism and narcotic addictions. With regard to alcoholism, for example, the amendments set policy by stating in part that

> . . . treatment and control programs should whenever possible: (a) be community based, (b) provide a comprehensive range of services, including emergency treatment, under proper medical auspices on a coordinated basis, and (c) be integrated with and involve the active participation of a wide range of public and nongovernmental agencies.
>
> The handling of chronic alcoholics within the system of criminal justice perpetuates and aggravates the broad problem of alcoholism whereas treating it as a health problem permits early detection and prevention of alcoholism and effective treatment and rehabilitation, relieves police and other law enforcement agencies of an inappropriate burden that impedes their important work, and better serves the interests of the public.

Clearly, the legal and institutional concept of the role of community mental health centers in American society was changing. The CMHCs began developing programs for treatment of alcoholism and drug abuse.

Concern about drug abuse, both in government and among the general public, continued through the late sixties. The Community Mental Health Centers Amendments (PL 91–211) were passed by Congress on March 13, 1970. The amendments served to extend federal support for CMHCs through fiscal year 1973, continuing the basic programs for alcoholism and narcotic addiction. In addition, expenditures for children's mental health facilities and services were authorized. The Act also provided for a higher federal share of the costs in rural or urban poverty areas while simultaneously encouraging the initiation and development of new programs there.

The Comprehensive Drug Abuse Prevention and Control Act of 1970 (PL 91–513) was a significant landmark because it pushed CMHCs further toward increasing the amount of effort expended in the direction of drug-abuse treatment and education. As written, the Act was designed to "provide increased research into, and prevention of, drug abuse and drug dependence; to provide for treatment and rehabilitation of drug abusers and drug dependent persons, and to strengthen existing law enforcement authority in the field of drug abuse.'' The Act's political and social implications were as significant as the changes it portended for CMHCs—not only was it significant in the Nixon Administration's policy on drug abuse and crime control, but it brought about considerable (perhaps subtle) changes in the way CMHCs viewed their respective roles.

In 1972, public perception of the problems of drug abuse in the U.S. had reached such startling proportions that Congress made a formal declaration of national policy on the issue:

> The Congress declares that it is the policy of the United States and the purpose of this Act to focus the comprehensive resources of the Federal Government and bring them to bear on drug abuse with the immediate objective of significantly reducing the incidence of drug abuse in the United States within the shortest possible period of time, and to develop a comprehensive, coordinated long-term Federal strategy to combat drug abuse.

The statement above came from The Drug Abuse Office and Treatment Act (PL 92–255), passed by Congress on March 21, 1972, a program of action designed ''to concentrate the resources of the Nation against the problem of drug abuse.''

Although the Act greatly stepped up the federal program to combat drug abuse on several fronts (including the creation of a National Institute on Drug Abuse), it amended the CMHC Act in passing. These amendments were designed to meet the additional staffing and program costs required by the enactment of drug program burdens. CMHCs were ordered to provide treatment for drug abusers under the strictest of confidentiality by June 30, 1972. PL 93–45, passed by Congress on June 18, 1973, and known as the Health Programs Extension Act of 1973, gave one year's authority to CMHCs to continue their activities.

By 1974, Congress was ready to overhaul completely the system designed to administer U.S. policy toward alcohol, drugs, and mental health. The Comprehensive Alcohol Abuse and Alcoholism Prevention, Treatment and Rehabilitation Act Amendments, enacted on May 14, 1974, was the tool by which it was accomplished. Within the U.S. Department of Health, Education and Welfare was established the

Alcohol, Drug Abuse and Mental Health Administration (ADAMHA), which was given the administrative responsibility of overseeing the activities of the National Institute on Alcohol Abuse and Alcoholism (which the Act had created), the National Institute on Drug Abuse, and the National Institute of Mental Health.

Title II of this act (PL 93–282) put the responsibility for the administration of ADAMHA, including the provisions of the Public Service Health Act and the Community Mental Health Centers Act, in the hands of the Secretary of Health, Education and Welfare.

The object of this legislation was to restore some kind of coherent administrative structure and organization of responsibilities to U.S. policy concerning alcohol, drug abuse, and mental illness. The Public Health Service Act and the Community Mental Health Centers Act had been amended so many times that policy and responsibility, especially regarding the principal foci of CMHC activities, had become chaotic, and in some cases, dysfunctional.

The latest significant act concerning public policy and mental health was PL 94–63, the Special Health Revenue Sharing Act. Enacted on July 29, 1975, it was designed "to revise and extend the health revenue sharing program, the family planning programs, the community mental health centers program, the program for migrant health centers and community health centers, the National Health Service Corps program, and the programs for assistance for nurse training . . ." Much like PL 93–282, this law's implicit purpose was almost as important as its stated intent.

The section dealing with CMHCs in PL 94–63 sought, in essence, to close some of the gaps in the wording of CMHC legislation by defining their character and programs more closely, clarifying the process by which, and the possiblities for which, grants may be obtained, and identifying the scope of services which CMHCs must provide (see Table 2).

Section 201 of the Act defines the term "community mental health center" as well as the scope of services which it must render. Mandated activities include inpatient services; outpatient services; day care and other partial hospitalization services; emergency services; programs of specialized services for the mental health of children and of the elderly; consultation and education services; assistance to courts and other public agencies in screening residents of the center's catchment area who are being considered for referral to a state mental health facility for

Table 2.

**Title III of PL 94-63: The Community Mental Health
Centers Amendments of 1975**

Authorized Support Programs	Authorized Appropriations	
Description	Fiscal 1976	Fiscal 1977
A. *Planning Grants*—assess the needs of an area for mental health services, design a CMHC program, obtain financial and other support. One year grants. Maximum of $75,000.	*$3,750,000*	*$3,750,000*
B. *Grants for Initial Operations*—eight years of support to centers, providing all required services; two years to centers which do not provide all required services but have a plan satisfactory to the Secretary to do so within two years. Maximum federal share, by year of support: 80, 65, 50, 35, 30, 30, 25, 25, in non-poverty areas; 90, 90, 80, 70, 60, 50, 40, 30 in poverty areas.	$50,000,000 (plus continuations through 1983)	$55,000,000 (plus continuations through 1984)
	(Continuation grants are also authorized for 1976-1982 for centers which (1) received grants under Sections 220, 242, 243, 251, 256, 264, or 271 of the Act as in effect before enactment of PL 94-63, (2) do not wish to receive a grant for initial operations, and (3) provide the required scope of services within two years.)	
C. *Grants for Consultation and Education Services*—grants begin with the fifth year of a center's operation, unless the Secretary determines that a center would be unable to adequately provide these services in the third or fourth year. Grants may be made to non-federally funded centers if they meet the service requirements other than consultation and education.	$10,000,000	$15,000,000
D. *Conversion Grants*—one or two years of grant support to centers with initial operations or financial distress grants which expect to have operating deficits for the reasonable costs of providing those mental health services newly mandated by PL 94-63 to enable them to meet the expanded service requirements.	$20,000,000	$20,000,000
E. *Financial Distress Grants*—up to three years of support to centers whose operations (or staffing) assistance is about to terminate because of statutory limits as to funding period and which demonstrate that without such continued support they would experience a significant reduction in the quality of services or be unable to provide all the essential services required by these Amendments.	$15,000,000	$15,000,000
F. *Facilities Assistance*—grants from allotments to states to pay the federal share of projects for the acquisition and/or remodeling of facilities for community mental health centers, the leasing of facilities for such centers, and the	$5,000,000	$5,000,000

construction of new or expansion of existing facilities for community mental health centers (but only in poverty areas). The federal share may not exceed 66⅔ percent of costs in nonpoverty areas, 90 percent in poverty areas.

G. *Rape Prevention and Control*—grants to carry out the purposes for which a new National Center for the Prevention and Control of Rape is established within the National Institute of Mental Health, including research, demonstrations, education and information, and training.	$7,000,000	$10,000,000
Total:	$110,750,000	$123.750,000
Total for fiscal 1976 and 1977:	$234,500,000	

inpatient treatment to determine if they should be so referred, and provision, where approrpiate, of treatment for such persons through the center as an alternative to inpatient treatment at such a facility; provision of follow-up care for residents of the catchment area who have been discharged from a mental health facility; and a program of transitional halfway house services for mentally ill individuals who are residents of its catchment area and who have been discharged from a mental health facility.

Centers must also provide a program for the prevention and treatment of alcoholism and alcohol abuse and for the rehabilitation of alcohol abusers and alcoholics, and a program for the prevention and treatment of drug addiction and abuse and for the rehabilitation of drug addicts, drug abusers, and other persons with drug dependency problems, unless the Secretary of Health, Education, and Welfare determines that there is no need, or no unmet need, for such services in such catchment areas.

Clearly the concept of comprehensive treatment in community mental health centers has changed greatly from its initial acceptance as U.S.-policy in 1963. These centers remain controversial, just as they were 13 years ago, and the interested parties can be expected to continue their bickering over the scope and methods of mental health care delivery. In the meantime the administrators, staff, and patients must make the best of the situation. Although the federal government has come a long way from its pre–World War II days of "benign neglect" of mental health care, the Golden Age has yet to arrive.

Paying for Mental Health Services

This section will deal primarily with the existing systems used in the United States to finance mental health care. Of the existing arrangements, we will discuss the increasingly important role played by the federal government, as well as the significant efforts of state and local governments, private health insurance and philanthropic organizations. Few sources exist which comprehensively attempt to seek out the roots of mental health care finances, so this effort owes a particular debt to *Financing Mental Health Care in the United States* (1973), the report of the American Hospital Association's Advisory Panel on Financing Mental Health Care, published by NIMH–HEW.

Role of the Federal Government: Major Programs. The expansion of the services provided by the federal government in the mental health field is well documented in legislative history. It is not a long history. It began, substantively, with the passage of the National Mental Health Act of 1946. As the demands for more and better mental health care grew, so did the responsibilities of the federal government. The assumption of ''a share of the cost of state and local mental patient services'' (p. 287) was a principal recommendation of the Joint Commission on Mental Illness and Health in its report, *Action for Mental Health* (1961).

The federal role has been growing steadily throughout the sixties and early seventies. A variety of mechanisms have been put into effect through which a part of the burden for caring for those with mental care requirements has been shifted to the federal government.

Medicare: Health Insurance for the Aged and Disabled. The 1965 Social Security Amendments gave financial access to health care for most Americans aged 65 and older. Under Medicare (Title XVIII) the benefits for mental health care are the same as for any illness—and thus subject to the same restrictions—in terms of hospitalization insurance.

There are certain circumstances which restrict mental health care under Medicare. While benefits for care in a psychiatric hospital are available under the same benefit period and cost-sharing conditions applicable to general hospitals, coverage is limited to 190 days of care in a person's lifetime.

Community Mental Health Centers are not certified as separate service providers under Medicare. If their inpatient facilities are not certified as participating under the hospital insurance plan, then all services provided there, including inpatient care, are subject to the limitations on federal financing for outpatient services.

According to available statistics, only a small proportion of total Medicare expenditures can be identified as going toward mental health care. It comes to approximately 1½ percent for each of the three fiscal years studied. The data also indicate that the major portion of reimbursement for hospital care involving mental health problems was made to general hospitals—generally about three-fourths of the payments for that purpose.

In essence, although mental health services only comprise a small portion of health care provided by Medicare, it has been argued that the system has greatly increased the role of the general hospital as a psychiatric resource center for older people and, in recent years, for the disabled. Many private insurance programs contain limitations on the hospital benefits available for the treatment of mental problems which do not apply to care for other illnesses. Also, Medicare has expanded the capabilities of general hospitals in the area of mental health beyond that previously available. Moreover, the Medicare program may have resulted in the appropriate classification of many patients who required psychiatric care but were treated under other diagnoses to assure insurance reimbursement.

There remain, however, a number of unique limitations which Medicare places on the coverage of services to the mentally ill. These restrictions include limitations on the length of care in psychiatric hospitals, on ambulatory mental health services, and on the services of psychiatric home health agencies and community mental health centers (centers are not viewed as separate service providers—they are required to meet the conditions of participation used for mental hospitals). These restrictions inhibit the development of individualized programs of continuing patient care.

Medicaid: Medical Assistance Program. Medicaid (Title XIX) was a second major program established by amendments to the Social Security Act through which federal funds are made available to purchase direct health services from a variety of providers for a portion of the American people. The object was the creation of a program of federal grants-in-aid made to participating states which, on a voluntary basis, could choose to pay for a portion of specific medical services for the "needy." These include those persons eligible for welfare assistance because of age, blindness, permanent and total disabilities, and dependent children. The medically indigent may also be included, if the state chooses.

Depending on the state per capita income, the federal contribution to the costs of health care ranges from 50 to 83 percent. The services offered by each state have to be approved by the HEW Medical Services Administration. However, although no state is permitted to refuse treatment on the basic diagnosis—eligible persons with a psychiatric diagnosis are entitled to the same services as all other types of patients in accordance with the various types of state plans—there is one significant exception: no federal funds are available for the care of persons between 21 and 64 years of age in psychiatric institutions.

Only recently have these services been available to those under age 21. Previous to the Social Security Amendments of 1972, authorizing federal matching care in psychiatric hospitals for Medicaid beneficiaries under 21, the support had been limited to patients aged 65 and over.

Much of the data available on Medicaid are outdated both by year and by program changes. However, as opposed to Medicare, which restricts the mental health benefits available to patients (these may not be of any great significance since persons 65 and over tend to be low utilizers of such services, except in the cases of chronic health conditions), Medicaid is a much more generous mental health insurance benefit, especially since it is legally forbidden to discriminate according to diagnosis.

Because it is a state-run program, Medicaid provides a wide range of options and selections from among which state decision-makers may choose in determining the health care programs and those to whom they are available.

To a degree, Medicaid has increased access to mental health services for a population group least likely to have other means of financing such care. Although there exists some federal support for the care of certain patients in psychiatric hospitals—a significant step forward from earlier days—lack of federal support for inpatient care in a psychiatric hospital, regardless of age group, seems an unnecessary discrimination against those with mental health problems who qualify for Medicaid support.

A major problem affecting the program's coverage of all types of health services is the uneven application of benefits from state to state. It has been suggested that Medicaid should attempt to develop a uniform level of coverage among the states opting to utilize it.

However, it would still fail to overcome prevailing inequities by which states able to match federal funds receive the bulk of Medicaid funds.

CHAMPUS: Civilian Health and Medical Program, Uniformed Services. CHAMPUS was set up by the Military Medical Benefits Amendments of 1966 to provide a broad insurance program for retired military people and certain dependents as well as certain active-duty service members. CHAMPUS beneficiaries have a cost-sharing plan with the federal government. The federal funds come jointly from appropriations of DOD and DHEW and are paid directly to the executive director of CHAMPUS, who, in turn, lets contracts to civilian service providers via fiscal agents.

The CHAMPUS program contains no limitations on care for problems of mental health that do not apply to all types of illnesses. The plans agreed to with the purchasers of such insurance contain the same concern for all conditions. A written plan of management is required for hospitalization extending beyond 90 days. Of the 22,227 persons applying for extended hospitalization in 1969, 14 percent were approved. Otherwise, any treatment deemed necessary by a certified physician is usually approved. The broadest possible definition of psychiatric care is employed, including special schools, camps, and other mental health resources generally not available to the beneficiaries of many other insurance plans. Another progressive provision included in the CHAMPUS coverage is the permitting of family participation in the psychiatric treatment of individual patients.

According to the Advisory Panel on Financing Mental Health Care of the American Hospital Association (1973), "CHAMPUS coverage would appear to offer opportunities for the development of flexible, personalized psychiatric treatment plans, based on clinically indicated needs for care" (p. 47).

Veterans Administration: Mental Health and Behavioral Sciences Service. Health care from the Veterans Administration (VA) is available to those who have served in the military services of the United States and have been discharged other than dishonorably. All kinds of care are supported in full by the federal government, both in VA facilities and, in certain cases, in non-VA facilities. Mental health care is provided to veterans on the same basis as is medical care for all injuries and physical illnesses.

The VA psychiatric programs represent the major system for the direct delivery of mental health services operated by the federal government; likewise they are entirely supported by federal monies. The VA system's inpatient psychiatric services are an enormous system, representing about 10 percent of all psychiatric beds in the U.S. Although long-term inpatient services tend to predominate at the VA, increased attention is being given to the concept of community treatment. It has been suggested that the relatively high costs per covered person, and utilization rates for days of care and length of stay, raise questions concerning the extent to which VA health care dollars may be financing maintenance/residential services that lead to a system discouraging short-term mental health care delivery (AHA, p. 52). A further criticism is that an expansion of the relationships between VA psychiatric facilities and other types of mental health providers can aid in a more economical use of mental health resources with less duplication of effort in some communities (AHA, p. 52).

Community Mental Health Centers. We have dealt with CMHCs at some length in this chapter, so suffice it to say that the CMHC construction and staffing grant programs of NIMH represent the principal focus of federal categorical support for mental health services over the past decade or so, the objective being the delivery of comprehensive mental health services at the local level. The CMHCs exist largely on public funds, receiving a certain percentage from the state and local community as well as a larger share from the federal government. The exact percentage that is federally assumed depends, to a degree, upon the relative ability of the community to pay. Studies have shown that in 1969, 80 percent of the $174 million total spent by CMHCs came from all levels of government, the rest coming from a variety of private sources.

The CMHCs were established to encourage a new approach to the delivery of mental health care in the U.S., one which stressed care in noninstitutional settings and the offering of preventive services. Certainly they have had a tremendous impact on the way psychiatric services are delivered in this country. Information available on the CMHCs indicates that the federal grants have had an impact both on the innovation of new services and on the integration of existing ones.

It is important to note that the CMHCs have had considerable difficulty in finding other sources of revenue to replace the federal share of their income, which by law must decrease in percentage over time. For the time being, this gap seems to be filled most often by state governments. Local government has offered a rather limited support for

CMHCs, owing to the relatively limited taxing authority they have for mental health programs and the lack of coterminous boundaries for both CMHC catchment areas and political subdivisions.

It is generally believed that in the near future some kind of federal funding will be required to keep the CMHCs alive. It is hoped that in the future, payment for personal mental health services will flow through the same kinds of mechanisms as reimbursements to other types of health care providers.

Other Governmental Agencies. In addition to the major components of the federally funded mental health care programs discussed above, there exist a variety of other programs in which the federal government has been attempting to improve the mental health care delivered in the U.S. A brief description of these programs follows.

In 1970 the National Institute on Alcohol Abuse and Alcoholism (NIAAA) was established within NIMH. Its mission was to assume responsibilities for federal activities concerned with alcoholism. Its initial grants were approximately $84.6 million. The formation of the NIAAA provided a focal point, not only for the coordination of federal activities on alcoholism, but also for the development of national policies concerning the problems of alcohol abuse and establishing priorities for combating these problems.

In the late sixties and early seventies there was a great deal of concern about the problems of drug abuse and the proliferation of federal activities in the field. A number of agencies, under a variety of legislative authorities, became concerned with law enforcement, public education, rehabilitation and treatment, manpower training, and research in the area. A National Institute on Drug Abuse was created within NIMH. In fiscal 1972, a total of $189.6 million was allotted to the various federal activities in this field, nearly six times the amount spent only two years before. Programs financed included the Community Assistance Grants Program (helping communities meet the costs of treatment for narcotic addicts and others with drug-abuse problems); the Narcotics Addict Rehabilitation Program; the VA battle on drug abuse primarily among U.S. Department of Defense employees and Vietnam veterans; and Law Enforcement Assistance Administration grants to state and local governments (helping to fight the war against drugs not only through legal means, but through education, rehabilitation, treatment, and other facilities). The now-defunct Office of Economic Opportunity awarded funds to Community Action Agencies

(CAAs) demonstrating competence in community-based drug rehabilitation programs.

Federal grants are made to state vocational rehabilitation agencies for the provision of services which will assist the physically and mentally handicapped to obtain or retain employment. The services provided include medical care, the coverage of basic living expenses during rehabilitation, and services to members of clients' families; they operate on a cost-sharing basis with the states. These services appear to offer opportunities for extending needed services for the mentally ill beyond those required in a strictly medical setting.

Assistance in financing mental health was provided by the federal government under the Comprehensive Health Planning and Public Health Services Amendments of 1966, helping states and local governments to plan comprehensive physical, mental, and environmental health services. The Hill-Burton program has been used to aid in the construction and modernization of hospital and medical facilities.

In sum, given the random and ad-hoc manner in which mental health policy has been developed, it is hard to disagree with the findings of the study, *Financing Mental Health Care in the United States,* which stated that "when one reviews Federal activities which support mental health services and facilities, it is apparent that continuing efforts are needed to improve coordination of programmatic efforts, to include mental health in general health programs without specific discrimination, and to insure Federal leadership and financial support for mental health program innovation and for the development of a basic national capacity to deal with mental health issues" (p. 70).

The Role of State and Local Governments. Almost all of the early work in the psychiatric hospitals field in the United States was done by state and local governments. During the early years of American colonial history, the mentally ill were ignored or left to fend for themselves in total banishment from the community. If they couldn't care for themselves, such methods as assigning responsibility for their care to the lowest bidder or jailing them in almshouses were common practice.

According to the study *Financing Mental Health in the United States* (1973), of the state and local funds, $1.7 billion (79 percent) was spent for care in state and county mental hospitals; $306 million (18 percent) was spent for services in other settings, such as outpatient clinics and nursing homes; $35 million (2 percent) was spent for facility development; and $16 million (1 percent) was allocated for mental health manpower training and research (p. 75).

State mental health programs have traditionally been financed by state tax monies from the sale of bonds for construction. Although some states have been more successful than others in raising the necessary revenues to fund mental health activities, there is general recognition that this is an appropriate state role. Legislation varies from state to state as to the liability of the patient for the cost of services in public mental health facilities, but there is a general recognition that patient care revenues represent an important source of support for hospital programs. Also, through a variety of projects, states have cost-shared with the federal government in providing mental health services to citizens. Federal grants have enabled many activities to continue to function, principally community mental health centers, services to alcoholics and drug abusers, and vocational rehabilitation.

One often cited problem among state mental health authorities is that state budgeting procedures may be rigid and unresponsive to requirements of mental health programs where approaches to appropriate care are changing rapidly. Besides budgeting, civil service regulations, purchasing requirements, and controls over facility construction and remodelling—even though applied in the best of intentions—often seriously dilute the usefulness of state civil service funds (AHA, p. 95).

On the other hand, state financing of mental health care is well established in the U.S., and unless a national program for financing health services (including mental health benefits) becomes operational, the states will remain the principal provider of mental health care revenues. However, because of the continuously increasing costs to the states, they may be expected to seek the expansion of arrangements for more efficient use of their own resources, to seek out greater federal funding for delivering services, and to share the responsibility of financing and delivering mental health services with local communities.

The Role of Private Insurance. Private health insurance has been a rapidly growing phenomenon in the United States. Of course, the type of protection received depends largely on the service, and according to the provisions of the particular insurance programs, it varies from complete coverage to very little coverage. In general, there have been limitations or exclusions in coverage for care of mental health problems.

While the role of private insurance in this area is undoubtedly expanding, these discriminations continue to represent a source of frustration to providers and an economic burden on the patients and their families.

The Blue Cross–Blue Shield plans usually provide health insurance on a cooperative basis, emphasizing group coverage. Today, all Blue Cross plans offer some hospitalization benefits for mental conditions, though there remains a significant diversity of plans. Owing to its traditional contractual relationship with general hospitals, Blue Cross coverage has lagged behind that offered by private insurance companies. For example, a common benefit for general illness under major group contracts is 120 to 125 days of care in a general hospital; for mental health problems, the common benefit is generally 30 to 31 days. In addition, coverage of physicians' services by Blue Shield appears to be largely limited to in-hospital care.

With other insurance companies, Follmann (1970, p. 63) reports that although discriminatory provisions against mental conditions in relation to other illness are still existent, there appears to be a trend in group coverage toward comparable benefits for mental health hospitalization. The biggest differences remain in outpatient care, for which the patient is generally required to pay a much greater percentage of the charges for group coverage programs than in other conditions.

Individual insurance policies generally provide less extensive mental health benefits than group coverage, according to Follmann (1970, p. 62), because with individually underwritten policies, adverse selection can be a considerable problem. Those most likely to need insurance will buy it, and, as such, it is difficult to keep the cost of protection within the range of most people. As a result, the coverage for mental conditions is probably limited to hospitalization and is likely to extend for fewer days than would be the case with other types of illnesses.

With independent plans, such as community group and individual prepaid practice plans, employer/employee/union plans, and private medical clinics, the organization and function of the services are so diverse that no generalization is possible about their coverage of mental health problems. However, the community group practice plans were studied at some length (Scheidemandel *et al.*, 1968, p. 65) and were found to have generally lagged behind Blue Cross–Blue Shield and insurance companies in their substantial coverage of mental health services, especially for outpatient care.

In sum, mental health care is insurable, both as inpatient and outpatient services. Conley, Conwell, and Willner (1970) estimated that private insurance paid about $502 million (or about 13 percent of the $3.8 billion total) for direct mental health services in the U.S. in 1968. It is estimated that per capita charges would be only 3 to 5 percent higher for the inclusion of mental health services.

Restrictions on insurance coverage appear to stem largely from concern about the cost of long-term custodial-style care. In terms of outpatient care, the concerns about the high costs of psychoanalysis are the focus of the problem. "As a result of these legitimate concerns, misconceptions of excessive duration and costs for all psychiatric care have prevailed, and unwarranted discriminations against mental health services in general have persisted" (AHA, p. 111).

Given the substantial difference between long-term and custodial care, and the rapid changes in psychiatric care in the past two decades (new emphasis on outpatient care), the removal of insurance provisions discriminating against outpatient mental health care is especially important.

The Role of Philanthropic Organizations. The role of private philanthropy in financing mental health care in the United States is small but important. It is a tradition deeply ingrained in America— always encouraged on the frontier and legally encouraged in the Internal Revenue Act of 1913 by the granting of tax incentives.

The extent to which donated money has financed mental health care in the U.S. has never been documented very well. There remains today no centralized measure of the extent to which philanthropy finances mental health programs. Conley, Conwell, and Willner (1970) estimated that the portion of the cost borne by private industry and individual gifts totaled about $127 million, or 3 percent of the total $4 billion treatment and prevention costs for mental health care in 1968.

Individuals, foundations, and corporations all give to support mental health programs to some degree. Deferred gifts represent 9 percent of all philanthropy in the form of bequests, life insurance, trusts, etc.

In recent years, because of the great boom in size and complexity of mental health programs stimulated by public money, contributions frequently have been overlooked as an important resource. Clearly, gifts will not soon become major sustainers of mental health programs, but their potential impact is greater than their actual magnitude, for they often represent the only unencumbered and unrestricted funds which can be used for developmental purposes. They might be available for capital costs, for social support systems (halfway houses), or for establishing linkages with other human service systems.

The Difficulty of Determining Costs. One of the biggest problems in the financing of mental health care is the question of identifying the various costs associated with mental health problems. Available data on some of the various aspects of these conditions are scattered among a plethora of public and private accounting systems. Where information does exist, it is rarely in a meaningful form, for it has been assembled only for administrative purposes.

Fein (1958) was one of the first to attempt to quantify at least some of the components of the cost of mental health. He estimated the loss of earnings by the institutionalized ill and the cost of care for those with mental health problems, both in- and out-patients, as $2.4 billion. Obviously these figures, even if correct, are extremely outdated.

In 1966, Conley, Conwell, and Arrill (1967) developed a more comprehensive approach by estimating costs of a wider range of treatment services and earnings lost from reduced productivity among the employed mentally ill for reasons other than "work-loss" days. They estimated the cost of mental illness at nearly $20 billion.

In 1970, Conley, Conwell, and Willner (1970), updating the earlier model by using different estimating procedures, pointed to costs of $21 billion, with $17 billion representing the cost of reduced productive activity alone, and $4 billion as the treatment and prevention costs. Contributions to financing the costs of treatment and prevention of mental illness were as follows:

State and local government	$1.7 billion	42%
Federal government	$1.0 billion	25%
Private funds and donations	$1.3 billion	33%

As such, public funds constituted a little less than three-fourths of the costs of the total. In terms of direct costs, state and local governments put up 43 percent, the federal government put up 22 percent, and the private sector provided 35 percent. Facility development was more than 50 percent financed by state and local funds. The Federal government provided about 91 percent of the estimated $93 million for mental health manpower development and 82 percent of the $110 million expended for mental health research.

The Budget of the United States Government for fiscal year 1977 is very discouraging in terms of funding for health. The 1977 budget request for the Alcohol, Drug Abuse and Mental Health Administration (ADMHA) is $622 million. The actual 1975 budget for ADAMHA was $1.056 billion; for general mental health it is $264 million, compared to an actual 1975 budget of $554 million.

In summary, long-term funding for mental health is on the way out. Access to mental health services for Blacks and other selected population groups will become more difficult. This phenomenon of gradually phasing out federal funds has been anticipated. Mental health programs should have begun long-range financial planning with financial managers over the past ten years. Ernest Harvey (1973, pp. 118–119) speaks of the mental health administrator thusly:

> The financing requirements [of mental health] demand that he be an innovative and efficient manager, a long range financial planner, and a salesman with *grantmanship* ability. He can expect both frustration and satisfaction from this complexing role.

The cutback in federal funds is indicative of the need for an overall, effective planning mechanism for mental health services which would include financial planning.

Issues in Policy Planning for Mental Health Services

A discussion of public policy and mental health would be incomplete without a discussion of health planning. Among the many issues related to the process of planning are (1) how to plan, (2) who should do the planning, (3) consumer participation, (4) legal issues, and (5) accountability. However, in this section, we will not discuss all of these issues, but will focus on the theory of the planning process and the National Health Planning and Resources Development Act of 1974 (PL 93–641). These issues have significance for the Black community as well as for the general health community.

Ralph Littlestone (1973, p. 9) has pointed out two models of health planning: (1) *rational planning*, which stresses the development of facts and their analysis; and (2) *participatory planning*, which emphasizes the planning process. These models may be subsumed under the heading of *social policy planning*.

Planning for mental health services will not be effective without well-trained administrators and managers with skills to manage the diversity and complexity of community mental health centers, clinics, and state hospitals (LeCompte, 1975, p. 97). Moreover, the paucity of Black administrators and planners in mental health facilities perpetuates a problem for the Black community in planning for mental health care.

In 1973, only 1 percent of all Blacks employed full-time in hospitals and sanatoriums funded by state and local government were in official or administrative positions, according to data from the U.S. Equal Employment Opportunity Commission. Three percent of all Asian Americans, 2.7 percent of all American Indians, and 4.9 percent of all whites were employed as officials and administrators (Humphrey, 1974, p. 44).

The Health Planning Process

Health problems are identified in relation to the population at risk in the planning area. Therefore, health problems have epidemiologic numerators, demographic denominators, and geographic boundaries. Geographic boundaries depend upon the mandate of the planning body, the location of health resources, political jurisdictions, transportation and communication patterns, population concentrations, and other financial resources. In speaking of the planning process, Reinke (1972, p. 53) observes:

> Health planning can be considered effective only to the extent that it produces a greater contribution to health status per unit of resources expended than would have been achieved in the absence of planning. Since resources are limited and some problems are more vulnerable to attack than others, the planner is challenged to develop a rational, practical, and efficient allocation of the scarce resources based upon realistic objectives and sensible properties.

Essentially, health planning (or any planning) is a delineation and specification of who gets what, where, when, and how much at alternative prices and costs. The activities undertaken by planners commonly involve:

1. assessment
2. forecasting
3. problem definition

4. systems analyses
5. goal-setting
6. alternative interventions
7. cost-benefit comparisons
8. implementation
9. evaluation

Outline of Approaches to Planning

   I. *Developing planning competence:* identification of the political power structure, health professionals, community residents, and other parties

  II. *Determination of planning policies and goals of all parties and governments involved:* getting your politics together

 III. *Collection and analysis of data*
    A. Source of data
      1. Existing data
      2. Collection of new data
    B. Kind of information and data
      1. Demographic data
      2. Epidemiologic data
      3. Economic data (cost accounting of specific health activities)
      4. Utilization of health facilities
      5. Productivity of health workers (all categories)
      6. Consumer demand (expressions) for health services
    C. Organizational framework required
    D. Personnel and facilities needed
    E. Costs in comparable financial terms and arrangements
    F. Standards and criteria for outpatient, inpatient, and ambulatory care services in the service area of concern

 IV. *Development of detailed plan with targets and standards*
    A. Involvement of local government and local groups in the development of detailed programs (centralization vs. decentralization of planning)
    B. Development of appropriate standards for performance of health system
    C. Specification of targets within stated time frameworks

V. *Implementation strategies*
  A. Specification of the conditions under which health plan-
     ning will be carried out with the greatest likelihood of
     success
  B. Establishment of procedures to get the plan accepted by all
     parties concerned
  C. Design of an effective model for community participation
     to include all categories and types of residents and par-
     ticipants
  D. Development of a mechanism to include health personnel,
     political leaders, and other consumers in the implementa-
     tion process

VI. *Evaluation strategies.* While the evaluation mechanism may not
    be a major part of most planning documents, it is one of the
    most important and difficult tasks to be incorporated into any
    health plan. Evaluation is necessary for effective planning for
    administrative purposes and specifically for revising the plan.
    Evaluation requires *objectivity* in the approach used and must
    be approached with ingenuity and innovative precision.
  A. Qualitative procedures
  B. Quantitative procedures

For a more detailed discussion of the theory of health planning and
the qualitative and quantitative aspects, see the references to Henrik L.
Blum (1974) and William A. Reinke *et al.* (1972).

Health Planning Legislation. The National Health Planning and Resources Development Act of 1974 (PL 93–641) demonstrates a growing
determination in Congress to motivate the system of health services
toward greater efficiency in utilization of resources. The Act was designed to overcome some of the weaknesses in earlier planning legislation (PL 89–749).

The goals of the PL 93–641 legislation provided the assurance of
adequacy and equity in the availability and access, quality, and efficiency of health services throughout the country. Putting these
rhetorical concepts into administrative practice is not easily accomplished. Moreover, the 1974 legislation was based on the
perspective of 30 years of federal experience with support of programs
for health services planning and development at the state and local

level. The Hill-Burton Act of 1946 was the earliest such legislation and expanded the capacity of short-term general hospitals in many communities. The Hill-Burton Act, however, made little progress in the establishment of systems based on a functional articulation of facilities and services within hospital service areas.

The 1964 Hill-Harris Amendments increased the number of area-wide planning agencies in metropolitan communities, but its impact on the direction of institutional development was limited. Establishment of Regional Medical Programs (RMPs) in 1965 mobilized substantial national interest in cooperative arrangements among health service organizations, research institutions, and medical schools to facilitate access to advances in diagnosis and therapy. Yet this legislation was not implemented in a manner that addressed the underlying problem of rationalizing services on a regional basis.

The Comprehensive Health Planning and Public Health Service Amendments of 1966 were designed to support planning for improvement and maintenance of adequate and efficient community health services. Here again the impact of the program on health service structure and costs fell far short of expectations.

The National Health Planning and Resources Development Act of 1974 (PL 93–641) mandates coverage of the entire country by an estimated 160 to 240 Health System Agencies (HSAs), which are accountable to state planning agencies and, in turn, to the U.S. Department of Health, Education and Welfare (HEW). This results in a provision for complete coverage of the country by planning agencies within a framework of closely articulated programs and effort at the three levels of government.

The 1974 legislation proposes to establish an adequate service area for local governmental jurisdictions in order to support a critical mass of manpower and facilities. The minimum population for Health Service Areas, established in Section 1511, assures a reasonable base of support for local planning units. Furthermore, the Act requires that Health Service Areas consist of geographically functional units with resources to provide all essential health services.

PL 93–641 also seeks to maintain the integrity of metropolitan communities. Local communities are composed of local governmental jurisdictions with anachronistic boundaries. Nevertheless, the communities are interdependent for human services as well as trade and commerce. Hence those striving for optimum availability, quality, and efficiency of utilization of resources would not argue with the basic logic of pooling resources of contiguous communities which make up a functional service area, "the community of solution" of the Commission of Community Health Services. Yet the inattention of PL 93–641 to the total deficiencies in this nation's health care from an organizational viewpoint appears to be a "band-aid" approach to health planning.

Effect on Mental Health Planning. The federal government will not make any allotment, grant, loan, or loan guarantee, or enter into any contract in the area of health without the designation of a State Health Planning and Development Agency. The growth of health programs and projects will be closely related to the politics of implementing PL 93–641 (see Section 1516).

Policy Questions: PL 93–641. Numerous issues and concerns have been raised about PL 93–641. These queries have significance for health providers, consumers, and policy-makers. The answers are yet to come. Selected examples of such questions follow:

1. A National Council on Health Planning and Development is to be created with the function of "developing and recommending national policies, recommending guidelines for appropriate supply, distribution and organization of health services."
   Issues:
   A. What goals will they define? What policies will be implemented? Are they to be based in part on the interests of the very poor and minorities?
   B. How much implementation authority will or should this Council have regarding the development and organization of health planning capacity? How will the implementation capacity of the National Health Policy Council affect the disadvantaged population?
   C. To what extent, in fact, will the Public Health Service be free to utilize their discretionary power to determine the recommendations of the National Council for Health Policies? Will the National Council for Health Policy have any real power?
   D. Who will be selected for the board? According to the proposed legislation, five members have to be non-providers, no more than three can be federal government employees, and so on. What are the implications of the selection process for the delivery of services to the disadvantaged?

E. To what extent will the board representation affect the manner in which they determine goals, and develop planning strategies and resource development strategies?

2. Health Services Agencies will be established. They will probably be designated in areas of population sized from 500,000 to 3 million and may go down to 200,000 in some cases, or go over 3 million if the service area is an SMSA with a population over 3 million. They may also be located on the basis of "a rational geographic region with a comprehensive range of health services available" and of a "character suitable for the effective planning and development of health services."

A. To what extent will the HSA's location be based on criteria which takes into consideration the location of the most *disadvantaged* portion of the population?

B. How much discretion can be utilized in determining their location? Apparently the governors will, in some cases, have considerable latitude.

3. One of the main functions of the HSAs is to "assemble and analyze data on (1) the status and determinant of the health of the residents; and (2) status of the area's delivery system and use of that system and plans for use of health resources and services." In the latter case, the HSAs review all federal assistance, review for continued needs, and make recommendations on use of Hill-Burton funds or facilities-use funds if Hill-Burton is allowed to lapse.

Issues:

A. How will the needs of selected population groups be determined and considered? Can federal regulations be developed when it is uncertain that such needs are considered?

B. Will the Statewide Health Coordinating Council (SHCC) and the HSAs shift the focus of power from the local governments and place it at the state levels? If so, will this remove the Black populations and other minority groups one step further from the administrative and planning process, since their ability to affect area-wide and state planning agencies is probably very limited?

C. Since the HSAs will probably be private, non-profit organizations, how will they be made accountable to the federal or state governments? If they cannot be made accountable, will

this not continue to perpetuate the impact of traditional elements on the planning process (e.g., control of private-sector
physicians and other related providers)? And will this not have
a negative impact on the planning of service and resource development and utilization as far as the disadvantaged or
underserved population is concerned?

4. A statewide planning agency (Statewide Health Coordinating
   Council) will be established with the responsibility of reviewing
   local HSA plans, state plans, federal grant applications, and
   approved state plans for formula grants.
   A. Since the legislation is somewhat loosely written, the SHCC
       would apparently have considerable discretion in terms of
       relating the plans to the very needy, to laying stress on par-
       ticular types of resource development activities as a means for
       implementation of the plan. To what extent can the SHCC
       utilize their discretionary power in order to ensure that a part
       of each plan deals with specific targeted needs, the most
       underserved, the sickest, and the hungriest?
   B. To what extent can, or will, the SHCC promote the
       development of facilities-use plans which can focus on the
       needs of the Black population and other selected groups?
   C. To what extent can, or will, the state SHCC monitor or review
       the various grant programs in order to assure quality of services
       and target these services on the very needy?

In order to assure proper planning and implementation of PL 93-
641, it is necessary to insist that the mandate for consumer involvement
in the legislation be adhered to. Low-income residents must be involved
along the entire spectrum of consumer participation in health care
(Sanders, 1975). Research studies have shown that community health
centers are better off in terms of health services provided and the overall
use of a facility by the residents (Thompson, 1972; Danaceau, 1975).

Consumer involvement in mental health has been concentrated at the
volunteer level with the exception of the Lincoln Hospital Neighborhood Service Center in New York City (Kaplan, 1973). The takeover
of this mental health center by the Puerto Rican and Black communities
of Harlem is one indication of the non-therapeutic aspect of consumer
participation (Thompson, 1974).

Facilities Planning under PL 93-641. Pl 93-641 is also to provide
assistance through grant allotments, loans and loan guarantees, and

interest subsidies for (1) modernization of medical facilities; (2) construction of new outpatient health facilities; (3) construction of new inpatient medical facilities in areas which have experienced recent, rapid population growth; and (4) conversion of existing medical facilities for the provisions of new health services. The Secretary will decide, by regulation, how the state agency will determine the need for medical facilities.

The following questions might be raised with respect to the relationship of facilities planning, the Black population, and other selected population groups:

1. What facilities will be modernized? How will the manner in which decisions are made affect selected population groups?
   A. Who will be served?
   B. In what geographical area?
   C. How will the facilities be utilized?

2. What facilities will be constructed? How will the manner in which decisions are made affect selected population groups?
   A. Who will be served?
   B. In what geographical area?
   C. How will the facilities be utilized?

3. What facilities will be converted, and how will these decisions be made?
   A. How will the conversion of facilities affect selected population groups in terms of facility utilization?

4. How will the medically underserved population be defined? (To a certain extent, this is already defined, such as in Title XIII of the Public Health Service Act or as designed by the Health Service Agency.) To what extent will there be an interpretation of the underserved, or the use of discretion? What are the implications of the use of discretion?

5. What are the implications of each of the various types of allotment formula? Where need is determined? How can this be affected by the manner by which the money is administered?

Policy-makers and health-makers are eagerly awaiting the final set of regulations for implementing PL 93–641. Meanwhile, Black health workers, other minority groups, and concerned policy-makers had better "get their politics together." Mental health is a political affair, as is all health care in this country.

Conclusion

Mental health care in the United States is controlled by an *elite* of physicians known as psychiatrists. These psychiatrists tend to be the major actors in implementing mental health policy. Psychologists and social workers are the officials and administrators in the elite model. Ironically, the majority of mental health services provided to the Black community and other poor people is provided by social workers. As many mental health professionals point out, poor people of minority-group identity cannot benefit from traditional psychotherapeutic modalities.

In studying the mental health of Black people, McGee and Clark (1974, p. 58) write:

> We find little difficulty in adopting as a black mental health model a person who is (a) musical, (b) given to superstition, and (c) religious. Such a person may indeed represent the antithesis of a white European model, but this does not mean that he is unhealthy.

Combining mental health research and public policy analyses should lead to the development and adoption of a mental health model advantageous for Black people and other selected population groups. In speaking of the "Black health crisis," Max Seham makes the following policy observations about health care in America (1973, p. 25):

> Although it is highly important to focus upon financing and improving the resources and facilities for the delivery of medical care, in relation to blacks, the Achilles heel lies in the periphery of medicine: it is the lack of human relations between the providers and the consumers.

Finally, it must be noted that public policy plays the major role in the allocation and distribution of mental health services. Technology and money alone will never solve the chronic social and mental disease of the poor health of Black people. A long-range, comprehensive program must include better education in health care, improved minimal levels of family income, improved housing, and the universal application of biomedical advances to benefit all Black, brown, and neglected Americans.

References

Abad, V.; Ramos, J.; and Boyce, E. "A Model for Delivery of Mental Health Services to Spanish-Speaking Minorities." *American Journal of Orthopsychiatry* 44 (1974): 584–595.

Allen, R. C.; Feister, E. Z.; and Rubin, J. G. *Readings in Law and Psychiatry*. Baltimore: Johns Hopkins University Press, 1975.

Allison, G. *Essence of Decision: Explaining the Cuban Missile Crisis*. Boston: Little, Brown, 1971.

American Psychiatric Association. *Modern Psychiatry, Diagnostic Manual of the American Psychiatric Association*. Washington, D.C.: A.P.A., 1965.

Anderson, J. E. *Public Policy-Making*. New York: Praeger, 1975.

Archibald, K. A. "Three Views of the Experts' Role in Policymaking: Systems Analysis, Incrementalism, and the Clinical Approach." *Policy Sciences* 1 (1970): 73–86.

Auster, S. L. "Insurance Coverage for Mental and Nervous Conditions: Developments and Problems." *American Journal of Psychiatry* 126 (1969): 699.

Ausubel, D. "Personality Disorder Is Disease." *American Psychiatrist* 16 (1961): 69–74.

Bellak, L. (ed.). *Handbook of Community Psychiatry and Community Mental Health*. New York: Grune and Stratton, 1964.

Bindman, A. J., and Spiegel, A. D. (eds.). *Perspectives in Community Mental Health*. Chicago: Aldine, 1969.

Blum, H. L. *Planning for Health*. New York: Human Sciences Press, 1974.

Boulding, K. "The Boundaries of Social Policy." *Social Work* 12 (1967): 3–11.

Braceland, F. J., and Stock, M. *Modern Psychiatry*. Garden City: Doubleday Image Books, 1963.

Braybrooke, D., and Lindblom, C. E. *A Strategy of Decision*. New York: Free Press, 1963.

Brunsgaard, J.E.J., Jr. *Financing Mental Health Care: A Survey of Reimbursement Policies, Procedures, and Sources in the Department of Mental Hygiene in the United States*. Washington, D.C.: George Washington University Press, 1969.

Caplan, G. *Principles of Preventive Psychiatry*. New York: Basic Books, 1964.

Conley, R. W.; Conwell, M. D.; and Arrill, M. B. "An Approach to Measuring the Cost of Mental Illness." *American Journal of Psychiatry* 124 (1967): 755–762.

Conley, R. W.; Conwell, M. D.; and Willner, S. G. *The Cost of Mental Illness, 1968.* Statistical Note No. 30. Washington, D.C.: U.S. Department of HEW, Biometry Branch, NIMH, 1970.

Connery, R. H. *The Politics of Mental Health: Organizing Community Mental Health in Metropolitan Areas.* New York: Columbia University Press, 1968.

Danaceau, P. *Consumer Participation in Health Care: How It's Working.* Arlington, Virginia: Human Services Institute for Children and Families, 1975.

Davis, M. I.; Sharfstein, S.; and Owens, M. "Separate and Together: All-Black Therapy Group in the White Hospital." *American Journal of Ortho-psychiatry* 44 (1974): 19–25.

Deutsch, A. *The Mentally Ill in America.* 2nd ed. New York: Doubleday, Doran, 1949.

Dror, Y. *Public Policy Reexamined.* Scranton, Pennsylvania: Chandler, 1968.

Dudley, J.R. "Citizens' Boards for Philadelphia Community Mental Health Centers." *Community Mental Health Journal* 2 (1975): 410–417.

Dye, T. *Understanding Public Policy.* Englewood Cliffs, New Jersey: Prentice-Hall, 1972.

Dye, T., and Harmon, Z. *The Irony of Democracy.* Belmont, California: Wadsworth, 1970.

Easton, D. *The Political System.* New York: Alfred A. Knopf, 1953.

_____. *A Framework for Political Analysis.* Englewood Cliffs, New Jersey: Prentice-Hall, 1965.

Etzioni, A. "Mixed-Scanning: A 'Third' Approach to Decision-Making." *Public Administration Review* 27 (1967): 385–392.

Fein, R. *Economics of Mental Illness.* New York: Basic Books, 1958.

Felix, R. H. *Mental Illness: Progress and Prospects.* New York: Columbia University Press, 1967.

Follmann, J. F., Jr. *Insurance Coverage for Mental Illness.* New York: American Management Association, 1968.

Forrester, J. "Planning Under the Dynamic Influences of Complex Social Systems." In Eric Jantsch (ed.), *Perspectives of Planning,* pp. 236–254. Paris: OECD, 1969.

Friedrich, C. J. *Man and His Government.* New York: McGraw-Hill, 1963.

Glazer, N. "The Limits of Social Policy." *Commentary* 52 (1971): 3–11.

Grob, G. *The State and the Mentally Ill.* Chapel Hill, North Carolina: University of North Carolina Press, 1966.

Harvey, E. C. "Financing Mental Health Services." In S. Feldman (ed.), *The Administration of Mental Health Services,* pp. 86–119. Springfield, Illinois: Charles C Thomas, 1973.

Hoff, E. C. "Dependence." *Encyclopedia of Mental Health,* Vol. 2. New York: Franklin Watts, 1963, p. 451.

Humphrey, M. "EEOC: Equal Employment in the Health Industry?" In T. Thompson (ed.), *Black Colleges: Resources for Educating and Training Health Services Administrators,* pp. 36–45. Washington, D.C.: Howard University, Health Services Administration Department, 1975.

Jahoda, M. *Current Concepts of Positive Mental Health.* New York: Basic Books, 1958.

Jahoda, M. "Toward a Social Psychology of Mental Health." In R. Krotinsky and H. Witmer (eds.), *Community Programs for Mental Health,* pp. 296–322. Cambridge, Massachusetts: Harvard University Press, 1955.

Jones, C. O. *An Introduction to the Study of Public Policy.* Belmont, California: Wadsworth, 1970.

Kane, T. J. "Citizen Participation in Decisionmaking: Myth or Strategy." *Administration in Mental Health,* Spring, 1975, pp. 29–34.

Kaplan, S. R. "Community Participation." In S. Feldman (ed.), *The Administration of Mental Health Services,* pp. 201–240. Springfield, Illinois: Charles C Thomas, 1973.

Kittre, N. *The Right to be Different: Deviance and Enforced Therapy.* Baltimore: Johns Hopkins University Press, 1971.

Kolb, L. C.; Bernard, V. W.; and Dohrenwend, B. P. (eds.). *Urban Challenges to Psychiatry: The Case History of a Response.* Boston: Little, Brown, 1969.

Laswell, H. D., and Kaplan, A. *Power and Society.* New Haven: Yale University Press, 1950.

LeCompte, G. "Planning and Administration." In E. J. Liebermann (ed.), *Mental Health: The Public Health Challenge,* pp. 97–101. Washington, D.C.: American Public Health Association, 1975.

Lindblom, C. *The Intelligence of Democracy: Decision-Making Through Mutual Adjustment.* New York: Free Press, 1965.

Littlestone, R. "Planning in Mental Health." In S. Feldman (ed.), *The Administration of Mental Health Services,* pp. 3–28. Springfield, Illinois: Charles C Thomas, 1973.

McGee, D., and Clark, C. X. "Critical Elements of Black Mental Health." *Journal of Black Health Perspectives* 1 (1974): 52–58.

Mechanic, D. *Mental Health and Social Policy.* Englewood Cliffs, New Jersey: Prentice-Hill, 1969.

Musto, D. F. "Whatever Happened to Community Mental Health?" *The Public Interest* 39 (1975): 53–79.

_____. "Mental Health: An All-Time Great Government Boondoggle?" *Medical Economics,* January 12, 1976, pp. 173–198.

National Commission on Community Health Services. *Health Is a Community Affair.* Cambridge, Massachusetts: Harvard University Press, 1967.

National Health Planning and Resources Development Act of 1974. U.S. Congress, House of Representatives, Conferences Report No. 93–1640, 93rd Congress, December 1974.

Noyes, A. P., and Kolb, L. C. *Modern Clinical Psychiatry,* 6th ed. Philadelphia: W. B. Saunders, 1963.

Reinke, W. A. (ed.). *Health Planning: Qualitative Aspects and Quantitative Techniques.* Baltimore, Maryland: The Johns Hopkins University, School of Hygiene and Public Health, Department of International Health, 1972.

Rich, C. "Special Role and Role Expectation of Black Administrators of Neighborhood Mental Health Programs." *Community Mental Health Journal* 11 (1975): 394–401.

Reissman, F.; Cohen, J.; and Pearl, A. (eds.). *Mental Health and the Poor.* New York: Free Press, 1964.

Ruiz, P., and Behrens, M. "Community Control in Mental Health: How Far Can It Go?" *Psychiatric Quarterly,* 17 (1973): 317–324.

Salisbury, R. "The Analysis of Public Policy: A Search for Theories and Roles." In A. Ranney (ed.), *Political Science and Public Policy,* pp. 151–175. Chicago: Markham, 1968.

Sanders, A. H. "Law, Accountability, Consumer Participation." In E. J. Liebermann (ed.), *Mental Health: The Public Health Challenge.* Washington, D.C.: American Public Health Association, 1975.

Scheidemandel, P. L.; Kanno, C. L.; and Glasscote, R. M. *Health Insurance for Mental Illness.* Washington, D.C.: The Joint Information Service of the American Psychiatric Association and the National Association for Mental Health, 1968.

Schon, D. A. "The Blindness System." *Public Interest* 18 (1970): 25–38.

Seham, M. *Blacks and American Medical Care.* Minneapolis: University of Minnesota Press, 1973.

Sells, S. B. (ed.). *The Definition and Measurement of Mental Health.* Washington, D.C.: U.S. Dept. of HEW, Public Health Services, Health Services and Mental Health Administration, National Center for Health Statistics, 1968.

Shore, M., and Mannino, F. V. *Mental Health and the Community: Problems, Programs and Strategies.* New York: Behavioral Publications, 1969.

Smith, O. S., and Gundlach, R. H. "Group Therapy for Blacks in a Therapeutic Community." *American Journal of Orthopsychiatry* 44 (1974): 26–36.

Szasz, T. *The Myth of Mental Illness: Foundations of a Theory of Personal Conduct,* rev. ed. New York: Harper & Row, 1974.

_____. "Stop Poking Around in Your Patients' Lives!" *Medical Economics,* June 1975 pp. 21–22.

Thomas, C. S., and Lindenthal, J. J. "Issues in Community Mental Health." *Administration in Mental Health* (Spring 1975): 66–70.

Thompson, T. "Community Involvement in Health: A Conceptual Approach to Evaluating the Consumer Participation Process in Neighborhood Health Centers." Ph.D. dissertation, University of Michigan, 1972.

_____. *The Politics of Pacification: The Case of Consumer Participation in Community Health Organizations.* Washington, D.C.: Institute for Urban Affairs and Research, 1974.

Tomes, H. "Meharry's Community Mental Health Center." *Journal of the National Medical Association* 65 (1973): 300–303.

Truman, D. B. *The Governmental Process.* New York: Alfred Knopf, 1971.

U.S. Department of Commerce, Bureau of the Census, Government Division. *Survey of State and Local Mental Health Finances.* Washington, D.C.: Bureau of the Census, 1970.

U.S. Department of Health, Education and Welfare, NIMH, Biometry Branch. *Preliminary Data on Expenditures and Source of Funds—Federally Assisted Community Mental Health Centers in the U.S., 1970.* Washington, D.C.: NIMH, 1971.

U.S. Department of Health, Education, and Welfare. *Interim Analysis of Results of Comprehensive Health Planning Agency Assessments.* Washington, D.C.: Bureau of Health Resources Development, Health Resources Administration, Public Health Service, 1974.

U.S. Department of Health, Education and Welfare, NIMH—The Advisory Panel of Financing Mental Health Care, American Hospital Association. *Financing Mental Health Care in the United States.* Washington, D.C.: DHEW Publication No (HSM) 73–9117, 1973.

U.S. Joint Commission on Mental Illness and Health. *Action for Mental Health.* New York: Basic Books, 1961.

Wasby, S. L. *Political Science: The Discipline and Its Dimensions.* New York: Charles Scribner's Sons, 1970.

Williams, R. H., and Ozarin, L. D. (eds.). *Community Mental Health: An International Perspective.* San Francisco: Jossey-Bass, 1968.

Willie, C. V.; Kramer, B. M.; and Brown, B. S. (eds.). *Racism and Mental Health.* Pittsburgh: University of Pittsburgh Press, 1973.

Witmer, A. H. "Insanity in the Colored Race in the United States." *Alienist and Neurologist* 12 (1891): 19–30.

13 BLACK MENTAL HEALTH WORK FORCE

Willie S. Williams, Ph.D.,
James R. Ralph, M.D., and
William Denham, Ph.D.

One of the major problems that exists in mental health today is the decline in the total support of training programs. This decline in support comes at a time when Blacks are just beginning to enter training programs in appreciable numbers. Along with the problem of numbers of Blacks presently in the professions and training programs is the problem presented by the geographical distribution of Black mental health manpower. Improper manpower distribution limits the type, level and amount of care received by Black patients. Levels of care may be determined by the numbers of times a patient is seen by a professional, a paraprofessional, a hospital aide, or other person. Care rendered by volunteer home visitors would also be considered as levels of care. The education of mental health workers often determines where they will practice and what position they will occupy. Although a variety of specialists (anthropologists, school counselors, and economists) provide different types of mental health services, the traditional mental health personnel (psychiatrists, psychiatric nurses, psychologists and social workers) have received training support for the past 25 years from National Institute of Mental Health (NIMH). In the fifties and sixties, large numbers of psychiatric trainees received all or part of their support from NIMH. Presently, NIMH supports training in 500 institutions; however, the amount of its support in Black institutions is limited. Since training is affected by type of institution, for example, Black colleges versus white colleges, and graduate versus undergraduate training, the impact of the lack of support affects both manpower and services. The role of Black colleges in the education of mental health workers together with topics mentioned above are among the more important problems and issues receiving attention in this chapter.

Historical Perspective

Because there are so few Black mental health professionals, Black patients usually must seek treatment from mental health personnel who may not be sensitive to the cultural and environmental circumstances of the patients. While Black Americans represent more than 11 percent of the total population, less than 2 percent of psychiatrists are Black; less than 2 percent of doctoral level psychologists are Black; approximately 11 percent of social workers are Black; and less than 2 percent of the doctoral-level nurses are Black.

A look at Table 1, which summarizes the Black trainee participation in mental health programs supported by the National Institute of Mental Health from 1948 to 1968, clearly shows one of the reasons for the shortage of Black mental health professionals. During this 20-year period a total of 22 Black psychiatrists, 15 Black psychologists, 32 Black nurses and 138 Black social workers were supported by NIMH funds. This extremely poor situation as far as trainees are concerned has been remedied only slightly in certain of the training programs. A more detailed discussion of the changes will be presented in the section on assessment of Black mental health manpower.

Table 1

Summary of Black Trainee Participation in
NIMH-Supported Training Programs, 1948–1968*

	Number of Trainees			Percent of Total		
	1948–57	1958–63	1964–68	1948–57	1958–63	1964–68
Psychiatry	3	3	16	1.7	.7	1.7
Psychiatry		6	9		1.5	1.0
Social Work	14	56	68	5.1	8.3	6.0
Nursing	4	8	20	3.0	6.1	3.5
Social Science			1			
Biological Science			1			1.1
Pre-Doctoral		3	6		1.0	0.9
Post-Doctoral						

* Preliminary report/follow-up survey of NIMH-supported trainees 1948–1968 (DMT).

Table 2 shows the total number of trainee awards made through the Division of Manpower and Training programs of the National Institute of Mental Health for fiscal year 1972. This table also shows the awards made to minorities and the percentage of minorities among the total awardees. The table highlights the efforts that have been put forth by various programs within the Division of Manpower and Training. For

Table 2.

Trainees by Discipline or Program for Fiscal Year 1972*

Discipline/Program	Total Awards†	Awards to Minorities‡	Percentage of traineeships to Minorities
Psychiatry	3342	387	12.0
Psychology	2241	369	16.0
Social Work	1476	726	49.0
Nursing	1287	205	16.0
Biological Sciences	428	39	9.0
Social Sciences	551	72	13.0
Experimental/Special	328	153	47.0
New Careers	93	64	69.0
Continuing Education	NA		
Fellowships for Research Training	NA		

* These figures were derived from the DMTP/MASB report, dated July 19, 1974, submitted in response to questionnaire item D. asking for a "breakdown by race and ethnicity of all trainees and fellows receiving training in NIMH funded programs for years 1971, 1972, 1973 and 1974 separately." The report indicated that "data on race/ethnicity of trainees are not presently available for any period other than that covered in this table." Also, the data for Continuing Education and for Fellowships for Research was not available.

† Figures in the Total Awards column are actual, and the report stated that "distribution by race/ethnicity is estimated on the basis of incomplete reports of trainee appointments received on form HSM-600-2, Summary Report of Trainees, for the budget period from July 1, 1972 through June 30, 1973."

‡ The figures for Awards to Minorities may be slightly higher than those shown above because the report noted that "numbers of trainees reported (by code) as 'American Native', a group intended to include only American Indians, Eskimos, and Aleuts, greatly exceeded the number of such minorities actually supported for training; it was obvious therefore that this category was used in many instances to report white, non-minority trainees. Since no data were available with which to estimate the numbers of 'American Natives' actually receiving traineeships, it was necessary to combine this group with the non-minority category."

example, the new careers program has made the greatest effort in the recruitment of minorities as shown by the fact that 69 percent of the awards were made to minority trainees. The Social Work program with 49 percent of awards, and the Experimental Special Program, with 47 percent, are a reflection of extraordinary efforts to reduce the problems of an insufficient minority work force. It can be seen below how these data relate specifically to Blacks.

Table 3 shows a breakdown of the percentages for each minority group from Table 2. The data are limited to the training grants for the fiscal year 1972 which supported programs for the school year 1973. The data reflect efforts only by the Division of Manpower and Training of the National Institute of Mental Health.

The Experimental Special Program made the greatest contribution to the number of Blacks in training programs for fiscal year 1972. The Experimental Special Program is not a specific discipline, but rather an attempt to provide for unique kinds of training for mental health service deliverers or researchers. As a result, the people trained may have specialities in one of the other core professional fields such as psychology, social work, or sociology.

Tables 4* and 5* give a historical perspective to the critical need for the training of Black mental health personnel. The number of Black professionals, as indicated in Table 4, is extremely low. When these data were collected in 1969, the move toward increasing the minority or Black mental health manpower had not come into full swing.

The percentage of minority group trainees during the period 1964 to 1968 is shown in Table 5. During this time, when there was a very small number of Black and other minority professionals, there was a slight decrease in the percentage of awards made to minority group members in social work and nursing but a comparative increase in psychology and psychiatry. The comparison of Table 5 to Table 2, however, reveals that some progress was made in all the mental health professions during the 4-year period. While minority representation in most of the disciplines has doubled, it has increased fourfold in social work.

The New Careers programs made the next most productive effort in fiscal year 1972 as far as the training of Blacks is concerned. Although

---

*The tables were originally listed in a special report to the Chief of the Center for Minority Group Mental Health Programs.

Table 3.

Race/Ethnicity of Trainees, by Discipline or Program, NIMH/DMTP, Fiscal Year 1972*

Discipline or Program	Negro or Black		Asian American		Spanish-Surnamed		Other† Minority		Non-Minority		Total‡	
	No.	%	No.	%	No.	%	No.	%	No.	%	No.	%
Psychiatry												
Graduate	63	3.1	48	2.3	93	4.6	80	3.9	1748	86.1	2032	100.0
Undergraduate	36	2.7	19	1.4	25	1.9	23	1.8	1207	92.2	1310	100.0
Psychology	260	11.6	17	0.8	62	2.8	30	1.3	1872	83.5	2241	100.0
Social Work	457	30.9	60	4.1	201	13.8	8	0.5	750	50.9	1476	100.0
Nursing												
Graduate	124	12.1	8	0.8	26	2.5	3	0.3	864	84.3	1025	100.0
Undergraduate	24	9.0			7	2.6	13	5.2	218	83.2	262	100.0
Social Science	47	8.4	6	1.0	12	2.2	7	1.4	479	87.0	551	100.0
Biological Sciences	7	1.5	13	3.1	9	2.1	10	2.3	389	91.0	428	100.0
Experimental/Special	118	36.1	2	0.5	33	10.0			175	53.4	328	100.0
New Careers	33	35.2	1	0.8	30	32.8			29	31.2	93	100.0
Continuing Education	NA											
Fellowships for Research Training	NA											

* Supported from fiscal year 1972 funds, for training in fiscal year 1973. Data on race/ethnicity of trainees are not presently available for any period other than that covered in this table.

† Includes trainees reported as "American Native" (American Indian, Eskimo, and Aleut).

‡ Data in total column are actual; distribution by race/ethnicity is estimated on the basis on incomplete reports of trainee appointments received on form HSM-600-2, Summary Report of Trainees, for the budget period from July 1, 1972 through June 30, 1973. Numbers of trainees reported (by code) as "American Native," a group intended to include only American Indians, Eskimos, and Aleuts, greatly exceeded the numbers of such minorities actually supported for training; it was obvious, therefore, that this category was used in many instances to report white, non-minority trainees. Since no data were available with which to estimate the numbers of "American Natives" actually receiving traineeships, it was necessary to combine this group with the non-minority category.

Table 4.

Health Professionals*

Profession	Total Number	Black Members	Percentage of Black Members	Source of Data
Physicians	305,000	6,700	2.2	Black members estimate based on NMA membership.
Psychiatrists	17,000	300	1.8	Based on APA survey, 1963.
Psychologists	15,565	304	2.0	Based on census, 1960
	24,473	489	2.0	Based on APA membership, 1966.
Social Workers	95,103	10,372	10.0	
Nurses	581,289	32,825	5.6	Based on 1960 census of professional nurses employed.

* Data submitted with DMTP report dated July 25, 1974. Originated in Manpower Study Section, October 27, 1967.

Table 5.

Trainees by Discipline or Program for 1964–1968*

Discipline/Program	Total Awards	Awards to Minorities	Percentage of Traineeships to Minorities
Psychiatry	929	48	5.2
Psychology	972	69	7.1
Social Work	1132	103	9.1
Nursing	579	31	5.4
Biological Sciences	92	2	2.1
Social Sciences	209	7	3.3
Pre-Doctoral	641	18	2.1
Post-Doctoral	106	0	0

* Data submitted by Chief, Survey and Reports Section PPEB, dated February 21, 1974, to Chief, Center for Minority Group Mental Health Programs.

these efforts are commendable, they point out the major problems of a disproportionate number of Black paraprofessional trainees and service deliverers. Paraprofessionals most often serve in non-policy-making positions and usually have their work supervised by professionals. Paraprofessionals are certainly important, but a larger percentage of Black trainees in professional programs is needed. The conditions that existed in 1972 were not representative of what existed in prior years or what has taken place since that time (see the detailed discussion in the section on assessment of manpower). Owing to the reduction in federal funds for training programs, there has been a considerable reduction in efforts to train additional Black manpower since the 1972 report.

The Center for Minority Group Mental Health Programs has provided funds for several training programs. These programs are based in each of five special disciplinary mental health organizations. These include the American Psychiatric Association, the American Psychological Association, the American Nurses Association, the American Sociological Association, and the Council on Social Work Education. The programs have been responsible for an increase in the number of minority trainees in several educational institutions.

Types and Levels of Care

The potential contributions of Black mental health practitioners become obvious as we review the literature regarding problems faced by Blacks in receiving mental health care. Sue and co-workers (1974), in a study of minority use of mental health facilities in the Seattle, Washington area, report that Black clients attended fewer sessions than white clients, terminated more often after the first session, and were more likely to see paraprofessionals. Lowe and Hodges (1972) found that alcoholic whites receive treatment, while alcoholic Blacks are disproportionately sent to prison. One reason that Blacks more often see paraprofessionals is, as indicated in the data above, that there are more Black paraprofessionals. These conditions signal the need for more Black mental health workers who can relate to the culturally and environmentally different lifestyles of the patients. While some aspects of Black cultural differences may be taught, other aspects can only be understood or perceived by having been a part of that cultural milieu.

The number of sessions in which blacks are seen by professional therapists depends on the nature of the problem and the race of the therapist as variables in treatment. Jackson and co-workers (1974) found that Black children were seen for shorter periods of time than were white children. The condition that frequently creates a problem for Blacks is the difference in the types of treatment administered. In a special report on inequities in mental health service delivery prepared for the Center for Minority Group Mental Health, NIMH, Fiman (1975) described the situation as follows:

> A number of investigators have provided evidence for differential treatment as a function of race. Gross et al. (1969) found that diagnosis and type of referral from psychiatric emergency rooms varied with the race of the client. They concluded that as the socio-cultural distance between clinician and client increases, diagnosis becomes less accurate and dispositions more non-specific. Cooper (1973) presents case histories to document the relationship between treatment and race. Lowenger and Dobie (1966) state that recommendations for treatment are related to the race of the client, as are the therapists' attitudes. Jackson et al. (1974) indicate that Blacks are more often seen for diagnosis only. Gilbert (1972) in a study of equity in community mental health centers found a number of differences in the delivery of services to Black and white clients.

This type of service differential should not exist. By producing more Black researchers to ask appropriate questions and obtain data for policy decisions, we can improve these conditions.

Gardner (1971) studied the relationship of race and effectiveness in the clinical situation and found that Black therapists, overall, were seen as more effective by the Black patient than were white therapists. When he differentiated categories of therapists, however, he found that the most effective therapists, as seen by the Black clients, were Black therapists who were sensitized to the cultural and idiosyncratic background of the Black patient. The next group, in terms of effectiveness, consisted of white therapists who were sensitized in terms of the client's cultural background and idiosyncratic factors. The third group was composed of Black therapists who were not sensitized or who had engaged in an identity shift or a denial of their own Blackness. The last group consisted of white non-sensitive therapists. With respect to identifying the kind of instruction best suited for training therapists to work with Black populations, the implications of Gardner's study are that Black institutions could accomplish this in two situations. One is in the training of Black therapists only, where the Black institution cuts across the range of ethnic, class, and regional orientations. Another is training all therapists who will be working with Black populations, whether the therapists are Black or white; the Black institution will expose the therapists to training with a range of Black clients who represent many of the life-space, life-style, and life-stage factors of the Black community.

Assessment of Black Mental Health Manpower

A number of attempts have been made to assess the Black mental health manpower. An initial attempt was aborted by the Office of Management and Budget in 1974. One of the more recent attempts has been made by the Center for Minority Group Mental Health Programs. It has been conducted informally by the minority fellowship programs funded by the National Institute of Mental Health at each of the following professional organizations: the American Psychological Association, the American Psychiatric Association, the American Sociological Association, the American Nurses Association, and the Council on Social Work Education. The directors of the minority group mental health training program within each of the associations have been requested to provide data regarding the number of professionals in the country and the number of students in training at all training institutions. This has been done with varying degrees of success.

Social Work. The best estimates of the number of Black social workers indicate that they have larger proportional representation than any other Black professional mental health group in this country. Table 4 shows that of 95,103 social workers, 10,372 are Black. This represents 10 percent of the total social workers in 1974.

Reports from the Council on Social Work Education show that there has been a relative increase in the number of full-time Black faculty in accredited graduate schools of social work. In Table 6, it is clear that the number of faculty varies by rank and time of appointment. Beginning in 1970, the 24 Black professors of social work represented 6 percent of the total number of full professors on faculties in schools of social work, while the part-time Black faculty represented 13.9 percent. In 1971, the percentage of Black full professors had dropped from 6 to 3.7 percent and from a numerical 24 to 17 Black full professors; however, there has been an increase in the number of Black associate professors from 51 to

60, which showed an increase from 8.8 to 9.6 percent. A similar increase was shown in the number of Black assistant professors—122 in 1970 to 155 in 1971, or an increase from 16.0 to 18.2 percent. The data show clearly that there has been a reduction of Black faculty with the rank of full professor in the various institutions. There has been an increase in the number and percentage of Black associate professors, assistant professors, and instructors from 1970 to 1973.

Table 6.

Black Faculty in Accredited Graduate Schools of
Social Work by Rank*

Year	Full Professor	%	Associate Professor	%	Assistant Professor	%	Instructors and Other	%	Part-time	%
1970	24	6.0	51	8.8	122	16.0	62	15.0	120	13.9
1971	17	3.7	60	9.6	155	18.2	44	13.3	112	13.5
1972	25	5.1	79	11.8	154	18.1	58	17.4	119	14.1
1973	27	5.4	85	12.3	170	21.1	58	18.8	109	12.2
1974†									128	13.2
1975‡									124	12.4

* Table developed from data in *Statistics on Social Work Education,* 1970, 1971, 1972, 1973, 1974, and 1975.

† Data were reported in a different form for 1974; consequently, the total Black faculty of 330 (or 15.1%) can be reported along with part-time faculty.

‡ In 1975, the report contained both graduate and undergraduate faculties. Full professors: 30 (5.7%), associate professors: 113 (15.1%), assistant professors: 162 (20.3%), instructors and other: 77 (25.7%).

For the years 1974 and 1975, the Council on Social Work Education developed a different method of reporting data. Consequently, we can only report a total Black faculty of 330 or 15.1 percent of faculty in graduate schools of social work. For the year 1975, the data were recorded on the basis of graduate and combined graduate-undergraduate social work programs. These data show that there were 30 Black full professors, which represented 5.7 percent, 113 Black associate professors, which represented 13.1 percent, 162 Black assistant professors, which represented 20.3 percent, and 77 Black instructors, or 25.7 percent of the total full-time faculty in graduate and combined graduate-undergraduate programs of social work. The difference between reporting for 1975 and for 1970–1973 is that the latter reports contain data on Black faculty for the graduate schools of social work only. The 1975 data have the graduate schools' Black faculty plus the entire Black faculty for schools that combine undergraduate and graduate programs. There were 124 part-time faculty which represent 12.4 percent of the total part-time faculty.

As shown in Table 7, the number of Black students in social work training programs rose from the years 1971 to 1972 and then began a steady decline through 1975. The number of Black M.S.W. candidates in 1970 was 975, or 14.5 percent of the total number of first-year candidates. There were 872 Black second-year candidates, or a total of 14.3 percent of the second-year total. The number of Black first- and second-year candidates increased to a high, in 1972, of 1,226 first-year candidates (or 15.8 percent) and 1,126 second-year candidates (or 15.4 percent). The numbers and percentages steadily decreased from 1972 to 1975. In 1975, only 933 Black first-year candidates (11.9 percent) and 1,093 Black second-year candidates (12.4 percent) were enrolled in M.S.W. training programs. Post-M.S.W. Black trainees have shown a steady increase, however, from 1970 to 1975. The numbers have risen from a low of 54 candidates, which represented 11.7 percent of the total post-M.S.W. trainees, in 1970, to 123, or 17.3 percent of the total post-M.S.W. candidates, in 1975. The information found in Table 6 gives a clear indication of the decline in interest and efforts to train Blacks in schools of social work at the present time.

Psychology. The most recent reports indicate that 190 Black males and 97 Black females, or a total of 287 Blacks, have Ph.D.'s in psychology. These data are based upon a membership study conducted by the American Psychological Association in 1974.

Since the report of Wispé and co-workers in 1969, a number of attempts have been made to increase the number of Black Ph.D.'s in psychology. Wispé reported in 1969 that 166 Blacks had Ph.D.'s in psychology. The APA report in 1974 indicates that 287 Blacks have Ph.D.'s in psychology, and an average annual increase of only 13.

In a report on women and minority students in graduate departments

Table 7.

Black Full-Time Degree Students Enrolled in
U.S. Schools of Social Work*

| | M.A. | | | | Post-M.S.W. | |
| | 1st Year | | 2nd Year | | | |
Year	No.	%	No.	%	No.	%
1970	975	14.5	872	14.3	54	11.3
1971	1,067	14.9	1,049	15.3	70	13.3
1972	1,226	15.8	1,126	15.4	87	15.4
1973	1,185	14.4	1,227	15.6	104	16.8
1974	1,004	12.2	1,093	12.6	113	17.4
1975	933	11.9	1,093	12.4	123	17.3

* Developed from data in *Statistics on Social Work Education*, 1970, 1971, 1972, 1973, 1974, and 1975.

receiving NIMH training grants, Stanley Schneider (1975) provides the following information:

> We do have some comparative data on minority students. In 1972, in response to a letter sent to all NIMH supported psychology training programs the returns showed that 10.5% of the students at that time were minority students. This proportion was based upon 9,014 students, of whom, 943 were identified as minority students. The 1972 survey included our pilot programs, which contained almost 39% minority students, and our field training programs, which had 12.6% minority students. The fact that several pilot awards were made to minority schools contributed to the high minority proportion in that category of grants. However, many of the pilot programs are at the less than doctoral level, and would not be included in the present survey. Also, the field training centers were omitted from this survey, the minority proportion comes out to 9.2% (721 out of 7,807 students). That is the universe most comparable with the one in the present survey. It included only one program in a Black school (Howard) which is also included in the present figures.

> We are left with a comparison between 9.2% for our NIMH supported doctoral programs in 1972 and 13% for the departments that contain these programs in 1974–75. It is very rough, but is suggestive of a direction, and that is positive. By any criterion, the situation is an improvement over the minority figures in the early sixties, which were less than 2%.

A further breakdown of these data (see table 3) shows that 11.6 percent of the minority psychology trainees were Black. This includes both master's and doctoral level students. However, the number of Black institutions providing master's level psychology training accounts for the larger percentage of the number of Black trainees.

Psychiatry. Data on Black psychiatrists indicate that there are approximately 400 Black males and 100 Black females, for a total of 500 nationwide. This is a very rough estimate based upon data from the American Psychiatric Association and the Black Psychiatrists of America. The Black Psychiatrists of America are conducting a more comprehensive and definitive survey of Black psychiatrists.

Table 8 examines psychiatric residential training programs over a period of four years. This material represents the school years 1972–73, 1973–74, 1974–75, and 1975–76. During this time the data show that there has been a very small percentage of Blacks in psychiatric training programs. There was a slight decrease in the 1973-74 school year from the previous year. The data show, however, that there has been a trend toward increased numbers in 1974–75 and 1975–76. This increase is possibly a result of the special efforts initiated by the Center for Minority Group Mental Health Programs in funding the project for the American Psychiatric Association's minority psychiatry programs. However, the data clearly demonstrate the need for more Blacks to enter psychiatric training programs.

Sociology. Data from the American Sociological Association (ASA) are very limited. An estimate based upon the A.S.A. census and on the

Table 8.

Psychiatric Residents, 1972–1976*

Year	Total	Black	% Black	Black Male	Black Female
1972–73	4699	92	2.0	65	27
1973–74	4739	88	1.9	61	27
1974–75	4821	110	2.3	77	33
1975–76	4789	131	2.7	90	41

* From *American Psychiatric Association Manpower Statistics*, 1976.

graduates of 1975 indicates that approximately 275 Blacks have a Ph.D. in sociology. Joan Harris (1975) reports that there are 8,270 graduate and undergraduate faculty in sociology. Of this number 13.1 percent, or 1,084 are Black. In 1974, the American Association for the Advancement of Science, in a scientific manpower commission report, indicated that 4.9 percent of graduate faculties in sociology are Black. It further indicated that Blacks tend to be in the lower ranks; 10.3 percent of the instructors were Blacks, and 1.2 percent of lecturers were Black, versus 4.5 percent of assistant professors.

Nursing. Data available on nursing are also very limited. The report by Fiman (1975) indicates that 47 Black nurses have Ph.D.'s. The categorization of nurses into the various subspecialities, such as psychiatric or surgical nursing, was not indicated (see tables 9 and 10).

The Role of the Black Institution

The Black institution occupies a key role in the development of the Black mental health specialist. There are several institutions now offering programs which would qualify for the training of psychiatrists at some level. Among these institutions are Howard University, Meharry Medical College, Charles R. Drew Postgraduate Medical School, and the newly established Morehouse Medical College. While the Morehouse Medical College offers only two of the four years of training required for an M.D. degree, it plays an important part in the training of Black students who will eventually become physicians.

At the present time there is a limited number of Black institutions offering doctoral degrees in one or more of the mental health disciplines. For example, Howard University offers the Ph.D. in sociology, social work, and psychology. Fisk University and Meharry Medical College are cooperating in the process of developing a Ph.D. program in psychology. Atlanta University offers a Ph.D. in the counseling area, but is contemplating dropping this program for one in community psychology. Texas Southern University may be offering the higher-level degrees at some future data. Other Black institutions offer master's degrees in several of the mental health disciplines.

The highest terminal degree in a given discipline, i.e., the doctorate,

Table 9. *

Source Table for the Percentage of Racial Minorities in Selected Disciplines

Discipline or Sub-Discipline	Degree	Total Minorities No.	Percent Total Minorities	Percent Black	Percent Asian	Percent American Indian and Alaskan	Percent Hispanic
Psychology	Ph.D.	1,021	6.0	1.2	0.8	0.1	
	M.A.	257	6.0	2.0	0.5	0.1	
Psychiatry	M.D.	752	4.3	1.2	2.6	0.1	
Biological Sciences	Ph.D.	3,507	6.6	0.9	4.8		0.8
Social Sciences	Ph.D.	1,494	6.2	1.2	4.0	0.2	0.7
Chemistry	Ph.D.	3,808	12.0				
Mathematics and Biostatistics	Ph.D.	2,329	15.0				
Nursing	Ph.D.	58	6.0	5.0	0.1		
Physics	Ph.D.	1,397	7.0	0.4	6.0	0.2	0.3
	M.A.	774	8.0	0.9	5.6	0.4	0.9
Pharmacy	Ph.D.	58	31.0	2.0	1.6		0.5
	M.A.	87	29.0	1.3	1.0		0.7
Sociology	Ph.D.	184	5.0	5.0			

* Reproduced from report by Byron T. Fiman et al. prepared from the Center for Minority Group Mental Health Programs–NIMH, "Development of quantitative indices, institutional change with regard to racial minorities and women in NIMH external program." May 13, 1975.

Table 10.*

Race and Sex of Individuals in Selected Disciplines

Discipline and Sub-Discipline	Degree	Total No.	No. Non-Minority		No. Minority		Percent of Total No.							
							Black		Asian		Amer. Indian-Alaskan		Hispanic	
			Male	Female	Male	Female	Male	Female	Male	Female	Male	Female	Male	Female
Psychology	Ph.D.	15,885	11,925	2,939	241	92	0.8	0.4	0.6	0.2	0.1	0.0		
	M.A.	4,240	2,456	1,527	80	43	1.0	0.9	0.4	0.1	0.1	0.0		
Psychiatry	M.D.	17,982	12,982	1,597	608	143	1.0	0.2	2.0	0.6	0.1	0.0		
Nursing	Ph.D.	964	22	884	3	55	0.3	4.5	0.0	0.1				
Physics	Ph.D.	19,772	17,371	473	1,342	55	0.4	0.0	6.0	0.2	0.2	0.0	0.3	0.0
	M.A.	10,275	8,808	528	701	73	0.9	0.0	5.0	0.6	0.4	0.0	0.9	0.0
Pharmacy	Ph.D.	187	120	9	8	0	2.0	0.0	1.6	0.0			0.5	0.0
	M.A.	303	192	24	8	2	1.0	0.3	0.6	0.3			0.7	0.0
Sociology	Ph.D.	3,090	154			30	4.2	0.8						

* Reproduced from report by Byron T. Fiman et al. prepared for the Center for Minority Group Mental Health Programs–NIMH. "Development of quantitative indices, institutional change with regard to racial minorities and women in NIMH external program." May 13, 1975.

is considered the basis for acceptance and promotion in a number of positions that have policy-making significance. For example, within the university structure, the important policy decision will be made by administrators and usually those people carrying tenure or professorial rank. The honor of professorial rank is most often reserved for those persons with the highest terminal degrees in a given discipline. Most top-level administrative positions are also reserved for those persons with a terminal or doctoral-level degree. In the federal government, persons in top-level administrative roles for an institute or agency frequently have terminal degrees or are advised and guided by study groups (Initial Review Groups) or other review groups and consultants to the special agencies. The role played by Blacks is becoming increasingly more significant as more Blacks with terminal degrees find their way into various committees or leadership positions.

One aspect of the mental health training programs must deal with the operation of Blacks in administrative roles and in policy-making positions. The development at certain Black institutions of specific programs which will deal with this type of situation provides another way for preparing these administrators. Programs at Black institutions should be adequately funded so that research can be conducted by Black social and behavioral scientists in Black institutions. It is most discouraging when Black scholars must leave Black institutions because tremendous demands upon their time for teaching and other necessary activities within the institutions have prevented them from continuing their scholarly endeavors in a significant way. The role of government and private agencies in establishing chairs at Black institutions becomes increasingly important in resolving these issues and problems. A significant first step in this direction has been the development of the postdoctoral fellowship program by the Center for Minority Group Mental Health Programs. It will permit scholars to take a year off at full pay or nearly full pay to conduct research.

Certain institutions should be identified, based upon their geographical location, their support programs, their student body, and their accessibility to other resources, as places where specific types of research and training may be conducted. In effect, research and special training may work better at some institutions than at others. Once these institutions are identified, a long-range funding program should be developed so that they can play particular roles in the training of mental health researchers and in the conduct of mental health research that has policy implications. It may well be that unified efforts among Black mental health caucuses could be developed toward this end.

The Black Caucus and other Black political agencies may be involved at an early stage in the development of such a project. Position papers relating to the needs should be developed and presented to the Black Caucus. Blacks in funding agencies operated by the federal government and by private foundations may be called upon to discuss the best method for obtaining the necessary financial resources. Blacks in administrative and faculty positions in Black schools and in major universities throughout the country may become involved in determining who should be called upon to develop these programs. Black mental health organizations, such as the Association of Black Psychologists, the Association of Black Nurses, the Association of Black Social Workers, the Association of Black Sociologists, and the Black Psychiatrists of America, should collaborate to develop an ongoing relationship with the Congressional Black Caucus to provide data, give testimony for congressional hearings, and develop a legislatively mandated program to meet the needs of an increased Black work force for mental health.

Summary

The paucity of data and the extreme difficulty involved in retrieving existing data suggest clearly that a new procedure should be developed to identify Black mental health manpower. There is a need to know where Black mental health professionals work. Information regarding the percentages of Black mental health workers in underserved areas with predominantly Black populations would be useful to social agencies, researchers, and educators. There is also a need to know how many Black mental health workers are in academic settings. Presently, social work has the most significant and efficient data base. The model used by the Council on Social Work Education in tallying the data should be duplicated by other professional organizations. Finally, but not the least important of the poorly researched issues, is the curriculum of various mental health training programs. While the literature is replete with articles expressing feelings among minorities that curricula do not reflect change to meet their needs (Longres, 1972; Turner, 1972; Gary, 1968; Robertson, 1970), Wittman (1974) reports (p. 1206):

The activist atmosphere of the 1960's led to greater concern for factors influencing the entire social system. Students in minority groups pressed for changes. Consequently, much more of the curriculum was devoted to studying the social forces influencing society and the means of changing social policy.

A well-designed study of the curricular content of the mental health professions and of mental health manpower as they relate to Blacks and to other minority groups should be conducted.

References

Cooper, S. "A Look at the Effect of Racism on Clinical Work." *Social Casework* 52 (1973): 76–84.

Fiman, G.; Peter, G.; Willen, D. L.; and Sinnett, J. D. "Development of Quantitative Indices of Institutional Change with Regard to Racial Minorities and Women in NIMH External Programs." Report prepared for the Center for Minority Group Mental Health Programs NIMH, Rockville, Maryland, 1975.

Gardner, W. E. "How Selected Personal Characteristics of Helpers are Related to their Effectiveness as seen by Black College Students." *Journal of Clinical Psychology* 11 (1971): 111–115.

Gary, L. E. "Social Work Education and the Black Community: A Proposal for Curriculum Revisions." *Social Work Education Reporter* 16 (1968): 47–50, 68–69.

Gilbert, J. "A Study of Equity in Providing Community Mental Health Services." Interim Report prepared for NIMH by Public Sector, Inc., New York, 1972.

Gross, H. et al. "The Effect of Race and Sex on the Variation of Diagnosis and Disposition in a Psychiatric Emergency Room." *Nervous and Mental Diseases* 48 (1969): 638–642.

Harris, J. "Women and Minorities in Sociology: Findings from Annual ASA Audit." *ASA Footnotes,* January, 1975, 4–5.

Jackson, A. M.; Berkowitz, H.; and Farley, G. K. "Race as a Variable Affecting the Treatment Involvement of Children." *Journal of the American Academy of Child Psychiatry* 13 (1974): 20–31.

Longres, J. "The Impact of Racism on Social Work Education." *Journal of Education for Social Work* 8 (1972): 31–41.

Lowe, G. D., and Hodges, H. E. "Race and the Treatment of Alcoholism in a Southern State." *Social Programs* 20 (1972): 240–252.

Lowenger, P. L., and Dobie, S. "Attitudes and Emotions of the Psychiatrist in the Initial Interview." *American Journal of Psychotherapy* 20 (1966): 17–32.

Robertson, M. E. "Inclusion of Content on Ethnic and Racial Minorities in the Social Work Curriculum." *Social Work Education Reporter* 18 (1970): 45–47, 66.

Schneider, S. "Women and Minority Students in Graduate Departments with NIMH Training Grants." Internal Report, Rockville, Maryland, 1975.

Sue, S.; Allen, D.; McKinney, H.; and Hall, J. "Delivery of Community Mental Health Services to Black and White Clients." Seattle, Washington: University of Washington, 1974.

Turner, J. B. "Education for Practice with Minorities." *Social Work* 17 (1972): 112–118.

Wittman, M. "Social Work." In Silvano Arieti (ed.), *American Handbook of Psychiatry*, Vol. 1, pp. 1200–1215. New York, Basic Handbook, 1974.

Wispe, L. et al. "The Negro Psychologist in America." *American Psychologist* 2 (1969): 142–150.

14 RESEARCH ON THE MENTAL HEALTH OF BLACK PEOPLE

Stanley H. Smith, Ph.D.

Studies of Black mental health must follow and abide by the basic methodological rules and procedures of research. The researcher must seek to examine and understand the principles, concepts, and methods of the scientific investigation as these relate to Black mental health. The basic characteristics of research, as given below, must therefore be adhered to and followed.

Research gathers new knowledge or data from primary sources. It places emphasis on the discovery of general principles. It is expert, accurate, and systematic investigation. The researcher uses data-gathering instruments which are both valid and reliable—they measure what they are supposed to measure and they do it consistently. Research is logical and objective, using every possible test to verify not only data collected, but also the procedures employed. Personal feelings, preferences, and biases must be studiously avoided. The researcher endeavors, therefore, to organize data in quantitative terms and express them as numerical measures. The researcher expends painstaking effort in the research activity and, in the process, suspends judgment in order to permit the data and logic to lead to a sound conclusion.

It is of the utmost importance, then, that research be carefully recorded and reported. All important terms and concepts must be operationally defined. All procedures must be described accurately and in detail. All conclusions and generalizations must be cautiously arrived at, taking into due consideration all of the limitations of the methodology, including the rules for data collection and possible errors of interpretation.

The model research design is, without question, an experimental one. A causal hypothesis is a *sine qua non* to this design. This hypothesis is a specifically stated relationship between two variables or units of measurement: one is an X variable which is a causal or independent variable; the other is the Y, or dependent variable. This research design must have at least two matched groups—a control group and an experimental group. This approach gets more precisely to the question of causation or etiology and/or the precise effectiveness of a social intervention or treatment mechanism. One of the real concerns always with this type of research is whether the determined factor is causal or just concomitant. The critical concern is whether it is an intervening variable which affects and influences in a constant manner both the dependent and independent variables.

Research on mental health, and appropriately on Black mental health, must be assessed and evaluated by taking the above concerns into consideration. Additionally, research on mental health, and specifically on Black mental health, must meet the same basic concerns of all research on social problems. By definition, research must recognize that social problems, including mental health problems, are multidimensional and multifaceted. Research should not focus primarily on the biological or the psychological functioning of individuals, but must attempt instead to place within a systems analysis framework the complex interrelationships of the person, the social situations, and the institutional and social-structural dimensions, recognizing also the conceptual commonalities and interconnections of social problems. The research scope has, heretofore, tended to be narrowly analytic and structured within a framework of uniqueness and, therefore, limited in its applicability and its conceptual usefulness. Research on Black mental health might conceivably have implications for, and be related to, race and racism, poverty, sex-role differentiations, socio-economic status, and community organization.

Such research efforts in the past have lacked methodological rigor and have been exploratory or, at best, descriptive in research designs. Failure to recognize the interrelatedness of social phenomena and social problems has not usually led to multivariate statistical analyses or to methods of longitudinal analysis, or at least to an appropriate combination of cross-sectional and longitudinal analyses.

More specifically, in mental health research, attempts are not usually made to establish meaningful relationships between drug addiction, alcoholism, suicide, job maladjustment and dissatisfaction, and mental illness. The tendency has been to treat each research problem area in isolation and to deal primarily with one level of analysis, usually the psychological, thereby virtually ignoring the biological and the social.

The present organizational structure and consequent research funding activity of the Alcohol, Drug Abuse, and Mental Health Administration (ADAMHA) of HEW are an appropriate demonstration of this basic philosophical thrust. It is of significance that even though recognition is given to the special research needs, concerns, and problems of minorities, the only existing organizational provisions are those made in the National Institute of Mental Health with the establishment of a Center for Minority Group Mental Health Programs. There are no comparable organizations in the National Institute of Alcohol Abuse and the National Institute for Drug Abuse.

Additionally, in research on social problems and mental health, there is a glaring paucity of cross-national, cross-racial-ethnic, and cross-cultural kinds of studies. The need is great for such kinds of research with comparable methodologies, thereby permitting meaningful comparisons and facilitating the control of specific variables and the evaluation of the precise impact of certain kinds of social interventions.

Other research problems which are related to investigative concerns dealing with mental illness revolve around the difficulties of operationally defining such important concepts as mental health, mental illness, and psychiatric (mental) disorders. These definitions become even more crucial when they are linked with behavior which carries with it certain stigma.

The concept of mental illness itself has been challenged. Thomas Szasz (1960, 1961) is the chief proponent of this attack. He takes the position that the phenomenon is not an illness and, therefore, the approach should not be in accordance with a medical model. Szasz conceives of mental illness as basically a problem of communication. Therefore, he advocates the abandonment of the concept by taking the strong position that mental illness is a myth and should not be considered as a medical entity. He further states (1960, p. 113):

> The norm from which deviation is measured, whenever one speaks of a mental illness, is a psycho-social and ethical one. Yet the remedy is sought in terms of medical measures which—it is hoped and assumed— are free from wide differences of ethical value. The definition of the disorder and the terms in which its remedy is sought are therefore at serious odds with one another.

Karl Menninger, on the other hand, defines mental health instead of mental illness by stating (1945, p. 2):

Let us define mental health as the adjustment of human beings to the world and to each other with a maximum of effectiveness and happiness. Not just efficiency or just contentment—or the grace of obeying the rules of the game cheerfully. It is all of these together. It is the ability to maintain an even temper, an alert intelligence, socially considerate behavior, and a happy disposition.

The difficulties inherent in reducing the philosophical concepts explicated in this definition to empirical referents—the end result of an operational definition—are readily apparent.

The concerns for the positive aspects of mental health are explored by Jahoda (1959) and by Parsons (1958). Jahoda develops six cardinal aspects of mental health in her book *Current Concepts of Positive Mental Health.* Of importance is the purposive effort to operationalize these concepts. Parsons deemphasizes deviancy and emphasizes the positive states of health. He points out that performance and behavior must be evaluated within the framework of the social structure. He makes a very important distinction between commitment and capacity by stating, "Finally, let me repeat that I am defining health as concerned with capacity, not with commitment to particular roles, tasks, norms or even values as such" (1958, p. 176).

The scientific usefulness and the definitional difficulty of good mental health, are recognized by Barton, who states that "The phenomenon of a superstate of good mental health, well beyond and above the mere absence of disabling illness, has yet to be scientifically demonstrated" (1959, p. 233).

Hoffman (1960) comes to grips with the multi-dimensional aspects of health by placing emphasis on the importance of the social environment and by taking into consideration, in the definition of health, the cultural context of values and, therefore, questioning the scientific value of the term. He is pessimistic about the possibility of any real scientific definition of the concept.

A significant number of the behavioral studies dealing with mental illness or mental disorders take diagnosis as given and then proceed to analyze the nature of the relationship between the diagnosis and the incidence, prevalence, and etiology of the particular disease. Subjects, therefore, are already diagnosed as mentally ill or suffering from a psychiatric disorder, a manic-depressive disorder, or schizophrenia.

The significance of these findings are, therefore, specifically related to the scientific accuracy of the diagnosis of mental illness or mental disorder. It is of significance that standard textbooks of psychiatry, as well as the first and second editions of the American Psychiatric Association's *Diagnostic and Statistical Manual of Mental Disorders,* do not give definitions of mental disorders. The definitional problem revolves around the fact that behavioral manifestations—and not pain, disability, or death—are the major diagnostic and definitional tools. Additional judgments have to be made concerning the undesirable nature of the disorder and the consequent nature of the diagnostic process. It is understandable, therefore, that no explicit definition of mental disorders is accepted universally by psychiatrists. Two models are usually used. One is to define a mental disorder normatively, taking into consideration the deviation from some norm. The other is to postulate a continuum from highly desirable (positive mental health) to highly undesirable (mental illness) and then make a determination of mental disorder to the highly undesirable end of the continuum. Both approaches are beset with possibilities of wide margins of error. The level of diagnostic agreement is usually high in limited cases, such as organic brain syndrome. Fair agreement is achieved in the diagnosis of psychosis and schizophrenia. The agreement is usually of a low level in the other cases and particularly in the diagnosis of psychoneuroses.

The diagnoses, definitions, and classifications become, therefore, increasingly difficult as the behavioral symptoms deviate from organic psychosis to psychoneurosis. Diagnosis or the lack of it becomes, as a consequence, progressively difficult and lacks consensus among experts.

Of particular significance to research on, and diagnosis and treatment of, mental illness is the process of labeling. Labeling is applied to many social problems, but it is in the area of mental illness that the implications are quite clear. Noteworthy in this effort is the attempt of Scheff (1963, 1966). He builds on the works of Lemert (1951), Erikson (1957), Goffman (1961, 1963), and Becker (1963). He attempts to show the applicability of the labeling theory of deviance to mental illness by developing a social systems model of mental disorder different from the traditional psychiatric disease model. Of significance is the impact of the label of mental illness on the reaction of people to those who are so defined. The implication is that the label itself determines how persons behave towards the labeled individual. In this context, Kirk states succinctly that ''The influence of a person's account of another person's misbehavior is thought to be particularly conditioned by the role and status of the labeler and his relationship to the person labeled'' (Kirk 1974, p. 10).

Jane Murphy (1976, p. 1019) applies the theory of labeling more specifically to mental illness by delineating the basic characteristics of the behavior patterns called mental illness from a labeling perspective. These characteristics are:

1. These behaviors represent deviations from what is believed to be normal in particular sociocultural groups.
2. The norms against which the deviations are identified are different in different groups.
3. Like other forms of deviation they elicit societal reactions which convey disapproval and stigmatization.
4. A label of mental illness applied to a person whose behavior is deviant tends to become fixed.
5. The person labeled as mentally ill is thereby encouraged to learn and accept a role identity which perpetuates the stigmatizing behavior pattern;
6. Individuals who are powerless in a social group are more vulnerable to this process than others are.
7. Because social agencies in modern industrial society contribute to the labeling process, they have the effect of creating problems for those they treat rather than easing problems.

David Rosenhahn adequately demonstrates the social aspects of the labeling process by referring to the experiences of eight sane subjects who were admitted to psychiatric hospitals and were diagnosed as schizophrenic and remained for an average of 19 days as patients until discharged as ''in remission.'' Rosenhahn argues that once the label of schizophrenic has been applied, ''the diagnosis affects the patient, family and relatives as a self-fulfilling prophecy. Eventually the patient himself accepts the diagnosis, with all of its surplus meanings and expectations, and behaves accordingly'' (Rosenhahn, 1973, p. 254).

Goffman attaches significance to the sociocultural aspects of mental illness by stating that ''the perception of losing one's mind is based on culturally derived and socially engrained stereotypes as to the significance of symptoms such as hearing voices, losing temporal and spatial orientation, and sensing that one is being followed'' (Goffman, 1961, p. 132).

Murphy (1976), however, substantiates the position that similar kinds of disturbed behavior are labeled abnormal in cultures other than that of the United States. This observation was based on mental health research conducted in a village of Yupik-speaking Eskimos on an island in the Bering Sea, among the Egba Yorubas, in Gambia, Sudan, and South Vietnam. Explicit labels for insanity were found to exist in these cultures. These labels refer to feelings, actions, and beliefs that are thought to emanate from the minds of an individual and to be essentially beyond the control of that person. The affected seeks aid from someone designated to give such relief. In these cultures the pattern consists of hallucinations, delusions, disorientations, and behavioral deviance which appear to indicate that the individual is "losing his or her mind" (p. 1027).

What compounds the picture, however, in the United States, is the stigma attached to the pattern, particularly as it applies to women and other minorities, particularly Blacks. For example, Helen Deutsch (1944), in accepting the stereotypes about women, takes the position that women are by nature passive-receptive and masochistic. From this kind of analysis, then, if a woman is competitive and aggressive, she is labeled as suffering from "penis envy," as neurotic and, therefore, abnormal, in spite of the fact that data appear to suggest the contrary; that in reality, women are less fragile psychologically and more able to cope than the stereotype above will lead one to expect (Bart, 1971).

In a similar vein, many behavioral scientists tend to overemphasize the psychopathology in minority groups (Sabshin et al., 1970) with a consequent deemphasis of their coping mechanisms and adaptability. In spite of the wide awareness of American life, there is a paucity of systematic, rigorous attempts to evaluate, with some degree of specificity, the precise impact of race on mental illness.

Stigmatized persons are considered deviant in a negative, pathological sense. The labels of mental illness and Blackness increase markedly the double-jeopardy dimensions of the stigma and the label. The values of the social structure attach significance to power, vigor, strength, success, and good health, and deemphasize and denigrate the weak, the powerless, the failure, and the sick. The sick person, as a consequence, is considered stigmatized, particularly when diagnosed as mentally ill. Stigma, according to Goffman, spoils normal identity and makes the development of positive self-concept or ego-identity difficult (Goffman, 1963). The double jeopardy stigma of mental illness and race markedly increases the difficulty of operationally defining mental illness and disorders and will continue to retard efforts to seek meaningful breakthroughs in the diagnosis and treatment of Black mental illness.

One of the basic assumptions which is made in research on Black mental health is that race and racism are crucial variables which influence the etiology, the prevalence, and the incidence of mental illness as it does the diagnosis and treatment plans of patients. Very few attempts have been made, however, in research to establish the kinds of controls which will delineate the precise relationships and impact which race and racism might have on mental illness. One of the reasons accountable for this failure is the absence and relative non-existence, of operational definitions of racism.

Attempts were made in a recent book on *Racism and Mental Health* (Willie, Kramer, and Brown, 1973) to define racism. These definitions, however, were not operational. On the contrary, each definition remained at a fairly high level of abstraction with virtually no empirical referents and, therefore, was not really testable. For example, Charles Pinderhughes (1973), in his chapter on "Racism and Psychotherapy," states that "The essence of racism lies in a relatively constant pattern of prejudice and discrimination between one party who is idealized and favored and another who is devalued and and exploited in a common relationship" (p. 61).

Pinderhughes develops the relationship between racism, mental illness, and psychotherapy by stating that:

> Black people in our racist society have had more opportunity than Whites to have early experiences of loss, pain and deprivation which can imprint tragedy-seeking scripts in their personalities. Moreover, our racist society makes psychotherapy far less accessible to the Black person who needs it (p. 66).

Commenting on the pathological conditions of Black communities, Pinderhughes states that:

> The serious pathogenic circumstances in predominantly Black communities contribute to three major mental health problems: usually large numbers of people need psychiatric treatment, serious resistances to treatment are frequently encountered, and patients must return to the same pathogenic circumstances which spawned their pathology (p. 67).

As a member of a study group of Black psychiatrists, Pinderhughes collaborated with them in defining white racism as a "paranoia in which dominant Whites and oppressed Blacks both believe in White superiority and Black inferiority in a folie á deux" (p. 85).

Claudewell Thomas and James Comer, in describing the adaptive strengths of Blacks and the double-jeopardy bind of the Black child, define racism as "the belief that race, or identifiable physical

characteristics related thereto, is the primary determinant of human
behavior and sets the limits for human accomplishment'' (p. 167).
They state further that ''Racism or ethnic prejudice, while it is often
expressed individually, is basically an intergroup phenomenon, the
malignant manifestations of which accrue to individuals only in the
context of their membership in groups'' (p. 167). They establish a
relationship between racism and mental illness by stating that:

> Because of racism, a disproportionate number of Blacks cannot enjoy
> the desirable quality of mental health to which they are entitled. Indeed,
> White racism—because it is the block between individual aspiration and
> opportunity—has created a great deal of mental anguish, has com-
> plicated mental illness, and stands as a formidable obstacle to the
> development of all kinds of mental health services (p. 168).

It is of significance that Thomas and Comer fail to distinguish between
racism and mental illness, and oppression and mental illness. A sound
research methodology must make measurable distinctions between the
two.

Thomas Pettigrew does no better than the others in operationally
defining racism by defining institutional racism as ''that complex of
institutional arrangements that restrict the life choices of Black
Americans in comparison to those of White Americans'' (p. 274). This
definition encompasses too much to be operationally useful.

Kramer, Rosen, and Willis, in a kind of summary approach to the
research relationships between racism and mental illness, conclude that
''There is much room for sound research in this area.'' They state that:

> All of this emphasizes the need for an intensive research effort to
> acquire facts needed to assess the extent of mental disorders among Blacks
> and other minority groups, to test hypotheses concerning the role of
> genetic and social factors in the etiology of mental disorders and the
> manner in which racism affects the incidence of such disorders and their
> duration, and to establish base lines against which to measure changes
> both in the extent to which racist attitudes and practices exist in different
> populations and in their effects on the persons toward whom these at-
> titudes are directed (p. 440).

Attempts by most of the scholars working in the field to establish
meaningful relationships between racism and mental illness fail to
throw significant light on the operational definitions of mental illness
and racism.

The Center for Minority Group Mental Health Programs of the

National Institute of Mental Health, in its attempt to encourage research and professional development on racism and mental illness, outlines three goals:

1. Delineation and analysis of the dynamic aspects of institutional racism at the operational level in mental health and human services agencies with a goal of developing specific and valid intervention methodologies. These guidelines take the view that racism is "any attitude, action, or institutional structure which subordinates a person or group because of his or her color." This is a difficult definition to operationalize.

2. Examination of the effect of White racism upon the majority population with an emphasis on identifying the deleterious psychosocial consequences.

3. Development of a pool of skilled professionals available to plan, implement and research programs designed to eliminate racism within a variety of institutional settings.

One of the first tasks of these professionals should be to define these important concepts operationally in such a way that they will be reduced to lower levels of abstractions and will have definite empirical referents. This has not yet been accomplished, but the research need is still great.

The difficulties involved in dealing with methodological issues in research addressing the area of mental illness are considerable. The rate of the systematic accumulation of a body of knowledge, which will narrow the margin of error in diagnosis and facilitate effective treatment, will, as a consequence, be impeded until these methodological problems are solved. It is difficult, therefore, to construct instruments which will accurately measure the incidence and prevalence of mental illness and increase the effectiveness of screening, particularly as these apply to Blacks.

As a consequence, serious questions must be raised about reliability and validity. It is within this framework that specific emphasis must be placed on the different dimensions of validity—content, concurrent and predictive.

In addition to the considerations already alluded to, it is equally important to take into specific account the psychosocial and sociocultural characteristics of the population to whom these instruments will be applied. How will variables such as sex, age, rural-urban dichotomy, and socioeconomic status affect and influence the construction of these measurement instruments? How specifically important are the variables of race and ethnicity? What specific changes must be made in the construction and implementation of these instruments in order to meet the special needs of specific racial and ethnic groups? If there are changes in the content and contextual aspects of these instruments, to what extent will meaningful comparisons between and among different racial and ethnic groups be impaired?

The assumptions that the researcher makes about Blacks and about Black mental health research are, therefore, of crucial importance in influencing all of the research steps, including the findings. A researcher cannot minimize the important role that assumptions play. What has the researcher or the behavioral scientist or the mental health professional taken for granted concerning Blacks and their mental health? What must the reader of the research product, the analyst, and the consumer accept as reasonable? Methodologically, the researcher's values and interests will affect the selection of the research problem area, the specific definition used, and the analysis of the problem. Assumptions made will also, by definition, influence the specific formulation of the hypotheses, the kinds of questions for which answers will be sought, and the determination of those variables which are dependent and those which are independent.

It must be emphasized that a diagnosis that one is suffering from a particular type of mental illness is, in methodological and operational terms, a hypothesis, and the treatment program will be contingent on the testability of this hypothesis. Effective rehabilitation, in this context, means that the hypothesis has been accepted. The nature of the assumptions made in a study or in a treatment program or plan affects and influences all of the research steps and procedures including the analysis and interpretation of the data and their overall functional value. There is great danger, then, when these assumptions are not made explicit or when the researcher or the analyst is not consciously aware of these assumptions.

Assumptions about the Black family by many behavioral scientists and professionals in the field of mental health have also affected and influenced the diagnosis, treatment plans, and rehabilitation of Blacks who have been classified as mentally ill. These assumptions have to be examined and made explicit. The basic assumption made about the Black family is that it is pathological. The conceptual and/or operational model used as a reference is the typical white family. The ethnocentric assumption is made, therefore, that the patriarchal type of family is typically and traditionally American and functionally preferred. As a consequence, the matriarchal family, the assumed characteristic of the Black family, is deemed non-functional and by definition pathological.

Indices of the Black family's pathology are designated as high rates of mental disorders, divorce, desertion, and separation. This categorical approach to the Black family is non-functional and fails to explain the psycho- and socio-dynamics of social interaction among Black family members. It is erroneous to refer to the American family on the one hand and the Black family on the other hand as monolithic. On the contrary, one sees different combinations and permutations of different types of families occupying different positions on a continuum running from authoritarianism of either the patriarchal or matriarchal brand at one end of the continuum to equalitarianism at the other end. One would therefore expect to find different types of families, different family rituals, different forms of marriages, childbearing, and socialization experiences to the extent to which Black families are found in rural and urban regions, North and South, with different socio-economic backgrounds and different educational experiences. Systems analyses are certainly in order to determine the different combinations of these variables which are seemingly conducive to a prevalence of mental disorders. These will certainly be useful indicators to the mental health practitioners as they attempt to diagnose and treat. For example, it may not be the function of the rate of vertical mobility that can be consistently correlated with the probability of mental illness. The critical factor might very well be the direction of the mobility, thereby suggesting that mentally ill persons tend to be more downwardly than upwardly mobile.

Broad judgments are made that there is an inverse relationship between socioeconomic status and the rate of mental disorders. Efforts are made, therefore, to concentrate on the prevalence of mental disorders among low-income Blacks as if they are monolithic. Among low-income Blacks, there are differentials in the rate of mental illness, just as there are fine gradations of stratification in the low-income category. There are, consequently, possibilities of upward and downward mobility in this segment of the population with differential consequences and probabilities of mental illness. Some concern can, therefore, be expressed for methodologically determining the particular social stratum among low-income Blacks which is most conducive to a high prevalence of mental illness.

Additional observations are made concerning the relationship between "intact" stable families and the low rate of emotional disturbances and mental disorders, and the high rate of such disorders among "broken" families. In these approaches, the traditional definitions of marriage and the family are usually employed. Thus significant light cannot be thrown on the more realistic dimensions of mental illness without a careful delineation of the role of the family. Behavioral scientists cannot make meaningful contributions to an understanding of the dynamics of human behavior if they continue to use the layman's terms and concepts with their emotional undertones. Concepts such as illegitimacy should be ignored operationally. Marriage and the family should be defined in functional and operational terms and not in terms of a culturally selected norm. Since marital status and family stability are increasingly considered important factors related to mental illness, it is important to strive for conceptual clarity.

Behavioral scientists are prone to define marriage or family in terms of its conformity to white, middle-class norms and not in relationship to whether it meets sociological and anthropological criteria. If a heterosexual relationship is not based upon clearly and officially defined marital rituals, behavioral scientists are reluctant to define the phenomenon as a marital or familial relationship. Rigorous observations of the behavior of low-income Black persons have pointed up many instances of enduring, mutually satisfying heterosexual relationships. In this kind of relationship, both persons have accepted childbearing, childrearing, and socialization responsibilities. The designation "incomplete family" (i.e., one headed by a female) is given because of the supposed failure of a unit to meet certain preconceived marital standards. Precise measurements of the nature and content of the social-interactive patterns of behavior will be extremely useful as determinants of mental status.

Increasingly, behavioral scientists, and particularly psychiatrists are finding it necessary and appropriate to involve the whole family in therapeutic relationships. Therefore, failure to take into consideration the different types of families in terms of role and function in the Black community would be a methodological limitation and would seemingly affect the effectiveness of Black family therapy.

There are significant methodological implications to be derived from a laboratory demonstration by a group of mental health professionals and workers. Such findings are given in a book entitled *Black Ghetto Family in Therapy: A Laboratory Experience,* by Sager, Brayboy, and

Waxenberg (1970). Certain essential questions were raised and answers sought. Among these were the following: Can a white therapist treat a Black patient or a Black family? Or, even more functionally, how can a White therapist most effectively treat a Black family and how can he be of greatest service to its members? The significance of this prospect evolved from the recognition that "we are failing to reach the urban Black millions, failing to develop workable methods for treatment and prevention" (Sager, Brayboy, and Waxenberg, 1970). More specifically, the authors were concerned with "the increasing difficulties middle-class white therapists experience in engaging Black 'multi problem' families in traditional psychotherapy" (p. 3). The findings of this laboratory experiment tended to substantiate the thrust of this study about mental health measurement problems of Black and other minority groups. Some of these findings are discussed below.

The need was underscored for the therapist, particularly the white therapist, to examine the assumptions made about the behavior of Blacks and other minority groups. According to the authors, "it is not uncommon for White middle-class professionals to approach the ghetto patient with an armload of stereotypes and myths and an outlook clouded by a long-standing pejorative view of lower-class culture" (p. 233). Many studies have examined this question with similar results (Kennedy, 1952; Waite, 1968; St. Clair, 1957).

Low-income Blacks place priority on survival and subsistence. They come or are brought, in to treatment as a last resort. Their needs have to be met immediately. Psychotherapy can only be effective after these immediate and urgent needs are met. The medical model of treatment is, therefore, not as applicable to this situation. In this case, what is expected of the professional is an accurate diagnosis and, as a consequence, a prescribed treatment program. The importance of this has been additionally highlighted by Bruce P. Dohrenwend, who states very specifically and meaningfully that "Many of the stress situations of everyday life, perhaps especially those associated with low-status positions of groups such as Negroes and Puerto Ricans, are themselves enduring, e.g., racial discrimination" (1967, p. 630).

"Spontaneous therapy," in cases of severe stress, is absolutely necessary. This necessitates acquiring the skills for the establishment of immediate rapport. It is important to know the language of low-income Blacks and to have a deep appreciation for the nuances of the language through a knowledge and awareness of the life styles of the group. J. D.

Frank has attached significance to this phenomenon when he discussed the difficulties of white therapists in establishing rapport with Black patients (1947). St. Clair, in his study, reported similar difficulties (1951).

The special resistance which Blacks bring to the therapeutic setting must be recognized. Sager, Brayboy, and Waxenberg state that "It can be disastrous for the therapist either to deny the suspicion and hostility of the Black patient or to feel guilty about the fact that these sentiments exist (1970, p. 224). More specifically, as so many white therapists are prone to do, the raising of the racial issue by Blacks cannot always be interpreted as resistance.

As previously indicated, external stressors are important factors in determining the nature and existence of emotional problems and disorders. Attempts must be made by the therapists to determine when coping mechanisms are in order or when it is necessary to initiate relevant social changes. The authors state that "Environmental factors are often more compelling behavioral determinants than are intrapsychic. If change is to occur, intervention should be aimed at stresses deriving from the patient's social conditions as well as at manifestations of intrapsychic pathology" (Sager, Brayboy, and Waxenberg, 1970, p. 230).

Since group and psychotherapy are so dependent on language as the basic tool of communication, it is absolutely necessary for mental health professionals to discard the stereotype about the limitations of the language of Blacks and consider the strong possibility that there is a verbal language which is not fully understood. Effective treatment must be predicated upon the skill and the accuracy with which this particular language is learned to allow for meaningful communication and symbolic interaction.

The Black vernacular vocabulary provides valuable insights into Black life styles and the history of some of the important dimensions of the Black experience. Anyone, therefore, claiming to know something of this experience and to relate at a fairly empathetic level with predominantly low-income Blacks, must be able to attach connotative and denotative significance to this language or argot. The instruments constructed must reflect this knowledge. The nature of the interpersonal relationship must be guided by it. This is very difficult for white behavioral scientists. According to Edith Folb, "Black vernacular vocabulary is clearly not intended for white ears" (1973, p. 19). It is considered a language of survival which all oppressed groups have had to develop. As a consequence, great value is attached to verbal dexterity in the ghetto—the ability to "rap." Because the vocabulary is a language of the street, it is used predominantly by the Black male.

Methodologies must be developed, therefore, to make content analyses of this language with a view to delineating its relationship to, and influence on, mental disorders, emotional content, and the ego-identity and self-concept of Black persons in the ghetto.

Bruce and Barbara Dohrenwend (1965, 1975) throw further light on the significant issues related to research diagnosis and treatment of mental disorders. They are cognizant of the fact that most of the research cases of mental disorders are not cases that are operationally defined as mentally ill, but rather ones that have already been diagnosed as mentally ill and are in treatment. This points up, according to the authors:

> The difficulty of interpreting the results of studies in which the fact of being in treatment constitutes the sole definition of disorder. Treatment rates vary, for example, with the availability of treatment facilities, and with public attitudes toward their use. Either could be responsible for spurious relations between sociocultural factors and rates of illness measured by number of cases in treatment.

In too many instances, clinical judgment is the basic tool used in the determination of the cases of mental disorder. It is difficult, therefore, and well nigh impossible to replicate with any degree of exactitude this dimension of the methodology, particularly in view of the fact that the diagnostic criteria are not usually described in any great detail. Nevertheless, the validity of the diagnostic process is hardly ever questioned. It is within this context that the validity of diagnostic instruments used in the classic community studies of mental health— the Midtown (Srole et al., 1962) and the Sterling County (A. H. Leighton et al., 1963)—can be assessed and evaluated.

In the Midtown study, the measurement of mental disorder considered the rating of the psychiatrists on a scale which ranged from "well" to five degrees of severity of disorder: mild, moderate, marked, severe, incapacitated. It is quite evident that the rating scale was skewed in favor of disorder. In the Sterling County study, the descriptions in the *1952 Diagnostic and Statistical Manual* of the American Psychiatric Association were used as the basic criteria for determining mental disorders, rather than using actual patients as the comparison norm.

According to the Dohrenwends (1965), "There is, then, much to criticize and improve upon in these past attempts to investigate the criterion-oriented validity of both objective and judgmental measures of untreated disorder . . . Foremost is the present fact that there are no generally agreed upon criteria of psychological health or disorder" (p. 593).

The Dohrenwends, then, attempt to compare the findings of a number of studies on mental disorders in terms of a pattern of relationships between the four sociocultural variables of age, sex, race, and socioeconomic status and rates of "judged psychopathology" (p. 594). They concluded that (1) there is no consistent pattern for the age at which maximum rates of mental disorders were found; and (2) studies were almost evenly divided between those reporting higher rates of functional psychoses, particularly schizophrenia, for women, and those reporting higher rates for men. Most of the studies, however, reported a higher rate of manic-depressive psychosis among women. Rates of neurosis are generally higher for women as contrasted with rates of personality disorder, which were found to be higher among men. It is of significance, therefore, that 14 of the 18 studies, with data on the relationship between social class and mental illness, found the highest rate of judged psychopathology in the lowest socioeconomic stratum. This relationship is consistent for schizophrenia and personality disorder but not for manic-depressive psychosis and neurosis.

Interesting attempts are made to interpret, not analyze, these findings by placing them in one of two theoretical frames of reference. One is social causation, meaning that it is the low status itself which is accountable for the disorder. The other is social selection indicating that persons with mental disorders find themselves in, or drift to, a low social status.

The latter position is comparable to, and compatible with, the notion that genetic factors are crucially important in the etiology of mental disorders. This position is also comparable to that of Jensen and Shockley concerning intelligence and genetic factors. It is, therefore, of contemporary interest and significance that the social selection theory of mental disorders is gaining some degree of prominence in spite of the glaring absence of rigorous research specifically to test this hypothesis.

Langer, however, takes the position that:

> It is the adult life conditions in particular that stimulate the develop-
> ment of high rates of psychosis in the lower class; for the childhood

conditions at least as reported by our respondents do not vary substantially between the classes.

This is a strong advocacy position for the personality defect of adult, low-income persons who are judged to be mentally disordered. The Dohrenwends attempt to be eclectic by taking the psychological, social, and environmental factors into consideration and positing that the pathological symptoms "represent transient responses by normal personalities to objective, stress-producing events, i.e., stressors . . . in the immediate environment" (1961, p. 598).

According to the Dohrenwends, there are three grounds accounting for the high level of symptomatology in the lowest socio-economic stratum. These grounds include (p. 599):

> First, evidence suggesting that stressors for which the individual cannot be held responsible are relatively pervasive in the lower class environment; second, observations that normal individuals exposed to stressors respond with symptoms which would ordinarily be classified as indicative of psychopathology; third, evidence of spontaneous recovery from these symptoms on removal of the stressors.

If, therefore, normal persons, when responding to stressful situations, show symptoms which might be classified as psychological disorder, then when is a classification of psychological disorder appropriate? The Dohrenwends deal with this by stating that:

> Stressor-induced symptomatic responses, judged by the individual and/or by other social agents to be harmful to the individual and/or to others with whom he stands in social relationship, indicate psychological disorder if the symptoms continue (1) after the stressor ceases to impinge on the individual, and (2) despite sanctions directed at the individual by social agents who judge the response maladaptive.

> This definition articulates within a single conceptual framework evidence concerning transient symptomatic responses to situational stressors with evidence from both clinic and laboratory which points to intractability to control by reward or punishment as the critical characteristic of symptoms indicative of psychological disorder (p. 602).

In support of the above proposition, the Dohrenwends suggest that the following be tested:

1. That a large portion of the symptomatology reported in field studies is induced by stressors in the contemporary situation.
2. That a large portion of such stressor-induced symptomatology is transient rather than persistent.

3. That transience of symptomatology varies directly with the extent to which it is defined as maladaptive.

4. That the extent to which such symptomatology is defined as maladaptive varies inversely with social class.

5. That the incidence of stressors in the contemporary situation varies inversely with social class (p. 603)

Such a research approach to Black mental health will move this research area away from the emotionally-laden stance now dominant, heighten the objectivity, and be potentially more productive in providing significant breakthroughs in this important area.

It is important, therefore, to explore further the role of stressful situations on mental disorders and psychopathology with some emphasis on the life events or combinations of life events. Dohrenwend (1975) raises a fundamental question in this regard when he asks: thusly: "What kinds of life events, in what combinations, over what periods of time, and under what circumstances are causally implicated in various types of psychiatric disorder?" (p. 384).

T. H. Holmes and R. H. Rahe (1967) were pioneers in measuring the relationship between life events and adaptive changes by devising a social readjustment scale with the basic assumption that life events, whether good or bad, demand adaptive changes. The scale consists of 43 life events with scores weighted in terms of the amount of readjustment which the life event demanded. The stress of adjusting to change then varied from a weight of 100, given to a death of a spouse, to 11, for minor violations of the law. These researchers found that an accumulation of 200 or more life change units in a single year led to an increased incidence of such diseases as peptic ulcer, infection, myocardial infarction, and a variety of psychiatric disorders.

Holmes and Rahe, in weighting the series of life events in the construction of the Social Readjustment Rating Scale (SRRS), instructed the judges as follows (1967, p. 213):

> You are asked to rate a series of life events as to their relative degrees of necessary readjustment. In scoring, use all of your experience in arriving at your answer. This means personal experience where it applies as well as what you have learned to be the case for others.

Despite the obvious difficulty in determining whether the life event was the cause, the symptom, or the consequence of illness and other methodological problems, recent research efforts by Hudgens (1974),

Paykel (1974), and Brown and Birley (1968) have indicated that various types of psychiatric disorder may indeed follow life events, including acute episodes of schizophrenia, suicide attempts, depression, and neurosis. Markush and Favero (1974) found a relationship between life events and mild symptoms of depression. Research efforts are being made to delineate the real differences among events, contrasting coping mechanisms among individuals and among groups—racial, ethnic, and socio-economic—that will affect the precise impact of the events and the coping mechanisms. When research is able to determine the precise effect which the racial variable has in determining the meaning and significance of a life event and therefore its stressful impact, a major breakthrough will be made on the understanding of Black mental health. The Langley Porter Neuro-Psychiatric Institute of the University of California in San Francisco is making great strides in this direction.

Rosenberg and Dohrenwend (1975) asked 172 students at the City College of New York to give readjustment ratings for 10 life events consisting of both desirable and undesirable events. These judges were 53 percent male and 72 percent non-Hispanic white with the remainder divided approximately equally among Asian, Black, and Hispanic ethnic groups. The results indicated that there were significant differences in the ratings of several events from judges from non-Hispanic white ethnic groups and those from Black, Asian, or Hispanic groups. It is clear that life events have different meanings for different racial and ethnic groups and, therefore, different ratings. Further research should delineate these differences with greater specificity particularly as these concern Blacks, and with specific indicators of how different definitions of life events, with different stressful ratings, might lead to serious illness, including mental illness.

This is logical in view of the basic assumption on which the Social Readjustment Rating Scale of Holmes and Rahe is based, namely, that a change in the normal life pattern of an individual makes it necessary for him or her to make a series of adjustments which are stressful in varying degrees. The accumulation of these stressful events will bring on an illness. The crucial concern is not the type of change but how disruptive the change is. The methodological need, therefore, is to measure the degree of disruption of the life patterns experienced by individuals. Holmes and Rahe (1967) developed indicators of the relative disruptive power of various life events and then computed the "readjustment demand scores" for individuals by summing the weighted scores of the life events experienced by the individual over a given time frame. The basic thrust is always on the perceived stressfulness of the life events.

Among the limitations of the SRRS of Holmes and Rahe is the fact that the list of stressful life events may not be complete enough to represent the broad spectrum of life events that might bring on illness. It is also believed that there is a differential impact of negative, compared to positive, life events. The Holmes and Rahe instrument does not distinguish between these two. As previously indicated, specific methodological attempts will have to be made to determine whether persons from different racial and ethnic groups perceive the seriousness of these life events differently. If they do, then different weights or scores will have to be assessed. Hough and co-workers (1976), found that Blacks, Mexican Americans, and Hawaiians generated rankings that did not tend to correlate highly with the Caucasian ranking, indicating that significant racial and ethnic differences exist in perceiving seriousness of life events.

In a study on "Life Events and Mental Status," Myers and co-workers adequately demonstrated a clear relationship between changes in the occurrence of life events in a two-year time frame and changes in psychiatric symptomatology. An increase in life events was associated with a worsening of the psychiatric symptoms. On the other hand, a decrease in life events was associated with an improvement in the psychiatric disorder. This study emphasizes the pervasive influence of external social forces and/or situations. According to the authors, the data throw light on "the tenuous balance between the individual's psychic economy and the social milieu within which he is forced to adapt." They further state (pp. 403–404):

> They demonstrate the importance of social and interpersonal forces frequently external to the individual in influencing psychological status. The sheer quantity of events alone seems to have a striking effect upon one's capacity to maintain a state of mental health.

Of significance is the report of Myers and co-workers (1975) on "Life Events, Social Integration and Psychiatric Symptomatology." In this report the authors examine the "relationships between life events, social integration and psychiatric symptoms in a community sample of 720 adults in New Haven, Connecticut" (p. 421).

The basic assumption of this study is that people who are integrated into the social system of the community are better able to cope with the traumatic impact of life crises than those who are not. The authors appropriately state (pp. 421–422):

> The level of social integration is associated with the relationship between life events and psychiatric symptomatology and changes in that relationship over two years. More specifically (1) among those reporting many events and few symptoms, the level of social integration is higher than among persons reporting few events, but many symptoms, and (2) among those reporting a net increase in events but a decrease in symptoms, the level of social integration is higher than among persons reporting a decrease in events but an increase in symptoms.

This frame of reference is very relevant to an understanding of the mental health of Blacks. It indicates that life events take place in a certain ecological system and that the cohesiveness of that system will influence coping mechanisms. There is, therefore, a complementarity between the development and organization of the person and that of the community. Erikson demonstrates full awareness of this relationship when he states that: "A mature psycho-social identity pre-supposes a community of people whose traditional values become significant to the growing person even as his growth and his gifts assume relevance for them" (1965, p. 231).

It is hypothesized, therefore, that if a Black community has been developed in keeping with the principles of community organization with a concomitant sense of "peoplehood" and feelings of belonging, plus the internalization of positive Black values, the coping mechanisms of the people there will be enhanced and the incidence and prevalence of mental disorders will be low. Efficient methods of diagnosis, treatment, and rehabilitation of the mentally ill must take into consideration and be able to measure, as accurately as possible, the degree of integration of the community from which the mentally ill person has come and to which he will be sent in the rehabilitative process.

As implied, great importance has been attached to the principles of community organization and community development. They throw some light on the incidence and prevalence of mental disorders and suggest conditions conducive to their onset and development. Definitions are, therefore, in order.

A community is herein defined as an ecological area whose boundaries can be demarcated and where the physical and psychosocial characteristics of the people make it distinctive in such a way that it can be differentiated from other communities. The members of a community have developed feelings of consensus and of *esprit de corps*. The implication here is that the members of a community share a common heritage and are aware of the importance and significance of this heritage to the continued survival of the community and the group. The continued growth and development of the community do not, by any means, rule out the possibility of conflict and change which are thought to be somewhat indispensable. The important point here is that conflict must be of a dialectical nature and the change must be orderly and somewhat purposive.

One of the fundamental aspects of community organization is the nature of the relationship between the basic social institutions and their social agencies. The ideal is that the basic social institutions, such as the family, religious, political, and economic organizations, are related to, and interrelated with, each other in such a way as to constitute a characteristic pattern. Basic social values of the community must permeate, be supportive of, and not be in conflict with, these social institutions.

Community development within this context is viewed as the mechanism for the achievement of community organization. The essence of this will revolve around social institutions and social values related and interrelated in such a manner that they are congruent, reinforcing, and supportive. It also implies a methodology whereby the people, through the different social institutions, must develop some consensual awareness of their needs and problems, see how these problems relate to each other and to the community, establish priorities, and accept basic responsibility through the principle of self-help for the solution and/or amelioration of these problems.

The intricate, *Gestalen*-like relationships and interrelationships of social institutions must be recognized. Community organization must, therefore, take into consideration the mechanism through which the people of the community, as they interact with each other in the different social institutions and agencies, develop a meaningful consensus, a group solidarity, peoplehood, and group cohesiveness.

Community control, where persons have a certain command over their resources; where they participate in the major decision-making process affecting their lives; where there is built-in accountability in every social institution and social agency, is a crucial element in this realization.

It is felt that a community which is organized, as described above, has a prevalence of persons who are generally satisfied with the community and possesses the following: racial pride and pride in "Blackness," a prevalence of feelings of positive identity and confidence in one's ability to establish command over resources and to determine one's destiny, and a belief in the importance of cooperation and mutual aid.

An organized community might very well be one in which there are relative absences of the kinds of stresses which might make it difficult for individuals who reside therein to cope adequately with them. If an ecological area is seemingly conducive to a prevalence of stresses, it might be a tip-off about its lack of integration and organization, and an indicator that a frequency of psychological and emotional disorders might be one of the resultants. Precise establishments of research benchmarks to measure community organization and social change, and carefully delineated social indicators to assess the degrees of satisfaction which the community provides, might be very important research dimensions in coming to grips with the problems posed by mental illness and psychiatric disorders.

As already indicated, recent studies have shown that behavioral adaptations to life events have been associated with stress. This, in turn, has been contributory to the onset of physical and/or mental illness. Some attention has been given to external factors, such as death of a spouse or loss of a job, which might be precipitants. Additional attempts have been made to take into consideration those configurational aspects of the community structure which might be conducive to stress.

M. Harvey Brenner (1973) addresses himself to "stressful precipitants within the social or physical environment which trigger maladaptive responses, understood as mental illness, at a temporal point that is proximal to the occurrence of the stressful event" (p. 1).

Taking as his cue the generalized finding that there is an inverse relationship between the rate or intensity of stress and socioeconomic status, Brenner states that "Increases and decreases in the incidence and prevalence of disease [are] related to some change in the ecology of the susceptible organism, i.e., alteration in the physical or social environment" (p. 3). Brenner sees the economic situation as a crucial index and, as a consequence, examined the research hypothesis that "A significant relationship exists between economic conditions and admissions to mental hospitals" (p. 7). He sees unemployment and not personal income as the primary indicator of fluctuations in the national economic welfare. It is of significance that unemployment which presupposes loss of income can be extremely critical during inflationary time periods. Thus employment may be regarded as a stress-producing condition, particularly when, due to relative deprivation, a substantial proportion of the population is living in visible affluence.

These findings, although not specifically explicated by Brenner, are particularly applicable to an understanding of the mental health of Blacks, among whom the unemployment rate is high generally, but reaches critical proportions when there is a downturn in the economy.

It is quite evident from all of the above that Black mental health research calls for different methodological approaches, for systems analysis, and for holistic approaches which will come to grips with and "tease-out" the precise impact of racism, oppression, socioeconomic status, nature of community organization, stress-producing life events relevant to Blacks, and other sociocultural and psychosocial factors which might contribute to the social disability of Blacks.

It is of importance, therefore, within this context to obtain a reading on the kinds of research which have been, and are being, conducted on Black mental health. Specific emphasis will herein be placed on the Black mental health research efforts which have been and are being generated in the National Institute of Mental Health and more specifically in the Center for Minority Group Mental Health Programs, which was instituted primarily to meet the specialized research and training needs of minority groups in the United States.

The Center for Minority Group Mental Health Programs was officially established on November 19, 1970, to serve as a "focal point for all activities, including programs of research and training, within the Institute, which bear directly on meeting the mental health needs of minority groups."

Prior to the establishment of the Center, more than half of the research conducted by, and under the auspices of, the National Institute of Mental Health (NIMH) employed the "deficit" or "pathological" model with the administration of assessment and measurement instruments which had not been validated on minority groups. This limitation negatively affected both diagnosis and treatment of minority groups. Priority was given by the Center to the following areas:

1. The stimulation and support of research and training designed to increase knowledge of minority group life styles, value systems— particularly mental health problems associated with these life styles—the relationship between minority-major groups, provision

of technical assistance to minority groups and communities, and a greater understanding of the evolution of adaptational or survival behavior of minority groups.

2. The stimulation and support of programs which are directed at increasing the number and improving the competencies of minority group members engaged in mental health research and training.

3. The training of minority group members for a variety of professional careers in mental health.

On December 10–11, 1971, an interdisciplinary group of Black mental health professionals and paraprofessionals convened at Meharry Medical College in Nashville, Tennessee, to assess and make recommendations with respect to goals and strategies for the operation and thrust of the Center for Minority Group Mental Health Programs in relationship to the mental health of Blacks. The following broad questions were addressed:

1. What is Black mental health?

2. What are the manpower requirements to achieve and maintain Black mental health?

3. What essential research is needed for the positive advancement of Black mental health from the present to the year 1980?

The overall conclusion from this conference was that there was a need to seek out the strengths of Blacks—the positive dimensions of Black behavior. The critical question, then, that must be asked of any training or research program, is whether the results can be used in meaninfgul social interventions to alleviate the conditions and serve the needs, particularly the mental health needs, of Black people.

With respect to research on Black mental health, the following recommendations and conclusions were derived from the conference:

1. There was agreement that much of the research on Black mental health had been conducted by white, middle-class behavioral scientists with their normative biases. As a consequence, there was a failure to take cognizance of the interrelated factors that were conducive to racism and, therefore, to Black mental health.

2. The conference recommended that a section be established within the Center to assess past research, to monitor ongoing research and

to place special emphasis on the functional utilization of research results relating to Black mental health.

3. An additional recommendation was made that a program of intramural research be set up as part of the Center operation to attract specialized investigators to conduct research on problems relating to Black mental health.

4. The conference further recommended that funding support by the Minority Group Mental Health Center be awarded for the setting up of interdisciplinary research and demonstration centers. These centers were to spearhead research on the problems of Black mental health. They were to be staffed with Black research scholars with methodological expertise to address the special problems of research on Black mental health.

5. A recommendation was also made that the Center for Minority Group Mental Health make the necessary provisions for the adequate publication and dissemination of the research findings related to Black mental health.

6. The Minority Group Center was charged with the responsibility for establishing a set of guidelines for research in the Black community. The hope was that these guidelines will serve as a model for incorporation into all research-oriented programs of the National Institute of Mental Health.

7. The Minority Group Center was advised to hold a series of meetings throughout the United States for purposes of discussing grantsmanship.

Some research areas relevant to an understanding of Black mental health were suggested. Among these were:

1. Child rearing practices in Black families.

2. Creativity in Black children.

3. Winners and losers (using a Black mental health perspective). How are adjusted Blacks differentiated from unadjusted Blacks?

4. The theory of dual economy (as related to the high degree of instability created by the system of public education).

5. The fantasy life of Black children.

6. Race and institutional racism as variables in research.

7. A new social psychology of adaptation of Blacks to urban settings.

8. School system and teacher behavior as conditioners of the affective and cognitive development of Black children.

9. Special populations (e.g., the aged, prisoners, hustlers, middle age Blacks, Black male/female interaction roles, the Black middle class, and Black leadership).

The Center for Minority Group Mental Health Programs operated with a budget of approximately $2,745,000 during fiscal year 1972—its first full year of operation. It is estimated that by the end of fiscal year 1976, it would have expended approximately $25,889,000. Of this amount, approximately $14,445,000 will be allocated for research, and $10,230,000 for training. These amounts were to meet the research and training needs of the major minority groups—Blacks, Native Americans, Spanish-speaking Americans, and Asiatic Americans— accomplished primarily by the funding of research and training proposals to be submitted and screened by the review committee set up for each minority group.

In addition, by the end of fiscal year 1975, five research and demonstration centers were established. Each center was to be organized by and focused on, a single minority group and was based within a university and/or community setting located in an area where there was a high concentration of the target population. Seed money of $200,000 for each year of the five-year grant period from the National Institute of Mental Health was used to establish these centers. These centers were expected to undertake basic and applied research related to the mental health needs of the specific minority group population. Additional funding was to be sought from public and private institutions for the expansion of the program of each center. The centers were also expected to provide unique kinds of basic data, technical assistance, and consultation to the programs of community mental health centers as well as to alcoholism, drug abuse, and other federal, state, and local human service programs. Two of these five centers were set up to serve the needs of the Black community. They are:

1. Mental Health Research and Development Center
   Institute of Urban Affairs and Research
   Howard University, Washington, D.C.

2. Fanon Mental Health Research and Development Center
   Department of Psychiatry
   Drew Postgraduate Medical School
   Los Angeles, California

The other Research and Development Centers for minorities are:

1. White Cloud Center for Native Americans
   School of Medicine, Department of Psychiatry
   University of Oregon
   Portland, Oregon

2. Asian American Mental Health Research Center*
   1640 West Roosevelt Road
   Chicago, Illinois

3. Spanish-speaking Mental Health Research and Development
   Program
   Department of Sociology
   University of California
   Los Angeles, California

The following are respesentative types of research grants related to Black mental health which have been awarded by the Center for Minority Group Mental Health Programs:

1. Title of Project: *Mental Health Profile of Blacks and Asian Americans.*

   To assess the existing services provided in the greater Seattle, Washington, area to Blacks and Asian Americans in the community mental health facilities—from the assessment the principal investigators plan to design treatment models which would be most effective for the two minority groups at question who are being studied. It is also anticipated that this study will yield a profile of predisposing and contributory factors which give rise to the Asian Americans and Blacks seeking help in mental health.

2. Title of Project: *Restudy of Absorption of Migrant Workers.*

   The principal investigator of this study is attempting to profile the experiences and processes involved in the assimilation of migrant workers, and to identify some of the mental health problems associated with their assimilation and absorption in their transitory status. He is also studying some of the experiences which precipitated

---

*Formerly at the University of California, San Diego.

the use of mental health services, as well as some of the deterrents to seeking mental health services.

3. Title of Project: *Ethnic Survey Program.*

The program is designed to gather data concerning the perceptions, needs, quality of life, and mental health status of ethnic minorities, including Afro-Americans, Asian Americans, Chicanos, and American Indians. The program also provides educational experiences and training for minority group students in research techniques such as sampling, experimental design, data analysis, interviewing, and report writing. These individuals participate directly in the research procedures of the ethnic survey, which is conducted through the mail, over the telephone, and through large-scale sampling techniques carried out in cooperation with demographers, survey researchers, sampling experts, and census personnel. The staff selects a small random sample for in-depth interviews to provide individualized information. Seminars and conferences are conducted to discuss revisions for the ongoing program, based on annual evaluations of such factors as the use of language in the survey procedure and the use of ethnic versus nonethnic interviewers.

4. Title of Project: *Self Survey of the Black Community of Topeka, Kansas.*

The investigator is developing a profile of Topeka's Black community to determine the needs, priorities, and possible solutions to its social, economic, and political problems. The study employs survey methods, personal interviews, questionnaires, and statistical analyses to ascertain the mental health needs of the urban Blacks, studies the manner in which funds are allocated for the purpose of meeting those needs, and investigates how the funds are spent. Blacks participate in the project either as staff members or as informants.

5. Title of Project: *Research Review of Black Mental Health/Mental Illness.*

The researcher is preparing a comprehensive review of all literature on Black mental health, interpreting each article and developing an annotated bibliography. Literature in or out of retrieval systems is being evaluated and categorized under biological attachments, cultural group belongingness, personal historical experience, and contemporary social/psychological experiences. The completed bibliography can be used as a guide for administering grants and for policymaking.

6. Title of Project: *Data Systems for Minority Mental Health Services.*

A prototype of a basic data system for minority mental health services is being designed, developed, implemented, and evaluated. The system allows an assessment of community mental health from the perspective of the treatment provided for minorities. Differential dropout rates from therapy, effects of cultural differences on therapeutic outcome, and the characteristics of therapists providing service to minorities can be assessed using the system. Other advantages of the system, particularly from the minority perspective, are that progress of minority clients can be monitored in a more efficient manner, therapist and client can be better matched to increase the success rate of therapy, and continuity of care can be facilitated.

7. Title of Project: *Community Health Survey Project.*

A survey is made of living conditions and health characteristics of Black persons living in rural Mississippi. A stratified, multistage probability design, developed by the U.S. National Committee on Vital and Health Statistics, is used to select respondents for the study. The survey instrument consists of sections covering demography, household sanitation, family and individual health and mental health, and early life experiences. The investigator conducts the study with controls, and other precautionary measures are made to insure the quality of the results. The objective is to elucidate the relationship between the array of independent variables and health indices.

8. Title of Project: *Attempted and Completed Suicide in East Harlem.*

The basic aim of this proposal is to determine any differences in various characteristics among Black, White and Puerto Rican suicide attempters in the East Harlem area of Manhattan. Demographic data, diagnosis, disposition and means of attempt will be obtained for all suicide attempters seen in the seven hospitals in the area for a period of one year. The rates for suicide attempts and completions for the three ethnic groups will be compared with an age and sex breakdown; differences among the three groups in method of attempt and completion will be explored.

9. Title of Project: *A Program for Metropolitan Culture Studies.*

An ethnographic study is made of the life patterns of Blacks and other ethnic groups (Polish and Italian) in Philadelphia. The emphasis is on Black community life in urban areas. The main areas of investigation are: allocational patterns, social organization and kinship; community institutions; settlement and migration patterns; response to cultural differences; definition of an Afro-American culture area; language and socio-linguistics; discourse, ritual and social style in the Negro community.

10. Title of Project: *The Absorption of Migrants.*

Substantial numbers of Mexican-Americans, Blacks, and whites have migrated to northern industrial cities and have been absorbed in their new home with varying degrees of economic and social success. The investigator is identifying the combinations of factors that control how quickly and how successfully the migrant is absorbed into the new environment. Data from a three-year (1959 to 1961) comparative study of Mexican-American, Black, and white migrants to Racine, Wisconsin, a northern industrial city, are the subject matter for this project. Fifty representative variables from the 1959 survey and 60 representative variables from the 1960 survey are analyzed by a Nucros computer program. Using these results, the investigator selects items for a resurvey of the original group. He also determines if there are clusters of people within various racial and ethnic groups who show distinctly different adjustment patterns in their respective groups.

11. Title of Project: *Epidemiology of Achievement and Psychiatric Status.*

    This research study has five parts: (1) completion of a longitudinal study; (2) development of a method for identifying representative samples of alcoholics and drug addicts; (3) an attempt to explain the discrepancy between Black and white suicide rates; (4) preparation of a handbook dealing with methods for longitudinal life history studies; and (5) a three-generation study.

12. Title of Project: *Transcultural Study in Discharge of Schizophrenics.*

    This investigator is studying the cultural factors involved in the discharge of schizophrenics to the community. The project is comparing the effects of a variety of social environments on schizophrenics.

Two research efforts which evolved as a result of the activities of the Center for Minority Groups Mental Health Programs are noteworthy in terms of adequacy of mental health care to Black Americans.

Stanley Sue and co-workers, in their study of "Delivery of Community Mental Health Services to Black and White Clients," threw some light on the nature of the inequities in the mental health care delivery system as it relates to the mental health needs of Blacks. One of the strengths of this study was the fact that, unlike many of the funded research proposals, it did not study the Black mental health aspect of the delivery system in a vacuum but more meaningfully and functionally in terms of its relationships to the service experiences of whites. Accordingly, the authors state that "Particular attention was focused on racial comparisons in regard to major service received, type of personnel rendering treatment, number of contacts with facilities, and a whole host of demographic and diagnostic variables" (Sue et al., p. 3). Data were collected from 13,450 clients who sought services from 18 community mental health facilities in the greater Seattle (King County) area. The following findings are of significance:

1. There was a tendency for Blacks to be assigned more frequently to inpatient rather than outpatient programs in comparison to white clients.

2. Blacks were more likely than whites to receive intake diagnosis.

3. Whites were more often engaged in group and family types of therapy than Blacks.

4. Paraprofessionals saw Blacks at intake more frequently and professional specialists saw Blacks less frequently than whites. This finding was also applicable to personnel involved in the therapy sessions. Blacks, then, are treated by less professionally qualified staff.

5. Blacks have less frequent contacts with mental health facilities than whites.

6. A greater proportion of Blacks dropped out of therapy after the first session than whites.

Generally, then, according to the authors, "Black compared to White clients attend fewer number of sessions, terminate more often after the first session, and are more likely to see paraprofessionals" (Sue et al., p. 12). Of significance, therefore, for future delineation, is the precise role of the race of the therapist as a factor in the rate of therapy termination. Such studies are absolutely necessary in delineating measurable indices of racism and thus facilitating the attainment of the important research step of operationalizing this important variable.

A study prepared for the Center for Minority Group Mental Health Programs which has implications for operational definitions and other important methodological issues and concerns is the "Special Report on Inequities in Mental Health Service Delivery," by Byron Fiman. In pointing out these research problems, Fiman observes that "while it appears that the evidence for differential treatment as a function of race continues to become clearer, there are still a number of methodological issues that prevent complete understanding of these complex relationships" (Fiman, 1975, p. 1). Of particular significance is the statement that "Definitional inconsistencies of the various aspects of the mental health delivery system make the comparison of different studies more difficult" (Fiman, p. 1). Some methodological device must, therefore, be developed to minimize these definitional inconsistencies and maximize the reliability and validity of the measurement instruments.

In examining the relevant literature, Fiman considered the following findings to be of significance:

1. More White children were admitted to psychiatric clinics for treatment than Black children (Jackson, Berkowitz, and Gordon, 1974).
2. Minority groups tended to be overrepresented in public mental health facilities (Williams and Carmichael, 1949; and Redick and Johnson, 1974).
3. Blacks were less prone to visit psychiatric treatment facilities even when they were referred and had made appointments (Raynes and Warren, 1971).
4. Diagnosis and type of referral from psychiatric emergency room varied with the race of the client (Gross et al., 1960).
5. Diagnosis became less accurate as the socio-cultural distance between clinician and client increased (Gross et al., 1960).
6. More Whites than Blacks are selected for insight-oriented therapy (Rosenthal and Frank, 1958).
7. The long-term psychotherapy patient is more likely to be White than Black (Wilder and Coleman, 1963).
8. Black families tended to be more dissatisfied with treatment and had more negative perceptions of the clinic and the therapist than Whites (Warren et al., 1972).

These findings certainly underscore the need for more rigorous methodological approaches to the issue of Black mental health.

The research proposals and projects sponsored by the Center for Minority Group Mental Health Programs generally lack the sophistication in research design and methodology conducive to significant "breakthroughs" in the area of Black mental health. The studies were largely exploratory or descriptive in design. This means that it is difficult to determine the precise impact which one variable or combination of variables would have on another variable. Research on Black mental health should strive to set up experimental designs with hypothesis indicating specifically stated relationships between variables—units of measurement. The design should make allowances for controlling variables either by having control and experimental groups or by the utilization of the kinds of statistical techniques that will allow an accurate utilization of multivariate analyses including analysis of variance and covariance. A computerized approach allows for the kinds of statistical activities which would adequately take cognizance of the complex interrelationships of the person, the social situation, and the sociocultural dimension. Reliable and valid instruments must be devised to measure important variables such as racism, oppression, social disability, and stress. Research designs should reflect more of the longitudinal type of study, although, in many cases, in the interest of time and the functional utilization of the results, the design might reflect a combination of the cross-sectional and the longitudinal.

The Research and Development Centers at Howard and Drew Universities are set up and structured to make contributions in the sorely needed methodological areas. The basic goals of the Research and Development Center at Howard University are congruent with the level of research expectation pertaining to Black mental health. These goals are:

1. The instituting of a multidisciplinary approach to the study of mental health in Black people. This goal recognizes the multidimensional and multi-faceted dimensions of Black mental health. As a consequence, it should be approached in such a way that it is not primarily biological, psychological or social, but meaningful combinations and permutations of all of these.

2. The encouragement of new approaches to provide mental health services in the Black community. This goal recognized the inequities of the service delivery system in Black mental health and, therefore, the need through research to minimize these inequities. The structure of the research effort will, by definition, be functional and practical.

3. The development of procedures for monitoring and evaluating research in this field. This will be accomplished through seminars, workshops, conferences and by printed publications such as those dealing with mental health from a Black perspective.

4. Providing technical assistance to those doing research on Black people.

5. Developing an operational definition of positive mental health for Black people.

This approach is of crucial importance. In the past, research on Black mental health, particularly when done by white researchers, has operated within the framework of the pathological. This assumption, as previously indicated, has affected all of the steps and stages of research, including the factual conclusions. The reverse change from the pathological to the positive has realistic possibilities for affecting the research process in an entirely different way.

As already implied, the Mental Health Research and Development Center at Howard University took the strong position that "The Mental health needs of Black people have never been adequately determined or assessed and, moreover, have been distorted" (Gary, 1975, p. 5).

One of the reasons given for this, without an operational definition, was racism. Some of the assumptions that, hopefully, research activities in the Center will dispute about Black mental health will be that Blacks cannot benefit from traditional psychotherapeutic approaches and that there is no real difference between Black people and persons of low socioeconomic status in the study of mental health.

The real justification, contrary to the assumptions above, is that the Black perspective, from which Black mental health should be studied will, by definition, place the research project in a different theoretical framework with significantly different possibilities and outcomes. Of additional significance in the approach is its systems analysis aspect in viewing the person as interacting with his total environment. Here, according to the annual report, "the approach is interdisciplinary and the focus is on mental health—on the coping strengths of Black people—not on mental illness" (Gary, p. 53). The specific goals of the Center are "To improve the delivery of mental health services in the Black community, to prevent mental illness, and to produce more effective treatment models for Black people" (p. 54).

These are indeed laudable goals, the realization of which will be contingent on a great degree of sophistication relating to research methodology, including the refinement of research instruments. This will be difficult because of the absence of a critical mass, at this point in time, of Black researchers with significant expertise in the area of Black mental health.

The research staff of the Center has been working on some research areas relevant to Black mental health, including the following:

1. Policy evaluation of community boards of community health centers

2. A study of factors which may account for some of the reported variations in mental diseases

3. Mental health and the Black church

4. Mental health in the Black community

5. The definition of mental health from a Black perspective

This Center, in terms of its operational plan, has the potential to be one of the outstanding centers in the world in relationship to research on Black mental health. Until it actually begins to conceptualize research problems within a systems analysis framework and thereby move significantly away from exploratory and/or descriptive kinds of studies, and construct tests for validity and reliability and implement specifically designed research instruments, the verdict about its contributory potential will have to remain out.

The Fanon Mental Health Research and Development Center is a multidisciplinary Black research and development center with a special focus on the mental health of Blacks. The Black family is the specific research unit of investigation, taking into consideration areas such as family growth and development and including patterns of child rearing and family organization survival styles. It attaches significance to the social milieu within which the Black family exists and functions and the totality of the psychosocial, sociocultural, political-economic, and biological and physiological forces which impinge upon and affect the family and its members. By definition, therefore, community organization and community development are considered to be basic processes in assessing the nature and scope of these functional relationships and interrelationships. The Center takes a very positive definitional approach to Black mental health by defining the mentally healthy Black person as "that individual who is active in the pursuit of goals which are harmonious with natural growth and which allow for survival of the cultural group with minimum injury to self or others; that person whose awareness allows her/him to deal effectively with any constraints (e.g., racism) of the social system" (King, 1976).

The Center has delineated eight research areas of emphasis. These are:

1. *Psychosomatic Correlates*

   Key Questions: What are the factors that dictate the mind-body equilibrium (health) or disequilibrium (disease) in Blacks? How do these factors interact in the individual, and in the collective?

2. *Developmental Models*

   Key Questions: What are the physical, emotional-cognitive, psychosocial and cultural parameters of the Black

developmental process and how are they manifested across the developmental life span?

3. *Cross-Cultural Relations*

Key Questions: What person-group behavioral themes transcend
and are the essence of Black cultural groups, and
how do these factors interact to predict competent Black individuals, families and groups?

4. *Intervention*

Key Questions: What are the measurement (diagnoses) parameters
to qualitatively measure the interactions of individuals with social/family worlds, the ecological
space and the social order, and how can effective
interventions be made to optimize the mental
health of the same?

5. *American Social Dilemmas*

Key Questions: How do the major American social dilemmas—
racism, militarism, sexism and ageism—affect
the Black individual and the Black family, and
what intervention strategies can be developed to
effectively resolve the same?

6. *Social Planning and Policy*

Key Questions: How do social policy decisions currently affect the
lives of Blacks and how can Blacks intervene in
this policy-making process to gain access to power,
equality and equity in the distribution of scarce
public goods (i.e. critical social pathways)?

7. *Community Building*

Key Questions: What are the social mechanisms used to perpetuate the collective powerlessness and colonialism
of Black communities, and how can interventions
be made to effectively foster self-determination
and collective action for individual gain?

8. *Research on Research*

Key Questions: What should be the philosophical premises, the
parameters, questions and methods that should

be used as the model of research for Blacks, and how can the necessary individual, professional, institutional, and community resources be developed to implement such a model?

There are specific research projects in each research area.

Specific Research Projects on Psychosomatic Correlates

1. The Role of Social Mediation of Anger in the Development of Essential Hypertension in Blacks
2. Epidemiology of Stress and Hypertension in Black Children and Youth
3. National Survey of Black Children's Health: Indices

The following is the content area of the research on Psychosomatic Correlates:

1. *Cosmic Realm*
   a. Biomystical processes
   b. Physiological indices of mental processes
   c. Mentalistic measures
   d. Paranormal phenomena
   e. Psycho-historical phenomena
2. *I-It Phenomena*
   a. Psychophysiological response styles
   b. Melanin and Black psychophysical processes
   c. Black stress and stress-coping styles
   d. Psychosomatic disorders
   e. Nutrition and psycho-physical functioning
   f. Emotions as precursor and as index of physiological processes
3. *I-Thou Phenomena*
   a. Black body image
   b. Black perceptual and cognitive styles as influences and consequences of psycho-physical processes
   c. Psychophysiology, development and socialization

The specific research projects on Developmental Models are:

1. Individual and generational changes in older Black adults
2. To be young, gifted and Black; divergent creative thinking, personality and ability among Black children

3. The adjustment problems of the physically handicapped adolescent and their values and mental health correlates
4. The body collage as a measure of body image
5. Adjustment problems in cerebral palsy

The research proposals of the Fanon Mental Health Research and Development Center throw significant light on the philosophical thrusts and the theoretical bases which will give the operational parameters of research activities relevant to Black mental health in the Center. The approach takes cognizance of the weakness of dichotomous, compartmentalized, and piecemeal traditional approaches of research on mental health, including Black mental health. The research activities of the Center are structured to be holistic and to be in accordance with the principles of systems analysis.

It is regrettable that the rationale for this approach is couched in political and not in scientific terms. Eastern and African cultures are given credit for monopolizing this holistic approach. Additionally, there are a number of concepts in this theoretical framework such as mystical and cosmic considerations, that will create some difficulties in operational definitions and, therefore, obviate the possibility of meaningful replication—one of the basic tenets of the scientific method.

For example, in a research proposal on "The Role of Racism as a Social Mediator of Essential Hypertension in Blacks," the operational definition of racism was given as "the state of affairs whereby the factor of race interacts with personal and social factors to influence the actual range of response options available to an individual or group to cope with socially induced anger or stress" (Myers, p. 1). This definition only succeeds, as is quite apparent, in moving the statement from one level of abstraction to another—empirical referents are absent.

It is of considerable research significance that this Center attempts to incorporate stress, life events, and coping mechanisms into its theoretical system and relates these variables to mental health and particularly to Black mental health and to hypertensive diseases. This is done by summarizing the relevant literature and taking the position in terms of major findings that:

> Psychosocial and socio-cultural stress differentially affect individuals according to some complex function that includes personal stress-coping styles, the amount of stress the individual may be exposed to as a function of the person's race and socio-economic level, the number of disrupting

and disquieting events that occur in the person's life, and the existence of larger socio-cultural factors that interfere with the individual's ability to control his life, to act assertively, and to discharge generated anger against legitimate targets. All of these factors appear to interact to create a style of coping with stress that is characterized by a constant state of alertness and a failure to achieve a resting state (Myers, pp. 2–3).

This approach, as already implied, has all kinds of possibilities for significant "breakthroughs" in the area of mental health in general and Black mental health specifically. What remains to be done is to ensure that the stressful life events are ranked and rated in terms of their relevance to Blacks. This has not been done. Another positive approach to this kind of study by the Center is the combination of cross-sectional and longitudinal designs in the research methodology. This approach significantly reduces the time frame for meaningful results.

The increasing sophistication of research and research methodology and the developmental stages of research on Black mental health call for a departure from the usual exploratory and descriptive types of research designs to more experimental research designs where causation or the precise impact of a social intervention can be determined. Even with some descriptive studies, the strides of computerization permit high level multivariate analyses with built-in internal controls.

There is great need, therefore, for a critical mass of Black researchers specifically trained to implement these advanced research and statistical techniques. This becomes particularly crucial when it is recognized that meaningful "breakthroughs" in research on Black mental health will come with the recognition that mental health is multidimensional, and multifaceted, and must be placed within a configurational system which recognizes the intricate but functionally meaningful relationships and interrelationships between the person, the human group, and the sociocultural environment, all interacting in terms of principles of community organization and community development. This holistic systems analysis approach is rigorously demanding methodologically. The two Black Research and Development Centers offer great promise in making significant contributions to the area of Black mental health research. A greater degree of collaboration between them, however, will be essential to this attainment.

If, therefore, the Center for Minority Group Mental Health Programs expects to facilitate research "breakthroughs" in Black mental health, it must do the following:

1. Establish more rigorous standards for the funding of research proposals.
2. Insist on research methodologies which are highly sophisticated.
3. Encourage unique but relevant combinations of longitudinal and cross-sectional designs.
4. Make special appeals for research proposals which try to determine the kind of social milieu or community organization not conducive to a prevalence of mental disorders.
5. Encourage the submission of research proposals which conceptualize the relationships and interrelationships between mental illness and drug addiction, alcoholism, job dissatisfaction, etc., as these indicate degrees of community disorganization.
6. Allow for research designs that are cross–racial-ethnic or cross-cultural.

Additionally, mental illness must be operationally defined in behavioral and, therefore, measurable and researchable terms. Life events with external stressors as empirical referents appear to offer great research promise. It is important, therefore, to relate these variables more meaningfully to the Black experience with the basic assumption that life events take place in a certain ecological system and, therefore, can be assessed within a framework of community organization.

In order to accomplish the above, the first order of business on the research agenda must be the production of a critical mass of Black researchers with expertise and sophistication to perform the research tasks described commendably and creditably.

References

Bart, P. B. (ed.). "Sexism in Family Studies." Special Issue, Parts 1 and 2. *Journal of Marriage and the Family* 33 (1971): 409–606.

Barton, W. E. "Viewpoint of a Clinician." In M. Jahoda (ed.), *Current Concepts of Positive Mental Health.* New York: Basic Books, 1959.

Becker, H. S. *Outsiders: Studies in the Sociology of Deviance.* New York: Free Press, 1963.

Brenner, M. H. "Economic Instability and Mental Hospitalization in the United States, 1922–1968: An Issue of Primary Presentation in Several

Mental Disorders." Paper presented at the 10th annual meeting of the American Public Health Association in San Francisco, 1973, pp. 1–25.

_____. *Mental Illness and the Economy.* Cambridge, Massachusetts: Harvard University Press, 1973.

Brown, G. W., and Birley, J. L. T. "Crises and Life Changes and the Onset of Schizophrenia." *Journal of Health and Social Behavior* (September 1968): 203–214.

Deutsch, H. *The Psychology of Women.* New York: Green & Stratton, 1944.

Dohrenwend, B. P. "The Problem of Validity in the Field Studies of Psychological Disorder." *International Journal of Psychiatry* 1 (1965): 585–609.

_____. "Social Status, Stress, and Psychological Symptoms." *American Journal of Public Health* 57 (1967): 625–632.

_____. "Sociocultural and Social Psychological Factors in the Genesis of Mental Disorders." *Journal of Health and Social Behavior* 16 (1975): 365–392.

Erikson, E. H. "The Concept of Identity in Race Relations." In T. Parsons and K. Clark, (eds.), *The Negro American*, pp. 254–279. Boston: Beacon Press, 1965.

Erikson, K. "Patient Role and Social Uncertainty." *Psychiatry* 20 (1975): 263–268.

Fiman, B. "Special Report on Inequities in Mental Health Service Delivery." Prepared for Center for Minority Group Studies of NIMH. McLean, Virginia: Human Sciences Research, 1975.

Folb, E. "Rapping in the Black Vernacular." *Human Behavior* 2 (1937): 16–20.

Frank, J. D. "Adjustment Problems of Selected Negro Soldiers." *Journal of Nervous and Mental Disorders* 105 (1947): 647.

Gary, L. *Annual Report 1974–75.* Washington, D.C.: Institute for Urban Affairs and Research, Howard University, 1975.

Goffman, E. *Asylums.* Garden City, New York: Doubleday, 1961.

_____. *Behavior in Public Places.* New York: Free Press, 1963.

_____. *Stigma: Notes on the Management of Spoiled Identity.* Englewood Cliffs, New Jersey: Prentice-Hall, 1963.

Gross, H. et al. "The Effect of Race and Sex on the Variation of Diagnosis and Disposition in a Psychiatric Emergency Room." *Journal of Nervous and Mental Diseases* 48 (1969): 638–642.

Hoffman, M. "Psychiatry, Nature and Science." *American Journal of Psychiatry* 117 (1960): 205.

Holmes, T. H., and Rahe, R. H. "The Social Readjustment Rating Scale." *Journal of Psychosomatic Medicine* 11 (1967): 213–218.

Hough, R. L.; Fairbank, D.; and Garcia, A. "Problems in the Ratio Measurement of Life Stress." *Journal of Health and Social Behavior* 17 (1976): 80–82.

Hudgens, R. W. "Personal Catastrophe and Depression: A Consideration of the Subject with Respect to Medically Ill Adolescents and a Requiem for Retrospective Life-Event Studies." In B. S. Dohrenwend and B. P. Dohrenwend (eds.), *Stressful Life Events: Their Nature and Effects* pp. 119–134. New York: Wiley, 1974.

Jackson, A. M.; Berkowitz, H.; and Farley, G. "Race as a Variable Affecting the Treatment Involvement of Children." *Journal of the American Academy of Child Psychiatry* 13 (1974): 20–31.

Jahoda, M. *Current Concepts of Positive Mental Health.* New York: Basic Books, 1959.

Kennedy, J. "Problems Posed in the Analysis of Negro Patient." *Journal of Psychiatry* 15 (1952): 313–327.

King, L. *Research Overview.* Los Angeles: Fanon Research and Development Center, 1976.

Kirk, S. T. "The Impact of Labelling on Rejection of the Mentally Ill: An Experimental Study." *Journal of Health and Social Behavior* 15 (1974): 108–117.

Kramer, M.; Rosen, B.; and Willis, E. "Definitions and Distributions of Mental Disorders in a Racist Society." In C. Willie; B. Kramer; and B. Brown (eds.), *Racism and Mental Health,* pp. 353–459. Pittsburgh: University of Pittsburgh Press, 1973.

Langner, T. S., and Michael, S. T. *Life Stress and Mental Health.* Glencoe, Illinois: Free Press, 1963.

Leighton, A. H. et al. *Psychiatric Disorder Among the Yoruba.* Ithaca, New York: Cornell University Press, 1963.

Lemert, E. *Social Pathology.* New York: McGraw-Hill, 1951.

Markush, R. E. and Favero, R.V. "Epidemiologic Assessment of Stressful Life Events, Depressed Mood, and Psychophysiological Symptoms—a Preliminary Report." In B. S. Dohrenwend and B. P. Dohrenwend (eds.), *Stressful Life Events: Their Nature and Effects,* pp. 171–190. New York: Wiley, 1974.

Menninger, K. *The Human Mind,* 3rd ed. New York: Knopf, 1945.

Murphy, J. "Psychiatric Labeling in Cross Cultural Perspective." *Science* 191 (1976): 1019–1028.

Myers, H. "An Epidemiological Study of Psychosocial Stress and Essential Hypertension in Black Children and Youth." Unpublished grant abstract. Los Angeles: Fanon Research and Development Center, 1976.

_____. "The Role of Racism as a Social Mediator of Anger and Stress in the Development of Essential Hypertension in Blacks." Unpublished grant abstract. Los Angeles: Fanon Research and Development Center, 1976.

Myers, J. K.; Lindenthal, J. J.; and Pepper, M. P. "Life Events, Social Integration and Psychiatric Symptomatology." *Journal of Health and Social Behavior* 16 (1975): 421–427.

Myers, J. K.; Lindenthal, J. J.; Pepper, M. P.; and Ostrander, D. R. "Life Events and Mental Status: A Longitudinal Study." *Journal of Health and Social Behavior* 13 (1972): 398–406.

Parsons, T. "Definitions of Health and Illness in the Light of American Values and Social Structure." In E. G. Jaco (ed.), *Patients, Physicians and Illness.* Glencoe, Illinois: Free Press, 1958.

Paykel, E. S. "Life Stress and Psychiatric Disorder: Application of the Clinical Approach." In B. S. Dohrenwend and B. P. Dohrenwend (eds.), *Stressful Life Events: Their Nature and Effects,* pp. 135–149. New York: Wiley, 1974.

Pettigrew, T. F. "Racism and the Mental Health of White Americans: A Social Psychological View." In C. Willie; B. Kramer; and B. Brown (eds.), *Racism and Mental Health,* pp. 269–298. Pittsburgh: University of Pittsburgh Press, 1973.

Pinderhughes, C. A. "Racism and Psychotherapy." In C. Willie; B. Kramer; and B. Brown (eds.), *Racism and Mental Health,* pp. 61-121. Pittsburgh: University of Pittsburgh Press, 1973.

Raynes, A. E., and Warren, G. "Some Distinguishing Features of Patients Failing to Attend a Psychiatric Clinic After Referral." *American Journal of Orthopsychiatry* 41 (1971): 581–588.

Redick, R. W., and Johnson, C. "Marital Status, Living Arrangements and Family Characteristics of Admissions of State and County Mental Hospitals and Outpatient Psychiatric Clinics, United States, 1970." Statistical Note 100. Prepared by the HEW Public Health Service, NIMH, Office of Program Planning and Evaluation, Biometry Branch, Survey and Reports Section, 1970.

Rosenberg, E. J., and Dohrenwend, B. S. "Effects of Experience and Ethnicity on Ratings of Life Events as Stressors." *Journal of Health and Social Behavior* 16 (1975): 127–129.

Rosenhahn, D. "On Being Sane in Places." *Journal of Science* 179 (1973): 250.

Rosenthal, D., and Frank, J. "Fate of Psychiatric Clinic Outpatients Assigned to Psychotherapy." *Journal of Nervous and Mental Diseases* 127 (1958): 330–343.

Sabshin, M. H.; Diesenhaus, M.; and Wilkerson, R. "Dimensions of Institutional Racism in Psychiatry." *American Journal of Psychiatry* 127 (1970): 787–793.

Sager, C. J.; Brayboy T.; and Waxenberg, B. *Black Ghetto Family in Therapy: A Laboratory Experience*. New York: Grove Press, 1970.

St. Clair, H. "Psychiatric Interview Experience with Negroes." *American Journal of Psychiatry* 108 (1957): 113–119.

Scheff, T. *Being Mentally Ill: A Sociological Theory*. Chicago: Aldine, 1966.

_____. "The Role of the Mentally Ill and the Dynamics of Mental Disorder: A Research Framework." *Sociometry* 26 (1963): 436–453.

Srole, L. et al. *Metropolis: The Midtown Study*. Vol. 1. New York: McGraw-Hill, 1962.

Sue, S.; McKinney, H.; Allen D.; and Hall, J. "Delivery of Community Mental Health Services to Black and White Clients." Unpublished report partially supported by the National Institute of Mental Health and its Center for Minority Group Mental Health Programs. Seattle: University of Washington, 1974.

Szasz, T. S. "The Myth of Mental Illness." *Journal of American Psychology* 15 (1960): 113–118.

_____. *The Myth of Mental Illness*. New York: Harper, 1961.

Thomas, C., and Comer, J. P. "Racism and Mental Health Services." In C. Willie; B. Kramer; and B. Brown (eds.), *Racism and Mental Health*, pp. 165–181. Pittsburgh: University of Pittsburgh Press, 1973.

Waite, R. "The Negro Patient and Clinical Theory." *Journal of Consulting and Clinical Psychology* 32 (1968): 427–433.

Warren, R.; Jackson, A.; Nugaris, J.; and Gordon, F. "Differential Attitudes of Black and White Patients Toward Psychiatric Treatment in a Child Guidance Clinic." *American Journal of Orthopsychiatry* 42 (1972):301–302.

Wilder, J., and Coleman, M. "The 'Walk-In' Psychiatric Clinic: Some Observations and Follow-Up." *International Journal of Social Psychiatry* 9 (1963): 192–199.

Williams, E. Y., and Carmichael, C. P. "The Incidence of Mental Disease in the Negro." *Negro Education* 18 (1949): 276–282.

Willie, C.; Kramer, B.; and Brown, B. *Racism and Mental Health*. Pittsburgh: University of Pittsburgh Press, 1973.

INDEX